IN FOREIGN FIELDS

IN FOREIGN FIELDS

Heroes of Iraq and Afghanistan,
in their own words

DAN COLLINS

Monday Books

A CIP catalogue record for this title is available
from the British Library

ISBN: 978-1-906308-07-0

Typeset by Andrew Searle

Printed an   by CPI Cox & Wyman, Reading, RG1 8EX

Contents

I went into a public 'ouse to get a pint o' beer,
The publican 'e up an' sez, 'We serve no red-coats here.'
The girls be'ind the bar they laughed an' giggled fit to die,
I outs into the street again an' to myself sez I:
O it's Tommy this, an' Tommy that, an' 'Tommy, go away';
But it's 'Thank you, Mister Atkins,' when the band begins to play,
The band begins to play, my boys, the band begins to play,
O it's 'Thank you, Mr. Atkins,' when the band begins to play.

Extracted from 'Tommy' by Rudyard Kipling

Preface

MODERN Britain can seem a strange and superficial country at times. It's a country where people whose sole distinction is that they have appeared on reality TV shows can become overnight millionaires, where pop singers lecture us on politics while Prime Ministers proclaim their love of 'The Arctic Monkeys' and where a football 'hero' spends more on his highlighted haircuts than the daily pay of a young soldier.

Meanwhile, out in the deserts of Iraq and Afghanistan, far from the comforts we regard as essential, those young soldiers are risking their lives every day.

For most of us, the greatest danger we face is of death from over-eating or drinking too much. For them, it's very different. They have no say in when and where they fight; to paraphrase Tennyson, theirs is not to reason why, theirs is but to do and, sometimes, die.

I wanted to give some of those who have served in Iraq and Afghanistan the opportunity to tell their stories, in their own words.

Almost every Briton 'on the ground' in those countries will be in harm's way many times during a tour of duty. Tales of courage, self-sacrifice and dedication to duty abound, and a library would be needed to do them all justice. So I sought out those recognised even within their own fraternity – medal winners.

By its very nature, the military honours system is imperfect. Many outstanding acts go unrewarded, unnoticed in the heat of battle or 'written up' unsuccessfully. However, to win the Conspicuous Gallantry Cross, the Military Cross or any of the other awards featured in these pages, you must have performed to a very high level. Many of the men herein – and Pte Michelle Norris MC, the sole woman entry – stood toe-to-toe with death and moved forwards in its face.

That is not say they were 'gung-ho' about their actions. Many, of all ranks and ages, had tears in their eyes as they recalled their experiences. A few had struggled emotionally since returning home. None had enjoyed the business of killing, and many showed considerable compassion for those they were fighting. All were profoundly proud of their service and their colleagues, and all expressed an almost identical sentiment which may be summarised thus: *This medal is for everyone who was there with me. Any of them would have done what I did...it just happened to be me.*

All were selected, at random, by me; the choice of one particular action and individual over others is emphatically not a comment on any award or person. I could have written this book ten times over with entirely different names each time.

Meeting the 25 interviewees was a moving, rewarding and humbling experience; my own unimpressive and unremarkable life was thrown into uncomfortably sharp relief as I talked to people who had travelled thousands of miles to be mortared and machine-gunned and hardly turned a hair. But strangely, given their uniform bravery and the nature of their exploits, the most impressive feature of the interviewees was their modesty. None had requested to be included; all were recommended by their superiors and all, indeed, required a degree of persuasion. (Incidentally, this book was originally going to be called *Heroes*; this was dropped after the heroes themselves told me the title would embarrass them.)

In Foreign Fields does not pretend to give an overview of the events in either country, or the wider geopolitics of the Middle East. Clearly, readers will have their own opinions about our activities in Iraq and Afghanistan, and I am sure the service personnel have theirs. I asked for and received no hint as to what these might be. They were, and are, professionals to their fingertips and bootlaces. 'We go where we're sent,' said one soldier, who might have been speaking for them all. 'It's not for me to question why I'm there. I get paid to do a job and I do it to the best of my ability.'

Of course, the Army are not the only armed service involved in Iraq and Afghanistan. The Royal Air Force and the Royal Navy (through the Royal Marines) have also done, and continue to do, sterling work. Thus, though inevitably the bulk of the stories herein are from the Army (including the TA), those services are represented, too.

I am grateful to the Ministry of Defence and its staff for assistance rendered in locating and contacting interviewees and in ensuring the requirements of operational and personal security were met. Memories of events which happened under stressful conditions some years ago are inevitably clouded; we have done all we can to ensure the accuracy of these stories.

Above all, I am grateful to all of the interviewees for giving me their time. My name is on the front cover of this book only because someone's had to be; all I did was sit and listen, and then edit, as sparingly as possible, their words. This book is by them.

In modern Britain, for the last 60 years at least, we have been fortunate in living without the horror of total, all-consuming war. We have no conscription or national service, our armed services seem more remote than once they did and our eyes have turned inwards. But as you read the words that follow, I hope you will remember that some of our people are living different lives to yours. I hope they make you feel proud.

Dan Collins, August 2008

The Medals

Conspicuous Gallantry Cross (CGC)

The CGC was instituted in 1993 and is second only to the Victoria Cross as an award for gallantry for all ranks across the whole armed forces. Recipients have usually put themselves at extremely high risk of being killed, and have acted with an order of bravery far outside that which would normally be expected.

Military Cross (MC)

The Military Cross is the third level decoration, granted in recognition of gallantry during active operations against the enemy. Again, the recipients will generally have been in great danger during the action for which the medal is awarded.

Distinguished Flying Cross (DFC)

The Distinguished Flying Cross is awarded for acts of 'valour, courage or devotion to duty whilst flying in active operations against the enemy'.

Distinguished Service Order (DSO)

The Distinguished Service Order is awarded for meritorious or distinguished service by senior officers of the armed forces during wartime, typically in actual combat. Since 1993, its award has been made solely for distinguished service (that is, leadership and command), since the introduction of the CGC as the second highest award for gallantry.

List of Abbreviations

(a fuller explanation of terms used is found in the Glossary)

2IC	Second-in-Command	JAM	Jaish Al Mahdi aka The Mahdi Army
ACK	Assistant		
AFV	Armoured Fighting Vehicle	KOSB	King's Own Scottish Borderers
AK	AK47 (or AK74)	LAW	Light Anti-Tank Weapon
AOR	Area Of Operations		
BATUS	British Army Training Unit Suffield	LBdr	Lance Bombardier
		LCoH	Lance Corporal of Horse
Bde	Brigade	LCpl	Lance Corporal
BRF	Brigade Reconnaissance Force	LMG	Light Machine Gun
		Lt	Lieutenant
Capt	Captain	Lt Col	Lieutenant Colonel
CoH	Corporal of Horse	LZ/HLS	Landing Zone/ Helicopter Landing Site
Col	Colonel		
Coy	Company	Maj	Major
CP	Command Post	MAK	Al Majar Al Kabir
Cpl	Corporal	NVG	Night Vision Goggles
CQMS	Company Quarter Master Sergeant	OC	Office Commanding
		Op	Operation
CSgt	Colour Sergeant	OP	Observation Post
EOD	Explosive Ordnance Disposal	Pax	Persons
		PRR	Personal Role Radio
FOB	Forward Operating Base	Pte	Private
FSG	Fire Support Group	QBO	Quick Battle Orders
Fus	Fusilier	RHA	Royal Horse Artillery
GMPG	General Purpose Machine Gun	RMO	Regimental Medical Officer
HE	High Explosive	RMTC	Chilwell Reserve Mobilisation and Training Centre
Intel	Intelligence		
IRT	Incident Response Team		

RPG	Rocket-Propelled Grenade	**UAV**	Unmanned Aerial Vehicle
RV	Rendezvous Point	**UGL**	Underslung Grenade Launcher
SA80	The standard British Army rifle	**USMC**	United States Marine Corps
SAC	Senior Aircraftsman	**VCP**	Vehicle Checkpoint
Sgt	Sergeant	**WMIK**	Weapons Mounted Installation Kit
SOP	Standard Operating Procedure	**Wng Cdr**	Wing Commander
Spr	Sapper	**WO**	Warrant Officer
Sqn Ldr	Squadron Leader		
TACP	Tactical Air Control Party		

Lieutenant Charles Campbell, MC
The Royal Regiment of Fusiliers

WHEN Coalition Forces finally invaded Iraq on March 20, 2003, the men of the Royal Regiment of Fusiliers were among the first across the border. And among the first of the Fusiliers was Charles 'Ollie' Campbell, a quiet and modest man with a broad smile and a hint of the Zambia of his youth in his accent. Campbell was 7 Platoon commander with Y Company of the First Fusiliers Battlegroup during Operation TELIC 1.

The day after the invasion, his platoon was ordered to secure a strategically important motorway bridge over the Shatt-Al-Basra waterway outside Basra, Iraq's second biggest city. Campbell led a dawn attack, his men fighting their way across the bridge on foot - armoured vehicles could not cross because it had not been cleared of explosives. With mortars landing all around them, and machine gun rounds and rocket-propelled grenades filling the air, they pressed home the attack against an enemy dug in on the far bank in good positions. Despite the odds being stacked against them, Campbell's light force got across and took prisoners. His citation says he "pressed home his attack, inspiring his troops by personal example, displaying no concern for his own personal safety."

The following two days and nights saw Lt Campbell and his men fight off near-continuous enemy assaults, while under mortar fire for at least 30 of those 48 hours. He "stayed calm and self-assured in command and... his men were able to repulse at least three well-organised and fierce attempts by the enemy to dislodge his small force from the eastern bank."

On the night of 27 March, 2003, Campbell led an assault force deep behind well-prepared enemy lines, showing "considerable courage and determination in the face of great personal danger" as his men sought enemy prisoners.

I'm 30 years old, married to Monica and I was commissioned into the Fusiliers in 2000 - probably influenced by my dad, who was always quite keen on me joining the British Army. I'd spent my early life in southern Africa, having been born in Zambia, and I was always an outdoors sort of bloke, so it was the kind of thing I was looking for.

I remember very clearly when 9/11 happened, and our company commander, David Milo, got us together the following day. He said, 'Gents, be in no doubt, this will change your lives. This is the biggest thing to happen since the invasion of Czechoslovakia in World War Two. It will have implications for the rest of your careers.' We were like, 'Yep, thanks a lot,' but of course subsequent events proved him right.

The citation refers to TELIC 1, the invasion of Iraq. At that time I was a Platoon Commander, in charge of three sections of 10 blokes within Y Company. As everyone did, we flew out to Kuwait and then spent a lot of time sitting round, trying to organise training and so on. There was a lot of corporate combat experience within the Regiment, and experience of the area, which was very helpful. Our Company Commander, Maj Paul Nanson, was just one of a number of men who had been involved in the first Gulf War, and their input was vital. They knew what the terrain would be like, they had a good idea of how the Iraqis would fight, of what their capabilities were... all vital stuff, which gave us all a lot of confidence. We weren't going into the unknown, we had blokes onside who had done it all before, and not that long ago. On the downside, a lot of the kit and equipment supply was chaotic but eventually everything was in place and, after three weeks or so, we got the word to move.

Our Platoon was the tip of the spear, as it were. And that was a tremendously exciting thing for everyone. It's hard to put across, without making war sound grand or glorious, but being the point Platoon of the Fusilier Battlegroup was... well, the blokes were keyed up and raring to go. We were going to be coming across the enemy first, albeit that they had been softened up hugely by bombing and so on.

We broke our way into Iraq, a mixed force of tanks, Warriors, engineer assets... over 1,000 men. My team's first job was to provide the protection for the Engineers as they bridged a huge ditch which marked the Iraqi border and then knocked through some electric fencing and a big three or four metre high sand berm. And then... nothing. There was a border outpost, but there was little or nothing coming from there and, in fact, we faced almost no opposition. It was bizarre. A huge armoured column speeding straight up these excellent roads... you could have been on the M4. Except that the surrounding terrain was flat desert, littered with wrecked tanks and other signs of death and destruction, there were oil fires in the distance and lots of bilingual road signs indicating we were heading towards Basra. I think it was the signs, more than anything... you knew you were in enemy territory, but where were the enemy? We were told the Republican Guards were making their way south with their tanks, and we went a day early in response to that, but we never saw them... I suspect they were destroyed from the air as soon as they moved.

Our mission once inside Iraq was to seize Basra airport and some crucial bridges - Bridge 2 for us - and put a block in, to close off Basra and protect the American flank to our west as they pushed north.

On 21 March, Y Company was ordered to secure a strategically important motorway bridge and ensure that it did not fall into enemy hands. The Company Commander decided to launch a dismounted dawn attack, with Campbell leading the point platoon.

We had stopped a kilometre short of the bridge the day before. It was a substantial concrete affair, carrying a motorway over a canal which was probably 25 metres wide. It's probably stating the obvious, even to civilians, but canals and rivers hold up your advance and bridges facilitate it, so it was very important that we took it and held it. One complicating factor was that we suspected it had been wired for demolition. It seemed entirely likely that the Iraqis would wait until we were half way across and then blow it.

We had a troop of three or four Challenger 2 tanks under Roly Graves, a guy I'd been at Sandhurst with. We dug in the night before, and Paul Nanson sent the tanks forward to provide protection. And all of sudden, Roly came on the net... 'Sighting... one-times-BMP... wait out!' A BMP is their equivalent of our Warrior, a Soviet-built armoured personnel carrier.

Next thing, there's a huge bang, the sound of a tank firing. Then Roly again: 'Contact... wait out.' Then, 30 or 40 seconds later: 'One-times-BMP, engaged and destroyed.'

I'm sitting in the back of my Warrior thinking, *S***, this is happening, it's not training, it's not a game... there's a guy out there, who I was in the same platoon at Sandhurst with, and he's just fired his tank and killed a bunch of people.*

And it happened throughout that night. The Iraqis were making a concerted effort to get to the bridge, and every now and then they would push another BMP forward, with the same result. Roly and his guys destroyed three or four more over the course of the next few hours and... fair's not the word... war isn't fair, and it shouldn't be, you want it to be unfair in your favour, but they didn't stand a chance.

It was a long night, though, actually, our own fighting was limited to the tanks. To our right, three or four kilometres down at the next bridge, it was all kicking off. There was a guy called Chris Head with

Zulu company, and you could see the tracer and hear the explosions and stuff flying around down there. I sat with my platoon sergeant, Chris Dodds, listening to this racket and the radio traffic on the net. Very excited. Nervous. And knowing we'd have to be across our bridge the following day.

Paul Nanson called me forward in the morning. 'Right, Ollie, we need to go forward, seize that bridge on foot.' We didn't know whether it was rigged for demolition and we needed eyes-on. So we get to the bottom of the bridge and dismount. Cpl Burrows' Warrior on my left, Cpl Black's on my right. The idea was we'd send a section across the left hand side first, then follow that with another on the right. If the bridge *was* rigged, we didn't want to lose half the platoon. I would go behind the lead section. It was about 6.30am, and already daylight.

The first section's dismounts were commanded by Cpl Drew Hayton, a great big bear of a man, an awesome rugby player and a fantastic bloke I got on very well with. He took his section forward and I was just behind him, with my signaller Chris Burden alongside. The lads called Chris 'Sally' because they said he looked like Sally out of *Coronation Street*... I'm not a fan of the show so I can't say, but physically there certainly wasn't much to him... he was a slip of a lad. You looked round the platoon, there were some young guys, but he was about the youngest of them all.

'Right, Sally, let's go.'

As soon as they were on the bridge, all hell let loose. The Iraqis on the other side were dug in and determined to hold it. Soldiers in machine gun nests began spraying the British troops, while mortar teams further back began dropping shells onto them.

We moved closer to the bridge and then dismounted, and we were immediately fired upon. You could hear the crack and thump of the rounds, and see the tracer screaming overhead. Luckily, they were lousy shots and their fire was all over the place. But I thought, *Blimey, people are shooting at me.* And it sounds ridiculously naive, but it took a while to register. I quickly snapped out of that. *There are people over there and they want to kill us. Right.*

We got away from the vehicles as quick as we could, because they attract fire, and started on to the bridge. Drew Hayton's lads were returning fire and we started seeing the Iraqis, either falling or withdrawing. It was still a difficult business, getting across. I remember at one point, I was kneeling on the Iraqi side of the bridge, shouting instructions to one of the sections, and I felt this tug on my sleeve. And it was Sally. 'Boss, boss, do you mind if we get into a bit of cover?'

'S***, yes, sorry Sally.'

Because wherever I went, he had to follow with my radio; we were both very exposed and for some reason - nothing to do with any bravery on my part, I assure you - I hadn't really twigged that.

So we hunkered down and called the next section up, Cpl Black's dismounts under Cpl Thomas, to take the right hand side.

They were pretty determined, throwing everything at us... machine gun fire, AK and mortars. We made it across so, technically, we held the bridge. But it was tenuous at best. There were lots of enemy... 50 or so of them in sandbagged sangars or dug in trenches, or popping up and down behind walls, to our front. We were under a lot of fire, now, it was more accurate, and it was effectively pinning us down. It would have made life more comfortable if we could have gone on and cleared those positions, but we had a strict limit of exploitation marked by a line of pylons and the Iraqis were just beyond that.

One of our guys, Drummer Carr, had a mortar land just behind him, a metre or two away, as he was crouched down. By rights, he should have been a dead man... he felt the heat from the explosion go past him but, miraculously, none of the shrapnel hit him. And, suddenly, one of the tanks came roaring across the bridge - they weren't meant to come across at that stage, in case it *had* been set for demolition - but he came steaming up and started firing, because he could see the pressure we were under. Drummer Carr, the poor bastard, was still wandering round all dazed and confused, and he was right next to the tank when it fired... he was now stone deaf and thoroughly bewildered, to the point where his section commander had to physically grab him and point him in the right direction.

The Challenger certainly helped us, and eventually we got the whole platoon across the bridge, dug in, along with a Warrior-load of Irish Guards under Sgt 'Milly' Butler who were attached to the platoon from the beginning of the tour. So my platoon is across, Tom Kibble's platoon had taken the airport without much resistance, and Chris Charnock's platoon were in reserve. We cleared the bridge from an explosives point of view and got the tanks across by about 10am, and Paul Nanson confirmed that we were to continue to provide the block.

With the bridge secured, the next problem was holding it.

That's when the counter-attacks started... lots of effective mortar fire and infantry sections trying to make their way up the sides of the motorway. Fair play to the Iraqis for fighting. You couldn't fault their bravery-stroke-stupidity, because they kept throwing themselves forward... sections of dismounted men or BMPs coming forward to take on three tanks, four Warriors... a total waste of their time and their lives. Luckily, although they were determined, they were not concerted. Among a number of attempts, I think they had three serious goes, whereas if they had got all their guys together and given it one real push, I think there's every chance we could have been overrun. As it was, they were getting to within 100 metres of us, I guess. Literally running towards us and firing AK47s. And of course we would just wipe them out. Cpl Hayden destroyed one of the BMPs with a LAW, and Cpl 'Buz' Burrows another with his Rarden. And still they kept coming. It sounds callous, but I didn't feel bad about that... it was me and my blokes or them and we did feel in real danger. But I did keep hoping they would see the futility of their situation and surrender.

It all really brought the best out of the lads. We had a little guy called Fusilier Donaldson, even smaller than Sally. One of those guys who was made by joining the Army, who found his purpose in life. He was in the Battalion boxing team, the Battalion football team, he was a really good cross-country runner, a very popular lad, and you could see his confidence just growing daily. He was the gunner in Cpl Burrows' Warrior, and at one stage a group of eight blokes were approaching their vehicle and getting dangerously close.

'Buz, there are eight men... '

'Yeah, hold on a sec... '

'But these eight men... '

Cpl Burrows had his mind on something else, which would have been equally important, and in the end Donaldson moved the turret round on his own initiative and shot the eight guys himself with his co-axial machine gun. A lot of initiative, from an 18-year-old bloke not long out of civilian life in Birmingham. Things like that... a lot of people say our recruits aren't as good as they used to be, but that's not my experience. The blokes I had were absolutely sound.

We had to go back to the CQMS for ammo resupply throughout the day. We'd crossed the border with loads, but we'd fired hundreds of turret rounds and thousands of GPMG and SA80 rounds, which gave me some idea of how intense it had been. Drummer Swain had had an LMG and he had used that to great effect, in particular.

It got dark around 6pm, and we started getting engaged with RPGs. That scared me. Several times I saw the red flash from one of them zip by between my Warrior and the next one to me, and thought, *Someone has got close enough and feels brave enough to fire those.* We would engage the RPG team immediately, but it didn't seem to put them off and we had another sleepless night. Though they didn't do much at night - our kit and equipment versus theirs... if it was madness in daylight, it was suicide in the dark. Totally futile, and even they could see that.

There were still mortars landing every ten minutes or so, two or three of them at a time, when they would call in their equivalent of a fire mission. Probably 100 rounds fired throughout the night. We knew they had a spotter nearby so we were looking out for him. He was firing from what is now called the Shia flats... buildings, slum dwellings, water towers. We had a pair of snipers looking for him and the tanks ready to fire if he was located. If you're dug in properly, unless a mortar lands right on top of you, you're safe. And the ground around us was boggy and marshy, which absorbs the impact and lessens the effect compared to, say, concrete. But it was nonetheless frightening. I was on the net to the 2IC Liam Wilson, saying, 'We need to find out where these guys are firing from,' and he said, 'How close are they landing?' And no sooner had he said that than one came in and exploded right beside us. The noise was enormous. I said, 'Did you hear that? That's how close.'

Myself and my platoon sergeant Chris Dodds would take it in turns, one monitoring the radio net while the other tried to get some rest. All through that day and into the night the Company were attempting to organise CAS - close air support - in order to destroy the mortar teams that were engaging us from the edge of the Shia

Flats. Eventually, and with great fanfare, a USMC Harrier arrived on task and promptly dropped the bomb about a kilometre short of the target! An hour later, though, four Cobra gunships, again courtesy of the USMC, arrived on task and proceeded to destroy the mortar team and just about everything else in range. That was a real boost to morale.

And at 10am the following day Chris Charnock's platoon came forward and we were withdrawn.

I remember Juliet Bremner, the ITN reporter, somewhere to the rear with a camera crew. Blokes were having a wash and a shave, or just chilling out, and she was trying to interview them. I felt that was not the time or the place. These fellows had come back from 36 hours of being shot at and shooting, and she was trying to get the 'how do you feel?' type of thing. I understand the need for the media, and particularly the need to let people back home know what's going on, but I felt things like this were a hindrance. Yes, they have their jobs to do, but the lads' jobs were slightly more important.

Lt Campbell's citation makes clear his MC was awarded for the above action and for a second, on the night of March 27, when he led a daring night-time raid well into enemy territory, with the aim of seizing an enemy prisoner. Cloud and choking smoke from distant oil fires meant it was almost pitch black, and the route to and from the target building was fraught with the danger of being compromised. Campbell "demonstrated considerable courage and determination in the face of great personal danger" and showed "exceptional personal example, bravery and coolness in command" during the operation.

The first thing I should say is that the citation says I led the patrol, but actually the Coy Commander Paul Nanson came out with us, so he led it, not me. Though it was very generous of him to give me the credit! We had sound defensive positions but one of the key principles of defence is that you maintain an offensive spirit, which means mounting patrols, finding and destroying the enemy and gathering intel. Plus keeping your morale up and, hopefully, sapping his. This particular patrol was a huge thing, 60 or so blokes in total. We started out from the bridge. Immediately in front of us was a kilometre, maybe a kilometre and a half, of mud flats - wet, cloying, clinging, clay-mud, like an east Anglian farmer's field, or the Somme. A mud desert, basically. No vegetation. Beyond that was Basra, beginning with the slum, shanty-town dwellings on the outskirts, and then moving into proper housing. The enemy were using these slum dwellings as their FOB from where to send their own patrols forward. It was dark, there was a lot of smoke. We patrolled into enemy lines and dropped off our fire support group - including a GPMG, a Minimi and a couple of snipers under the command of Sgt Rutherford - before approaching the target dwelling. We took up fire positions and then Cpl Hayton went forward with his section and he and a couple of his blokes broke into the house... just kicked the door down and went in. Very brave - bear in mind, they were expecting armed men to be inside. And they found them. There were a couple of guys in there, sleeping with their weapons. One of them escaped out of the rear of the building and was shot by the fire support group and Hayton leapt on the other guy as he reached for his weapon and bundled him out. The sound of the shots had stirred up more enemy, and they started firing, but as we left the building they were engaged by the FSG and our artillery, and that was curtains for them. So, a successful outcome. The Iraqi bloke was taken back to our position. He was terrified, a gibbering wreck, poor fellow, but I think he eventually realised that he had actually been the lucky one. The idea was to get information from him, to establish their strength and locations, and also to send out a message... You're not safe anywhere, this is what we can do: we can drag you out of your house in the middle of the night if we want. And actually that message was much more important than any info we could get out of him.

Not long after that, we went down into Basra proper. We were prepared for a massive battle but it never happened: the Iraqi Army and the Saddam loyalists obviously saw the writing on the wall and had basically melted away. And in their place were just thousands of happy people. We were welcomed, literally, with open arms. The reception we got was awesome. I mean, only a fool would say everything has been perfect in Iraq since then, but those early days confirmed very clearly that we had done something for the good of those people.

Lt Campbell completed Operation TELIC and returned to the UK, where he later discovered that he had been awarded the Military Cross for his bravery and leadership.

I didn't think much about it at the time, but I remember when we got back, we went on leave and I flew out to Spain with my mum and dad; they'd just bought a house out there and it was going to be a nice, relaxed family holiday. And poor mum, bless her, she hadn't got the key to the house. It was 10 or 11pm, we were stuck outside and I just lost it with her... I'd just come from an environment where everything is very abrupt, life or death, and I think it was that, and the stress of everything, coming out of me.

The medal... I felt faintly embarrassed, to be honest, and a bit disappointed that guys like Drew Hayton got nothing. It's hard to describe, sitting here in the UK and having a cup of tea, but going behind enemy lines... I know that sounds a bit melodramatic, but that's what it was... and going into this house, and *not* shooting the guy, which would have been the easy option, and bringing him out... absolutely incredible bravery, for me. Cpl Hayton could easily have been killed and, to be honest, I'm annoyed he wasn't recognised. While I think I did a decent enough job, to me that sort of individual act was outstanding. Anyway, I got the boys all together after I was awarded the MC and said to them, 'I'm wearing this, but be under no illusion - it's you fellows who won it.' It was a medal for the whole platoon, no doubt about that, and I think they can all feel very proud of themselves. The Iraqi forces were not the strongest the world has to offer, but they put up a determined fight and were themselves very brave; any of my blokes could have been killed or seriously injured on and around that bridge, and they got on and did their jobs well with that knowledge.

Lieutenant Chris Head, MC
The Royal Regiment of Fusiliers

AS Charles Campbell and the men of 7 Platoon, Y Coy were assaulting their bridge, Chris Head and 10 Platoon of Z Coy were tasked with taking and holding another strategically vital bridge some three or four kilometres to the east.

Head, a friendly and engaging man with a self-deprecating air, watched as others raced ahead of him on the opening day of the war, resigned never to seeing any action.

But before long he found himself in a similar situation to Campbell.

He and his men arrived at their bridge expecting to find it taken by an American tank unit who had arrived some time before. In fact, lacking the infantry support essential to the task, they had been beaten back. Head and his men stepped up to have a go and succeeded where the US forces had failed, Head leading his platoon in what his citation describes as "a devastating dismounted attack on enemy positions, including revetted tanks, anti-tank guns and dug-in infantry."

As with Campbell's position, the Iraqi Army launched a series of counter-attacks; Head "reacted swiftly and aggressively, always to the fore of a robust defence and constantly in range of the enemy's weapons. He showed courage under fire, determination and inspirational leadership throughout the fierce and unrelenting engagement, motivating and inspiring his men for many hours; his selfless courage belied his age and experience."

I joined the Army straight from uni - I don't come from any sort of military family, but I'd been in the cadets at school in Reigate, and then the UOTC (University Officer Training Corps) in Southampton, so it seemed to be the obvious thing to do. I had a pretty hectic time after I commissioned in August 2001. I was lucky to arrive in the Battalion just as we went to Canada for BATUS, which really was in at the deep end, and I'd only just got back and caught my breath from that when I went off to Belize on a jungle warfare exercise. Then the drums started to beat about Iraq and we started training in earnest for the invasion: the Battalion became the Lead Armoured Task Force in November 2002.

At the time the war started, I was a 24-year-old lieutenant, a platoon commander with Zulu Company, which was part of the First Fusiliers Battle Group.

The First Fusiliers Battle Group was the first British element to cross into Iraq. Our other rifle company (Y Company) came up against a bit of opposition, which got the Engineers very excited because it was the first opposed crossing in many years, but it was very quiet for us. We actually got a bit despondent; we'd had this flurry of excitement when we opened up the border, and then we sat in our trenches and watched every man and his dog go by and disappear off into the distance. It felt like the war had happened and we'd missed it.

The plan for our Battle Group centred on a group of four bridges across one of the main waterways on the southern outskirts of Basra, the Shatt-Al-Basra Canal. Obviously, bridges are vital in this sort of situation; if the enemy hold them or blow them, it can cause major hold-ups.

The plan was that Z Coy would take over Bridge Four from an American unit called 1st Tanks, which would get there ahead of us, capture it if required and sit on it until we arrived. We didn't anticipate any problems, based on what had gone before, so it would be a nice genial hand-over from the Americans before they headed off, presumably towards Baghdad. We would then hold the bridge and get decent suntans while probably not firing a shot in anger.

Our company consisted of 10 Warriors, three attached Challenger 2 tanks and assorted ambulances, supply vehicles and other odds and sods. Myself and my Company Commander, Maj Duncan McSporran, were the lead element and the first two Warriors to arrive at the bridge; the bulk of the company was slowly making its way up, and would have been around 20 kilometres behind us at that point.

We halted some distance away, close to the 1st Tanks position, which was on our side of the bridge. That was interesting: they were supposed to be *on* it, and across the other side, and ready to hand it over to us. It turned out they actually hadn't been able to take it - in fact, they'd been beaten back off it by some pretty fierce resistance. Being a Cavalry unit, all they had were tanks, with no infantry; and you can't capture bridges with just tanks - no matter how advanced the technology, you need soldiers on the ground. So it was very much still a live battle; it turned out that the ITN reporter Terry Lloyd had been killed there a few minutes before we arrived. The wreckage of the vehicle he'd been in was lying smoking by the roadside, and there were a number of dead Iraqis in the road, some very badly burnt.

In the near distance, a kilometre or so away, we could see the outskirts of Basra proper. There was smoke hanging over the place, and US helicopters zipping across the city, firing missiles. Somewhere not too far away, an ammunition store had caught fire, and thousands of rounds were cracking off, so it sounded like there was a huge firefight going on. Further away, out in the desert, we could see huge plumes of smoke, from burning oil wells and Iraqi vehicles which had been destroyed, and there were US tanks and more Cobra helicopters pouring fire into the distance. We couldn't actually see the opposition, but they were clearly there. My gunner, Fusilier Wynne, described it perfectly. He said, 'F*** me, sir, it's like we've just driven on to the set of a war film.' It was. Everyone was a bit in awe of this spectacle, to be honest, and I was just very grateful that I wasn't on the other end of it.

The bridge itself was a big concrete affair, like a motorway bridge back home, only much wider - the water was around 250 metres across at that point. It carried the main arterial road between the south of Basra and Kuwait, a four-lane highway called Route 6, and to get up onto it you had to drive along a circular slip-road. The surrounding area was dotted with the traditional small Iraqi buildings, made from a sort of mud and white stone construction - little shops, petrol stations, a few houses here and there and a massive warehouse complex on the home bank. This was a big, walled-in enclosure, the size of, say, three football pitches, full of multi-storey warehouses of modern construction.

We pulled off onto some wasteland and Duncan dismounted and went off to speak to the Americans. Not long after, he returned. 'You've got to go back and get the rest of the Company,' he said, so I turned around in my Warrior and trundled back to fetch them. It was perhaps 10-15 kilometres now. I needed to do that rather than contact them by radio and talk them in because of the confusion - there were only one or two main routes coming up from Kuwait and all the Americans and British were piling up these main roads as quickly as they could and diverting off in different directions. There were vehicles and troops everywhere and the potential for confusion was high. We didn't want them missing us. We were back pretty quickly and then it got even more confusing, because all the American tanks started leaving and moving back through our Warriors.

Duncan quickly reviewed his plan, which now involved us capturing the bridge instead of just holding it. 12 Platoon, four Warriors, would secure the home bank, including the warehouse complex, and 10 Platoon - my platoon - would go over the bridge and secure the enemy bank.

We had a few minutes to go back to our platoons and get our Section and Vehicle Commanders in, tell them the news and give them a quick set of battle orders. Suddenly, a few guys who were usually bolshy and full of bright ideas were looking at me with slightly ashen faces. I strongly suspect I was a bit paler than usual as well. Till then, everything had gone pretty peacefully; now we were actually going to have people trying to kill us, and that's a sobering thought. My Warrior Sergeant, Cpl Daglish, was really on the ball, and snapped us all out of our moment of sobriety, dishing out orders to the vehicle commanders, and helping me formulate a plan for our Warriors once I'd dismounted with the platoon.

12 Platoon went first. We couldn't see much sign of the enemy still, but as soon as they went down the road they came under fire from the warehouse complex on the home bank. Two or three enemy armoured vehicles also appeared on our side of the water, from where they had been hidden under the bridge - I think there were a couple of MT-LB armoured personnel carriers and at least one BMP, which carries a 73mm gun which could disable a Warrior.

Straight away, you could see that this wasn't going to be easy. The 12 Platoon dismounts were quickly out of their vehicles and assaulting the warehouse area, bayonets fixed, and our three Challengers moved up to dispatch the Iraqi armour which had appeared. We were still 800 metres back from this, so I moved us into a position from where we could bring our 30mm cannons to bear on machine gun nests and other positions I could see inside the complex. Back there, at the limit of small arms fire, we were exposed but not in much real danger and I felt pretty detached, working with the gunner, just loading the cannon, checking its lay, watching the strikes and, when I got a sec, letting the guys in the back know what was going on. Detached but quite excited, I supposed, because we were firing live rounds and doing what we'd joined the Army to do.

Duncan went down to assess the situation and realised that, due to the size of the complex, he would need more support. So I left my other three Warriors in the control of my Warrior Sergeant and drove down there, parking up on the edge of the complex. There was a huge amount of noise, because the 12 Platoon dismounts were clearing each room in each building with grenades and lots of fire, and behind us the tanks were finishing off the vehicles under the bridge. I jumped down, my signaller handed over my webbing and rifle with my bayonet already fixed, and we ran off to find Duncan. It didn't feel particularly dangerous, despite all the lead and shrapnel flying around, because most of it was ours - we had the initiative.

By the time I located Duncan, it became apparent that 12 Platoon had pretty much dealt with the complex after all. We helped secure the area and moved the whole Company into it, Challengers apart, because it gave us an element of security and a staging point. And then we gathered our thoughts. We'd had our first engagement, and come through it with no injuries, apart from the odd bump or scrape, which was good. There were few Iraqi casualties - a lot of them had very sensibly fled.

The light was starting to fade now, not helped by the thick, choking, black smoke from the oil fires, and as we stood there it became apparent that there were Iraqis still over there and that they were preparing to blow up the bridge. We'd known they might do this, and we certainly would ourselves... if you can't defend it, deny it at the last moment. It suddenly became very important that we got over to the other side of the bridge and captured it. That was my Platoon's job.

There was no room for sweeping desert tactics. As you got nearer to the water, the terrain either side of the road was mud with a crust on the top; it was very soft and a complete no-go for armoured vehicles, which would have simply bogged in. The only way forward was to zip up the slip road. We remounted in our four Warriors. There was a short delay while Duncan organised some mortar illumination rounds, which light up the battlefield for short periods, and then we really went for it, doing 40mph or 50mph. Partly we wanted to surprise them, partly we didn't want to end up in the canal if they did destroy the bridge. It had a massive camber to it, like a giant humpback, and it reminded me of being on a roller coaster: you get more and more nervous as you near the top and it's out of your control. Because of my position in the turret and the angle of the Warrior, I couldn't even see the road - all I could see was the sky and all these flares. It was very unnerving, actually. We got to the hump in the middle, and then we tipped downwards and at last we could see what was ahead of us. There was a long road leading down into the city, with buildings dotted either side of it and a large compound - it turned out to be a technical college - about 800 metres up on the left-hand side. More importantly, we saw the muzzle flashes from dozens of enemy weapons in trench positions either side of the road immediately after the bridge. The closest were probably 50 metres away, and it was mostly AK47s. We later found out they had RPGs, but they didn't seem to use them for some reason.

Head's citation tells how despite "accurate and heavy" enemy fire, and "despite the very real danger of the enemy successfully initiating their demolition and being under fire from the enemy already, he seized the initiative by calmly and swiftly leading his platoon on to and over the bridge. He then led them in a devastating dismounted attack on the enemy demolition party, thus disabling their equipment and ensuring the capture of this

> key element of the enemy's defence. Disheartened by the action
> led by Head, the enemy abandoned the entire position,
> including anti-tank guns and dug-in infantry positions."

We drove straight over some of their explosives as they detonated them in an attempt to destroy the bridge - fortunately, they destroyed neither the bridge nor our Warriors - and opened fire with our machine guns to suppress the enemy positions. We then dismounted to assault them. There were a lot of rounds flying around, but the guys attacked so quickly and aggressively that the nearest enemy troops surrendered almost immediately, and we quickly got into a prisoner-handling scenario. Then, as we sat there, we came under fire from a collection of buildings about 300 metres down the road.

I launched a platoon attack, with the guys very aggressively going into these buildings and clearing them, one by one. There were a lot of rounds coming back, lots of green tracer all around, but we were gradually getting the job done. All the time, the Company Commander was on the radio because we had a very strict limit of exploitation; there were air strikes into Basra planned, and we were not allowed to go any further than 800 metres forward of the bridge. It's hard to restrain soldiers when their blood is up; we all wanted to go on, because we were now coming under fire from enemy positions still further down the road. Fear had gone out of the window and it was pure aggression and adrenaline. But we had to get back, so we fire-manoeuvred back to the Warriors. As we did so, the 30mm cannons suppressed the distant targets.

Once remounted, we pulled back to the bridge, still on the enemy's bank, and moved into tank scrapes which had been dug by the Iraqis. The other three bridges were off to our flanks, and they were obviously involved in action themselves - we could see air strikes in the distance - but our bridge was quiet now.

We dealt with our prisoners, and it was interesting to actually see the enemy. They were a group of very scared, cold, wet, muddy guys who had been ordered on pain of death to stay on that bridge and stop us crossing it, and you couldn't help but feel sympathetic to them. They looked terrified of us, so we tried to reassure them that they were not going to be harmed and packed them off back to Company HQ, which was now the warehouse we'd taken a few hours earlier.

We entered this very long period of uneasiness. It was pitch black by now, and we were expecting a counter-attack at any moment. We were either in our Warriors or in trenches, all using our NVGs to scan the area ahead for enemy activity. An anti-tank detachment, equipped with Milan, was brought up to bolster our defences. We just sat tight. No question of anyone sleeping.

The most worrying thing was when an American UAV, something like a Predator, flew over. At the time the NBC (Nuclear, Biological and Chemical) threat was still perceived as being severe, and there were a number of dead Iraqis in the road. One of them seemed to be wearing a respirator or gas mask of some sort, which of course fuelled everyone's fear that chemical weapons would be used. Later, and on closer inspection, the 'gas mask' turned out to be some sort of plastic container which had become fused to the man's face with heat. One way the Iraqis might deliver any chemical or biological agent was via a light aircraft, and we mistook the UAV for one of those. So we all masked up and put our NBC suits on and went through the mandatory waiting period while guys conducted tests to see if something had been dropped - it was a really nasty feeling, and about an hour before we were given the all clear.

Almost simultaneously, another company on another bridge unmasked and one of their guys collapsed. The Platoon Sergeant ran over and saw he had all the textbook symptoms of nerve agent poisoning. He straight away took out the guy's combo pen and gave him his injection. It came over the radio that it was NBC black at their location, and someone's gone down. It transpired that he had heat exhaustion. No slur on the sergeant - the symptoms are almost identical, dilated pupils and so on, and who would take a chance? The soldier was fine, fortunately.

After an uneasy night, dawn came. We were all on edge, waiting to see what the day would bring and, at first light, we were confronted by throngs of people trying to leave Basra, people who had become refugees overnight. There were hundreds of them, more than a thousand at various points. They wanted to come over our bridge, but our mission was to hold it and allow no-one over. Trying to keep them back was a nightmare. The road was the width of the M1 motorway back home, so we parked the four Warriors up and used mini-pipe fascines - hard plastic tubes we use to fill in ditches in rough terrain - to make a barricade, and physically blocked the road with that and the guys themselves. We didn't have any of the public order kit, riot shields and so on, that they have in Iraq now, we just had to keep pushing people back.

Some of them began to get very agitated and we had to be very restrained, because one or two started getting violent. You looked at these people, just ordinary Iraqi mums and dads who were fleeing with their kids and babies from a combination of the Iraqi forces and our air strikes, and you couldn't help but feel a lot of sympathy for them. But also, all the time you're wondering if someone might use the crowd as a shield to get near with an AK, or what you're going to do if the enemy start shelling you while you're surrounded by all these people. Pretty stressful. It got to the stage where we fired warning shots. We didn't have any intention of shooting anyone, but we needed to put across the message that they weren't coming over that bridge. Eventually, they started to thin out.

As we'd feared, that two or three hours of jostling and mayhem had allowed the enemy to set up an attack behind them. All of a sudden, a counter-attack started and then the crowd really did thin out.

Initially, it was indirect fire, with mortars landing to the left and right of us. At first we thought it might be friendly fire... *Who's firing that? What's going on?*

It sounds ridiculous, but it took us a few moments to realise that we were being fired on and to get back in the Warriors. And that was the start of a long counter-attack which made us realise that they were very keen on this bridge, and that there were still enough Iraqis around who wanted to fight us.

The intensity of the mortar fire increased. It's horrible stuff, indirect fire. It rains down on you, you can't tell where the next one will land, so it really saps your morale. There would be two or three a minute for a period of five minutes, and then nothing for 10 minutes, and then it would start again. We also came under small arms fire. A lot of Iraqi armed forces had made it into the big technical college campus just down the road and they were setting up medium machine gun posts on the roof and hosing the Warriors down. It was ricocheting off the armour and sending up dozens of little dust spouts in the crust of the ground around us, and several civilians in the remnants of the crowd went down, dead or injured.

There began a game of cat and mouse which lasted for the next six hours or so. Ideally, we'd have charged down the road, smashed into the compound and dealt with them, but we were on a short leash because of the limit of exploitation. So we'd identify a particular machine gun position, send one or two Warriors to race down the road, engage it or dismount the guys in the back and let them deal with it, and then zoom back to where we were supposed to be.

At one point, a soft-skinned truck full of Iraqi troops screamed down to the college and they jumped out with AKs blazing. At a range of 400 or 500 metres, that was as near to suicide as you get - we destroyed them before they'd got rid of half a magazine. We were constantly moving to avoid becoming static targets and in the turrets we were working till the sweat was in puddles around our feet. The atmosphere in the turret was electric: machine guns and cannons were going almost non-stop, and every time there was a lull we were tearing open more ammunition boxes and heaving the empty ones over the side. Each Warrior had a turret load and a half of ammunition, half a load more than it was designed to carry, but despite that if the engagement had lasted much longer than it did we would have needed re-supply.

I remember how calm and professional the radio chatter was in my headphones; in particular, Duncan and the sergeant major were always very measured and reassuring when speaking on the net. My turret, however, rang with the shouts of myself and Fus Wynne as we screamed gunnery commands at each other, and demands for more ammunition to the guys in the back. In gunnery training, you're taught to shout specific, disciplined military commands. Once we qualified, my gunner and I had got into the habit of just chatting to each other in the turret - we didn't need the commands in Canada or Germany. But as soon as the heat was on it was like a switch being flicked and we were straight back in the classroom and shouting those textbook commands. Meanwhile, as Platoon Commander, I had constant reports coming in from the other vehicles in the Platoon, from the Company Commander and the tank Troop Leader, and, likewise, was keeping them updated on what was happening. It was really busy, with so many different voices in my ears and things to think about, but Fus Wynne was a real star, helping me out whenever he could.

It got so heavy that a few of the guys got excited and wanted to pull back. *Come on, sir, this is ridiculous; let's just get off this bridge*, sort of thing. But I just reassured them and reminded them, either face-to-face or via the radio, that, no, our mission was to hold it and hold it was what we were going to do.

Suddenly, matters took a turn for the worse.

There was a lull in the battle, I got out to have a word with some of the guys and someone handed me a brew. I was about to take the first sip when there was the loudest explosion somewhere behind me, and I was almost knocked over by an enormous pressure wave. I crouched down, covered in mud and debris, going, 'What the *f**** was that?'

It was different to anything we had encountered up until then - bigger and much scarier. I dropped the tea and jumped into the turret of my Warrior to get a look, as another two or three of these huge explosions happened within 20 or 30 metres of my vehicle. It turned out they were tanks, though we couldn't identify them at first. Although we didn't want to - at all - myself and another Warrior pushed down the road to try to see what it was, maybe lure them out.

Suddenly, we caught sight of three T55 tanks around the small buildings. The T55 is an old Soviet tank, obsolete by modern Western standards, but nevertheless it is a tank and I knew if we took a direct hit from one of them it was curtains for us. We began to engage them with our cannon, at a range of around 1000 metres away; that sounds a long way, but is well within the Warrior Rarden cannon's effective range. They were very well camouflaged and moving around to avoid being hit, though they might as well not have bothered - I was watching our 30mm rounds just bounce off them, having no impact at all. I got on the radio, looking for some US Cobra helicopters, but they were busy, which was mildly upsetting and quite worrying because, eventually, these Iraqi gunners were going to range in on us.

Our tanks had stayed on the home bank of the bridge; quite rightly, Duncan was reticent about them crossing over because we really didn't want to lose them. But suddenly, amidst all the ringing ear drums and panicked faces, a very calm voice came over the net. 'Don't worry, guys... I've got this.'

It was the Troop Commander of our three tanks: his Challenger II came up over the bridge, bounded down the road, zipped past us - they can really go very quickly when they need to - and fired three times while on the move... bang, bang, bang. Three shots and three enemy tanks destroyed. They didn't even have time to get out and run away.

He came back on the radio. 'Happy with that?'

I said, 'Yes, I'm happy with that!'

Then he was off back to the safety of the other side of the bridge.

It was a fairly devastating expression of superiority, an unequal battle of 1950s technology against the 21st century's best main battle tank, and things quietened down after that.

I remember looking at the smoking wreckage and wondering why they hadn't just given up and gone home. It was a bit like the guys jumping out of the trucks and firing AK47s at us. My gunner and I just sat there and said, 'Can you believe that they are going to take us on like that?' We just hit the fire switch, and that was it. I didn't feel bad about killing them, or the guys in the tanks being killed: they were trying to kill me or the guys in my Platoon, trying to stop me going home to my fiancée, and they chose to fire their weapons at me. What I am aware of, though, is that they probably didn't want to fight. I volunteered to join the British Army. It wasn't quite like that under Saddam. Most of them were probably pressurised by the regime and

27

didn't have much of an option: fight or have your family kidnapped. It's just a shame that, once things were obviously going our way, more of them didn't just jack in and go home. There comes a point where it's not worth fighting if you're going to die and you're not even hurting the opposition.

The whole thing lasted through that day. It was so intense, I had this feeling that my body was in overload and that it was just adrenaline that was keeping me going. We'd been up two nights and we all felt really, really frazzled and just wanted it to stop, just so we could close our eyes, but that's not really an option when mortars are landing 15 metres away. You have to keep going. Eventually, it started to get dark again and there was a bit of a lull and Duncan came on the net and said he was going to send 12 Platoon over to take my place so we could have a breather. Typically, just as 12 Platoon came over the bridge the mortar fire started again. All of my commanders had got used to it and were almost flippant about it by now, but the other guys were like, 'What the hell's going on?'

The other platoon commander asked me whether we could get together for a face-to-face chat and I said, 'No chance... not unless you want a face full of shrapnel. Good luck.'

And that was it, we were back into the compound and finally got some kip.

The following day, the Iraqi resistance lessened and the bridge remained in Coalition hands; the war had moved north and was well on the way to being won.

We were so lucky. How none of our guys were killed or injured I will never know. I suppose it was partly to do with their experience and training. Those enemy tank crews were not necessarily trained men, they were remnants of a conscript army, possibly reservists who had been press-ganged. They were probably very scared and didn't really know what they were doing. Their small arms fire was wildly inaccurate, but then at times so was ours. Having fired my own rifle in anger in these engagements, I do know that with the adrenaline pumping, and just a blur to aim at, a muzzle flash and an outline of a person 200 metres away, you end up just wanting to fire as quickly as possible, to put as much ammunition in his general direction as you can. Everyone does it. It's even of tactical benefit - suppressive fire, it keeps the other bloke's head down, so it has an effect even if it doesn't always kill him.

I certainly wouldn't characterise the Iraqi Army as useless. They had some very brave soldiers, obviously, and elements of them were very good at fighting a guerrilla insurgency, as we later found out. They were just not very good at fighting toe-to-toe, but then it wasn't a level playing field.

As regards my medal, sometimes I have to pinch myself. I often can't believe I got it, particularly when you hear the stories about how other guys earned their MCs or similar awards. You think, *I'm not really sure that I am in the same league as him*. To my mind, I just did my job and I don't know what else I could have done. Someone, somewhere, thought it was appropriate that I got a Military Cross but I tend to think it was really a recognition of the whole platoon, and the way they stood up to be counted in a protracted and very fierce battle. There were two MCs and a Mention in Dispatches awarded from that action. Staff Sergeant Johnson of the Royal Engineers got an MC for going up onto the bridge and stripping out all the main explosives, because it would have been disastrous for our mission had they exploded. That was very brave. And Sgt Hornsby got the MiD. I like the fact that there were several awards because I do believe it was a team effort.

Sergeant Mark Heley, MC
Corps of Royal Engineers

AS the Fusiliers were working to secure the area around Basra, other forces were pushing further north.

Among them was Mark Heley, an experienced Patrol Commander in the Reconnaissance Troop of 23 Regiment (Air Assault).

His job - with his team - was to provide engineer-based intelligence for 16 Air Assault Brigade. Sgt Heley and his patrol were mounted in un-armoured, stripped down WMIK Land Rovers, and operated well in advance of the main body of the Brigade throughout the ground war. Of the 21 days of hostilities, there was only one day when he and his patrol were not 'danger close' to the enemy and they often found themselves miles from friendly forces.

On March 23, on a joint patrol with the Brigade's Pathfinder Platoon, Heley and his team became cut off from the Brigade 40 kilometres behind enemy lines. They had been sent north to check out an airfield which was being touted as a possible drop zone for soldiers from the Parachute Regiment. Advancing beyond Coalition lines - where US Marines and the US Army were stuck in very heavy fighting - they hit the road.

It was dark, and almost immediately they were ambushed in a carefully-prepared killing ground. It turned out to be the first of many such traps they would drive through. Astonishingly, no-one was injured, but eventually it became clear that heavily-armed enemy forces were now out hunting them. As they approached a village where the Iraqis were preparing a huge final ambush - which would likely have been

a death-trap - Heley and his colleagues pulled off the road into the pitch black desert. They watched a convoy of heavily-armed Iraqis race by; trapped, they realised their only option was to fight their way back south. In their path lay the same ambush killing grounds they had already battled though.

I joined the Army at 16 and was a sergeant at the time of Operation TELIC 1. I was Patrol Commander for an advance recce element of 16 Air Assault Brigade, made up of guys from the Royal Engineers and members of Pathfinder Platoon. Our main job was to advance ahead of our own lines to see what the enemy was up to. We were operating in an infantry role, but the idea was that we would be able to relay-back Engineer-specific intelligence about things like bridges, roads and minefields. The British Army has always liked boots and eyes on the ground, where the Americans, say, prefer to rely more on satellite photos and other aerial recon. To my mind, there's no substitute for a bloke seeing things with his own eyes.

We'd also bring in fire from the artillery on to enemy armour, where necessary, and pick up intelligence from talking to the locals after the Iraqis had pulled out of a given area. I remember one time there was a little girl who was badly burned and we treated her. It was simple hearts and minds stuff, but it worked - in those early days, it was like it was when they liberated French towns in the Second World War... flowers and happy people everywhere. We'd get shot at a bit, but nothing too bad. One time when the CO turned up to speak to us we got sniped, but at the time we had two snipers of our own with us and they took the guy out.

On March 23, we were south east of An Naziriyah, which is a town about 150 kilometres - about 100 miles - inside Iraq. Another 150 kilometres north there was an airfield at a place called Qal At Sukkar. The plan was for elements of the brigade to jump in to this airfield, to give our forces a foothold further into the country. In the event, the weather was too bad, with sandstorms and poor visibility, so this was changed to a drop using helis. Anyway, our patrol was tasked with recce-ing this airfield. It had been used in the previous Gulf War, and also in Saddam's war with Iran, so it needed to be checked for mines and other ordnance. Plus, obviously, potential enemy forces. They must have known it was a likely spot for us to go into.

We got on to the main highway that went up to An Naziriyah. At that point, we were behind the Yanks, who were up ahead and hopefully pushing on through the Iraqi Army. Ideally, they'd go up past Qal At Sukkar and we could just slot in behind them and secure the airfield.

In fact, American forces had run into serious opposition at An Naziriyah and were fighting for their lives. Armoured vehicles had been destroyed, a large number of men were dead and others wounded.

As it turned out, we got to An Naziriyah and the Americans were still fighting, and fighting hard. There was a lot of resistance and we sat with one of their recce elements and watched the US Marine Corps Cobras getting stuck in. It wasn't all one way by any means: the Marines were soaking up so much heat it was unbelievable. It was like a scene from *Hamburger Hill*... burning vehicles and buildings everywhere, and hundreds of US soldiers.

Well, we couldn't sit round all day, so at about 4pm we moved up. The country is criss-crossed by rivers and canals and there were a lot of bridges we'd need to cross on the way to Qal At Sukkar. We got to the first one, and halted - obviously you have to be extremely careful when you're driving through the lines, especially when there is still a lot of fighting going on around you. Brigade would have been in touch with the US command, letting them know we were coming, but you still proceed with caution and identify yourself.

This particular group of Americans had run into a determined lot of Republican Guard at this point and had basically come to a standstill. They were good fighters, some of the Iraqis, very good in fact. Quite often it was only our superior technology, air power and armour that made the difference. This group of Yanks had taken a lot of casualties - they had 10 or 20 blokes dead, more injured. The other side of the bridge, you could see an M113 armoured personnel carrier had been taken out, it was sitting there smouldering, with all inside killed. We got out to talk to the US commander and as I stood there a little Iraqi lad came over, with rounds going off not very far away, and handed over a set of dog tags from one of the dead Marines. I remember thinking it would have been a fantastic photograph, *Time* magazine stuff, except that people would have thought it was stunted-up.

The American said, 'Where are you guys going?'

We said, 'We're going up there.'

He looked at us like we were mad. 'You're going up *there*? In *those*?'

There were nine of us, in three open-topped WMIK Land Rovers. Obviously, they're very vulnerable but we could move quickly and we weren't that worried. Our best defence was speed. It's very hard to hit something that's going fast, especially with an RPG or even a rifle.

'That's RPG Alley,' he said. 'Every time we go down here we get hit. Be careful.'

So we moved up - I was in the middle Rover - and within about two minutes there was a pop and we had a puncture. There was a lot of debris and fragments all over the road. We can drive flat for a while, so we carried on and not long after we got to another bridge. There were more Americans here, and a couple of Abrams tanks sat there. It turned out that this was the Coalition limit of exploitation for the night.

We needed to change the flat, because if something happened we'd be right in the s***, so we got cracking. The tankies saw what we were trying to do and they came up alongside us and shielded us on the bridge while we swapped the wheel, which was good, and it wasn't long before we were on our way again. It was getting dark, now, and we had night vision on. The feeling was that the Iraqis probably wouldn't have such good equipment, or any, so that gave us a big advantage. But we were on edge, after what the American officer had told us: you think, *Any minute now*.

After a while, we came to a village split by the main drag. The street lights had all been shot out, except for a couple of hundred metres where they were on; as we hit this lit area, we took some incoming fire, an RPG over the top of the vehicle, and a few shots. It felt sporadic, like they weren't all that interested... as though they'd heard all the fighting down the road but they knew it was over for the night so they were just chilling out.

But as we got further on down the road and went through more villages - all with the same pattern of a stretch of road which was lit up - the fire got heavier and heavier each time, and it became clear that these were deliberately-prepared killing grounds and the Iraqis were communicating with each other, letting the people a couple of Ks further on know we were coming. It got quite surreal... almost like being in a war film or an exercise.

In all they fought through six major contacts, each of them carefully-prepared; a hail of RPGs, machine gun fire and even anti-aircraft rounds were fired at Heley and the others. As they cleared the final one, a large group of heavily-armed

Iraqi forces were speeding along the road behind them, hoping to trap the patrol in another killing ground further ahead.

We'd got about 40 kilometres when a couple of cars came past us. We couldn't engage them, but it was clear that they were scouts. They nipped ahead, did a U-ey and came back before peeling off into what looked like some sort of base. At that point, we decided to get off the road. Turns out this was a very good idea, because we were just short of a place called Ash Shatrah, the next large town north of An Naziriyah and we think we'd have been hit very hard there if we'd carried on. We plotted up in the darkness in a palm grove, a river to our backs, facing the road, just waiting.

A few minutes later, six or seven vehicles, civvie cars and 4x4s, sped past; in the back of one of the pick-ups was a 12.7mm Dushka, a Russian-made heavy machine gun, and the rest of them were full of blokes with weapons.

We didn't have a pop at them, because why expose yourself? Obviously, they were now well aware that we were in the area and given that we were now a long way ahead of the last US forces we'd seen we were quite vulnerable and exposed, and we needed to think about extracting. It was very quiet, except for this dog barking constantly from somewhere among a few houses not far to the south of us. We set up the satellite comms so we could get back to Brigade and ask for some air cover to bring us back in.

It takes some time, so while we were doing that one or two daft ideas got thrown around.

There was a young officer with us and I think he had read too many thrillers, to be honest. He said, 'Have you got any explosives with you?'

I said, 'You know I have.'

We had a lot of plastic explosives on board - probably 50kgs plus - so that we could clear any mines on the airfield.

'What we'll do,' he said, 'is we'll blow the vehicles, swim the river and tab to the objective.'

I just looked at him.

Then one of the Pathfinder lads said, 'Or I could go down to the house where the dog's barking, we'll steal a car and some clothes and all that, and we'll jump in it and drive back up the road.'

I just thought to myself, *This isn't happening*. It's always a mistake when you give people too much time to think.

Just then, Brigade came back to us and said they couldn't give us any air. That was a little bit disheartening. We were a bit stuck there, out on a limb 40 kilometres ahead of the Yanks, behind enemy lines and they weren't willing to put any air cover up.

Eventually, they realised they would have to brave the ambushes they had already driven through.

The officer, me, an ex-Signaller Pathfinder corporal called Tricky and Nathan Bell - the Pathfinder Patrol commander, a Parachute Regiment sergeant who also got the MC - got our heads together and came up with a plan. Which was simply to drive straight back down the road the way we'd come. Our thinking was that they wouldn't be expecting us, because the last time they'd seen us we were heading north with their mates in hot pursuit, so the element of surprise, plus our speed and the firepower we had, meant we should be OK. We went back to the vehicles and I briefed my guys as regards all the actions-on, what should happen in every eventuality, so everyone knew what was happening. Then we moved back on to the road. We used lights this time, so that we could go that bit quicker, and just waited for it.

As soon as we came around the first corner, we saw the lights where they'd lit up the killing area, and all hell broke loose.

It was like being on the range, but down the wrong end. There were bullets flying everywhere; there were dozens of them shooting at us from about midnight to nine o'clock. Some of them were firing from the darkness down alleyways, and all you could see was the muzzle flash, but others - who hadn't really thought it through - were visible in the street lighting. We could see them in trenches dug in in front of the houses and in the houses themselves. There was a hell of a noise and loads of tracer zipping over our heads. There were a lot of RPGs, too - the rear vehicle saw one go under ours and bounce off and explode and another four went over the top of us.

We immediately responded. The guy on our .50 cal, Al Edin, was having problems with it. It's a really important piece of kit, especially in situations like that. The .50 cal round does a lot of damage - it's half an inch in diameter and they say that if it even passes within a certain distance of you it will do something. You fire that at people and they are in serious trouble and they don't want to know. But within a couple of rounds he had a stoppage and ducked down. I yelled at him, and he got back up, went through the drills, cleared it and was OK. And straight away I can remember big holes appearing in these houses and chunks of masonry exploding everywhere, which felt good. You always want to be giving it back to them. I was on our front-mounted GPMG, doing the same thing.

Heley was himself struck in the chest with an AK47 round; his citation says he "merely carried on returning fire."

I didn't realise it at the time, but an AK round went through my TAM (Tactical Aide Memoire) and into the pistol I had on my chest webbing, striking where the cartridge comes out of the ejection port on the weapon, smashing that totally and ending up buried back in the book.

I've still got the book at home - that and the pistol probably saved my life. Funnily enough, I took my family to the Imperial War Museum shortly after the war, and there's a section there with things like that - a cup that saved a guy, a helmet with a big dent in it and so on. And my youngest lad piped up, 'Hey, dad! You've got something like that!' And everyone started looking at us, which was a bit embarrassing.

As I say, at the time I wasn't sure what had happened. I was returning fire on the GPMG and it just threw me off, knocked me back. I said to the driver, Ginge McLaren, 'I think I've been hit!' But it was confusing, because I didn't feel anything. And I quickly dismissed it as I had other things to worry about.

Somehow we got through it with no injuries or serious damage, though the vehicles had all taken multiple hits, including one to the GPMG on the rear Rover, and a couple of guys later found rounds in their Bergens. For some reason it was our night - they were just bad shots, I think. I'd like to think that if it had been the other way around, we would have taken three Land Rovers of Iraqis out and stopped them quite quickly.

After the first contact, we noticed cars on the side tracks stopping and flashing their lights, obviously to signal to people at the next ambush that we were on our way, which wasn't massively reassuring.

At one point, a pickup truck pulled across the road to block our way, but they left a metre or so gap between us and the verge so we were able to nip round it. As we did so, we opened up on it and shredded it, as we did on a few vehicles that tried that. If we stopped, we were dead, simple as that, so we weren't stopping for anyone.

It was a massive adrenaline rush; you always wonder how you'll react to being under fire. I had been shot at before in Bosnia and Northern Ireland but that was nothing compared to the weight and intensity of this. For years you train for it, and all of a sudden you're there. I didn't really feel scared, probably because of the adrenaline and there wasn't time - I was just very focused and calm. I do remember repeatedly thinking, *I have got to get through this for my wife and the boys.* My wife and I have been together since we were 15 or 16 - 22 years - and I've got three lads. I didn't want to die out there, miles from them.

We got through, and every ambush we hit after that was exactly the same, only more intense. They came roughly every four or five kilometres. The last and worst one we think was a barracks: we were opened up on from there by an anti-aircraft gun. Not a Dushka, it was something much bigger than that. But as I say, at the speed we were going, up to 60mph, we were hard targets to find. I was using the GPMG quite sparingly, just squeezing off three to five rounds at each target. Even so, I got through about 800 rounds. Of course, in the same way it's hard to be hit, it's hard to hit people at speed, so I couldn't really tell what effect we were having, other than we were putting rounds into their positions and it was making them keep their heads down. There was a hell of a lot of AK and machine gun fire, as well, and the walls of this barracks were no more than 50 metres back from the road, so it was very close range stuff.

We pushed through there and passed a bus coming back the other way, I think carrying injured from their front line. We took a left fork, to bring us back round to where the Americans were, and there was one last bunker on that corner; they opened up on all of us as we went by. We were all massively high on adrenaline and all three vehicles poured masses of fire into that bunker and completely destroyed it.

The next danger we faced was the Americans. We slowed right down, kept our lights on and pushed all our guns away from us, holding our hands out where they could be seen. Nathan Bell went forward in the front vehicle, got out when he was challenged, told them who we were and brought us forward, and that was it.

The Americans were brilliant. They were going, 'You guys... we're so glad you're OK!'

They were quite emotional, actually, having lost so many of their own men that day.

They said: 'You guys are crazy driving in those things.' They couldn't understand the concept of no armour.

We stopped in the middle of the Americans, or just behind their line, and got into our sleeping bags. No-one had said anything up until then. And as we lay there, we all just looked at each other and burst out laughing. We were like, 'F***ing *hell*, can you believe what just happened?'

This incident was just one example of what his citation calls his "outstanding leadership and extraordinary resilience and bravery." It goes on to say: "He always volunteered for the most demanding patrols and despite the dangers managed to relay timely and critical information back to the Brigade. Sgt Heley is one of a very rare breed; able to overcome his own fears in spite of the threats around him and yet lead by personal example."

I went back and I wrote up the two young guys who were in my vehicle, the driver Spr Ginge McLaren and the gunner LCpl Al Edin, for medals. They were both Engineers, only in their early 20s, and they didn't lose it. Ginge was really scared, particularly at first, which was understandable, but I kept talking to him constantly - 'You're a good driver, keep going!' - and he did a brilliant job. Al had a nightmare on the .50 cal when his weapon jammed, but I could see why, you're stood up there, a hell of a target. But again, he got back up and came through it. Two really good lads.

I was a bit embarrassed to be written up myself. I was older, more experienced and felt really I'd just done my job. To be honest I was going to reject it, but I went in and saw Lt Col Chris Tickell, our CO at the time. He's a brilliant bloke, a brilliant commander whom I'd known since he was a young lieutenant, and he sat me down and explained how he felt maybe I did deserve it. The medal stays in its box in a drawer, and I certainly don't mention it unless someone asks, but it was a great honour to get it. I had a really good day at Buckingham Palace, meeting the Queen; I took my wife, her mum and my mum. My wife's mum absolutely loved it. She's getting on a bit, really loves the royals and loved being there, so that was nice.

I left the Army not long after TELIC 1 and, funnily enough, I'm now back in Iraq working in private security, chaperoning people in and around Baghdad. Iraq was, and continues to be, an eye-opener for me. Life out there... there are people dying every day, and when my son comes home with a problem at school, you think to yourself, *With the best will in the world, that is absolutely nothing.*

People in the UK have no real worries. The Iraqis have no electricity, no water; there are people dying left, right and centre, being blown up. But I talk to people at home and I don't think that they are that bothered or interested. If there's a big car bomb, and a lot of people die, and it's reported, yes. But everyday stuff doesn't really get written about. I don't think the majority of the public give a toss about Iraq or even our squaddies, which is bad. I'd like to think I'm wrong but I don't think people are that bothered.

My wife says I've changed since Iraq. She's probably right. It's not the thought of killing people - I would never go looking for it, but if it is a case of, if I don't do it to him he is going to do it to me... well, I don't want to die. I like living. I don't know whether that's wrong. I know it bothers some guys. One thing it does, it puts it all into perspective. I think I have changed, but it's for the better. Life is too short, that's my attitude now.

Lieutenant Simon Farebrother, MC
1st The Queen's Dragoon Guards

A WEEK after Mark Heley's exploits, British forces were still involved in fighting their way north to Basra, Iraq's second city. Simon Farebrother, 2nd Troop Leader, C Squadron Queen's Dragoon Guards, was working with the Brigade Recce Force and 40 Commando to clear Route 6, the main highway.

In their way stood Abu Al Khasib, a small town which was, effectively, a suburb of Basra. Farebrother's troop was ordered to seize a bridge to the east of the town to secure lines of communication and divert the enemy from the main axis of 40 Commando's attack, which was to come from the south.

In the early hours of 30 March, approaching the bridge in the dark, the BRF were engaged with RPGs and small arms, so Farebrother immediately pulled forward to give fire support into a bunker at a range of only 50 metres with his 30mm. The position suppressed, Farebrother and Cpl Armstrong, the commander of the other vehicle in his section, then crossed the bridge and began to put down suppressive fire on buildings on the far bank with 30mm and 7.62mm.

Just as it appeared that things had quietened down, an RPG was fired at short range at Cpl Armstrong, exploding on the asphalt a metre short of his hull. He reversed but in so doing ended up in a ditch and threw a track. The section therefore found themselves immobilised and isolated on the enemy bank, with the sun rising and exposing the two vehicles to more enemy fire.

I'm 28 and originally from Cranbrook, in Kent. I have no military background since WW2, where my paternal grandfather was a conscientious objector and my mother's father was in the Desert Rats. I think he was a tank commander.

Before the invasion, I'd been training at BATUS in Canada and afterwards had taken the opportunity to go skiing with the Regiment in Verbier. About half way through the trip, we got a call to say we were being recalled from skiing to deploy to Iraq. This was in January of 2003.

C Squadron, commanded by Maj Henry Sugden, would be attached to 3 Commando Brigade, with my troop attached to their recce element, the Brigade Reconnaissance Force. B Squadron would do rear ops with Division and A Squadron would be the recce unit for 7 Armoured Brigade.

We were in Kuwait a couple of months before the invasion. We were acclimatising, by default, while we waited, getting used to living out in the desert, next to your vehicle, eating rations, and doing a lot of training with the Marines and the Engineer elements of the BRF. The BRF is not far off Special Forces level... they were a highly-motivated, multi-skilled recce force drawn from the Royal Marines, the Royal Engineers and Gunners from 29 Cdo. It was quite an amazing time: there were vehicles as far as the eye could see, a lot of American kit, and you felt sure you were part of something almost unprecedented in scale.

The plan was for 3 Cdo Bde to be inserted via an amphibious landing onto the Al Faw peninsula. This was a bit odd from our point of view, because using tracked vehicles - Scimitar and its variants - we had not really done amphibious landings before. C Squadron had three Sabre troops of four Scimitars, a support troop of four Spartans and a troop of guided weapons vehicles equipped with Swingfire missiles, plus Squadron HQ vehicles. That's a lot of kit to get onto a beach. But the US Marines... their 15th MEU outfit had a fabulous bit of kit, a huge ship equipped with large hovercraft called, in that inimitable armed forces way, 'Landing Craft, Air-Cushioned - Heavy', abbreviated to LCAC Heavies. These could take four Scimitars and deliver them to the sand, so we spent weeks rehearsing getting them on and off.

Then the whole plan was changed. Our designated destination, codenamed Red beach, right by Al Faw town on the south coast, was found to have been heavily mined. I presume the SBS or someone else had taken a look... anyway, that was off. The LCAC Heavies are very expensive pieces of equipment, and the USMC were understandably chary about the possibility of losing them. Instead, we were to be inserted further up the coast, using some old-fashioned British landing craft from HMS Ocean... *Saving Private Ryan*-type things from 50 years ago, which weren't quite as flash as the LCACs but which did the job perfectly well.

Invasion day came. A Squadron like to claim they were first on Iraqi soil, but we were floating in a grid which was within Iraqi waters before that, so we reckon we were there first. It's a source of some discussion within the Regiment!

No-one wants to make an opposed landing on a beach, and the Tomahawk cruise missiles and Coalition air forces had done a great job of softening up the Iraqi defences before we went in. We had maps of our landing area and inland, all covered with mortar positions, anti-shipping missile launchers and other enemy facilities; each day during the two-month build-up, more and more of them were just being crossed off the maps by our Squadron Intelligence Officer, James Davidson. It was very morale-boosting, and, as it turned out, very important. Our landing was all a bit chaotic. There had been lots of roads and little concrete jetties which we could have used, but these had all been denied by the enemy, so we had to go onto the beach itself. A number of vehicles came off the landing craft and immediately bogged in on the soft sand. People were just sitting there with their tracks whizzing around, unable to move. The vehicles that had made it onto land proper, as it were, had to tow the others out; had we had to do that under fire we could have been looking at a real disaster. One vehicle, Callsign Zero Echo, bogged in on its side in the water, and the blokes had to get out and swim to shore. Interestingly, when the tide went out, we found that the vehicle was surrounded by mines. I was never quite clear as to whether they were new ones, or ones left over from the Iran-Iraq wars... we were just grateful that none had detonated.

Once we got everyone off the beach and formed up, we set off towards Al Faw town. We'd landed on the south west corner of the peninsula and we were supposed to go and link up with 3 Cdo Bde recce force. We would clear first the peninsula and then Route 6, the main road heading north to Basra and beyond. We would stop at Basra, turn to face the city and stop anything coming in or out on the south east side of the city while the main force caught up with us.

Our maps showed a track which led to Al Faw, so we got on that and set off. The whole area was deserted, and covered with spent munitions, bomblets, shell casings, destroyed Iraqi vehicles and army buildings. You could see that the Coalition air had really done a very good job and it also looked, to my eyes, as though a lot of the positions they had destroyed had been empty, things hanging over from the country's previous conflicts. We travelled along this track for around 17 kilometres and then, quite suddenly, it stopped. And so did we. We were just thinking about what to do next, when my troop sergeant, Sean Pawlin-Gardner, came on the net, saying '20... stop!' I turned round to look at him, and he pointed to my track. There was a Chinese anti-tank mine right there, a foot or so away. Big enough to destroy our vehicle and everyone inside. LCpl Evans dismounted to check the underside of his vehicle and felt something catch on his leg: it was a piece of wire attached to another mine. His commander, Cpl Dave Armstrong, had to jump off and cut the wire away, and it turned out there were loads of the things all around us. This presented a bit of a problem. We'd obviously driven into a minefield, probably a historic one. We couldn't just cut off across country towards Al Faw, and we couldn't even turn around, as we couldn't be sure the mines were not right alongside the track - all we could do was to reverse the whole way. Which we did, for 17 kilometres. So far, our involvement had been something of a comedy of errors.

Eventually, we made it to Al Faw after nightfall, along a cleared road, and found the Commando brigade which was there. They were very, very busy. There was a lot of incoming and outgoing mortar and tracer fire, and Marine troops were out and fighting enemy positions all around. There was a lot of proper resistance, which was a bit of an eye opener - we'd experienced nothing like that. It was around then that we had a major shock. Many of the BRF blokes were flying in on four US Marine CH46 Sea Knight helicopters - small Chinooks, effectively - and one had crashed. Eight guys had died, with four American crew, and among them was the OC, a chap called Maj Jason Ward. The BRF Sergeant Major, WO2 Stratford, and the Signals Colour Sergeant, CSgt Cecil, also died. It was very shocking; we'd been rehearsing with that very unit and had got to know those guys well. Jason in particular was a very nice chap, very welcoming. They were great soldiers to work with, we loved it, and to find out that this large group of them had gone down like that was a real shocker. Not like losing people from your own squadron, but close to. I doubt they knew anything about it, but it was still hard to take.

I met up with the BRF 2IC, Capt Chris Haw, who had now taken over from Jason, and we spent a noisy night in Al Faw and then set about moving up Route 6 the following morning.

To our west, the rest of our Squadron advanced very quickly; they came up against nothing, and recce works quickly, so they actually covered in a day what they were expected to cover in a week, with 29 Cdo following up behind them. They pulled up just to the south of a place called Abu al Khasib, which was a township on the outskirts of Basra, the last major settlement before you hit the city itself, and waited there.

On our side, we didn't come across much ourselves, certainly early on. Route 6 is a lovely, big concrete road, akin to the M1, and obviously you can move really fast on it. I stuck my Troop Sergeant on there, and my section of two vehicles moved up on another, smaller road a couple of kilometres to the right, and we worked along the banks of the Shatt-al-Arab, criss-crossing and working in tandem, and clearing through the villages and palm groves and farm settlements as we headed north. We either found no-one at all, or we found local people who were happy to see us. There were no Iraqi Army, insurgents or anything similar until we reached a position just shy of an old fort, where we were fired on. So we traversed right and put a lot of fire into it, and there were a lot of white flags, and people scurrying away, and that was over. From then on, we encountered more of that sort of thing... fleeting attacks, someone would fire a few rounds, and then a pick-up truck would fly up Route 6, heading north like a bat out of hell. Because elements of our own squadron were ahead of us, I would be able to talk to them and say, 'There's a white Toyota pick-up, it's just fired at us, three blokes in the back, it's heading your way,' and they would sit and wait till it came by and then destroy it.

We made decent progress and were told to go firm around nightfall. We were given a choice of two grid squares from which to choose, the idea being that these would be clear of Coalition air activity and, therefore, safe. One was in a town, the other was in the desert; we didn't fancy leaguering-up in a populated area, so we went for the desert. We arranged our vehicles into defensive positions, pointed our turrets out in the direction of potential threats and surrounded ourselves with Claymores. These were great new toys we'd not had before - high explosive surrounded with ball bearings, a fantastic anti-personnel weapon, triggered by a guy with a clacker. With double stag on, we slept a pretty nervous night - bear in mind that there were only 12 of us and we were probably 20 kilometres in advance of the nearest friendly forces, so well behind enemy lines.

Next day brought more of the same. We had a friendly reception from most of the villagers, most of whom looked astounded to see us. They were Marsh Arabs, and had suffered badly under Saddam - the marshes were being drained, tens of thousands had been displaced, so we did all that stuff of rolling over posters of Saddam, that sort of thing, just to show them whose side we were on. We ended up on the limit of advance of Route 6, south of Abu al Khasib, at which point we were detached from the BRF and flicked back over to the Squadron.

Abu al Khasib was to be the scene for Operation JAMES, which saw 40 Commando tasked with taking the place. It had army barracks and a sizeable Sunni population, and the thinking was that if we were going to get serious opposition anywhere, that was where it was going to be.

As I say, the rest of the squadron had arrived there on the first day and been told to halt. We put in an OP screen in a line, looking out at what was ahead of us. There were Iraqi Army positions in and around the suburbs, and they had eight or nine tanks hidden in scrapes, clumps of trees and behind sand berms, anywhere from two kilometres to five kilometres away. We're talking pretty old hardware - mainly T55s. They would roll out and have a pop, and then roll back in, and their gunnery was of the old school, bracketing method - one shot would land short of you, the next would land behind you and the third would be on you, except that we would move after the second and they would miss. The T55 is an old tank, but its round would destroy a Scimitar, and we couldn't really destroy them, so we had to call in air support. A friend of mine, a troop leader called Arthur Chamberlain, got a Mention in Dispatches for being chased around by, and directing fire onto, these tanks, and Sgt 'Scouse' McDonald, our Forward Air Controller, also did a great job, and was also awarded a Mention in Dispatches. We had F16 jets, Lynx helicopters from HMS Ocean and A10 Warthogs, and the effect was just extraordinary; the noise A10s make, in particular, is frightening and, to be honest, I felt slightly sorry for the Iraqis. What we had was so overwhelming. Manned bunker systems, a mix of concrete, rebar and earth, were being flattened by our artillery. You'd call in a fire mission and it would be overwhelming... the whole area explodes, the earth shakes. Then a lot of white flags would come up, so we'd stop. We couldn't go forward to take prisoners, because of our no-fire line, so ambulances would come along on their side and scoop people out. Then a line of taxis would deliver more people - I suspect they were probably young lads from Basra who were being coerced - and it would all start again. It was an extraordinary situation and it was the only option we could take. They weren't the Republican Guard, but they were still firing at us and even a granny is dangerous in a T55 or behind an artillery piece.

I remember one particular fire mission I called in with the USMC. It took 40 minutes to arrange, to ensure there were no aircraft flying through the artillery shells, and it eventually came back that I was going to get 18 guns, a Regiment of US Artillery 155mm towed howitzers, firing 30 shells each... five to adjust and 25 for effect. An unheard of weight of fire, to British ears. The 29 Cdo boys provided illumination so I could see where the rounds were landing, and the fire mission started. The five rounds to adjust were perfect, so I told them to proceed for effect. They used a mixture of point detonation, air burst proximity and bomblets and some illumination, and it was unbelievable. The phrase 'shock and awe' came to mind. All you could hear was the rounds roaring overhead and then these huge thumps when they detonated... I could feel my chest being punched by the force, even at a distance of several kilometres, and the earth was shaking. LCpl Evans, my gunner, and I looked at each other and said, 'Bloody hell.'

Afterwards, I was asked for a battle damage assessment. All I could say was nothing moving any more. But sure enough, next morning a load of taxis turned up and refilled the positions. It was frustrating; one felt we were just sitting there, hammering people who were probably being harangued into it. But then, as I say, we had no choice, because they were firing at us.

Behind us, 7 Armoured Bde had cleared their bridges, and people were pouring over from the west. On March 30, Op JAMES began.

Our mission was to clear and secure Sennen bridge, which was located to the east of Abu Al Khasib. It needed to be taken prior to H Hour, which was 2am, because it provided a potential escape route. Any civvies who wanted to get out could leave towards Basra, which wasn't being closed off, but we weren't going to allow armed men to escape. This wasn't really a typical recce task, to be honest. Normally, we'd mark a bridge and secure the home bank, and someone else would punch through before we nipped ahead of them again. So it was a pretty novel use of our light armour, but then it was a relatively flimsy construction and wouldn't have taken the weight of heavy armour.

We were told to expect about a section strength, about eight people, so that gave us pause for thought, the fact that we were going to be opposed. But we had what amounted almost to a creeping barrage of artillery ahead of us, so we were reasonably confident that whoever was there would have been pretty much dealt with before we arrived.

As they reached the bridge, with two Royal Engineer WMIK Land Rovers, they came under fire from a sandbagged bunker on the home bank of the river.

The Engineers put down some fire while mortar illum went up. That turns night into day... I could see the bridge, houses nearby and the bunker, with the guy inside engaging the Engineers. I said, 'Gunner, traverse on, six rounds automatic,' and he put six rounds HE into the bunker at a range of 50 metres, which stopped the chap in his tracks. The Engineers then very bravely whizzed straight over, and we followed. As we went, we started taking fire from the sides. What had happened was that the defenders had mostly scooted down under the bridge and waited out the artillery, which had been airburst, anti-personnel stuff. Once day broke you could see the whole bridge had been peppered, but it hadn't really hurt them. However, their resistance only lasted for a few moments, and they quickly surrendered to the Engineers who took them back to the home bank, leaving us on the other side.

We were still taking incoming from buildings out to the front of us, so we pushed out, putting down suppressive fire. Cpl Armstrong was slightly ahead of me, and suddenly there was the most enormous explosion as an RPG hit the road just in front of him. He immediately got some rounds down and reversed, as he should, but in doing so he went off the road and slid down the bank of the bridge. When he then tried to turn to come back up, he threw a track in the loose ground. So he was stuck there.

That was the first moment I thought, *Bugger*.

I sent a contact report back to Chris Haw. He sent the two Engineers WMIKs back over to give us some immediate protection, because the Scimitar is vulnerable when static.

We were taking fire from some nearby houses, so I used our 30mm cannon to punch holes in these buildings and the Engineers were in and cleared them before going up onto the roofs to provide sniper cover. Meanwhile, we towed Cpl Armstrong's vehicle back up on to the road and I jumped out and set about trying to help fix the track. I wanted to be able to speak to the blokes, and I needed to be close to them. Fixing a track is a 'how long is a piece of string?' job... you have to take the track off, split it down, lay it out and put it back together, then fix it back on. Depends on a number of things, and it took us a good half hour.

All the while, sporadic small arms fire was coming in and we were conscious of people with RPG launchers milling around in houses 300 metres or so away, looking for fire positions. Obviously, I'd lost my 'eyes', being out of the wagon, but I could still talk to my operator, LCpl Evans. He was scanning his arcs, saying 'I can see, 400 metres, the yellow house, a guy there with an RPG... and to the right of him, another one.'

By remaining with Armstrong's vehicle, Farebrother "demonstrated leadership of the very highest order. He placed the lives of his men before his own, retrieved the situation and ensured the success of the mission."

To be honest, I didn't really think about the incoming rounds. You could hear them cracking off overhead, or whizzing by, but the shooters were being suppressed and we were all concentrating on the job in hand. At one point, Chris Haw came across the bridge and said, 'I think you ought to stick a helmet on, mate,' but I couldn't because

I needed my crew headset on to stay in touch with the vehicle. I think my clearest memory is actually of how calm Cpl Armstrong was: he'd just had an RPG explode very close to him, now here he was changing a track under fire. It was bloody hot work, track-bashing while wearing body armour, and halfway through we stopped for a breather and cracked open some 7Ups we had in the back of one of the Scimitars, which I guess was mildly surreal, looking back.

There was an amount of human shielding going on, with young kids and teenagers all held out in front of the RPG teams, so LCpl Evans had a difficult decision as to whether he could shoot. Where it was possible to do so, we were destroying them and we effectively either killed them or drove them away. The battle lasted, I suppose, about 45 minutes.

And then the sun started coming up, and the atmosphere changed. Suddenly, the locals started coming out and were very friendly. Absolutely no anger in our direction. We had been forced to destroy some of their houses, but we had pushed some bad people out of there and they were pleased about that. They were eager to tell us that a house on the home bank was owned by a local big wig, a brigadier, so we searched that and found a lot of armed men, about 30, all hiding and properly scared. It turned out he had been given a lot of money by the Ba'ath Party to defend that bridge, and a bigger search uncovered a lot of AKs and suitcases of dinars, about three million of them, which then was quite a lot of cash, about £20,000. Lot of pics of Saddam there, lots of Ba'athist posters and so on, so actually quite a good little find, and they were all taken away by the intelligence guys.

By securing the bridge, Farebrother and the Brigade Recce Force ensured that the conditions were set for Op JAMES. His citation says that "the use of armoured recce as intimate

support was novel and dangerous but, by aggressive use of fire, Farebrother ensured that the initiative was never lost to the enemy."

Some months later, I had a message to go to see the CO. Like anyone, I suppose I expected a bollocking... *Oh, right... what have I done?* But he sat me down and told me I was going to be awarded a Military Cross. To be honest, I was flabbergasted. I have no doubt whatsoever that any other troop leader in my situation would have done the same as I did. Yes, it would have been easy for me to have been hit by the small arms or the RPGs coming in, but you could say the same of any of the blokes, here or anywhere else where they came into contact with the enemy. I was like, 'Why me?' Of course, it wasn't just me: Chris Haw, of the BRF, and the Squadron Leader, Henry Sugden, also won MCs and there were a number of MiDs, so there was a real buzz around the Regiment. And, obviously, though I was faintly mystified, it felt great. I rang my parents, who are not from military backgrounds so they didn't really understand what I was going on about. To be honest, neither did I - I went and read up about the medal, and past winners, and that was humbling, to say the least.

The investiture was a fantastic occasion. I took my mother and father and my then girlfriend, now wife, Diane to Buckingham Palace; it was a bit like a graduation without the clapping... quite sombre, actually. Prince Charles was presiding and, since he is the Colonel-in-Chief of our Regiment, that was rather nice. I got my three minutes with HRH, and - as most people are - I was amazed at how well-briefed he was. His equerry would whisper your name in his ear, and then he would launch into, without sounding silly, some quite intelligent questions, which made clear he'd read the citation and fully understood the background.

And then we went off for lunch and got thoroughly hammered with lots of my friends, to end a great day.

You get asked what you saw, and how it's affected you. My father, for one, was expecting me to come back from Iraq a changed man, I think. To an extent, I did. I grew up, certainly. You've seen and done things which are pretty horrible, killing people, at the end of the day. But I treated the whole thing, even seeing dead bodies, pretty clinically. I never wanted to kill anyone, but it happens in war, sadly. And while it puts the general irritations of life into context, I've been quite able to deal with it all: I believed in what we were doing, the lads all did their best, as did I, and that was good enough for me.

Lance Corporal Justin Thomas, CGC
Royal Marines

WITH others like Simon Farebrother and his men working to clear the area around Abu Al Khasib and secure bridges and other strategically important sites, the Royal Marines, supported by Challenger 2 tanks and Scimitars, were launching Operation JAMES. Named after James Bond, this involved 1,000 men and was designed to trap an Iraqi force of up to 3,000 who were well dug-in in the streets and houses of the suburb.

Justin Thomas, a GPMG section commander in Manoeuvre Support Group of 40 Commando, was among the 'Bootnecks' taking part in the operation.

A wiry Welshman with what one Royal Marine officer described as 'the levelest head I've ever seen', Thomas and his colleagues had been choppered-in behind enemy lines to help seize oil fields at the start of the invasion.

They'd then fought their way across the country to the outskirts of Basra - when they suddenly found themselves surrounded and outnumbered in a built-up area.

I joined the Royal Marines at 19 - my dad had been in the Royal Engineers, and I'd always wanted to be in the forces - and found myself out in Iraq as part of the original Operation TELIC.

I was in Manoeuvre Support Group; we had six GPMGs in two sections, amalgamated with three anti-tank troop sections into a mobile fire support asset for the entire Commando unit. The anti-tank boys were equipped with Milan, a mounted missile system which will take out any vehicle on the battlefield from an open Jeep to a main battle tank, or could also be used for busting open houses and walls during assaults. In each GPMG section there'd be a gunner and a loader for each gun, plus a corporal, a gun line commander, in charge. With the stripy (sergeant) and troop boss and the lads in the anti-tank group, there'd be 36 to 40 blokes in all.

I was a GPMG section commander; although I was only a lance corporal, for virtually my entire time in 40 Commando I was acting up as a corporal. The GPMG has been in service since the 1960s and is a tremendous weapon. It uses 7.62mm belt-fed ammunition, and is pin-point accurate once mounted on a tripod: you can take people out two miles away, no problem. Or you can use it in a light role - you take it off the tripod and have it on a bipod, with the gunner prone or the gun on a wall or something similar. It's less accurate then, because the tripod has buffers on it, hydraulic cylinders that deal with the vibration and recoil, but you're still talking a high level of accuracy at 800 metres. Finally, it can obviously be mounted on the vehicle - we were using Austrian-made Pinzgauers, a 4x4 that's a bit bigger than a Land Rover. They're not armoured, so we'd stripped all the back out of them so we could fire out of the back and get off quite quickly if need be. You can fire at anywhere between 650 and 1000 rounds a minute, depending on your requirements, and we'd balanced ours at around 750. The idea is that you tend to fire in short bursts of 3-5 rounds, though in combat that can go out of the window a bit.

Together, we would support Alpha, Bravo, Charlie or Delta Companies in major assaults, or go out with the Recce Troop to push forward and look for the enemy. Given the amount of firepower we had, and our anti-tank capability, we could take on an awful lot of targets and units, in greater strength than us, and still cope with the contact.

We entered Iraq right at the start. Our task was to secure an oil Manifold and Metering Station on the far eastern side of the Al Faw peninsula oil fields. A key objective for the Coalition was to stop Saddam from wrecking the oil infrastructure, because clearly the oil revenue was going to be very important for the Iraqis after the war was over.

We'd been rehearsing in the Kuwaiti desert for weeks, and we knew the place like the backs of our hands from satellite and aerial recon images. We flew in by Chinook in the dark. Not a particularly comfortable experience - you're jammed in, wearing your body armour, carrying weapons and lots of ammunition and water and so on, and you're flying low and fast. One RPG strike, even a few AK rounds in the wrong place, and it's all over, so that's on your mind a bit. Actually, while we were on our way in, we nearly collided with an American Black Hawk... our pilot had to take evasive action to avoid what would have been a large loss of life. And we landed in a hot LZ... we came straight off the chopper and found ourselves near an enemy bunker system and we were in contact, which was interesting. The Troop assaulted the enemy positions immediately, with my section taking out a bunker and an observation tower. I remember Paul Baird and Dale Anderson getting loads of rounds down, so many that we were all deaf afterwards. We ended up taking twenty prisoners there, and Paul spotted a high-ranking officer hiding amongst the soldiers, which was a good find. The Troop took 120 prisoners in total, and after several hours the area was secure, so we spent the rest of the night in defensive positions in case of counter-attack.

The next day, we moved on to clearing missions down on the coast, through all the bunker complexes. The idea was that if Basra fell, being the second largest city in Iraq, then word might spread and up north in Baghdad it might be a bit easier for the Americans.

The Commando had contacts all the time - everything from low level conscripts or people being forced to fight, through well-trained and organised infantry, all the way up to the Iraqi special forces and, even more dangerous, the Fedayeen, who were Saddam's right-hand men and had nothing to lose, basically. Obviously, the conscripts weren't that impressive, but the Fedayeen and the Special Forces, they don't lose much ground when they fight you, and some of it was pretty hard going. At some points, and particularly up by Basra on the day I won my award, they had more troops than us and better weaponry... more heavy machine guns, more sniper rifles and more mortars, and they were using it quite effectively.

The Brigade lost people but, fortunately, 40 Commando didn't. We suffered minor casualties, like burns and a bit of shrapnel here and there, mainly from enemy artillery and mortars. Quite a few lads did get shot, but were lucky in that the rounds hit the ceramic plates in their vests. Guys survived who otherwise would have been killed, for sure. It was astonishing, mind, that no-one was killed. I'm not exaggerating, there were hundreds of rounds coming close to all of us on any given day. Hundreds. You would feel them whipping past your head or see them hitting nearby. You'd be lying behind a piece of cover and dirt would be kicking up into your face a few centimetres away. Or you'd have RPGs bouncing in front of your feet and not going off because the ammo was faulty... you wouldn't have been able to count the number of times you could have died.

It was strange thinking about it afterwards and you don't dwell on it, to be honest. I don't know whether it's just luck or what, but after a while, after it has happened to you so often... I don't know what it is... you get used to it. A lot of the effect of being under heavy fire in contact, it hits you much later. At first, you don't know what to expect and you're really excited, not scared. I did two tours of Northern Ireland, two in Afghanistan, but I'd not really been shot at before... a few pot shots, nothing spectacular. This was massively different. But once you know what's coming... I remember feeling weak at the knees before one of the big contacts, because I knew what was round the corner. I think a lot of guys did. Don't get me wrong, even days down the line, we were still excited about getting into contact. It got to the point where, if you had one or two days of not being in contact, you missed it. But it was scary. I never experienced the shakes, but I felt weak afterwards, when I thought about what had just happened. *Oh my God!* you think, especially after a contact where you've spent a day fighting. It's pretty horrendous when you come out of it.

By March 30, Thomas and his colleagues had reached the outskirts of Abu Al Khasib, the start of the suburbs to the south west of Basra; Operation JAMES was launched.

We were pretty knackered. We'd been fighting or patrolling almost constantly for the 11 days to that point, apart from a lull when this huge sandstorm blew in and stopped everything for about three days. It was the worst weather I've ever experienced. You literally couldn't see for the sand, and the wind was phenomenal - it was blowing vehicles down the road. At one point, our windscreen glass was concave with the pressure - you just thought it was going to implode on you. So we hadn't had much kip... an hour here, an hour there, sometimes two or three days without sleep. But you just function. You're used to it. It's like that on exercise, where you might go four or five nights without sleep.

Our objective was to take and hold numerous crossroads and bridges on the main road into Basra, plus some enemy barracks. We moved up to our start line at night, with some armour from the Queen's Dragoon Guards attached to us for the initial assault. There was a pre-planned bombardment by 29 Commando, on known enemy positions, with the 105 mils putting in about an hour's-worth of fire, and then we started to go forwards.

Because of the fire power we had, we were on our own, on the extreme left flank of the Commando, with only the enemy and the city of Basra to our left and north. We were eight or nine kilometres from the centre of Basra, and for want of a better expression, and a few of us said it, it looked like the set of *Full Metal Jacket*: lots of palm trees and sandy-coloured buildings, with smoke and flames in the distance and scorched, destroyed enemy armour and positions everywhere. And in the distance, hundreds and hundreds of houses, as far as the eye could see.

Early on, we hit a minefield but the enemy had been careless, or in a rush, and had just strewn these huge anti-tank mines and lots of little anti-personnel jobs all across the roads, without even digging them in. So the Royal Engineers came up with a vehicle that's basically like a bulldozer, and that just shifted them off the road - if one happens to go, it's designed to take the full force - so they could be detonated later. So we moved through that and carried on.

All the roads were raised up high, like two metres above the surrounding land, and the further in we got the more vulnerable we all felt. We were silhouetted, for one thing. Then there was the chance of accidents. Say there's a sudden contact and the driver turns quickly, you can overturn. And that did happen. The Pinzgauer is brilliant, very stable, but even one of those can't go over a steep bank at 40mph... it's only going to be disastrous.

They hadn't blown the bridges, which was surprising, but it's two-fold, they need them as well. We actually only had to fight for a few. The Recce boys had a hard time with some of the Iraqi Naval Special Forces, where they took a long time to dislodge, but mostly they didn't even try to hold them. Maybe they were pushed back so quickly they didn't have chance, maybe they had just decided not to bother, even though they were obviously key objectives. Whatever the reasons, they seemed to prefer falling back on Basra. Same at most of the crossroads; we got sporadic contact, but nothing major. We found a few arms dumps, some of them had been blown, some hadn't, and from time to time we'd take light arms and give it back.

It really started when we got up close to the first of the houses. We came up a long road, with date palm groves to the left and right. We could hear Delta Company on the net; they'd advanced pretty quickly, without too much problem. Turns out that was because a lot of the opposition had just punted over to our side, and that was why we ended up getting so badly hit ourselves. The contact started half a K out from the houses and progressed up to a proper battle as we got closer.

We're out of the vehicles as soon as it starts, because the vehicles are a real target, and we left those some distance off with a few of the lads manning the gimpys to cover us while we went forward on foot. We got to the houses and started clearing the gardens, with the enemy very close; we could hear Iraqi soldiers on the other sides of walls at times, so it was close quarter stuff. Our troop boss was mindful of the fact that we were heading into a FIBUA situation, that they were trying to suck us in, but we pushed in quite a way to take the fight to them, anyway. It wasn't ideal. We were overlooked in every direction by buildings, single story things up to two and three storeys, all higgledy-piggledy. You'd come under fire and drop into a drainage ditch, and then look up and find that you were overlooked by a two-storey house. Next thing you'd be on a patch of waste ground, and be totally exposed. Plus the enemy knew we were coming and were prepared for us.

It wasn't a clean environment, which made it harder. By 'not clean', I mean there were a lot of civvies rattling around, and families and children coming towards us, despite all the lead flying around - mostly looking to us for help. They're obscuring the enemy and, at the back of your mind, you're also wondering who they are. For instance, a day or so before, a number of American soldiers had been killed at a checkpoint where two women, one of them pregnant, had blown themselves up. So even people who look harmless, you have to be careful with.

You've got all this going on in your head, and you're in contact, and you have to make split second decisions. So you're warning them to keep away, you don't want them anywhere near you. And sometimes they were carrying badly injured children, and they want help.

I've told my wife Heather about this, it's not something I hide from her and, to be honest, it doesn't distress me thinking about it. I don't know why. We're all different, I guess; some of my mates it hasn't affected, and others it has. We've seen the enemy dead afterwards, in areas where we've been in contact, and I couldn't let it bother me. It is not the nicest thing in the world to see, mind.

As I say, it made it harder to fight. We had strict rules of engagement, designed to protect the civilians. And rightly so, no-one wanted to hurt any civvies. Unfortunately, war is war and you take as much care as possible but sometimes... well, that's life. I don't think we killed any civilians, we were very, very careful, but if the enemy are in a civilian area and they are giving it to you, at some point you have to give it back to them and, hopefully, the civvies will have evacuated.

The fire got so heavy that it was constant. The rounds were ricocheting off the vehicles, off walls, off the ground right in front of you, cracking off just past your head or landing right next to you.

The Marines had unknowingly come up against an enemy in battalion strength and found themselves under heavy fire for three hours.

I remember hearing 'Contact front!' on the net, and then 'Contact left!' Which wasn't too bad. But then I heard 'Contact right!' And when 'Contact rear!' came over, you start to think, *Yeah, the s***'s hit the fan, here.*

We were surrounded and massively outnumbered. There were 40 or so of us and I heard afterwards, either from the 29 Commando ground radar or the thermal sight in a Challenger, that there were two hundred heat sources all round us, in bushes and ditches and buildings.

Some of the enemy you'd see, other times it was just muzzle flashes in a dark room or in the trees. And you'd just return massive weight of fire to suppress whoever was taking you on.

We could see RPGs coming out of the houses and gardens. In your head, it happens in slow motion, but in reality it's a millisecond. You see the flash and you think, *S***!* Then before you know it, it's gone over your head. I know I said a lot of them didn't go off, but a lot of them did and we had some very close calls. I remember one of the lads, Daz Hennessey, I turned round and he took an RPG to the left. It exploded a maximum of two metres from him. And we thought, *He's dead.* But the cloud cleared, and he was still standing. And he was just about to move to his right and another RPG went off right next to him again, and he walked out of that one as well. Obviously, shrapnel can go in any direction, and he was just incredibly lucky. I remember me and my mate Paul Baird jumped on the back of one of the wagons at one point and an RPG came in behind us. There was a little wall, about a foot high, two or three metres from us and it landed and detonated the other side of that. The wall took the entire brunt of the explosion. If the guy firing it had had his weapon elevated by a couple of millimetres it would have hit the wagon and taken us both out, no problem.

Fast as the RPGs were being fired at us, the Milan lads were putting missiles into the buildings they were firing from and there'd be this huge explosion and you knew you weren't going to have any more trouble from there. But straight away, another guy would pop up on a rooftop, and it would be 'RPG!' all over again.

It was all very chaotic. As a section commander, I had two nets on me - the troop net, the personal radios that everyone uses, and then another radio with better range so I can go to my troop commander. There are numerous people talking on the net at any one time - sitreps, where contacts are coming from, what they are, what positions to take out. Call signs go out of the window, you just recognise people's voices, you're best mates with a lot of them, and it's almost like a game of football - like guys shouting 'Man on!' You're trying to keep track of all of that, trying not to get disorientated, watching the ammunition situation, reacting to the enemy, commanding your blokes. Our orders had pretty much gone out of the window, too. You can have an objective, but once you have contact it's just a fight. You try to hold on to that little bit of organisation, but soon it's no longer a troop attack, it may not even be a section attack. At some points, there is just you and another bloke fighting together, fire manoeuvring. At times, it broke down to the individual, we were just skirmishing.

Eventually, we managed to extract. It was absolute chaos, *Keystone Cops* stuff, really... everybody on any wagon and just get the hell out of there, just firing in every single direction to try and suppress the enemy. I think the boss called in artillery, and we moved out under each burst. The blasts from the 105 are phenomenal, especially on Tarmac and hard surfaces. The killing radius is easily 100 metres, pieces of shrapnel the size of your fist or forearm, all the way down to splinters. You'll be chopped in half if you get hit by a big piece.

And we regrouped 800 metres to a kilometre down the road. We had a look at ammunition scales and redistributed it as needed, so that everyone would go back into whatever was going to happen on an even basis. There was talk of reinforcing us with a company from 42 Commando so we could go back up and try and take the bridges and the crossroads in the suburbs. And it went quiet for half an hour or so, so we took the opportunity to get some food into us. I remember I didn't actually feel hungry, even though we'd been fighting since about 4am and it was midday or later by now, so I only ate a few biscuits from my ration pack. Water was more important - it was the end of March, so it wasn't scorching, but it was hot enough - but even there I don't think I had more than a bottle. I remember taking my windproof smock off and sitting down for five minutes, just trying to relax. The bosses were having a bit of a conflab to decide what to do next - either re-issue orders or do it off the cuff, just advance to contact and deal with the problems as they arise. A lot of the troop were in cover, with some wagons on the road providing an overwatch. To our right was desert, with some big structures in the distance which Delta Company had cleared, and to our left, 200 or 300 metres away, was a tree line with lots of date palm groves and other greenery.

Suddenly, they came under sustained fire from a new and undetected group of enemy troops some 350 metres away.

They opened up on us with mortars at first. They knew what they were doing: they wanted to keep our heads down, and mortars do that to you. It's dispiriting stuff, mortar fire, like artillery, because there's often not much you can do except sit there and take it. It ceases to be amusing after about ten minutes and it can actually break you.

If they're close, you might hear the shell going into the barrel, with a 'dunk' sound, or you might hear it whistling through the air. Sometimes you can even see it. Then it whizzes in and there's a 'crump' when it impacts. If it lands on a road, you're looking at death anywhere within 20 or 30 metres, possibly even further. If it lands in sand and mud, the blast radius is much reduced, so we were immediately getting off the road and taking cover. Then they started hitting us with anti-tank rockets, probably the Russian Spigot, which is a wire-guided thing not dissimilar to Milan - the missile is actually trailing a wire behind it, and the operator watches through his scope and navigates it in to the target. An armoured fighting vehicle from the Queen's Dragoon Guards, I think it was an FV432, had come up to help us and they hit that right on the front, a few metres away from me. There was a massive bang and lots of smoke and flames, and the lads in the AFV battened the hatches straight down. Then they got hit again and they didn't hang around long after that. There was other armour there - a Scimitar and a Challenger 2, and they weren't firing. One of our lads got up on the Scimitar, under fire, and said to the commander, 'Are you going to use that thing or what?' He's got this 30mm cannon sitting there, and that's a battle winner: you put a load of 30mm rounds into defended positions, a tree line, whatever, it doesn't matter who they are, they're not going to hang around for very long. It just really ruins your day. But for some reason, he wouldn't use it. I imagine it was because of the possibility of collateral damage, but we weren't best pleased. Not long after that, the armour withdrew and we were on our own.

By now, there's lots of small arms coming in. There's a heavy machine gun firing at us from somewhere and they've got a sniper going as well. And there are the RPGs. I remember, just above me there were some electricity wires and a lot of the RPGs were being fired too high, coming in and hitting these cables. Sparks would be flying everywhere and these 3ft missiles would just spin off at crazy angles and explode somewhere.

Funnily enough, the lads were pissing themselves laughing about it all, despite how serious it was. There was a British journalist with us - not attached, he got left with us by others - and I remember him saying how nuts he thought we were. We were lying in these ditches, RPGs were just missing us, people were taking rounds in their day sacks, and we were all pissing ourselves. It was just so funny - I can't explain why, it just is for some reason.

But it was actually starting to look pretty bad. We're still pinned down by the mortars. They'd suppressed us good and proper. A few of the lads were trying to return odd bits of fire with their personal weapons but we had our heads down so we couldn't see the target and were basically ineffective.

I never thought they'd overrun us, because they'd have had to come into the open and stop their own fire, and we'd have cut them to pieces. But it was only going to end one way at this rate: sooner or later, those mortars or the RPGs or the sniper or the machine gun were going to find us and we'd start taking serious casualties.

With the air around him filled with lead and shrapnel, Thomas made a decision: he got up and ran to the nearest vehicle. Climbing onto the back - now in full view of the enemy - he got behind the pintle-mounted GPMG and started returning fire. Completely exposed, and with the enemy fire now concentrated on him, he was risking his life. Dozens of strikes peppered his vehicle and the surface of the road around it was chewed up and littered with debris.

I thought, *Hang on... there's nobody firing here. They're hammering us, and that's wrong.* So I ran to the nearest wagon and just climbed up on to it and started looking for them, basically. As soon as I was up there, I could see where some of their firing points were and I was able to engage them with the GMPG. Just putting a belt of ammunition on and hosing it down. Picking where I was firing, and giving it a good long burst, either until the belt ran out or the gun had a stoppage. Stoppages are the nature of the beast with a belt-fed weapon - it can be a case not extracting properly, or a bit of link falling down into the working parts, or a problem with the propellant... the GPMG fires better dirty, with bit of carbon on the gas regulator, but you still get stoppages. So I'd clear it, start again and carry on until I ran out of the belt. You're supposed to change your barrel every 400 rounds because they get too hot and can actually melt. They start to droop slightly, the next round explodes in the barrel and suddenly you've got a big problem. And I've seen barrels on the way to that - I've seen them go translucent, to the point where you can see tracer rounds zipping down the barrel. But I knew from experience that you can easily put a few thousand rounds through a weapon and nothing happens to it and, anyway, I couldn't operate by the rule book here. I just didn't have time to worry about it.

I mentioned the power of a GPMG earlier. The Iraqis were in houses but that was providing them with next to no cover. The rounds from a GPMG will go through concrete and keep going. Most of the time, I couldn't see whether I was hitting people, but I was firing into machine gun positions and RPG points. I'd see their tracer coming out, or RPG flashes, so I'd fire a long burst in there and everything would stop. Then it would start up somewhere else. I remember I saw a large group of enemy in a house so I let them have a really long burst; it literally demolished the house, like sawing through the stone.

After a few moments, Gary Lancaster jumped up next to me and started feeding the ammo to me, which made me more effective.

The citation continues: "With his No 2 feeding ammunition, and with no protection afforded by the vehicle, LCpl Thomas single-handedly returned a heavy weight of sustained fire for a continuous period of nearly 15 minutes to enable 20 other members of his troop to safely move into cover and to regroup.

As small arms and rocket-propelled grenades landed all around him, his courage and determination did not waver in the face of considerable threat to his own life."

At one point, I saw an RPG flash about 300 metres off, at about 11 o'clock from us. Like I say, there's no time to react, other than to think, *Oh no.* And this bloody thing passed right between me and Gary and exploded off in the distance behind us. We were only three feet apart and I saw it pass. Unbelievable.

It was probably round about then I thought, *F***ing hell, enough's enough now... I've got to get down from here.*

It was getting stupid, the amount of fire that was coming towards me and Gary, and I was just thinking, *It's only a matter of time.* We were just a massive, immobile target. It wasn't just the RPGs, though more of them were being aimed at us. There was a machine gun I couldn't find which was walking fire towards us. I know about machine guns and if someone has tracer rounds loaded it's only a matter of time before they click onto the fact that they're firing high or short or whatever. There were numerous strikes on the road and he was getting closer, and we weren't going to have any second chances if he found us. There were small arms as well, and a distinctive sniper weapon, single shots, a bit louder than an AK, so it wasn't really a tenable position for much longer.

We'd been lucky, really. There've been plenty of people in history who have done that kind of stuff and been slotted straight away, before they even touched a trigger.

So I shouted to Gary and we jumped off and rejoined the section. By now, the rest of the lads had started coming into it anyway, and the enemy's weight of fire started dropping. And it was hell for leather, then. We dropped a number of houses with the Milans and called in a helicopter strike to hit the sniper's building. That was destroyed, and it took the sniper with it. And within a matter of minutes the fight had turned right around and it was game over.

I have no idea how long the whole thing went on. Time loses its meaning when you're in that sort of situation. What I do know is the ammo supply for the next day was 47,000 rounds of 7.62. That is a phenomenal amount of ammunition and it takes a while to get through that much; it's not just a quick thing, with stoppages and changing belts and so on. One of my mates, Andy Gibson, put down about 11,000 rounds on his own. I think I'd used up 7,000 or 8,000 myself by the end.

To cap it off, the boss put in for artillery and some sort of air strike went in, Harrier GR7s I think. As soon as that was done, about half an hour later, we were back on the wagons and went straight back up to where we'd been surrounded and started fighting again, and we went on until 2am or 3am the next day. We were only a couple of hours short of being 24 hours in contact.

I think the whole day did show the Royal Marines in a pretty good light. Initially, we had a team of US Marines with us, Forward Air Controllers. I remember they were talking about bringing in a B52, rerouting it from Baghdad, believe it or not, and basically dropping bombs. We were only 350 metres from the enemy! They were virtually calling an air strike on themselves, and us. We said, 'No thanks... you're having a laugh. We'll enjoy the rest of the party on our own, ta.' They couldn't handle it. I'm not bigging our lads up but, like I say, we were laughing half the time during the contacts.

LCpl Thomas's citation says his "leadership in combat" was "of the highest order" and adds: "But it was an individual act of immense bravery and exceptional courage which distinguished him from his contemporaries as worthy of lasting recognition."

In terms of the medal, I didn't actually think I'd done anything all that special. I had a lot of people come up to me afterwards saying, 'What the hell did you do that for?' Lads were saying, 'I wouldn't have got up there for the world.' My opinion was... well, my mate Gary Lancaster got up there of his own free will, with no means to fight back, and that was more amazing, in my book. The sole thing in his mind was just to hand me ammunition in a totally exposed vehicle, with all the Iraqi attention drawn to us. So he had plenty of time to think about all that, whereas I'd just gone and done it without thinking.

I knew a few of us had been written up for things though Gary didn't get anything, which was a real shame. I thought I might get a Mention in Dispatches and while, to be quite frank, it wouldn't have bothered me if I'd got nothing, to be awarded a CGC was pretty amazing. The troop boss, Capt Lynch, and Cpl Pete Watts each received Military Crosses, and there was a DSO and a handful of MiDs. I think that shows the ferocity of the fighting, where to a lot of people they think the invasion was a walkover. In the big picture, maybe it was. But down on the ground, little units of blokes were fighting very hard indeed.

Sometimes I wonder whether I did enough to earn it. There were plenty of other guys going forward in all the assaults, who never ever took a backward step, and who got nothing. Other times I think, *Well, I didn't write myself up for it.*

Regardless of the medal, what your peers think of you is much greater in my eyes. I knew I was alright as a corporal, I was quite experienced and all that kind of stuff, but the one demon I wouldn't have wanted is to get up in the morning and not be able to look at myself in the mirror. To wonder, deep down, whether I really did the best I could for my mates. You prove yourself to yourself, and you're happy.

I left the Marines not long after, and I joined the police in South Wales. I wouldn't rule out rejoining at some point, but I'm happy where I am. I've got married and had a baby, and being in the forces isn't ideal for a married man.

Even through all the contacts that I got into over there, regardless of any s*** we chucked into the villages to clear the enemy, civilians still came to us, and not their own side. We blew up houses, but they still came to us. They wanted the regime changed, especially in Basra with the religion down there, they did want change. So I think it was all for the good, despite the fact that things have gone bad since.

One thing I would say, I didn't personally have any qualms about killing people. It's what we were there to do. We were extremely determined, professional people who did our jobs to the best of our abilities. I know a few lads who suffered afterwards, but the after-care the Armed Forces get now is much better than it used to be.

Corporal of Horse Glynn Bell, MC
The Blues and Royals

WITH the war won, the Coalition forces set about mounting a peacekeeping operation. For Glynn Bell, a Scimitar Commander in the Blues and Royals, the invasion and the subsequent fighting had been relatively quiet - he had scarcely fired a shot in anger. (His Squadron, though, had suffered a pair of tragedies, with the deaths of LCpl Karl Shearer and Lt Alexander Tweedie in an overturned vehicle and, infamously, that of LCoH Matty Hull, 25, in a so-called 'friendly fire' incident.)

On June 24, 2003, however, that changed for the worse. Two sections from 1st Battalion the Parachute Regiment were patrolling in the town of Al Majar Al Kabir, some 250 miles south of Baghdad, when they came under attack. Separated, low on ammunition, pinned down and surrounded by hundreds of armed men, they found themselves in a desperate battle for their lives.

CoH Bell's troop was tasked to deploy as part of a larger Battlegroup Quick Reaction Force to extract the Paras. As they entered the town, 200 people began firing at them from all directions, with rifles, heavy machine guns and RPGs. Undeterred, Bell and his men pressed forward, supported by a Para multiple which was also trying to fight its way back into the town.

Waiting for them were 200 armed men and a barrage of RPGs and bullets.

I'm 39, I live in Chertsey with my wife, Alison, and our two children, David and Annie, but I'm originally from Guildford in Surrey. I've been in the army 19 years. I remember watching the TV when I was about nine and seeing the Blues and Royals at the Trooping of the Colour; I liked the blue tunic and the scarlet plume and decided there and then to join the regiment when I was older.

I'm a Warrant Officer currently working in London on ceremonial duties with the Household Cavalry Mounted regiment, but in early 2003 I was out in Iraq as a Corporal of Horse, which is, in layman's terms, a sergeant commanding a Scimitar armoured scout vehicle and the three other vehicles in my particular Sabre squadron.

We had deployed to a camp in Kuwait two or three days after Valentine's Day, just prior to the invasion. I remember thinking, even in February, *Crikey, this is hot.* It was a fairly nervous time in some ways - we were carrying our respirators at all times because of the perceived threat of gas attacks, and there was just the general anticipation of being about to go to war, and not really knowing what it was going to be like. But I wouldn't say I was physically frightened, because there was nothing in front of us and I always felt it might be sorted out politically before we crossed the start line. Really, it was a matter of trying to prepare the troops as best we could for every eventuality.

As well as our famous ceremonial duties in London, we also work in a formation reconnaissance role, in Scimitar scout vehicles and their variants. So we would be out in front of the battle space, providing information back to the required level of hierarchy. The information that we give the commanders is what they use to formulate or confirm their plans for the main force coming through. Thus, we knew if it did all kick off we'd probably end up in quite exposed positions. But our job is to see and not be seen, so the hope is that we'd not have to fire any shots, and I never did until the very end.

Just before the war started, we had what we call 'sanitisation'. Any documents containing information about you or your families had to be bundled up and put in storage in Brigade HQ. That included any letters, and any mail you got after that had to be burned. The last letter I got came the day before crossing - it was from my then girlfriend Alison, saying that she was pregnant with our first child. To burn that was difficult.

I spent a while talking through things with my lads. We had to be careful about rules of engagement; where there were civilians or civilian vehicles, we had to make sure we only engaged people who were promoting themselves as a threat to us personally. Military vehicles, they were obviously fair game. We talked about the dangers we'd face; I tried to get them to think of it as an ordinary range package... just stay alert, keep looking through 360 degrees and not just forwards.

The invasion actually went well for the Coalition forces, generally, but not for the Squadron, with the three lives we lost. Matty Hull unfortunately died in the blue-on-blue with the American A10 and then, a few days later, Karl Shearer and Lt Tweedie were killed when their Scimitar slid down a crumbling bank and overturned.

But before too long we were assisting in a post-conflict situation. It felt slightly strange - one day we're at war and fighting each other, the next we're helping Iraq to rebuild its infrastructure and looking forward to getting home. I'd say the place was mostly friendly at that stage, with most of the Iraqis pleased to see the back of Saddam and looking forward to a new country. Obviously, there were pockets of serious trouble, though.

On 24 June, Bell's troop was tasked to deploy to extract a platoon from 1 Para that was pinned down under heavy fire in Al Majar Al Kabir. The patrol, led by Sgt Gordon Robertson,

had been surrounded by a large, hostile crowd in the densely populated market area of the town; they had been stoned and had attempted to disperse the angry people with baton rounds but had then been fired at by at least two gunmen using the crowd as cover. They had returned fire and had immediately come under sustained attack from more gunmen hidden in nearby buildings, injuring one of the Parachute Regiment soldiers. Their vehicles were then destroyed by rocket-propelled grenades and the men had withdrawn to a nearby building, where they were surrounded.

We were based at Al Amarah, probably half an hour away. About three or four days beforehand, we were on the scale-down to come home. We'd handed in all our ammunition and had started to hand over the vehicles to the Light Dragoons, who were coming out to replace us. Everyone was geared up for going home. Then we got the call that two Para multiples were in trouble in Al Majar Al Kabir. While the region was reasonably friendly, Majar was very volatile.

There was a panic on, everyone in a flurry to get back some of our ammunition and also take down extra ammo for the Paras. We were in a frenzy loading up the vehicles, getting a quick set of orders, and then it was straight down to the highway. On the outskirts of Majar, probably 600 metres away, we stopped. It was all quiet - we couldn't hear much shooting, and we started to fear the worst. It later transpired that they were so low on ammo by this point that they were firing single shots only, and then only when they absolutely had to. We met up with a C Company, 1 Para commander, a Major. His multiple had managed to fight its way out of the contact, and now they were going to go back in with us to get the rest of their guys out. We handed out fresh ammunition to them while the Major confirmed the situation and discussed how we should go in there, and the last sitreps that had been received indicating where his Paras were. By this time, they had been in contact, and surrounded, for an hour. We fanned out into our lines of advance and started out, leapfrogging and caterpillaring forwards. The idea is that in any two vehicle grouping, one vehicle is always stationary and therefore in the best position to return fire or suppress the enemy. You can't fire on the move, look through the scopes, as well as trying to map read, and negotiate the ground and tell the driver where to go. Caterpillaring means driving to the rear of the vehicle in front and then waiting while he goes ahead, obviously covering each other. Leapfrogging just means you overtake the front vehicle and go firm a little further on, so he can do the same for you.

The difficulty in a place like Majar was knowing who the enemy were. Potentially, it was anyone, just normal people in the town could, potentially, be snipers. The whole place was crawling with guns and weapons, and anyone could duck into a house and come out with an AK or a rocket-propelled grenade launcher. Lots of firing points for snipers, lots of cover... we're going into a built-up area. So we were all nervous and very watchful, and battened down inside the vehicles.

As soon as we entered the town, we started taking incoming. Later on, it was estimated that around 200 enemy were involved; there were people everywhere, and they all had weapons. I mean *all*. Anyone who didn't want to know had clearly got themselves out of the way and were under cover somewhere. In a way, that made it easier for us - but if they were shooting from behind a wall, or inside a house, how did you know who was on the other side? Many of the buildings were made of mud bricks, and our rounds were just going straight through them, so you had to hope there was no-one in the way other than the guy you were targeting. Though we were very accurate, because our weapons system is bore-sighted, so the rounds go exactly where the sighting system says they will. And it's not like you're hosing people down - it was very short bursts, and the guys you were aiming at were taken out. Of course, as soon as they went down, someone else would step up, often picking up their weapons from where they were lying, so it was constant fighting.

Initially, they were using small arms, mainly coming from our nine and three o'clock, and it carried on all the way in. A 7.62mm bullet won't penetrate a Scimitar, but it's not a pleasant thing hearing live rounds hitting your sides, and one or two of the vehicles had their periscopes shot out which obviously doesn't help. The main worry was RPGs. The Scimitar is a lightly-armoured vehicle and a direct hit from an RPG could have immobilised us, with the added risk of serious injury to whoever was nearest to the point of impact. On top of that was the chance that it would set fire to the diesel and ammunition stored inside. So you're driving along, thinking, *Please don't let us get hit by an RPG*. Luckily, that didn't happen, though one detonated between my vehicle and the call sign to my left, and a couple of others bounced off without exploding. Trust me, it's quite daunting watching someone physically put a launcher up onto his shoulder and point it at you. But once they did that they posed a clear threat, so we were able to engage them and we took quite a few out. We worked out later that between nine and 11 RPGs were fired at our vehicle, those were the ones we knew about and counted, so someone was watching out for us that day.

Sgt Robertson and his 1 Para men had now been in the building for 45 minutes. They had beaten off numerous assaults from a determined enemy, many of whom had managed to get within 20 metres of their position and some of whom had even tried to batter their way through the walls to attack the multiple. An attempt to extract them using the Air Reaction Force had been made, but it had been beaten off under heavy machine gun fire, sustaining seven casualties. Ammunition was running very low - many soldiers had less than one magazine left - and CoH Bell and the rest of the relief force were still some distance away. Robertson decided to extract from the building, under heavy fire, and head north to attempt to link up with Bell and the Blues and Royals.

We didn't actually know where the beleaguered Paras were, so the first thing we tried to do was establish comms with them, to try to get them to steer us into their location... if they could give us details of any prominent landmarks near to where they were, we could head in that direction. Comms weren't great, they had actually been split into two groups and they were not in brilliant ground - they had their heads down, they were taking sniper fire and couldn't really see a lot to give us too much help. They described a hollowed-out hangar, with only the metal girder skeleton left, which was near them, but we couldn't see it because we were in a built-up area ourselves.

At least we knew they were still alive, and still able to defend themselves. Both the company commander and myself were speaking to them, and I remember hearing the anxiety in their voices. When the Paras are getting anxious, you know they're in trouble - they said they were getting very, very low on ammunition and clearly they were concerned about being overrun. Given what happened the same day with those poor Redcap lads *(in an unconnected incident on the same day, six Royal Military Police soldiers were surrounded in a police station on the other side of Al Majar Al Kabir and murdered)*, they were right to be concerned, obviously. It's amazing how resourceful soldiers can be, but they were down to their last few rounds, not all that far from where the only option would have been to get up and run as fast as they could. That's a very, very lonely place to be. I could imagine it as I was talking to them.

There was a Gazelle scout helicopter up too, trying to find them for us. It sounds easy, but don't forget they were camouflaged and in cover - even from above they would have been hard to see.

Eventually, they found the trapped sections and Bell pushed forward to extract the besieged soldiers, in what his citation describes as "an act of significant bravery - he was on open ground and fired on by small arms, heavy machine guns and rocket-propelled grenades. One hit from the latter would likely have destroyed his vehicle, and all inside it. He knew full well the danger because as he advanced bullets smashed the observation episcopes around his cupola and his vehicle was nearly destroyed by heavy calibre fire."

After probably half an hour, we did locate one of their two positions. Someone looked through a little gap in some houses we were driving past and saw a runner who had been sent out to find us. And at pretty much the same time, the Gazelle came up and gave confirmation that they had also seen them. They were in and around a little 4ft-wide stream running through a ditch, all absolutely soaking wet and returning fire as best they could at a large number of enemy located in houses and other positions as close as 50 metres or so away.

We got as close as we could, and then set up either side of the road. The first thing we had to do was get out of our vehicles and resupply them with ammunition. We were still being engaged ourselves, and I remember the fear I had about opening my turret in those circumstances. It sounds odd, but in a way it's worse to be in a vehicle - it attracts so much fire and is so much of a target, whereas on foot you can make yourself small, get behind a wall, get into a ditch, be hard to see and hard to hit. So getting out was a horrible thing because you knew there would be rounds flying around you immediately.

We started breaking out the ammo while our gunners put down suppressive fire with our GPMGs. The Paras sent some lads up to collect the ammunition and, once they were resupplied, the weight of fire from ourselves and them combined very quickly started winning the firefight and quietening down the firing. As the enemy started keeping their heads down, the Para multiple was able to disappear very quickly, extracting back while we went forward to draw the fire from the militia before extracting ourselves.

With the other section still trapped, Bell advanced again, drawing fire while his troop leader moved to a flank to extract the remaining soldiers from the firefight. With all dismounted troops safely under hard cover, Bell and the rest of the troop remained in position to give covering fire for the final extraction of the whole force.

We located the second group of Paras and re-engaged the enemy while our other call signs went forward. They got to where the lads were and got some of them out on foot and others up and onto their decks so they could drive them out. I remember seeing these Para lads lying and sitting on the engine deck by the driver - the only thing shielding them from fire was the turret, so they were very exposed, but it was the quickest way to extract them. All told, the whole thing probably took 90 minutes.

You look back and think, *I killed people there*. Which wasn't something I ever thought I'd do. But it's the old saying, it's either them or me. Would a bloke I shot with an RPG have cried too many tears if he'd managed to get his weapon onto me and killed me instead? I doubt it. He'd probably have been celebrating. I certainly didn't celebrate anyone dying, but I didn't beat myself up about it because any life I took was taken to save lives on my own side.

I'm very lucky to be, as they say, an old pair of leather boots. But I do think sometimes, when I'm watching the TV or the kids are running around, *Have I taken a father away from his children?* That's a hollow thought. But as I say, I doubt they'd have worried too much about me if it had been the other way around. So, yes, you think about it, but you have got to let it go. Particularly at the time, when everything's still happening in front of you. There are lives on your own side in danger and you don't think about the enemy. Which is quite a sad way of looking at it, I suppose.

Mostly, we were shooting people from a range of maybe 250 metres to 800 metres. That's a long way, but with our sighting systems, which are 10x magnification, we'd get a very close look at them... you'd see people's facial expressions, see them talking, looking and pointing over, maybe laughing at us... then you'd see a bloke pointing his weapon at us and he would be engaged. So you see the people die, too. And it's not nice.

One thing sticks in my mind - there was an ambulance driver, bless his socks, from their side. All through the various firefights he was driving up and down the road bringing out casualties and taking them... wherever, I don't know. Now, we can't fire at the ambulance, and they knew that, but there was so much firing... if you've already got rounds in the air and he drives into them... well, you can't physically stop them, and he must have known that. I think if anyone deserved any medals from that day it was that guy there. He was really, really brave.

As we were leaving, it was weird. A lot of people, it must have been about 60 per cent of the town, came out and started clapping and cheering. But not in a hostile way, it seemed genuine, to me. So I wondered whether the people attacking us had actually come in from somewhere else. We'd obviously killed people, and if you've killed locals you'd expect that to alienate their friends and family and neighbours.

Subsequent intelligence reports indicated that the attack on the 1 Para soldiers had been carefully planned, and that a number of fighters had indeed moved into the town that day for the express purpose of attacking a Coalition patrol. To the credit of the British troops, local sources reported that the enemy was exceptionally impressed by their tactical conduct and the accuracy of their marksmanship.

We got back to Al Amarah, and everyone was on a high. For our troop, we'd never fired a shot through the war phase and then, finally, right towards the end... I don't know whether it was a high point or a low point. I'd say in my eyes it was a low point, not firing in war and then here we are in peacetime... but everyone came back, none of the Paras or our lads was hurt *(though there were some injuries aboard a Chinook which was hit by RPGs as it attempted to assist the trapped soldiers)*. Everyone was buzzing through adrenaline, and then it was taking all the ammunition back off again and going back to normal everyday life again.

And before long, we were back home, and you're in Tesco or watching the football on telly, and the whole thing is like a big, surreal dream. No-one around you, no-one in the streets outside, no-one knows what you were doing just a few days before. Quite strange.

Bell's citation ends: "Despite the ferocity of fire, and despite his vehicle almost being destroyed by RPGs, Bell led the successful extraction effort. Throughout the action, he displayed enormous courage. His leadership was, on its own, worthy of merit. His courage and tenacity under fire was central to the safe extraction of the platoon. Without his personal intervention and bravery, the trapped sections could have been

lost to the enemy and his initiative to move forward to extract them undoubtedly saved many lives." (Sgt Gordon Robertson of 1 Para was later awarded a Conspicuous Gallantry Cross for his actions on June 24.)

The medal was a strange one, too. Yes, I suppose we put ourselves in harm's way to help the Paras out. But then that's what we do. I couldn't have said no even if I'd wanted to. Yes, I was in danger. But so were the Paras, and it's not as though they all got Military Crosses. Most of all, why did I get picked out? I didn't do much different to anyone else, to my mind. There were two other guys in my vehicle, for instance. So I certainly don't feel like a hero. I couldn't have done the job that I orchestrated without everyone underneath going through their own levels of bravery to do it. If I got one, everyone should have.

I got offered three dates for my investiture... it was a bit spooky, because one was Alison's birthday, the second was on the day we were due to fly out to Antigua to get married and the third, the one we chose, turned out to be my son's first birthday. It was a good day. Within our regimental duties we meet the Royal Family frequently, and I'd probably already spoken to the Queen 15 or 20 times throughout my career. Obviously, you don't know her personally, but she's the kind of person who takes the time and trouble to know the people who work for her, and she seemed to recognise me, and spent quite a while chatting to me, which was really nice. On investitures, our regiment are used to line the stairs going up to meet Her Majesty, and they used all my troop to line the stairs going up, which was really humbling and did make me feel proud.

Due to the ballroom having limited seats for all the attendees of the recipients, you are limited to three guests; it would have made a very memorable day if my son could have been there on his first birthday but children under a certain age are not allowed in. Both my parents and wife-to-be were there to see it, which was a very humbling moment for me... to be presented with a medal in Buckingham Palace by Her Majesty Queen Elizabeth II in front of my mother and father and Alison. Amazing.

If I could, I'd like to take this opportunity to thank all ranks of D squadron who deployed on Op TELIC 1 for all that they did, and to express my deepest sympathy and warmest feelings to the families of the few who did not return to barracks: Lt Alex Tweedie, LCoH Matty Hull and LCpl Al Shearer. Never forgotten.

Corporal Shaun Jardine, CGC
King's Own Scottish Borderers

SIX weeks after the horrific murders of the six RMPs in Al Majar Al Kabir - and after Glynn Bell and his colleagues had helped the men of 1 Para to escape from a mob in the town - Shaun Jardine was commanding a fire team employed as the Immediate Quick Reaction Force for the Al Uzayr Security Force Base, not far away in Maysan Province.

Shy, skinny and softly-spoken, the young Scot was nevertheless an experienced NCO, having joined the Army as a boy soldier. The Security Force base was a small outpost in the village of Al Uzayr, a Shia backwater halfway between Basra and Al Amarah and the final resting place of the Hebrew prophet Ezra, also revered by Muslims.

On the morning of Saturday August 9, the men were busying themselves, some cleaning their weapons, others on guard duty or eating breakfast, when a huge firefight suddenly broke out 300 metres north of their position. They could hear a prolonged and intense mix of heavy machine gun and small arms fire, and Jardine and his team immediately deployed to investigate.

Almost as soon as they left the compound, they were engaged by two enemy positions 100 metres to the west; at the same time, other elements of the Al Uzayr Multiple, which had also deployed, came under fire to the south.

Pinned down, with no reinforcements available and with his team's position becoming untenable, Jardine's citation describes how he took the offensive, charging straight at the blazing enemy guns.

I come from Dumfries, in south-west Scotland. I'd got to about 15 or 16, there weren't too many opportunities for young lads round our way and I was getting fed up at home so I joined the Army. It was almost a spur-of-the-moment thing - I wasn't from an Army family or anything. I joined at 16, initially serving with the First Battalion King's Own Scottish Borderers, now amalgamated as part of the First Battalion of the Royal Regiment of Scotland.

We went out on TELIC 2, after the initial invasion. I was 21 at the time we landed, mid-June 2003. We arrived in Basra and then drove down to Kuwait to get acclimatised for a couple of weeks. Coming from Scotland, we definitely needed that. It was roasting hot, around 100 degrees in the shade, and a wee bit different to the weather back home. But we didn't actually get to finish that fortnight. A week or so after we arrived, the six Royal Military Policemen got murdered in Al Majar Al Kabir, so we were fast-tracked to move up earlier than planned. There was a lot of activity to try and find the killers, and make sure everyone knew the British Army was in control, and so they needed plenty of boots on the ground.

We made our way up through Basra towards Camp Abu Naji. The way it worked was we rotated on a four-weekly basis. You did a week of guard duties in Abu Naji, just having guys on stag to make sure it was secure. Then we worked a week on patrols of all the villages, where we'd go out with the police, carry out arrests and searches if necessary, set up VCPs and generally be a presence. Following that, we did a week guarding an ammo compound just outside Abu Naji - mainly to make sure none of the locals were trying to steal the brass from the munitions. The fourth week was spent down at the the Al Uzayr Security Force Base, an out-station roughly 70 or 80 kilometres south of Al Amarah and the same distance north of Basra.

It was a very small camp, an old police station in the shape of a squared-off figure eight, with courtyards in the middle. Around the whole compound, five or 10 metres from the building, there was a perimeter wall. If you looked over the wall you would see the village of Al Uzayr itself. It's a pretty poor place, sitting on the banks of the Tigris there in the middle of the marshland that runs down to the Iranian border, which isn't far away at all. The houses were mainly mud brick jobs and the whole place looked pretty beat-up - it had been in the front line in the Iran-Iraq war. There was only one real street, where you'd see people selling fruit and vegetables or livestock. The only thing that stood out is there was a big shrine to the prophet Ezra which had a blue dome and a big wall around it. The whole place would take 10 to 15 minutes to walk through, tops.

We had a platoon of about 26 KOSB, and three guys in each of three Scimitars of the Light Dragoon Guards, so there were only about 38 of us all in. You were a little bit cut off in there, so everyone was quite wary, but if the s*** really hit the fan, reinforcements were not that far away. Both the camps at Abu Naji and Al Amarah had Quick Reaction Forces on five minutes' notice to move, so they could have flown down in a quarter of an hour or so. Saying that, at that time, although we obviously had some trouble, it wasn't the very hostile place that it became a year or so later. In theory, it was deemed to be the safest of the areas because it was so far south and there was no Sunni and Shia thing going on.

We would patrol the immediate area of the village and then strike out into the other villages and the marshland round about. We were just showing a presence, and obviously looking for weapons and insurgents. You have to remember, Saddam's own police and Army had sort of vanished, so there wasn't that much formal law and order apart from us.

The locals were perfectly friendly most of the time. The kids, particularly, were always flocking round us, grinning, chattering away, looking for sweets and stuff. It was harder to tell whether the adults wanted us there - they were a bit more guarded. But certainly not openly aggressive or threatening.

Of course, there *were* people who didn't want us there. It had all kicked off two nights before. I had taken a six man patrol out around the village in a Land Rover, and we had been shot at from a number of rooftops. The rounds were close enough, probably AK, and we de-bussed from the vehicle and tried to locate the shooters. But we couldn't so we went back and reported it. There were no casualties, but we were slightly shaken up. That was the first time we had been shot at in that area.

The next night, another patrol was out and as they pulled out on to Route Six - the main road from Basra through to Al Amarah - they got heavy incoming fire from the other side of the road, again from the village. They also de-bussed and started to return fire. It's always sketchy, particularly in the dark, but from the muzzle flashes and noise they thought there were between ten and twenty insurgents. I deployed with six more guys towards the south, and we swept them out of the village, on to the other side of the road and over around 300 metres of flat, open ground to a farm complex. They were firing at us all the way. It's not something you ever really get used to, but the cliché of the training taking over is right, it does. The natural reaction is to freeze, and a few of the young lads - I'm talking 18 or 19-year-olds here - did do that a bit. It was perfectly natural - they had never been out on the streets and been fired at before. I'd be telling them to move here or get over there and they were a bit sceptical about moving. They can hear the rounds ricocheting nearby and they don't want to walk into one. But the worst thing you can do is just stay in one place, so we got them going.

Once we'd got the insurgents out of the village and into this farm area, there wasn't much more we could do. We weren't using NVG, just our rifle scopes, and because it was dark, and given our numbers and lack of knowledge as to theirs, we couldn't really clear the area, so we left it at that until the next morning. We got intelligence that we had killed and wounded a few of the enemy and, again, we'd not taken any injuries.

It was the next morning when the main thing happened. A team went out to clear the area and as they were returning, just as they got back to the control base, there was a lot of gunfire to the north east of our position. It was a mixture of heavy machine gun and small arms. You can hear the difference. Heavy machine gun is an awful lot louder and when it is fired over your head you hear the thump of the weapon and then a much louder crack as the round passes over. I was on Quick Reaction Force, dressed and ready to go, so I grabbed my guys. The sentries on our roof shouted down that they'd spotted some enemy up to the north east of the camp, on the other side of the river.

There was only one bridge across the river, and Cpl Jardine and his men had to cross it to get to the enemy. This was extremely hazardous; the bridge would channel them into a narrow killing ground in front of the enemy guns. Despite knowing this, Cpl Jardine and his men did not hesitate.

I moved out with my team - there were five of us, including myself. As we were moving up the road, we received incoming fire from the opposite side of the river, which was about 100 metres from our position. We started fire-manoeuvring over some waste ground until we came to the river. We were still unclear as to exactly where the enemy were, or how many of them there were. Because it was broad daylight, the muzzle flashes were much less vivid, but we were seeing clouds of dust coming up as people ran about. However, we couldn't just fire willy-nilly into those clouds because this is a village and there are innocent people and even kids about. So we would try to work out where the rounds were coming from, then scan the area through our rifle sights and, if we saw someone armed, we would then fire back. We'd also move around ourselves, trying to draw their fire so that we could observe or hear where it was coming from. Eventually, we fought our way over to the river. Many of the rivers in this part of Iraq have raised banks to prevent flooding, so that offered us some cover. There were cracks in the mud eroded by the weather or high water, and I got myself in one of them and located four positions on the opposite side of the river.

There was a bridge across to my left, about 100 metres away. It was raised up 15ft or so over the water, and a heavy machine gun - a Dushka, I think - was set up underneath there. It was firing diagonally towards us and our camp. There were three guys at that position and a pick-up truck parked close by. On the bridge itself was one guy with an AK47, lying behind a small mound of earth. There was another guy 30 metres to his right and a fourth one further down the river bank. They were on raised ground, in good positions. I identified all the targets to my four guys and we started suppressing them. The idea is that you kill them if you can, but if you can't you put enough rounds down on them that you either scare them away or keep their heads down while someone else can get close enough to kill them.

As the KOSB soldiers began suppressive fire, the insurgents with small arms closed up, with two men now on the bridge and one just to the side, leaving two positions. Cpl Jardine allocated three of his soldiers to suppress these, and then assessed the situation. The enemy were in well-prepared positions and were proving very hard to hit. If his men

stayed where they were, they risked other enemy forces potentially outflanking them and assaulting them from the rear. Retreat was not an option. He decided he had to get across the bridge.

Myself and Pte John Clark, now LCpl Clark, got up on top of the ridge and started running along to the bridge. We were very exposed at that point but that was the only way onto it. As we got up there, another group opened up on us from a large military building further north but on the same side of the river as we were on. They were 200 metres away, we estimated there were 15 to 20 weapons involved and they were accurate - the rounds started landing around our feet, in amongst the pair of us. I grabbed John and we slid back down the steep bank and crawled over to a pile of rubble for cover. I poked my head up and had a look and saw there were loads of people in this building firing at us. I got on the radio to the platoon commander and said, 'We need some support here... we're getting contact from this military building in the north... I suggest you move on to Route Six and cover us from the school.' There was a school building which looked directly into this new insurgent position. So Cpl Tony Currie and LCpl Chris Potts deployed with a few privates to this building and started suppressing them. Meanwhile, John Clark was using his Minimi on them. The other guys were still suppressing the original three positions - there was a lot of gunfire going off all around. Once Tony Currie's team were in position, they took over suppressing the building and I started thinking about getting back up onto the bank and trying to get onto the bridge. It was one of those moments when you just have to do it. No-one else was able to get across there, so it had to be me.

I was probably scared half to death but, to be honest, I can't remember how I felt. I just knew that something had to be done.

Around this time, a white pick-up truck moved up towards us, had a look and then turned and drove away. I kind of saw it out of the corner of my eye, but well enough to see that there were armed men inside. They could have been the local police - who we thought we could trust - but they could also have been more insurgents, so they forced my hand. As soon as I saw it, I thought *I've got to do something now, just in case.*

I left John with the Minimi to cover my rear. The Minimi is quite inaccurate if you're trying to fire it on the move anyway, and it offers a lot of fire support - 5.56 belted, up to 1,000 rounds a minute with a range of 800 metres. So he was better employed where he was; if the vehicle came back, or the guys in the building had another go at me, he'd give me a chance.

Cpl Jardine's citation explains what happened next: he charged three men who were firing automatic weapons at him. "Despite intense and accurate heavy machine gun fire, he assaulted the first position alone, killing two of the enemy and capturing their weapons. The third enemy fled. Jardine then proceeded to suppress the depth machine gun position, whilst calling forward the remainder of his own Team to join him. At this point a third enemy position was identified to him. Jardine's team located this position and proceeded to lay down fire on both positions, allowing the remainder of the multiple to move forward. At this point the enemy disengaged from the action and withdrew."

I got back up there and just ran as quick as I could until I got to the bridge. The lads doing the suppressing were brilliant, they kept the enemy down until I actually got on there.

I started running across the bridge. I was about 30 metres from the two guys on top of the bridge and they had seen me immediately. They were lying down, prone position, and firing at me as I ran; I saw their fingers on the triggers, then the muzzle flashes and then I could hear the rounds zipping past. I remember thinking, *Why are they not hitting me?* But they were firing on automatic and while the AK is a good weapon it is quite inaccurate. Luckily. Obviously, I was moving as well, which made their job harder.

I got to within 15 or 20 metres of them and I just thought, *I'm going no further*, here. I dropped to one knee, aimed, fired one round, quickly moved onto the second, and fired again. I'm a reasonable shot, but the sight system on the SA80 is such that, at that range... well, you *could* miss, but you'd almost have to be trying to. I just aimed at the body and in both cases my rounds went in to the chest, under the arm and came out of the back of the neck. Both guys were instantly dead. I didn't see what happened to the third guy, but apparently he ran away and vanished behind some mud huts. I did see the truck that was next to the machine gun drive away. It hit the road and just kept going, and we were on foot so we couldn't chase them to make an arrest.

The truck was still in range, but the fact that it had disengaged meant that we couldn't fire upon it. It was frustrating, of course; they can drive away, come back the next day and kill five of your mates. But I can understand the reasons for the rules. Everything was done with the aim of minimising death or injury to anyone. We would never fire unless fired on first. I think it spoke volumes for our discipline.

I moved back across the river, and Chris Potts was firing UGL grenades into the military building, because they were still engaging us. Obviously, we needed to clear it. One of the Scimitar armoured fighting vehicles came up and we parked it in the middle of the waste ground observing the back exit. But while we were doing that they must have extracted because when we actually went to clear through there was no-one left. There was a lot of blood, but no bodies or weapons - they had obviously taken them with them.

We recovered the bodies of the two men I'd killed, together with their weapons. You can't just leave bodies in the middle of the desert. You have got to pick them up and deal with them. And as soon as we got back, we had to write statements detailing exactly what had happened and how they had died. The Army thoroughly investigates any shootings by soldiers and they needed to make sure that we hadn't just murdered people in the street. The doctor, the padre and whoever else wanted to jump on the QRF helicopter came down from Abu Naji. The padre had a chat with the young guys - I say 'young guys', I'm talking about the 18-year-olds, but I was only 21 myself! - to make sure they were all OK. I was attending sitreps at the time, and I never really got to speak to him, but that wasn't an issue for me. I'd done what needed to be done when I shot those blokes. It was either them or one of us, probably me, so it never bothered me. Even now, while it's not something I like to ponder over, I think I made the right decision.

When I joined the army I was a quiet, shy person, and I don't think I've changed since, so getting the medal was a little bit... embarrassing, I suppose. Once we came back from TELIC 2, we moved straight across to Northern Ireland and I was told I had to go back and see the CO. I thought, *Oh, no, what have I done?* It turned out that he told me I was getting an award for my actions. I was a bit, like, 'Why am I getting it and some of the other people are not?' Although another guy got a Military Cross for the night before, and we got one Mention in Despatches for the night before as well. I mean, I'm very proud to have it, but John Clark and Chris Potts and all the other guys in the team all played their parts. I kind of feel that some of the others should have been given something as well. They did just as much, and I feel that everyone should have been recognised in some way. They were standing beside me, giving me their support. If it wasn't for them, who knows what would have happened?

Worst thing is, I never told my parents what had gone on. Partly, I never thought anything of it. I was just doing my job. Partly, I didn't want to worry them. They were shocked - they didn't know a thing about it until the newspapers started phoning them and asking them what had happened. My mum still hasn't seen the full citation, so I'm going to be in trouble when she reads this book.

Lance Corporal Christopher Balmforth, MC
The Queen's Royal Hussars

THE following year, the Queen's Royal Hussars were out in Iraq. Among their number was Chris Balmforth, a rugby-mad junior NCO from the Midlands. The country had been reasonably calm for some time, but on April 4, 2004, a prominent supporter of the maverick Shia cleric Moqtada al Sadr was arrested. Violence exploded on the streets of southern Iraq to a level not seen since the invasion 12 months previously. Well-armed insurgents repeatedly attacked Coalition Forces with rocket launchers, anti-tank weapons, grenades and machine guns.

Four days into the uprising, LCpl Balmforth was providing top cover to the first of four Land Rovers which were leaving the city's Al Jameat Police Station, where they had been training members of the Iraqi Police Service.

As the vehicle turned a corner, it was met by concentrated fire from five gunmen armed with machine guns and rocket launchers. At a range of around 15 metres this proved to be devastating: the driver was shot through both his thighs, and his ankle was shattered, and the vehicle was seriously damaged. From the top cover position Balmforth returned fire immediately, buying time for his colleagues.

I'm 27, married with a young baby, and I live in Birmingham. I joined the Army 10 years ago as a 16-year-old boy soldier. My dad and my uncle were in the regiment before me - my uncle was a recce troop commander in the first Gulf War, and he was in a Scimitar which was destroyed by an American A10 in a blue-on-blue. He survived, but he had shrapnel in his leg, a big hole through his helmet - it got blown off, and the only reason it didn't take his head with it was he didn't have the chinstrap done up - and had part of his wrist ripped away... they stitched it to his chest to keep the tissue alive and now he has chest hairs growing out of his hand, which is quite funny.

When I first got over to Iraq, I spent my first three months up in Maysan. For a while, I think we were actually the furthest north of all British soldiers, up above Al Amarah in a little camp at a place called Al Sharki, stuck right out in the desert, but mostly we were at Al Amarah. Through all our time there, we only ever came up against demonstrations, mostly out near the Pink Palace, the local municipal HQ... people complaining about a lack of jobs and that sort of thing. I think we had one RPG incident, where someone was seen near the camp with a launcher. I was guard commander that night; I remember Trooper Wilks fired his GPMG to deter them, and they scarpered before they got the RPG going; as they fled he fired a flare, and the bloody thing nearly went into our cookhouse. We still laugh about that. So it was really, really quiet.

On any tour, you're a bit apprehensive. It takes a couple of weeks to learn about the area and feel at home, and eventually you just get used to the place and the level of activity and it just becomes normal. I'd have to say that it was so easy that our drills started to slacken and we became a little complacent.

Then we went down to Basra. We were based in Basra Palace, a nice big camp, lots of space and beautiful compared to what we had been in, and it was still quite chilled. We started working with the SOD (Special Operations Directive), the Iraqi special police. Our job, basically, was to teach them how to be special police. They were proper cowboys. We were only trying to teach them basic skills, like, when you go out on patrol make sure that you load your weapon in the loading bay, silly little things that we get taught very early on but which they just couldn't understand. They'd cock their rifles at anything, or you'd catch them squinting down their barrels from the wrong end, and you don't need to be a squaddie to work out why that's a bit dodgy. It started to get a bit difficult between us and them, I thought, because they didn't like us coming in and telling them, sometimes a bit forcefully, what to do and how to run their police station.

The way they treated their prisoners was completely different to the way that we would have done it. They used to bring people in in the back of their trucks, and they would be tied up and gagged. They had a big frame that they could strap people to, lots of stuff like that, and we got rid of it straight away, as soon as we got there. I don't know about the rest of the lads, but it started to get a bit worrying for me. I would look at the way these blokes operated and think, *That's not right*. They used to patrol in balaclavas because they are special police and they don't want to have their faces seen, but it hardly helps reassure the local people.

They didn't like us getting rid of their little toys and changing the way they did things, and they started to get a bit anti. It got to the point where our lads were going, 'Hang about, this lot could cause a lot of problems for us.' I think we all thought that they might be a threat, rather than be on our side. You can't completely trust anyone out there, to my mind, and I personally think that they had something to do with what later happened, though that's only speculation. Anyway, all our earlier complacency disappeared, and we started to 'up' things. We started cocking our rifles as soon as we left camp, we were a bit more alert and we started to vary our routes into and out of the camp.

On April 4, the uprising began and on April 8, Balmforth and his colleagues were working at the Al Jameat Police Station.

A really, really strange thing happened on the day. We were at the cop shop, we usually went there for two hours or three, max, and were doing our usual bits and pieces... get the prisoners out and walk them around, talk to them and find out why they were in there and see how things were... when one of the police wagons came in. And in the back of the wagon was, of all people, a backpacker from New Zealand.

I mean, we were like, 'What the f*** are you doing here, mate?'

He'd taken it into his head that he wanted to find out for himself how bad things really were in Iraq, and he'd just been out, walking round the streets. Absolutely mad - asking to be kidnapped and beheaded, basically, because no-one would have believed that story. Luckily for him, the SOD had picked him up. And he was even luckier we were there when they arrived back with him, otherwise they might have sold him on to some really unpleasant people. He was a right tit - he would not accept that he'd been stupid, he just kept saying 'Oh, it's not as bad as everyone makes out.' And we ended up having to hang around, trying to convince him to come back with us, because we couldn't have left him there. We ended up staying for an extra two hours before he finally agreed, and looking back I wonder whether that gave the bad guys the time they needed to get into position. We were all pretty annoyed with this backpacker.

When we finally left, we took a different road to the one we'd arrived on, but there were only three major routes that you could use and it was all ideal ambush territory... loads of houses, it was in a residential area, barriers on the roads which you had to stop, get out and deal with. So it was a really slow process. There were four Land Rovers. I was in the front one, the Troop Leader's thin-skinned Rover, there was a snatch wagon behind us with the Troop Sergeant inside, then a bit of a gap, then the Squadron Leader's vehicle and the other one. We headed along one of the roads, you took a left, then a right and you came to the main drag, a dual carriageway. You had to turn right there and as we turned, they were waiting for us in a small copse of trees off to the right hand side. They were so close - literally maybe 15 or 20 metres away - that we didn't really even notice them at first. The first thing I remember was seeing an orange glow, and then hearing a bang and a subsequent explosion somewhere behind us. It all happened so quickly that my first thought was that an IED had gone off, but actually the orange glow was the muzzle flash from a rocket propelled grenade launcher, and the round had hit the front right hand side of our Land Rover, had failed to detonate - though it took out our front offside tyre - and had just spun off down the road and exploded behind us. Almost simultaneously, they opened up with at least one RPK - their equivalent of our GPMG. The rounds from that bounced off the snatch Rover behind us, which, funnily enough, was the one this New Zealand idiot was in. We later found it had taken 14 rounds but, luckily for him and the lads inside, the armour kept them out. Though I believe the Kiwi was s****ing himself, and very rapidly changed his tune about how dangerous Iraq was.

We weren't so lucky in my vehicle. As we accelerated out of the ambush, a load of AK47 came in and hit my driver, Trooper 'Pikey' Pike, in the legs. One shattered his ankle, the other went through the thigh at the top of his knee, out the other side and into his other leg. Another round went through the Troop Leader's map: he had it in his hand at the time, so he was a very lucky boy. He still has the map to this day as a little souvenir of the time he was about three inches from being cut in half by a 7.62mm round.

I immediately returned fire from the top of the vehicle, trying to suppress them. It was all very blurred. You knew the rounds were coming from over there somewhere, and you knew they were the men who were trying to attack you, but my vision was quite blurred, everything went slow... I certainly couldn't describe each individual's face or anything like that. I didn't actually feel scared, which was odd - that all came later. At the time, it actually felt like an exercise drill. It was like, this is what we have been trained for, so you just crack on. The training really does take over. I can't even remember taking off my safety catch. I was just returning fire. The drills kicked in.

I was using an SA80, the Mark II, the newer one. You don't put it on automatic unless you go to assault a position, and as you go into the bunker or whatever you switch across. So I was just firing at my normal rate, which is one round every four seconds or so. You just keep your finger on it and on, off, on, off, on, off... and just fire one aimed shot at a time. Though I wasn't sure whether I was actually hitting anyone at that point, it was a question of getting as many rounds as I could get into that general direction for suppressive fire.

There was a second top cover with me, Trooper 'Mac' McMahn, and he had a Minimi, which is a light machine gun, a stubby Gimpy, which puts down a hell of a lot of rounds. As soon as we started taking incoming, the interpreter and a TA guy who was with us had dived to the bottom of the vehicle, to find some cover, and one of them knocked Mac's legs so he came down into the wagon and nearly dropped his Minimi. He just managed to keep hold of it and get himself back up top. He fired a couple of rounds, and then the bloody thing had a stoppage... absolutely the worst moment for that to happen.

Meanwhile, Pikey was in no state at all, but he had somehow managed to jam his foot right down on the pedal and start wanging it across the road; he hit the concrete central reservation, mounted it and got the vehicle over the other side, despite his situation and on only three tyres, and sort of carried on through some rubbish on the other side. A great bit of driving. I think the Troop Leader pulled the handbrake on to stop the vehicle rolling into a river - it was a sort of evil-looking purple colour, full of dead dogs and dirty nappies, so that was good.

Once the badly damaged Land Rover had come to a halt, Balmforth continued to return fire while his team pulled the wounded driver to safety.

The Troop Leader leapt out and grabbed Pikey, dragged him out and down, and I jumped off the wagon. The central reservation barrier was concrete and about a foot high, and the road on our side dipped away just slightly and gave us a bit more cover. I'd say the enemy were about 50 metres away now, in and around the group of trees, so I got myself into a decent firing position and started looking for targets. The TA guy, Kev, came over with his rifle but I sent him off to help sort out Pikey. The last time Kev had given anyone morphine he'd had the thing the wrong way round and had injected his own thumb, so maybe not the best of ideas at the time, but he got the job done. Mac set himself up about five metres to my right, trying to clear his stoppage, and the interpreter picked up Pikey's weapon and made as though to get along aside us. He was a top bloke, half Egyptian, and just wanted to help us out, but we told him to put the weapon down and take cover. He is not part of the British Army, he's not supposed to get involved. So he just took cover, and I think he felt a bit lost and helpless, a bit distraught.

I still wasn't exactly frightened, but I did start to feel very exposed. There was such a lot of fire incoming that you think it's only a matter of time, or start worrying about whether you're going to get engaged from the rear. The Rover behind us had left, just driven out of the ambush. The two behind had stopped at the junction, briefly engaged the insurgents, but had then also left. I don't think they could see our vehicle was disabled at that point.

Fairly quickly, a lad called Trooper King had got out of the Squadron Leader's Rover and run back up to the junction, and I got eyes on with him. He saw us, and I was able to explain our predicament with hand signals. So he and a couple of other lads, Cpl Povey and Evo, LCpl Evans, started engaging the enemy. That worked out perfectly for us, because they were now taking fire from two directions and they started to panic themselves.

> Balmforth's citation describes how he then "broke cover, and with complete disregard for his own safety assaulted the ambush position. Three enemy gunmen were killed in the action, a fourth was critically injured and others got away."

A number of them had been hit, and I saw a bloke firing at us while running towards a minibus. He'd have been about 30, in local dress. I took him on the move, shot him in the chest and he went down. Immediately, you sort of assume he's out of the game and start looking for other targets. But out of the corner of my eye I saw him roll over, and he got back up and raised the weapon again. So I shot him again, this time in the face. He went down again, and at that the rest of them all started dropping their weapons and legging it. They all piled into the minibus, dragging some of the dead and injured with them, and just drove off in a cloud of dust; I had my weapon trained on them the whole time, and it would have been easy just to empty the magazine into the vehicle, but the direct threat had passed - I had to let them go. That's the way it is.

Around then, a Warrior tipped up; my sister was in the Army and some of her friends were in there which was slightly strange... seeing people I've been out for beers with, and here I am, I've just killed people and had people trying to kill me. I explained the situation to them, and we started securing the area, putting a perimeter in. It had all gone quiet and there was just one of the insurgents there, the guy I had shot twice. I went over to him. He was rolling around, reaching his arms up to me, calling for help, big time. I covered him with my rifle while one of the other blokes went up and removed his weapon, and then we assessed him. He was obviously in a bad way. My second shot had taken away most of the lower part of his face, and he was gasping for breath through the hole where his mouth had been. He closed his eyes, and I got a first field dressing out and applied pressure to the wound. We secured the area, and my sister's regiment took that over whilst I went back and helped Pikey back into the Warrior. We put the Iraqi bloke in as well, and off they went.

We had a look at the scene. The ambush had obviously been very carefully prepared - there were lots of weapons and RPGs all neatly lined up. They must have been waiting for a good while before we got there. We were concerned that they might have placed booby-trap IEDs on them, so we got the relevant teams out to make sure everything was safe.

The Military Police arrived. I was interviewed and had to make statements about what had happened, and justify the shots I had fired. In fact, we were interviewed three times... at the scene, then as soon as we got back we were spoken to as a group, and then a further individual interview straight after that. It makes me angry when I hear people talk about the Army, and soldiers ill-treating prisoners and stuff. I've never seen anything like that, and if I think about my own experiences... being grilled by the RMPs over whether I should have returned fire on people who were trying to kill me, and whether it was justified, and then seeing how we tried to save the life of the Iraqi prisoner... soldiers in the British Army, to me, behave as close to impeccably as you possibly can in a place like Iraq.

The only thing that did upset people was they put the Iraqi bloke in the hospital bed next to Pikey. Right next to each other, and the Iraqi could well have been the bloke who actually shot Pikey. I remember the Squadron Leader coming up and he was fuming and said he wanted something done about it. It was only a couple of hours later when he came back and said, 'It's alright, the guy's dead now.'

I felt bad about him dying, and the others. I don't feel guilty, exactly, but I do still feel sorry for what happened. If they hadn't come out that day to take us on, they could still be at home now with their wives and kids. I still have nightmares about what happened... I've punched and kicked my wife in my sleep, woken up covered in sweat, got myself all worked up. I used to take it out on her big time, she was a saint for putting up with me. I had a flashback, just one. We were in Germany and going on leave, and I was driving back to the UK. We got on the autobahn and we were coming over a rise, and the sun was setting right ahead of us, very low down. And the sun was just this big, orange glow, right in front of me, and it took me straight back to the moment the first RPG was fired. It looked exactly the same. And I started crying and shaking, and I just managed to get the vehicle on to the hard shoulder. And everyone was like, *You OK?* And I just sat quietly for a few minutes, and then it went away. And thank God, it's not happened since. These days I'm a lot better, but I avoid watching the news because anything about Iraq or Afghanistan upsets me, it just winds me up. As do civilians arguing about rubbish.

The ordinary Iraqis... I didn't like them, to be honest. They encouraged their children to throw rocks at us every time we went past and made it very clear we weren't welcome. This isn't just a few, it's all of them, that I saw. They were glad to see the back of Saddam but they needed law and order and the insurgents and militias were trying to stop the authorities and ourselves from providing that. The guys who ambushed us, and those insurgents... they used dirty tactics, and it wasn't really a fair fight. But then I wonder if another army came into our country, would I do the same? Yes, I probably would, if I was brainwashed and didn't understand that they genuinely wanted to help us. Which I think was the problem.

Balmforth's citation describes his actions that afternoon as "exceptional" and adds: "He was instrumental in protecting his comrade's life and regaining the initiative in very dangerous circumstances against overwhelming odds. His bravery, self sacrifice and leadership was an inspiration to his Regiment and acted as a significant deterrent to other would-be attackers."

The medal was amazing and great closure for me; I hope the rest of the team get their closure, because the medal was a symbol of what we all did that day. As I'm sure everyone who ever wins a medal will say, it wasn't down to me that we got out of there OK. Kingy and the guys who came back to help played a major part, as did everyone else. And Pikey... what he did was brilliant and very brave. Ignoring the fact that he had been shot and forcing his foot down and getting us over the central reservation... imagine how much pain he was in. I reckon he saved our lives. Funnily enough, that day he didn't want to go out on patrol, he said he could feel that something was going to happen. Sadly, he was right. He's since been medically discharged; the marrow from the shattered bones poisoned his blood, and he was touch and go for quite a long time. I've been out drinking with him fairly recently. He still walks funny and he says he has nightmares to this day.

I'm actually leaving the Army myself, now. Not as a result of what happened, I've just done my 10 years and I want to get out and try something else before I'm too old. But I'll never forget the lads and I have nothing but good memories to take with me, bar one bad afternoon.

Major Justin Featherstone, MC
The Princess of Wales's Regiment

JUSTIN Featherstone's Y Company was located in Cimic House, Al Amarah, in Iraq's Maysan province, between April and September 2004. Cimic House was the headquarters of the Civilian Military Co-ordination team in the area, which had been relatively peaceful despite some incidents such as those involving 1 Para and the Red Caps at nearby Al Majar Al Kabir the previous year.

However, 1PWRR's arrival to replace The Light Infantry coincided with the Mahdi Army uprising, which had sparked the violence that saw the ambush on Chris Balmforth's Land Rover.

Attacks against Coalition forces increased by one thousand per cent and Cimic House, a small and isolated compound, was surrounded and cut off. Re-supply was difficult and dangerous; one attempt to do so resulted in six casualties to the company and those forces attempting to re-supply them. In the space of 16 weeks, the compound was subjected to hundreds of indirect fire attacks from mortars and rockets, and the base sangars were repeatedly hit with short range RPG and small arms fire.

Featherstone - described by soldiers who served under him variously as 'a legend', 'completely mad' and 'a man you'd follow anywhere' - is something of an adrenaline junkie, who has led dozens of Army mountaineering and whitewater rafting trips. So it's no surprise that he personally led a large number of night-fighting patrols into the heart of the town's Mahdi Militia-controlled estates, taking his dismounted troops though the warren of poorly-lit buildings, across dangerously open waste ground and even over rooftops to find and kill the enemy.

They found themselves in firefights virtually every day, facing RPGs, heavy machine guns, small arms, IEDs and snipers, often in combination. Featherstone's citation explains how, "while under this heavy weight of incoming enemy fire, he would calmly direct his troops and return fire himself, and lead rapid and aggressive follow-ups, often in the face of heavy enemy resistance. This repeatedly brave personal leadership saw his company seize a number of heavy weapons, mortars and numerous rocket-propelled grenades and kill a number of the enemy forces. Featherstone showed personal courage, inspirational leadership, calmness, professionalism, determination and endurance over a protracted period."

I originally joined the Army on an 'O' type engagement, which meant training as a private soldier, and I did a series of attachments as a private before attending Sandhurst a year later. I was commissioned in to the Royal Hampshire Regiment in 1991, which was subsequently amalgamated in 1992 with the Queen's Regt to form The Princess of Wales's Royal Regiment. I'd served as a Platoon Commander, Coy 2IC, Intelligence Officer, Air Adjutant and Ops Officer, as well as leading and participating in a number of mountaineering, trekking and whitewater kayaking expeditions around the world. I'd also served on ops in Northern Ireland, Congo and Kosovo, and had commanded a company in the 2nd Battalion, before I took command of Y Company and we found ourselves in Iraq.

When the invasion was over, the Iraqi forces had essentially melted away. Behind them, they'd left a huge political and security vacuum, so the Coalition Provisional Authority, a temporary government, was set up. This was an administration run by Iraqis but with our support, and the local base, for Maysan, was in Cimic House in Al Amarah. That was home to us - Y Company, fire support, 130 to 135 men - and members of the CPA who were under our protection.

It was the former governor's residence, a three-storey building surrounded by a wall, and it would have been a very opulent place in its day. He'd had lions in the compound at one time, there were nice verandas and a lovely view of the Tigris, which curled around the back of the property a matter of yards away. To the front was some waste ground and then 100 metres away was the town. It had obviously been fortified - there were Hesco Bastion blast walls around the property and sangars built out of steel, concrete, Hesco Bastion sections and sandbags in the compound and on the roof. Probably 250 metres by 50 metres at its widest. With the river to your rear, it would have been easy to defend in a traditional, knights-in-a-castle way. In a modern warfare sense, it was a nightmare: there was only one route out, as both the front gate and the side gate converged onto a road in front, which made your exit and return potentially dangerous. And people could hang around on the other side of the river and shoot at you, and you couldn't get at them - there were only two bridges across. Still, it was what it was and when we first arrived there was internet access, and even air conditioning, and there was a hope amongst some of the boys that we would be spending our time working on our suntans and doing lots of hearts and minds work.

I'd gone out on my recce in December and things had been OK. Yes, there had been lots of riots, jobs and food protests - Londonderry 1982 stuff, only worse, exceptionally violent affairs with RPGs and AKs being fired - but as far as relationships with the Brits were concerned, there was a lot of love in the air.

When we arrived to take over from The Light Infantry in April, that had completely changed. They had been facing a steadily increasing level of violence, and there was a real feeling that the honeymoon was over and that things were beginning to smoulder, particularly up around Najaf. To an extent, it was understandable. Coalition forces had been there for some time and the people were seeing no tangible benefits, other than the removal of Saddam. The Coalition had lots of very impressive and important projects ongoing, and were really trying to make a difference, but these projects were all long term - six months, a year, more than a year, major, multi-million pound infrastructure projects. The Light Infantry beforehand, and now ourselves, were doing the best we could. But if you're an 18-year-old, and part of a 14-strong family with no work, it just doesn't wash. They think, *We've got these tossers on the street, with their tanks and their helmets and their machine guns and their British flags, and they may be polite, but they've done bugger all. They've painted a few schools, and provided a few school books. We've still got open sewers, only a couple of water treatment plants and we're still pumping water out of the Tigris.*

Unemployment was running at 85% and inflation, for staples such as cooking oil, was at 380%. That is a major deal. So we had a dislocated youth, in an already fractured country, and the loss of traditional tribal values because of the urbanisation in that area under the previous regime. The call to militancy, where you are going to get $50 for every 24 hours that you fight, or $50 for every bomb that a three-man mortar team fires... that's good cash, especially when you consider that the average salary was $8 a day.

So it was fertile ground for trouble makers. If you take electricity, Saddam had done no maintenance work on his power stations for 37 years. He hadn't touched them. To get power back on with our local power station, we had to shut down quarters of it for long periods. There was hugely reduced output to make the thing a viable, proper power station again. But of course all the people see is that the Brits have come and taken away our power. As much as you try to educate people that it *had* to be done, the message can easily be twisted and used for nefarious ends. Note, the insurgents never tried to blow the power stations up. If you cock it up in Iraq, and do something like that, your neighbour will just shoot you, so they had to be careful too.

It was such a shame, because the people themselves, largely, were lovely. Al Amarah and the surrounds had a population of 386,000. Of those only 200 people were Sunni, about 200 Christian and about 2,000 Zoroastrian. So the huge majority were Shia, which meant we had none of the sectarian fighting that there was in the American sector and further south. We had good, honest Shia Marsh Arabs, proud and fiercely loyal people. If you won them over, they were intensely loyal to you, as well. And brave beyond belief. We had 18 locals at Cimic House - interpreters, plumbers, electricians, cooks, police and so on - during August, by which time it was like hell on earth. I had to physically hand over the 14-year-old cook-hand to his family because it was too dangerous for him to be there and he wouldn't leave. We had a deaf and dumb gardener, who came with the building. He was a real liability because he couldn't hear the mortars and rounds coming in - his family had to come and drag him out, too, and he didn't want to go, either. Our local plumber and electrician used to run up and down between contacts and try and sort out where the water pipes had been blown or shot away, or patch up the electrics; at one stage, they even ran out to the junction box in the road to try and get a cable into us during a lull in the middle of a firefight. They didn't go home at all during August, they chose to stay with us. Two of my interpreters, one of whom was a poultry pathologist and vet by trade, stuck with it the whole time. I had about six interpreters at first, and not all of them stayed - which was perfectly understandable - but those two were by our side, day in, day out. I had six Iraqi coppers. They were meant to be on rotation, but they never left. Just refused to. Stood by us the whole time. One of my coppers found out that a

PRR radio from the previous battle group had been lost and that the Mahdi Army were using it to listen in to our patrols. It only had a radius of a couple of hundred metres, but it was still irritating because it could be the difference between success and failure for ambushers. This policeman put on a dirty dishdash and shemagh, and secretly followed the Mahdi Army patrols for seven days. On the seventh day, he jumped on the bloke with the radio, pinned him down with a pistol and then ran two kilometres back to base with the radio in a carrier bag. He did it on his own, against 17 heavily-armed men with RPGs and machine guns. I mean, staggering stuff.

Iraqis are stereotyped as mischievous, disingenuous, disloyal, thieving, mean, self-centred types, so I really want to get across the message that the great majority are actually good, incredibly brave and loyal people. Out of the 386,000 in Al Amarah, there were probably 3,000 who were prepared to fight and get involved with the Mahdi Army. Plus another 3,000 up in Najaf. So 6,000 out of perhaps 800,000; that's a small percentage of the population, considering that the whole country was inflamed at the time. But no-one is interested in that story.

When there was nothing happening, we would go out and try to win the locals over. The great and the good of the area were the CO's business, so I spent a lot of time meeting the grass-roots - the drug abusers, the criminals, the underclass, the widows, the traders, the tea-stall holders. People needed support to do the basics, so I created a small business regeneration scheme. The idea was we would set people up in business if they came from families where there was no work at all. People would come to me every two weeks with six nominations and an estimate of what it would cost to start the business. One man wanted rent money for a shop, another for a fruit stall. Another needed an angle grinder and a welder to set himself up as a mechanic. There was an accountant who wanted a second-hand PC for his business. One bloke wanted a second-hand fishing net, an old boat and an outboard motor to start him and three mates up as fishermen. Another wanted some painting materials, because when they have weddings they don't take photos, they commission portraits. He was the most successful of all the businesses, actually - the last one you'd have thought would work. All in all, we created 109 small businesses, all for less than $500 apiece. The money came through Brigadier Andrew Kennett. He fought tooth and nail - the rules said money couldn't be allocated for the benefit of individuals, and it had to be approved at Westminster and then in Washington. But he did it, he got me $78,000 within a week.

The other side of the coin was that the community representation and the formation of local businesses created a stream of intelligence, the volume and accuracy of which I had never encountered before. People were just coming and telling us things, specific information like, 'Mohammed has got X thousand dollars, he's operating out of this house, he's rounded up 150 men and is planning two mortar attacks tonight. This is a sketch map of where we think they'll be.' That level of detail. The amount of goodwill was amazing. Sometimes, it would be by mobile phone because they didn't want to come in while we were fighting, or they didn't want to be seen as a friend of the British Army. But others would brazenly walk right in. We had Imams coming up the street trying to turn back the Mahdi army. On five separate occasions, we even had locals take up arms against the Mahdi army. One time, they saw a mortar being set up and they forced them out of the area before they could fire at us. On another, they beat up a group who were about to have a go. If you can imagine the locals stopping the IRA in Londonderry, it was like that, only braver. Here you were talking about 10 or 12 people stopping groups of between 20 and 50 guys, armed with just an AK each. Incredible bravery.

Despite the goodwill generated by the work of Featherstone and his troops, Y Coy were mortared every night, and often during the day, from their arrival, and the attacks accelerated as the weeks went by. Things came to a head in August, when Moqtada al Sadr was surrounded by US and Iraqi forces in the Shrine Imam Ali in Najaf. The Shia militias rose up in anger and in Al Amarah attacks on the compound escalated to the point where hundreds of insurgents were launching daily full frontal attacks on the beleaguered British troops.

May was very busy and it got worse and worse until in August it really developed. The US forces were within touching distance of the second holiest site in Shia Islam and it was an explosive mix.

On August 5, we had planned to go out to visit some of the businesses but we got an urgent phone call telling us not to come. By 1900hrs, five of the seven police stations in the area had been over-run by the Mahdi Army. By about 2000hrs, the road between us and Abu Naji had about 500 armed fighters on it with anti-tank mines and a series of anti-armour ambushes, cutting us off completely. All that in a space of half a day. It was like being at Rorke's Drift, or the Alamo.

We took 600 mortar rounds to Cimic House between August 5 and 26, including a group of 19 incoming rounds in 42 minutes. The compound was relatively small, so it's a miracle no-one was killed, but we were pretty careful. Anyone who wasn't on sentry duty was in the sangars and didn't move around. We went down to one hot meal a day so that people only had to move to the cookhouse once. We had to move the kitchen inside the cookhouse, which was just a room really, because first the trailer kitchen, and then the tent kitchens, were both blown up. One of the chefs, Cpl Lewis Dodds, almost lost a leg in one of the explosions.

We felt isolated, and I was given the opportunity every day to withdraw if I wanted to. I said no. Firstly, I didn't think the troops would have wanted to leave. And two, I knew that we could hold it. Tenuous, but we could.

It usually kicked off at about 1400hrs. We would be sniped at from the north bank of the river, and maybe take some machine gun fire, and then we would start to get mortar attacks. They would come from north of the Tigris, from Majidir in the east, and then from the south east and the south west, near a mosque, using a ripple effect to fix us. This would carry on until about 1900hrs, sometimes later, and then they would launch ground attacks, getting to within 10 metres of our walls on many occasions. You're talking 20 or 30 guys running up and getting that close, with another couple of hundred firing from the doorways and alleyways to our front. The day would end with a load of mortar rounds until about 2300hrs.

We killed a lot of people, but I have no problem with that whatsoever. Actually, that's not quite true. No sane person wants to kill anyone and the first act of taking life is a crossing of the Rubicon, the point at which you have become dislocated from the rest of society, and, indeed, the rest of the Army as well. Your life is irrevocably changed, you can't rewind the tape. My first was in a large scale contact in Majidir, with blokes on the roof, firing down at us. Contact is always very confused, so you may have discharged your weapon at the enemy but there may have been half a dozen of you in a group shooting at the same man. It's impossible to say, *I did that*. The big moment is when you fire a round and you know that your round has felled that individual. But it didn't really leave a marked effect because for me, my overwhelming fear was what was going to happen to my soldiers. It was a good honest contact. *I've been engaged first. I've just taken human life. Now what's happening over there?* It is always a thinking point, for any soldier, but luckily I was always too busy to mull too much. I had 14 Fijians in my company, many of whom were very religious, mostly Roman Catholic. For them, it was always a moment where they needed to have a bit of 'me' time, to think.

The way most people rationalise it is, particularly with our rules of engagement, you're always in a straight 'me or them' situation, like they're sticking an AK through the wall and blazing away at you. So it's really quite easy... almost a no-brainer. You don't have huge difficulty with it. They are trying to attack me and over-run my base. So it isn't something that has left me with lasting misgivings.

In the face of the growing violence, Maj Featherstone and his men struck back.

When we had first arrived, whenever something major happened we were told to close down, for obvious reasons. The moment you start going out, you antagonise them and you're vulnerable and more likely to have casualties. But being under intense indirect fire is very emasculating - there is this inability to respond, and you just sit and cower and wait for something random to happen to you. It's very bad for morale. Psychologically, I reckon the company could have stuck about eight weeks of that before going to pieces. I mean, one of our lads took virtually direct hits in sangar three on three separate occasions. He had to be dug out on the second - he was uninjured but half-deaf and totally dazed. That is quite a quick route to combat stress. There is also dignity and pride to consider. *We're the British Army and we're not going out to face an enemy?*

So I approached the commanding officer, Lt Col Matt Maer, who was based in Abu Naji. That was only seven kilometres away, but at times when it was really bad it might as well have been 700 kilometres. Some of our re-supplies took seven days, others took ten days and were full battle group ops, needing Warriors and tanks to get into us. Pte Johnson Beharry won his VC for one of our re-supplies, a corporal got shot through the lung and there were another six casualties just to bring us food, ammo and bottled water and take away stuff that needed repairing.

I said I wanted to plan deliberate offensive operations at the time and place of my choosing, in the configuration that I chose. Both Matt Maer and Brig Kennett said, 'Not a problem, tell me what you need.' Both men gave me a level of support and empathy from the chain of command that I could only have wished for.

From that, Operation Caiman was born. We mounted about 50 night-time raids. I took out all but five, and my RSM Dale Norman also missed out on very few, and only then because he was on leave. We struck as far as 14 kilometres north east of Cimic, varying our methods - sometimes infiltrated by assault boat, other times dropped off by Warrior, still other times dropped off by Snatch. We'd always patrol on foot. Being in Snatch or a Warrior, you're a big target and you're not agile. Myself and all of the Toms preferred being light for design - minimum kit, maximum ammunition, maximum water, so we could move as quickly as the enemy. If they went on to a roof top, we could fight from a roof top. We could see all around and we could talk to the people who would point down the street and tell us where the enemy were.

We varied our tactics. One night we'd set up ambushes. The next might be a full-on, company-scale attack. As a result of those, we captured a couple of truck loads of ammunition, a number of prisoners who are all languishing in the Iraqi legal system as we speak, and obviously we killed a number of enemy and destroyed a number of their ambushes. Crucially, we sent a very clear message that we owned the ground, particularly at night. We ruled the night. Numerically, we were vastly outnumbered but we had better-trained and more disciplined men and superior technology. Our night vision was superb, whereas our intelligence was that they had two pieces of night vision for their whole organisation. We had UAV capability, we had thermal imagery which could reach from the top of Cimic house to some of our locations, and we also had air power. If you can call the AC130 Spectre US Special Forces gunship in on enemy positions, that is a very potent force indeed.

There was a marked positive effect. The enemy became less brazen and really thought twice about having a pop. For a month, when we started, they never fired their mortars when we were on the ground because they didn't know where we would be. The local people and the police saw we were in charge, and they grew in confidence, to the point where the police started to come out with us on these operations.

We had a total of 188 major contacts. And I didn't record anything as an individual contact unless there was an exchange of at least 100 rounds, it just didn't count. It was all reported, but it didn't go on the statistics.

Some of those contacts were six to eight hours long.

I was desperate not to lose one of my soldiers. I wasn't worried about myself, being under fire never vaguely bothered me or my sarnt major. What's the worst that could happen? If you die you're not going to know anything about it. You could fall off a mountain, like I have done before. It's no good thinking that way, so it never bothered me. What the awful, nagging, aching worry was, 24 hours a day, *If I had given a different set of orders would that soldier now not be injured or dead? If we do this tonight, and two people end up dead, will it have been worth it?* That is so wearing.

In the event, we were very fortunate. The company took 12 casualties, from very serious injuries to quite minor things. We had one terrible accident - Pte Chris Rayment was killed on sentry duty at

Cimic House, when the drop barrier at the entrance to the compound came down on his head. That was a real tragedy. Chris was one of the most popular soldiers in, not just the company, but the Battalion, and it was a massive body blow to the Company. I liked him a great deal. He was the life and soul of the party, and was one of the few soldiers who had been to my parents' house, for example, after a kayaking trip. He was killed on August 4, the day before it all went mad, so the soldiers didn't really have any time to grieve and I could only allow a tiny pall bearer party to go down and put him on to the Hercules in Basra. No-one went back for his funeral, bar those who were on leave at the time, so it was very tough. You have to watch soldiers in that situation: one's biggest fear is that they will be angry and have a thirst for vengeance. But, actually, the blokes weren't like that and it was never an issue. I think it goes back to the fact that we lived and breathed the city, and we knew that not every guy out there was a bad guy, that actually many of them were on our side. There was this level of genuine empathy with the local population.

Some of the raids stick in your mind. There was one on about August 17. I had about two thirds of the company out with me, three platoons-worth, and we were heading back in. We got to a well-lit street near Yugoslav Bridge and the dogs started barking, so they knew we were there. It was about 0200hrs and we got ambushed from three separate positions: two medium machine guns 300 metres away to our rear and six AKs 50 metres to our front. I remember an RPG passed just over mine and Pte Adam Somers' heads, fizzing and whooshing off into the darkness, and a home-made blast bomb detonated about five metres behind us. Not one of their better efforts, luckily. We shot the lights out and did a full frontal assault. I went right flanking so I could hit a wall and go alongside it, and gave the orders on the radio as I went. I moved very fast and just as I was to the front of the enemy position, and was removing the pin from my grenade, there was a tap on my shoulder. It was Pte Somers. 'Boss,' he said. 'Look behind you.'

And there was no-one there. The explosion had blown the lead from my radio and all my fine commands had gone nowhere. Somers had realised what had happened, and had followed me and protected my every tactical bound. He was a sniper, so he didn't have an SA80, he just had a L96 sniper rifle, a bolt action rifle designed for one shot, one kill at 600 metres to 800 metres. So he'd been running behind me, rapidly manipulating the bolt, and dealing with the enemy all the way up until that position. That was an amazing thing - he wasn't prepared for his OC to go on his own and with the barest of kit had come with me all the way.

Another time we were going through Majidir. They were trying to make it a no-go zone, and we weren't having any of that. So I started doing patrols through the town, about 70 blokes, with four Warriors in support. We came over the first bridge to the east and a couple of rounds were fired as the sergeant major crossed with his team. We advanced to contact and as we approached a little roundabout all hell broke lose. There were armed gunmen across the roof tops everywhere, 40 or 50 of them, well-prepared and up high. It was 2230ish and there was a lot of ambient light, but there was a lot of cover, too - low concrete walls, corners of buildings, doorways. Our immediate action involved kicking in doors and getting up on the roofs ourselves - the next day, you would come back and apologise and pay for the damage to be fixed, which made a big difference.

Ian Caldwell, the Colour Sergeant in charge of the Recce Platoon, came over to me and asked me what I needed him to do. There were several alleyways ahead of us, with a good 15 to 20 enemy down there so they outnumbered him. But we needed to deal with them, so I sent him and his multiple down there. He went without questioning: I remember feeling that weight of responsibility in my mind, that I could be sending them off to die. As I say, this was the very reason why my sergeant major and I went on almost every single fighting patrol, because we didn't want to ask our soldiers to do something we wouldn't do ourselves. We had to take our position in the firing line - often one of us would be point man, the first person crossing open ground. None of us are indispensable, and it was important to send a message to the lads that they weren't cannon fodder, and that their lives mattered to us, and that we would do what they did and more, if needs be. Ian and his guys were exposed by light, with rooftop gunmen still all around them and the odd RPG being fired off, but they went down there and they won that firefight. It was just quite incredibly brave. Then we brought the Warriors across so they could use their chain guns on the guys on the roofs and that closed everything off and we were away. Again, remarkably, no dead on our side.

It was during a re-supply mission to Cimic House that Pte Johnson Beharry undertook one of the two actions which saw him win a VC - the first non-posthumous Victoria Cross to have been awarded since 1969.

It was May 1, and we hadn't been re-supplied for some time because of the danger. There had also been a major arrest operation that preceding night *(details of which are in the following chapter)*, where we had arrested 14 suspected militia operatives, so the whole city was a bit of a hornets' nest anyway. The convoy had had to hook around over Yugoslav Bridge and go north to come back down to us through Majidir and the first thing we heard was the sound of chain guns going off, and then the contacts started coming up over the net. We started to get mortared as they fought their way through to us and by the time they got to Cimic House they had taken several casualties. Beharry's Warrior had been hit by several RPGs, with a few of the guys inside being injured, and he did well to get it to us. The commander had been hit and Beharry and Dale Norman helped pull him from the cupola. One of our guys, LCpl Barry Bliss, had been shot through the lung as we tried to assist them through and secure their entrance. There were at least 150 enemy in the area by now, and 30 Alpha, Bliss's multiple, called for assistance. They were under fire from all sides, particularly the rear, in a place called Baghdad Street, a long and narrow road enclosed by tall houses and with shops and market stalls alongside it. As it happened, the last unit we had in the box to send out was a group of TA lads. They were a mixed bunch - a mechanic, a MoD civil servant, a butcher, a couple of unemployed guys, a trainee accountant, university students - and they were absolutely brilliant. They were dispatched under the command of Sgt Steve Cornhill and Steve Marsh, one of my recce corporals, and they fought an action without communication for 35 minutes. They were getting hemmed in by burning barricades and were under fire the whole way, but they fought across rooftops, down through houses, alley to alley, street to street, for about an hour and a half until they got to where Barry Bliss was. Absolutely brilliant, and even more so when you consider they weren't regulars and didn't actually have to be there. Outstanding. The Warriors could then get to him, and within 15 minutes of that he was in the heli and away. That was pretty slick. He made an amazing recovery, by the way. He was on the ground for 90 minutes after being shot through the chest and at the time we thought there was a very good chance of him dying. He still smokes, too.

Back at Cimic House, we were unloading the supplies. Not easy. The back hatches of the Warriors were thrown open and boxes of stuff were lobbed in the general direction of our front gate. We got a chain of lads together and just passed the stuff, hand to hand, as the enemy fired at us, while our lads on the rooftop sangar and anywhere else with a vantage point returned fire.

Once the Warriors were emptied they just set off out of there. If it had been bad coming in, it was worse when they left - they got absolutely malleted, all the way out of the city. We had sight of them for about 300 metres and then they turned a corner and they were gone, and all we could hear was the stick they were taking. One of the Warriors actually got immobilised about 100 metres down from us - we couldn't go to help, because we only had Snatch wagons available and that would have been an act of suicide. The crew got out and into another vehicle, and we had to post snipers to keep people away from it till it could be recovered a day or so later.

There were lots of memorable moments that August. Some are memorable for odd reasons. I remember being in the top sangar, looking for the enemy so we could direct some counter mortar fire on to their position. We'd recently got permission to use 81mm - until then, no-one was allowed to use indirect fire within a city. The RAF were not allowed to release in a city, either, so all air-delivered fire came from the US Air force. Everyone bad-mouths the Americans, but they were our life-savers on a number of occasions. Anyway, I was looking to direct some fire. It was incredibly hot up there, and I was really thirsty. I just turned around, picked up a bottle of water, slurped it down... and it was piss. Sniper Juice, to be exact. The blokes were up there for hours at a time, so they would wee in the water bottles. I turned around and looked at the sergeant major, and he just looked at me. I thought, *What do I say?* Well, there wasn't much I could say. 'Whose piss was that?' I said. It was Pte Somers' piss, apparently.

Another thing that sticks in my mind, we were sniping at an individual who just wouldn't go down, despite being shot twice. He kept getting up and picking up his rifle and firing back. It was tragicomic, there was a ghastly humour in his movements, and I found myself laughing, and almost simultaneously being instantly horrified at such a reaction to the taking of life; such inappropriate physical reactions, reactions you would never have in the cold light of day, are common in such extreme environments. He was killed with a third shot.

It was a hell of a tour, TELIC 4. A lot of people thought Iraq was going to be fairly easy but that six months disabused them of that. But, despite all that went on, we were disappointed to leave. We had a bit of a send-off, with people from the community committees, some of the guys we'd set up in business, tribal sheikhs, right down to a few of the local common thieves and drug addicts. There were even three members of the Mahdi Army - they would have been lieutenants, effectively. I think they came out of respect for us. We'd had some pretty ferocious fighting, particularly that three-and-a-half weeks in August when we didn't have a day off, and they recognised that, despite that, some good had been done by us. There was a community centre in Majidir which was rebuilt during our tenure, with our funds. They painted a silhouette of Moqtada al Sadr on the side and underneath they stencilled, '*With the compliments of Major Justin.*' They saw no irony in this: yes, we were two diametrically-opposed individuals but as far as the Mahdi Army were concerned, al Sadr was the fellow that they followed but the cash came from this boy here. It was a very logical, unsentimental, almost clinical approach, typical of the marsh Arabs: *You've done things of practical value, so we are here to thank you and recognise that. But we will still want to kill you tomorrow.*

It was emotional, leaving. We handed the place over to the Iraqi authorities and I've never been back. I'd like to, one day.

I think about that tour and the people I met there all the time. A lot of the Iraqis were tremendous people. All of the soldiers I had under my command were fantastic and it is almost invidious to name individuals. But people like my company ops officer Steve Brookes, my reconnaissance platoon commander Simon Doyle, my sniper platoon commander CSgt Danny Mills, and Cpl Daz Williamson who took over from Danny, the mortar platoon commander Paul 'TJ' Hooker and his replacement, Lt Swales, straight out of Sandhurst, CSgt Cliff Lea my Anti-Tank Platoon commander, and ops NCO Jamie Maitland, a TA WO2 from the Lowland Regiment... these guys were just awesome, as were the multiples of A Coy 1 Royal Welch Fusiliers and A Sqn Queen's Royal Lancers, who also supported us in Cimic House (I also commanded A Coy 1RWF for 10 days when they relieved my Coy from the line) and Maj Charlie Curry, who relieved me for six days of August, during the heavy fighting.

If I had to pick out one man, I have a tremendous feeling of gratitude to WO2 (now WO1) Dale Norman, my CSM, who provided a degree of friendship, support, courage and inspiration that I could never have dreamed of; he remains one of my closest friends and he was the rock and heart of Y Coy.

But it's the ordinary Toms I'll remember most. I joined the Army for the privilege of commanding and serving with the best soldiers in the world. Because of my seniority, I am now in an instructing role at Sandhurst and I will never have that opportunity, to command men in battle, again. That's what I will miss the most, to the point where I've actually decided to leave the Army. I don't want to sit behind a desk. I've no interest in the bureaucracy of that, necessary as it is. How can I spend time worrying about my triplicate return for my motor mileage expenses?

I made an effort to go and talk to the soldiers at all times - that one-to-one is important. You need to know that they buy into you as a person, and that you have bought into them 100% as Pte Lee, as opposed to some random squaddie. Then, when you look to them to follow you they will. And they did. That was the most amazing thing. Ambush in front of you, you start moving, and you know, without looking behind you, that the soldiers are with you. The door goes down and they are through. It is a very liberating feeling. A feeling that everything has come together into a unity of performance. Pure cohesion. It's magical. People say that modern recruits aren't what they were. Bollocks. Yes, modern kids suffer more from lower leg injuries when they come into training, but that's because no one walks to school anymore. They don't wear shoes, they wear trainers. It is not because they're weak, it's because life has changed. We live in a different society. In terms of their cardio vascular performance, I think they are fitter than previous generations, certainly at Sandhurst. They are fast. They run quickly. When it comes to marching with weight then, no, people aren't doing heavy manual work, they're not becoming farmers at 14. But they soon pick it up. And I'm not sure that even the Falklands generation could operate the same level of technical kit at the lowest level that we do today, or that they could learn the same smatterings of Arabic as quickly as my boys did. They were superb; they behaved in the highest traditions of their grandfathers and I will never forget them. In terms of closeness, unity, cohesion, and a sense of being a band of brothers, I will never experience that again. The sheer pride and privilege of commanding that company will never be bettered for me, in my life.

The medal, obviously, is very much for them. I know that I earned it, because I was out every night being shot at, but so were lots of other people. I wish there was a unit citation, but they were never going to give out 130-odd Military Crosses. I wrote a number of soldiers up - about 15 - and was quite disappointed that we didn't do so well on the medals. But then not everyone can be recognised. I just feel that my medal has to be seen as recognition for everyone who was at Cimic House. I would not have been empowered to do the things that I did without the knowledge that those soldiers were behind me, or in front of me, or to my side.

Every medal casts its shadow.

Warrant Officer Class 2 Mark Evans, MC
The Royal Welch Fusiliers

WITH the violent Mahdi uprising underway, British forces - such as Justin Featherstone's troops in Cimic House - were coming under regular and fierce attack.

The men of 1st Battalion The Princess of Wales's Royal Regiment battle group hatched a plan to strike back, with a major night-time search-and-arrest operation codenamed PIMLICO. It was carried out in the maze of narrow streets and alleyways which made up the city's south-western housing estates in the early hours of April 30, and was aimed at arresting insurgents and confiscating their weapons, ammunition and bombs.

Mark Evans, a father of three from Rhyl with a modest, matter-of-fact air, was tasked with co-ordinating the arrests, moving prisoners and the exploitation of the search - a "complex and difficult task in a hostile environment" which he carried out "with huge professionalism and great skill".

At first, the Operation went very smoothly; in pitch black conditions, the soldiers moved almost noiselessly through the streets and broke into a number of target buildings, arresting known terrorists and seizing arms.

However, at first light - just as they reached the final target and uncovered a major cache - the enemy forces realised the British were in their midst.

We'd got to Iraq in early April and had just taken over Camp Abu Naji, just south of Al Amarah, from the Light Infantry. The LI hadn't had any real trouble and it was very quiet for us early on, too.

We did a few routine patrols in our soft hats - we'd only wear helmets inside the vehicles as protection in case of a road accident - trying to get to know the locals, give the kids sweets, that sort of thing. We got a mixed reaction. A lot of people seemed pleased that we were there, and they'd come up to us and talk to us. Some had a bit of pidgin English, and a few of us knew the Arabic for 'Hello', and we had interpreters with us, so we got by. Mostly, it would be a shy grin and they'd want to have a look at your kit and weapons and stuff. A few others were a bit more standoffish, wouldn't want to catch your eye or would be off indoors when you approached. But I'd have to say there was no real hostility.

However, there were some serious insurgents operating in the area and they were launching mortar and rocket attacks on our base and on Cimic House. We had to keep our wits about us, have our body armour and helmets with us at all times and be prepared to dive for cover if there was incoming.

With the constant threat from these attacks, and with British patrols increasingly coming under attack from ambushes and roadside bombs, Operation PIMLICO was mounted to disrupt the large and experienced bomb-making and terrorist cell operating in the area.

There was a housing estate just outside Al Amarah, only two or three kilometres from our base, called the Kadeem. I'm originally from Rhyl in North Wales and this estate was about the same size as Queen's Park back home. Which won't mean anything to anyone who doesn't know the Queen's Park, I suppose. It was a real rabbit warren of a place, a jungle of small houses and shops, many with mud walls, and narrow streets intersecting the main roads. Open sewers ran alongside the roads, full of effluent and household rubbish... the smell, in the heat of the day, was unbelievable. A very poor place, a lot of unemployment, a lot of broken down buildings and old cars and rubble and stuff everywhere. This was where the insurgents were located and were firing from.

Op PIMLICO was a company operation, about 120 blokes, and the plan was for us to move through the estate sequentially, hitting a number of target houses which we'd go into, search and make any necessary arrests. We knew who we were looking for - we had good intelligence from locals who were supportive of what we were trying to do. But actually finding them, finding their houses, was going to be pretty difficult; it's not like doing a search through Rhyl, say... there are no house numbers, no street names, it's going to be pitch black, early hours of the morning and we are relying on aerial photos to pinpoint the relevant properties.

The night in question was April 30, which happened to be my birthday. It had rained like a monsoon all evening, which didn't help because the non-Tarmac roads all turned to mud and slush, and the stench of the sewerage ditches, all full to bursting, was intense. It was really hot and humid, very uncomfortable for the blokes in their combat clothing, body armour and carrying all their gear.

A Company - my company, I was the Company Sergeant Major - was the search ops team. We had A Squadron Queens Royal Lancers held in the rear with their vehicles, ready to come in and pick up any ordnance that we found and then take it back in armoured Land Rovers. And then in reserve, just in case the s*** hit the fan, we had C Coy of the Princess of Wales's Royal Regiment in Warriors. I think it was about 2am we gathered together on the square, mounted the Land Rovers, did our final checks, got a quick final set of orders from the OC and then we left under the cover of darkness and made our way to an industrial area about 800 metres short of the Kadeem estate.

We pulled in and put the vehicles into a safe area guarded by the QRLs. We picked up all our kit - we had things like ladders, sledge hammers and shovels to enable us to gain entry and get on to roofs and to help with our searches - and got into our groups on the start position.

We had seven teams and 14 target houses, and we wanted to hit them as close to simultaneously as possible. Each team had Royal Military Police attached to make the arrests and handle the legal side of things while we dealt with the searches. We wanted to try and maintain the element of surprise, so it was all as quiet as possible: get to the house, throw a cordon around it to make sure no-one escapes or lobs anything out of a window and then knock on the door. If no-one answers, in we go. The doors tend to be flimsy, one boot and you're in. You have to remember, this is not a war situation. These are civilian homes we're entering, so while we were going to be as firm as we had to be, everything had to be absolutely spot on. We weren't going to go in there and trash places: there would be women and kids in there, and no-one wanted to cause any unnecessary upset. So we'd be forcing entry if necessary, quickly locating the males of the house, placing them together in the centre of the property and plasti-cuffing them.

Quite stressful stuff for some of our young Toms - these were some dangerous people we were after, and bear in mind that almost everyone in this part of the world has an AK47 under the bed. So whether they are good people or bad people, bashing your way into their house at 2am is not as simple or as safe as it sounds just saying it.

The OC then co-ordinated our departure and off we went. And we moved through and found plenty of materiel. An ammunition technician officer would make sure the ordnance was safe to move, and then it would be loaded up and taken away, as would any detainees.

A number of arrests were made and significant quantities of weaponry and ammunition seized. As the soldiers reached the last target in the middle of the estate, a major cache of munitions was found, including approximately 60 mortar bombs, 120 mortar fuses and numerous rocket-propelled grenade warheads.

Our final objective was a bus station, probably the size of a five-a-side pitch; there were a couple of buildings with a high wall around them and a couple of buses parked up inside. We had two platoons there at that stage - one handled the security outside and the other gained entry to carry out the search. Given that no-one lived there, we were wary that they might have booby-trapped the place, that was in the back of my mind, but we knew that they were using it quite regularly as somewhere from which to fire at us so it was unlikely.

At this stage it was just starting to show the first signs of dawn and people were starting to wake up... the calls to prayer were starting and it was obvious that, whereas we'd been able to operate in secrecy to that point, now the locals were going to be aware that we were around. And we had a substantial find, about half a ton of kit stashed on one of the buses. At the same time, we started having problems with our comms... whether it was the weather, or the fact that the area around was very built up, I don't know, but we had trouble getting in touch with the QRL to get them to come in and pick up the kit. The OC said, 'Look, I'll go back to where we can get comms and get the QRL in.'

So off he went with his guys, leaving one platoon of two 12-man multiples at the bus station. I had a signaller with me, and one or two others, so I think there were 28 of us in total. The idea was that we would sort through the haul prior to confiscation and also make sure that no-one came to take it away.

He'd been gone quite a while, it was getting lighter all the time and people were soon going to start having a nose at us. I wandered over and had a word with the platoon sergeant, a lad called Greg Plimley. I was going, 'Time's marching on, here, Greg, what do you reckon?'

He was thinking the same thing. We were getting quite vulnerable now. There were a few houses that overlooked us and there was plenty of time for them to set up a shoot on us. It would only take 15 minutes or so for them to get some lads with RPKs and RPG launchers into high positions overlooking us. So we started going through our options. If anything happens we can either fall back into the bus station, or we take over that house, or we extract along this route... stuff like that. All the time, keeping an eye on the blokes, making sure they were alert, in good positions.

The weird thing was, at that stage, it was still very quiet. There was no-one around, as far as we knew no-one had noticed us, but the training and the experience from places like Northern Ireland was all there... we just had a sense that something was going to happen. And the lads did, too, you could see it in the way they were acting. There was no relaxing, no feeling of, 'We've done it, the job's finished.' They knew the severity of what could happen and the potential danger.

After about half an hour, the two Land Rovers arrived. We said, 'Right, let's get this kit loaded up.' It took a while, and just as we got the last bits and pieces inside, a burst of automatic fire came in towards us from a rooftop. It was close - I heard the crack of the rounds as they came past, and Mr Neal got some shrapnel in the face from where some of them struck a wall near to him. A number of the blokes had just dived straight into whatever cover they could find, and in a few cases that was into sewerage ditches. There were quite a few guys who smelt a bit after that; one lad, Neil Roberts, actually went right under and was completely covered, from head to toe, in human excrement. Not nice at all, but better than being shot. Luckily, thanks to a combination of our drills, a bit of luck and their lack of skill, no-one was hit. Their tactic was basically to spray off some rounds on automatic and hope. It was probably AK, and the shooter was 30 to 40 metres away; the lads immediately returned fire in his general direction and we got the vehicles out of there immediately.

This extraction became a company level withdrawal in contact; the majority of the company remained with the OC and were able to extract through a series of contacts to the relative safety of the edge of the estate. Evans and the balance of the company were pinned down by increasingly heavy fire.

I stopped the lads and said, 'Let's just look where it is coming from and fire aimed shots only.' We had limited ammunition, we didn't know how this was going to develop and we didn't want to get into the position of firing in the direction of someone's house, with innocent civilians hanging around in the background. I had a quick shout round and we identified the rooftop it had come from but he'd obviously got his head down straight after firing. We waited a couple of minutes, just seeing what would happen next, and, sure enough, there were more bursts of fire, and this time they were coming in from several locations. Obviously, more people had turned up. We pulled the guys who were providing external security off the road and into the bus depot itself, because they were quite exposed out there. The bus station had quite high walls so we were reasonably safe in there for the time being. Parts of it were overlooked by some other houses behind us, so it would not have been a tenable position for very long, but it was OK temporarily.

We got the commanders in and had a chinwag while the signaller tried to send a contact report to let people know what was happening. Unfortunately, the radio had gone dead, possibly because he'd dislodged the battery when diving for cover, and we couldn't get comms. Comms were pretty bad anyway. I got him, said swap the battery, and got the lads concentrating on keeping the enemy heads down.

We had two choices: assault their positions or withdraw. We didn't want to launch ourselves into a potential assault, because we didn't know what we would be getting ourselves into, particularly in a built up area like that. So the best thing to do was to withdraw and make our way back to the edge of the estate where the Warriors would be. It meant exposing ourselves, because we had to come out of the bus station, but it was the only option. We ditched the ladders, the sledge hammers, everything that was replaceable, and made ready to leave. After a quick head-to-head we determined our route; Lt Neal took point, Greg Plimley would bring up the rear, and I would shuttle backwards and forwards, and make sure that we stopped at junctions, did our head counts, were going in the right direction, and stuff like that. Common sense.

It took us between 40 and 50 minutes to extract from the estate, firing and manoeuvring all the way. We broke out of the bus station and then ran through the maze of little streets and alleyways, often wading through ditches full of s***, firing and being fired at, all the while trying to keep our bearings and decide which way to go. Get to a junction... do a head check... get in a fire position with all-round defence... check the GPS and find out where we are on the grid... get the signaller to get comms to give the Warriors a grid so they could come in and give us a hand. We came under a lot of harassing fire from multiple locations. You would get bursts of fire of 20 to 30 rounds coming in from a rooftop, followed by another 20 to 30 from down an alley or behind a low wall... they were basically just emptying magazines at us, and you'd see and hear the rounds landing, hitting walls or pinging off the road near you. Amazingly, nobody was hit.

As we moved out, they were following us, at times running down parallel streets, trying to get round in front of us, trying to surround us. Obviously, they knew the area a lot better than we did. We tried to stay away from exposed areas, waste ground, major junctions. We didn't want 30 lads trying to sprint across 30 metre gaps, open to fire. So we took a really circuitous route through the estate, going through the sewer system here, through someone's garden there, over a house somewhere else.

I couldn't tell you how many of them there were. It was still very early, sort of first light, so you'd see a shadow run across a narrow alley and the muzzle flash from the AK as he did so... then he'd be gone.

Evans' citation says: "With a cool head in a far from cool situation, he led the break out. Under a huge and continuous weight of ferocious and accurate fire, he led his men through the myriad of flooded streets, open sewers, drains, alleyways and, at times, over roof tops, at each and every stage displaying exceptionally courageous leadership. He would fall to the back of the group to motivate the slower members and engage targets harassing them behind, and then run back to the front to ensure that the correct route was followed."

I was trying to ensure that we didn't get split up, and that everyone had his head up and was engaging the enemy. All the while thinking, *If it all starts to go pear-shaped now we will be in that house there.* You're constantly updating your plan. The strangest thing was I wasn't scared. You'd think you would be, and I'd certainly imagined this sort of situation, and imagined the fear. But if anything, there was laughter between me and the other sergeants... just giggling at the ridiculous nature of the situation we were in... weighed down with all our kit, wading through ditches full of s***e, with people shooting at you, you had to laugh, didn't you?

Don't get me wrong, I'm not saying I'm some sort of superhuman with no fear... later on, when I had time to think about what had happened, I thought, *Crikey, that was close*, and I did feel a bit shaky. But at the time, we didn't have chance to get scared, or think about anything other than the situation we were in and how to deal with it. I've got three boys, aged 11, 8 and six months, but I didn't even think of them... it's all about the younger lads you're with, making sure they're OK. And the young soldiers were outstanding. I think it had something to do with the leadership - from the corporals, sergeants and the officers. You could see it. They would look in, as if to say 'This isn't great', but they'd see that the officers and the NCOs were not fazed and then think, *Well, if he's OK, then we're OK*.

We came to the edge of the estate. By this time, it was light. The twilight in the Middle East passes very quickly, and it was like someone had switched a light on. And you could see the heads of people moving around and firing. It was obviously better for us, because we could pinpoint our targets and try to put them down. How many we killed, I'm not sure. We never went back to check whether there were any bodies or anything like that. It was just a case of, *Let's get out of here*. Our last exit road out was one hell of a long, wide road, it must have been 200 metres long. At the end of that road there were the PWRR Warriors but we had to run a gauntlet to get to them. They couldn't come in, because with our comms intermittent, we were asking for blue-on-blue.

We fire-manoeuvred down the road, and it was around now that we started taking incoming RPGs as well. Fortunately, no-one was hit: a lot of them skipped away and detonated some distance from us, others didn't explode at all. And we made it to the Warriors. A few of the lads hopped inside, obviously scared and wanting to feel safe, but that caused us problems when we did our head check. Eventually, we found them, got them out and moved off the 800 metres or so down the road to our own vehicles, with the Warriors covering us.

We got back to camp, did all our checks, everyone was OK, cleaned the weapons, reissued ammunition. The lads had showers and changed, which was important. And we got our heads down for a couple of hours, but we were soon back up and out to carry out a routine patrol in one of the villages... just a check on the local police station and have a look around. We were absolutely knackered, but that's what being in the Army is about at times. They were pretty hostile in this village, too. Lots of throat-slitting motions, and bricks thrown over walls at us. As we were leaving, we got to a bridge over a river and took incoming from three RPGs and small arms fire. We were in soft-skinned, open-topped Land Rovers at the time: one of the RPGs passed between two of our vehicles and the others hit the river bank and exploded, so we were lucky.

So shot at twice in one day. I remember thinking that evening, *Is this what it's going to be like for the whole of the six months?* And it pretty much was. Our patrols were contacted regularly and Camp Abu Naji was so regularly mortared that they renamed it Camp Incoming.

In many ways, our experiences in Northern Ireland helped us, especially in dealing with opportunists and people planting IEDs and so on. I did two two-year tours and four six-month tours of Ireland and there were similarities.

The citation continues: "Throughout, he remained cool, calm and assured and displayed outstanding and brave leadership... His outstanding and brave leadership certainly saved lives." Typically, Sgt Maj Evans doesn't see it quite like that.

When I was first told I was getting the medal, I was gobsmacked, speechless, I really didn't have a clue what to think. When I got over the shock I thought, *Do I deserve it?* I felt guilty because other people hadn't been recognised. It's quite hard to get your head round. But the guys who were there on the day in question were chuffed to bits for me, and one or two of them reassured me that I did deserve it, so that helped that process. On the citation, it says that my actions saved the lives of my soldiers and the other people around me, and I suppose I did contribute to that. We did come close to losing people, but we all got out OK, so that was a result.

I'm from an Army family - my dad spent four or five years in the Artillery, my mum was in the WRAC and my sister was in the Royal Signals and married a guy in the Paras. My granddads were killed in World War Two. I've been in 20 years, I love it and I hope I can stay in till 55. I love the camaraderie - within a company it's like a family, and the six months that you spend together you tend to bond quite well. The majority in my company were from Wales, we had a South African and a guy from Trinidad and Tobago, but they were mainly Welsh, so there was a great sense of bonding and togetherness. Very hard to find it anywhere else, to be honest, and hopefully I'll be able to be a part of that till I retire. I've just been promoted to WO1 and my hope is to go for a late entry commission to captain in the future. At the moment, I'm working in training in Brecon, but I'd like to go back to my battalion... they're on standby for Iraq or Afghanistan and I'd love to get back out there. It's what I joined the Army to do. I know there are some people who join up and when they're told they are going off to war or on operations, they're not so keen. I joined the Army to be on the front line. You're not trained for anything else in the infantry.

Sergeant Christopher Broome, CGC
The Princess of Wales's Royal Regiment

SOUTHERN Iraq was now a very dangerous place to be, and the men of the 1st Battalion The Princess of Wales's Royal Regiment were coming under relentless attack.

Chris Broome was a senior NCO in the Regiment, a Warrior commander with 17 years' service whom many junior soldiers looked up to - despite the fact that, as he himself says, his own experience of being under fire to that point was non-existent.

Sgt Broome's job was to resupply the beleaguered Cimic House in Al Amarah, where Maj Justin Featherstone and his troops were under siege, surrounded by suicidal Mahdi Army fighters. Convoys were repeatedly attacked by the insurgents; Pte Johnson Beharry won his Victoria Cross for his work on such missions, and it was Broome who cradled the seriously injured soldier in his arms after he was almost killed by a rocket-propelled grenade.

It's commonly accepted that all the men of 1PWRR fought like the 'Tigers' they are, but one platoon, says the citation, had the hardest time of all: that platoon was Chris Broome's, and he was always to be found at their forefront, repeatedly putting his own life in grave danger to save those of his men.

He "demonstrated gallantry, leadership and courage far beyond that reasonably expected of one in his position," the citation adds, "fighting the enemy from his Warrior and on foot... He led his men with courage and valour and his selfless, modest approach has been an inspiration to his men, his peers and his superiors."

Sgt Broome's Conspicuous Gallantry Cross was awarded for a series of actions, each of staggering bravery.

I'm married with a couple of kids, I'm from Dover, and I've been in the Army 20 years now. I went out to Iraq with the regiment as part of TELIC 4. Up to that point, Iraq had been a bit of a sunshine tour - obviously, there had been some major incidents and a number of deaths, but by and large it was quiet. Particularly down in Basra, guys had been going down to the market and buying their little furry camels and tourist stuff. It was the place to go and get some sun.

During our tour, that all changed very much for the worse when the Mahdi Army uprising started.

Our job early doors was to re-supply the guys in Cimic House in Al Amarah, take them food, water and ammunition. Obviously, the enemy knew we'd be coming, there were only a few routes in and only one way into the compound, so every time we went in we knew we were going through prepared ambush positions. And they did ambush us... bloody hell, they hit us hard. We had days of it. So it was decided that, on May 8, after escorting a convoy in, we would mount Operation WATERLOO, where we'd go back out into the town and get a grip of it. The week before, Johnson Beharry's Warrior had been really badly malleted in the town - multiple RPG strikes, the blokes inside all shaken up or hurt - and Johnson had driven a kilometre and a half with his head out of the vehicle and rounds everywhere, while injured himself. That was one of the two actions which won him the VC, so you can see how much it was kicking off.

Op WATERLOO was an early hours operation involving 30 Warriors, four Challenger 2 main battle tanks and more than 400 soldiers, supported by RAF Tornado jets and a US AC130 Spectre. Battles went on through the night, and, once day

broke, Broome and his colleagues set about maintaining law and order, through a framework of street patrolling which often resulted in pitched gun battles with pockets of heavily armed militia.

We found ourselves out on the Blue Route. Most of the mapping systems for operational tours are colour coded; there will be, say, four main routes and various junctions with numbers on them. So, for example, Blue Five could be near a mosque, Blue Four could be a crossroads. You get on the net and say, 'I'm at Yellow Two,' and everyone knows where you are. The Blue Route was where Johnson had been hit, though we were going the opposite way along it and we had a Challenger 2 tank with us. It's an aggressive move, to show the locals, 'OK, we've had a fair fight, but we're in charge now, and this is what we've got.'

We had Mr Deane (2nd Lt Richard Deane, MC) at the front, then Cpl Joe Tagica in the next Warrior, the Challenger in the middle, then myself and finally Sgt Adam Llewellyn at the rear.

About half way down the Blue we were planning to cross on to Yellow and that meant driving down a narrow side road. We got to the turning. It was tight and, while it wasn't crowded, there were a fair few people out, hanging around the little market stalls and carts, leaning on car bonnets, just watching us. Mr Deane and Joe got round quite easily but the Challenger had problems making the turn, with his barrel getting in the way. I think he was experiencing some engine problem as well. I went ahead, Lewy stayed behind, and we got our arses against the rear of the nearby buildings to cover the tank as he manoeuvred.

This is definitely not ideal. You do not want to be stationary in a place like this. There were a lot of locals milling around, now, and more arriving by the second, as they could hear the tank moving back and forward. Not everyone in Al Amarah was hostile by any means, but there were a lot of Mahdi Army there and as you sit in the turret, you're thinking, *Any minute now...* You're waiting for the first RPG, the first burst of AK, so you're scanning the rooftops, watching the people... some of them are on their mobiles... are they calling the gunmen in? There's a lot of chatter on the net. 'What's that bloke carrying? Looks like it might be an RPG... he's ducked into that building... watch that.' Your personal weapon is to hand, you're scanning your arcs, the gunner is doing the same, and everyone is very, very keyed-up.

Of course, no-one expects the attack to come from kids, do they? But as we were sat there, a couple of boys, no older than nine or ten, got on top of a flat roof which hung over Lewy's turret and dropped a petrol bomb in on him.

The drivers had battened down the hatches from the start on WATERLOO - that was something we'd tried to avoid, because it just gets too hot in a Warrior and you need the air - and only the commanders were out. But it was a bloody good job they had because it saved others from being hurt.

Lewy jumped up, totally ablaze and screaming in pain, leapt off the top of his vehicle and set off running down the street, before hitting the ground and rolling around, trying to put out the fire.

All of a sudden, the place went ballistic. Everyone in the street ran out and started cheering and jeering and shouting. We'd shaken the place up a bit, and it was like this was their first chance at payback. They had an injured soldier in front of them.

The area of town they found themselves in was a Mahdi Army stronghold, full of men armed with heavy weapons, mines and rocket-propelled grenades. But Sgt Broome's citation says he "did not hesitate to put his own life at risk

to save the life of his colleague. Showing total disregard for his own safety, he dismounted and chased Llewellyn until he caught up with him and put the fire out with an extinguisher from a Warrior."

I grabbed a fire extinguisher, said to my gunner, 'You're in control now, JC, you need to crack on,' and just jumped out of the wagon and ran after him.

My main thought, apart from to put the flames out, was not to let him run into the crowd, not to lose sight of him. Hostage-taking is their number one goal, and we didn't want that.

I got to where he was and sprayed him down to put the fire out. The crowd backed away a bit. His shirt and most of his trousers, being cotton, had just burned straight off him and he was sitting there in his CBA with his skin dripping off him from the burns. He was in a lot of pain. Lewy is a robust soldier, he's a big lad and he can stand his ground, but it doesn't matter how old you are, or how hard you are... if someone throws burning petrol at you and sets you alight, you can be the hardest man in England and you'll be like a little boy, you'll be in trouble. And he was in trouble. He was in a lot of pain. He's a really good mate of mine and I hated seeing him like that.

I got him back to his Warrior. By that time, the rear had opened up and we put him in there. I'd gone through my whole Army career without ever being in that sort of situation. You do all the first aid tests, every six months, and they say, 'A guy's in pain, what do you do?' In the classroom, it's all so simple. In real life, it's totally different... the guy's just gone straight up in flames in front of you, your hands are shaking, he's clearly in a lot of distress, he's moaning and writhing around, there are people outside shouting, there might be gunmen on their way, your hands are sweaty and greasy... you have to make yourself stop and think.

Morphine was the first thing that we had to administer, and water. We found out that morphine doesn't work quite as quickly as you'd think it might. I gave him a shot, and it didn't seem to make any difference. That played on my mind for quite a while. We were doing our best, but it wasn't really helping him.

Then we got the water from the inside of the vehicle - there are bottles and jerry cans of the stuff, obviously - and poured some of that on to him. Big mistake - it was hot, because the vehicle was hot (it could reach 70C inside the armoured vehicles in the heat of the day), so we were basically scalding him. He was in agony, poor Lewy. It was a valuable lesson, that. I think they're trying to sort out cooling systems or cooling boxes to have cold water in Warriors, now.

The guys in the back, a guy called Pte Sewell and a Fijian called Bruce, they administered first aid and looked after him as well as they could. They took hold of his head and turned it away from his body, and kept telling him he was fine, telling him that of course his arms hurt but that he was OK, he was just in shock. They did a really good job. Lots of the lads there who did just as much as me, they didn't get mentioned again.

From there on, someone shouted that the turret was on fire so I jumped up on top of the vehicle and used the extinguisher on the Warrior itself. The crowd was growing all the time, stones were being thrown and it had the potential to get very unpleasant indeed. I put Lewy's headset on and said we had to get out of there. Ironically, the Challenger had already moved and gone. He was completely unaware of what had happened behind him. To be fair, the lads inside my own Warrior were unsure, too, being battened down in the back. And it had all happened so quickly, and we'd been so frantic to get to him, that the comms hadn't been great.

I went to get on the net, and as I did that I saw Mr Deane's vehicle on its way back - he'd realised something was going on. I had a quick chat with him, and the decision was taken to go to one of the police stations nearby, which we used as a joint base, to get Lewy casevac-d from there.

I was panicking, to be honest, because there was a good chance in my mind that Lewy might die. I think Mr Deane must have heard the panic in my voice, because he was about 200 metres in front of me, just smashing cars out of the way. We'd try not to do that ordinarily - because why inflame the locals? - but it was clear that they were well aware that we had a casualty aboard and were deliberately slowing down and stopping in front of us to hold us up.

Credit to all the guys at the police station, they were lined up like a racing car pit when we arrived. I just drove in, the rear doors were opened, and other people started administering first aid and took control from there on in. Maj Coote, our CO, and the Sergeant Major, Dave Falconer, came down, got on the radio, and organised a Chinook to come in with an IRT aboard. The company based there went out to give all round defence, the Chinook came in and took Lewy and myself away to hospital - I had a few minor burns and some scratches and stuff, but nothing like as bad as his injuries. While we were in the air, they stuck him on a drip and whatever was in that finally gave him some relief because at last he closed his eyes and relaxed.

From the moment the helicopter touched down at Basra, the work was outstanding, from the initial medical treatment, to the day they put Lewy on a plane to Birmingham. We were taken off on stretchers, rushed to the casualty room and put on beds. There was only a small curtain between me and him, done deliberately so we could see each other, which helped me a lot though he was now completely out of it. I was very upset and in shock myself, and before I knew it all my clothes had been cut or ripped off and there was someone playing with my ears, someone else bending my legs, someone asking me how many fingers I had... they worked outstandingly.

After about an hour he was in theatre, and they were finishing up with me.

From what I saw there, I started being more optimistic that Lewy would pull through OK. I remember saying afterwards to some of the lads, if you're in trouble and you can get IRT to Basra, if you can just hang on, you're going to be taken care of. It was quite encouraging and soldiers do need that. As it happened, six of my guys were already there. One had been shot and the other five had been fragged a couple of days before; they put us all on the same ward, all from the same platoon, together with some other guys who'd been injured on Op WATERLOO... it was emotional, a few tears were shed, but it was good to be together.

Lewy's brother, who was down in Basra, came in to visit him and couldn't believe what he found. Basra, at that time, late spring, was still basically a sunshine tour. People were almost oblivious as to what was going on in Al Amarah, where it was all getting very unpleasant after the battle for Fallujah, when the insurgents had all come south. Of course, not long after that, it went further south to Basra, so that the back end of the tour, from late July or early August onwards, it was just as lively for them as it was further north.

Lewy's made pretty much a full recovery. He's got a good sense of perspective about it - he thinks, 'Yeah, got injured, part of the job, still alive, could have been a lot worse... there are people a lot worse off than me,' and he has just got on with it. He's got married to a lovely woman called Jo, he was only going out with her when it happened, and had his two years on the Y list, doing an office job. Funnily enough, those of us who didn't get injured look back on what happened with a lot of aggression... like, who would get kids to drop petrol bombs on a bloke? But he's a lot more relaxed.

On 14th May 2004 the company was deployed to the Danny Boy permanent vehicle check point near Al Majar Al Kabir.

Danny Boy was a permanent VCP we set up on a bend in the dual carriageway running south to MAK, which was where the six Redcaps had been killed the previous June (on the day that Glynn Bell and Gordon Robertson had won their awards). The idea was to show the Iraqi Police how a proper VCP should be run, and what it could achieve. At that stage, their VCPs were a few bollards and sandbags, often set up at points where you'd have to ask yourself, 'Why?'

MAK was a bit of a no-go area - it was hard getting Warriors and Challengers in, so we'd only go there if we had to. Risk-versus-reward. On May 14, one of our patrols was contacted on the outskirts and it started a bit of an uprising in the area. Down in Abu Naji, we were quite unaware of it. We were getting mortared - nothing unusual there. The mosques were singing away - again, nothing unusual there, though it turned out that the message coming out was, 'This is an uprising, kill them!'

I was part of the QRF that day, and when it all started I was told to go to a place called Red One, a bridge I'd been to loads of times, to put in a VCP. So me and Joe Tagica paired up and went down there, got to the bridge and just sat there, looking for anything that was coming in or out that day.

All of a sudden, Maj Griffiths came down in a s***ty old Land Rover with some of the Argyll and Sutherland Highlanders. He was quite shaken up, and his vehicle was so full of bullet holes it was like something out of a cartoon - how no-one had been hit I don't know. He pulled up, showed me his map and gave me QBO (Quick Battle Orders). There was a platoon somewhere south of Danny Boy, under Lt Passmore, the Ops officer, which had been pinned down by 70 or 80 militants. Maj Griffiths had been with them, and had managed to drive out of the ambush, but the guys were still in heavy contact. The plan was that Joe and I would get down to Danny Boy and hold there while we tried to establish their exact location, and another two Warriors - Sgts Dave 'Peter' Perfect and John Green - would chase me down. We'd extract casualties and give fire support.

We could hear on the net that the platoon on the ground had taken casualties and as we got to Danny Boy, we were ourselves ambushed from the right hand side. Pete and John Green just carried on through, and that was the last we saw of them - they got involved in their own personal battles, and finally met up with the call sign on the ground about half an hour later before assisting in their extraction in some very heavy fighting of their own.

Joe and I stopped, reversed up and started dealing with the ambush. There were 60 or 70 of them and they had picked an outstanding spot - they were firing at us from the other side of a roadside embankment and a deep, V-shaped drainage ditch, and all we could see was the tops of their heads and the RPGs coming down at us.

Within a matter of minutes, my vehicle caught fire with the weight of RPGs we got hit with. Then the engine started stalling. Pte 'JC' Fowler, the gunner, was engaging, and all the time I'm thinking, *What have they got?* When Johnson Beharry's wagon had been hit in one of the actions which led to his VC, it was by something like our Milan anti-tank weapon. It had gone straight through the centre of his Warrior and caused a big hole and a lot of damage, and all I could think was, *This is ideal country for Milan*. We were close to stationary, on open ground... if they'd done it to Beharry's Warrior in a town centre, then exposed like we were, it didn't bear thinking about.

It became clear that we were going to have to get the guys out of the back and get them into and across the drainage ditch so they could close with the enemy. I spoke to Cpl Brian Wood and said, 'Mate, you need to get your dismounts out... I'll do what I can from here but the wagon's damaged and you're pretty much on your own. Fix bayonets, get out and go right, push in to the ditch for cover. Good luck, mate.'

Without a second's hesitation, he and his lads got going. Brian won Military Cross for his actions on this day, and it was very well-deserved.

By this time, another Warrior had come in, I think that was Lt Plenge, and the Sergeant Major was on the net to me, saying, 'You've got a company plus a Challenger en route.'

Brian Wood met up with another set of dismounts led by Cpl Mark 'Billy' Byles, and they led their blokes, with bayonets fixed, up the embankment and then down into the drainage ditch. Very brave - they were assaulting a numerically superior enemy in well-prepared positions. I lost sight of them, and then they reappeared at the top of the ditch and started engaging the enemy, with JC using our 30mm cannon to help as best he could.

Just then, my driver, Pte Taylor, said, 'I've got complete power now.' The engine was working again. And, all credit to him, he said, 'I reckon I can get across that ditch.'

The angle really didn't warrant a Warrior crossing, but I said, 'OK, but don't get us bogged in or roll us.' Because then we'd really have been sitting ducks.

Before I knew it, he'd put his foot down and driven the Warrior up the bank. We tipped down into the ditch at a crazy angle, hit the bottom of the ditch and just flew back upwards and out over the top of the bank. He smashed the front of the Warrior, he came down so hard, but we were now on the same side as the Iraqis.

They were using big chest-high wadis, channels in the ground cut out by the heavy rain, as trenches. Brian Wood and Billy Byles got the guys to the right of our Warrior and we started going through the enemy positions, using us as fire support, suppressing them, then taking their positions. It was what we'd always practised for.

By the time we got to the first wadi, I couldn't depress the Rarden barrel any lower to engage them, so I reversed slightly to get a better angle, but by then Brian and Billy were in there. I couldn't see what was going on, and for a while no-one reappeared, which was concerning. Plus they were taking a lot of incoming.

Broome realised that the limited number of soldiers on the ground were struggling. His citation says: "He dismounted and, without a personal weapon for his own protection, moved around the battlefield under heavy, accurate enemy fire to take control of the situation. His courageous action and leadership under fire ensured that there was no loss of momentum and undoubtedly prevented friendly casualties."

I jumped out of the Warrior and ran over to the ditch myself. I found the lads were fine, they'd killed three enemy and taken four prisoners, who were face down in the dirt but not tied up at this point, and were already starting to suppress other positions. I took control of what was going on on the ground, and left my driver and JC to crack on.

I looked around the trench; there was just an armoury of weaponry there. I swear that every man had about two AKs, and there were around six RPGs, too. There were warheads and ammunition everywhere, and water and food. Very well prepared. There were also some very dead people. It was the first time I had ever seen anyone dead - the same with the rest of my guys. The surviving Iraqis - they were only young lads - were very scared, but then so was I. My heart was beating so hard I had to undo my CBA.

I had a bottle of water on my belt kit, and the first thing I tried to do was offer the prisoners a bit of water. Yes, they'd been trying to kill us a few moments before, but I think I wanted to reassure them that we weren't just going to top them, that we play by the rules. I said, a mix of pidgin Arabic and English and gestures, 'This is water... I need a bit, yes? You need a bit, yes?'

One took a sip, the others didn't, they were just in shock. They cannot have expected us to assault their positions so quickly and effectively.

I said, 'I need to blindfold you, yes? I need to tie your hands behind your back. You need to stay here with me.'

And we cuffed and blindfolded them, using their clothing to cover their eyes, and then separated them from the dead, turning them away while I searched the bodies.

It was all still incredibly loud, you had to shout at someone only a foot or so away. We're still under fire and, behind us, our lads and the Warrior are firing into other positions. There's a lot of shouting and screaming, and people talking on the net... 'You need to push along this ditch this way... You need to cover over there... You need to get fire support on this position...' It was quite unnerving, because there were a lot of rounds flying around and you didn't know what was outgoing and what was incoming.

The way I'm saying this, it sounds like it was all really quick and confused. It wasn't. It was actually all very slow and methodical. Everything seemed to slow right down, it was just how we had rehearsed it so often.

All of a sudden, the driver shouted out, 'The company battle group is on its way down.' I picked up an AK47, crawled along the ditch and rolled up and over the big drainage ditch and made my way down to the main road so I could cover the enemy with the AK while Maj Coote and Sgt Maj Falconer pulled in with the rest of the company.

Maj Coote got his Warrior up on the embankment - he was exposed, but it gave him a good overview - and started getting involved, and I led Dave Falconer back to the position I'd just come from. We unloaded the weapons as best we could, and he rechecked the three dead bodies. The Chally had turned up, as promised, and I saw him let off a HESH (High Explosive Squash Head) round. Somewhere in the distance, a Toyota van with an anti-aircraft gun on the back just disappeared in an explosion.

We then started to move into the enemy's second and third positions. This was where Brian Wood and Dave Falconer won their MCs. They were outnumbered, but they engaged both positions by themselves, with me and 'Spud' Tatawaqa - a big, strong Fijian private, one of many lads I felt privileged to serve with - in pursuit. The Iraqis were hidden in little bends in these channels, and they kept jumping out with their rifles and every time Brian and Dave would put them down. Then another bunch of guys would stand up and the same thing would happen. And gradually, we got the upper hand and it all started to quieten down, until there was just sporadic fire.

We'd been in contact for about four hours and it was getting towards dusk now.

We started a withdrawal. Maj Coote told us to break clean and start to peel back to Abu Naji. We took our four prisoners back to the sergeant major's Warrior, and then a message came over the net that they wanted the enemy dead brought back, too. The thinking was that they could have been involved in the Redcap murders, and we might be able to identify them, whether from DNA or their faces where possible, back at camp. I think there had been a bit of confusion - I think HQ thought there were only a couple of them. In fact, there were nine just from my position, a couple from another position and about 20 from where Peter Perfect was.

Dave Falconer said. 'Chris, the bodies need to go in the back of your Warrior.'

This is where it starts to get a bit messy. Me and my team started collecting the dead and loading them into the wagon, as dignified as we could. Still with the odd shot from distance incoming.

It was quite hard, physically. The expression 'dead weight' came to me more than once. I wasn't too keen on picking them up by their hands. I didn't want to make skin-to-skin contact, I had little cuts and grazes all over me and they were covered in blood and I didn't want contamination... there's a lot of hepatitis and other conditions out there. So we'd try to grab their clothes, but some of them were not small, and because their clothing was loose they would just fall out of their clothes... It wasn't nice work. A couple of them, we had to roll them in ponchos and pick them up that way. They had been hit by my 30mm chain gun and when you get hit by those rounds there's not a lot left. One poor guy only had half a face, one eye hanging down over his cheek... he'd been clipped with a 30mm. Another was completely shredded. We were picking up body parts.

I've heard suggestions that lads laugh about things like this. If I can reassure anyone, no-one laughed or joked about the mess that we made. It was quite horrible, not a laughing matter at all. No-one wanted to kill people, and no-one was happy about it afterwards.

Eventually, we got all the nine dead in the back of my Warrior and returned to base, with my dismounts obviously travelling in other wagons. We pulled up and tried to open the back, but it was jammed. Somehow, one of the corpses inside had shifted and was preventing the doors from opening. It became clear that someone was going to have to go in through the turret and open it from inside. If you think about that for a moment - it's scorching hot, we've got bodies and bits of bodies, which have been in the heat for several hours now. Imagine the smell inside the vehicle. Plus, it's pitch black, and whoever goes in there is going to be clambering and slipping around over the dead.

Pte Taylor, my driver, volunteered for the job. I think he felt he'd not really got involved, being in the Warrior all the time, but that was wrong, he'd done a brilliant job that day. But anyway, in he went. He was in there for longer than anyone would have wanted, and he finally got the door open a bit, not the whole way, and squeezed out. And unsurprisingly he completely freaked out and just ran off into the distance.

We got the door open; it was a hellish, horrible scene in there. We got the bodies out, all covered in blood and matter ourselves, and they were taken away to see about this ID.

And we stood there, all covered in blood and stuff, soaked through, sweating, filthy, feeling like vomiting. We had to get our kit straight off and burn it, and then all take long, long showers. And then we went for blood tests for hepatitis. They all came back negative, but there was a long period of worrying about it, when I, certainly, got slightly paranoid.

It had been a massive day. It wasn't just our little area... further south, there were people involved in their own contacts. For example, Billy Byles had gone off to join another fire team... he was also awarded the MC, as was Peter Perfect, which gives you some idea of the scale and ferocity of the fighting.

The whole of Al Majar Al Kabir had basically come to stand its ground.

They outnumbered us, but our weapons, training and tactics saw us through. They didn't expect us to push through that open ground so quickly. But it's just what we do in training, in Canada, Poland, Salisbury Plain. There was a lot of chat flying around, saying we'd carried out the first bayonet charge since the Falklands. It's all very nice, but it wasn't a bayonet assault. We had bayonets on the rifles because we just do in that situation. You get out of the back of the Warrior in a dismount, you don't know what's there, you only know from what someone is telling you in the turret via the net... there might be someone within bayonet range, so you have it on there.

On 11th June 2004 Broome's Warrior was stationed at the Broadmoor Coalition Force Base in Al Amarah. On this occasion, his Warrior was tasked with one other to pursue a mortar team who had just attacked Broadmoor.

We had two bases in Al Amarah - one was Cimic House, under Maj Justin Featherstone, and the other was Broadmoor. It was a prison, and we used it as an outpost and holding area.

On this particular night, we got mortared, as usual, and we were tasked with going out to arrest the mortar team. It was predictable, and there was a risk of ambush, but what else do you do? Johnson Beharry's Warrior was ahead of mine and, sure enough, we got ambushed somewhere on Red 8. We saw the initiations, and then the explosions as his vehicle was hit. I saw three strikes and one of them detonated on the frontal armour about six inches from Johnson's head. He was quite badly injured, obviously, though at the time I had no idea what the situation was because his Warrior stopped and then reversed, which is nothing unusual. Then it stopped at a funny angle against a wall and I thought, *OK, they're in trouble.*

I still had no idea how serious it was. It turned out that, somehow, with blood in his eyes and a gaping head wound, he'd managed to reverse out of the killing area and he came to rest some way back. Then he'd lost consciousness. His commander, Lt Richard Deane, was also temporarily incapacitated - he'd been up out of the turret looking through his night sight when the grenades had hit - and a number of his dismounts were also hurt. No doubt at all that Beharry had saved the lives of the guys he was with, and that was the second part of his Victoria Cross. A good lad, Johnson, and we were all delighted for him when it was announced later.

The enemy sensed that they had damaged the vehicle and the ferocity of their small arms, machine gun and RPG fire increased dramatically. Despite the risks to his own life, Broome once again showed total disregard for his own safety by jumping out of the relative safety of his own armoured vehicle and climbing up onto Beharry's Warrior.

I drove up and put my Warrior between him and the enemy. I could see six or seven terrorists running from alleyway to alleyway, and they were using the cover to engage us with RPGs and AKs. I got out of the Warrior, and jumped down. I could see Mr Deane in the commander's turret of Beharry's Warrior: he had a big gash in his head and was covered in blood, but he was still firing. The gunner of that Warrior, Pte Troy Samuels, was also injured, with thankfully minor head and leg wounds from where the blast of the RPG had travelled through the escape tunnel beneath and behind the driver *(Warrior drivers can leave the vehicle through the hatch to the front of the vehicle or via a tunnel behind them, exiting into the rear interior and then to the outside; Pte Samuels, a 27-year-old Jamaican, was later awarded a Military Cross for bravery in another action).*

I tried to climb up to see how Johnson was but as I did so I just fell over, for no apparent reason. I thought, *Weird, what happened there?* Then I realised I'd been clipped by a couple of rounds, which had gone through my webbing and spun me round. They hadn't hit my body or hurt me at all, I was very lucky.

It was clear that they had sensed we were in trouble. Normally, we would fight or we would withdraw. We certainly don't hang around. They were thinking, *Why has that Warrior stopped?* They started getting more confident, and more and more people were showing up. The whole street started getting louder and louder.

I got back on top of the Warrior. By now, there was a bloke there from that vehicle called Cooper, and Cpl Brian Wood and a lad called Irvine who had got out of mine. I could see Beharry was badly hurt, so I dragged him out and down, got him on my shoulders and carried him into my wagon. Cpl Wood and the others were putting down fire, giving us some all-round defence, but there were rounds coming down all over the place. I laid Beharry down in the back, with his head in my lap. He was in a bad state. He was conscious again, but looked like he'd lost the top half of his skull. Cooper, who didn't even have a driving licence and had never driven a Warrior before, jumped straight into Beharry's seat and got that vehicle started.

I administered what first aid I could - which wasn't a lot - and put the headset on to speak to Capt Sweeney, our Ops officer. I said, 'I've got a Priority 1 casualty and two Priority 3s.' Priority 1 is men who will die without urgent medical attention; Priority 3s, in this case Lt Deane and Pte Samuels, are walking injured. 'I can't make it to Abu Naji, I'm going to have to make it back to Broadmoor. It isn't looking good. I can see the inside of his head, here.'

Brian Wood had jumped in, he'd shouted at Mr Deane to get down, he was covered in blood, and with JC still fighting the battle upstairs in the turret we drove out of contact. We were under RPG and small arms fire all the way back to Broadmoor. It was as though the whole street had gone, 'F*** it, there's a gunfight going on out there, let's get amongst it.'

They were trying to send reinforcements down to us, but I held them off. No point. I was cradling Beharry in my lap, just talking to him. We gave him morphine, which you are not supposed to do for head wounds. I got a bollocking for that, but he was in a dreadful state and I honestly thought he was going to die anyway. It was probably the worst injury I had ever seen where the guy is still alive - I said to Irvine, who was crying his heart out, 'This isn't good.'

We made it back to Broadmoor and handed him, Mr Deane and Troy Samuels to the medics, and they were put into ambulances and escorted with armour to Abu Naji, and then flown on to hospital in Basra and, in Beharry's case, Kuwait.

Again, Broome's selfless disregard for his own safety and composure under enemy fire had saved the life of the driver and crew.

It took me a long time then to calm my guys down. Everyone was upset and some were crying, tears of anger as much as anything. They wanted to get back in the Warriors, go back down that street and mallet it from side to side. It got a bit scary, actually; I was trying to get the blokes to make safe, unload their rifles, and they were like, 'Why does it always happen to us?'

We'd lost a number of people and they were getting aggressive. Yes, there was still a mortar team out there, but the mortar team was just an excuse to get back out.

For me, it was probably the calmest I've ever felt. It was my job to be the platoon commander and say, 'Yes, lads, I know, but at the end of the day, we've got another two months until the end of this tour and that mortar team can wait... let's go through our drills, let's unload our rifles, let's check our ammo.'

That carried on for about two days, trying to calm them down. Everyone was devastated. The OC warned us that Johnson might not make it, but said that an American medical team, neurologists and other experts, had been flown in to work on him. That brightened a few people up but at the back of my own mind, because I'd seen him close up - I had his blood all over my legs - I was sure he would die. Sitting in the Warrior, with his head in my hands, I remember thinking, *There's no way you can put this lot back together*. It was like a jigsaw, with lots of pieces missing. Luckily, I was wrong, of course. Thank God, he made a very good recovery.

A day or two later, when his Warrior was getting stripped out and cleaned down, because it had blood and everything in there, they got his helmet. That saved his life. It was in dog order. There was enough shrapnel inside that you could just about build an RPG with. The whole tail fin was found where he'd been sitting.

How the hell he had reversed out of there I will never, ever know.

I had no idea about Iraq before I went. My wife Lynsey had a baby daughter on April 6, and I flew out to Iraq on the ninth. I didn't even want to hang around with them, because I thought I'd be straight back anyway. I thought it was going to be like Kosovo or Ireland... it isn't that bad, there's a big lump of soldiers, so they start looking for guys to send home. *Who wants to go on a course?* Right, we'll send you home. *Whose wife has just had a baby?* Me. Right, send you home. I was entitled to paternity leave, and I thought I'd get there and they'd say, 'Things are alright, not much going on apart from the sun-tanning,' and I'd be back to the UK in a week or two. I'd even packed some weights and some muscle powders and was looking forward to working on my tan.

And all of a sudden, this has all gone off.

I'd gone through 17 years of my Army career at that point and never even cocked a rifle in anger. I'd just done courses. But everyone looked at me and called me 'Uncle Stick'. I was one of the father figures in the team, and they all relied on me. And when it went lively and noisy, they really did look at me then. And I thought, *Blimey, these guys think that just because I've done 17 years' service, I've got experience.* Which I hadn't. I'd been on nine tours of Northern Ireland, and never been shot at once. It was hard holding it together. You do it because you have to, you've got to be there for your blokes, but then you think, *When am I going to get time for myself?*

There were quite a few times when I would wander off somewhere, have a little cry, a little grizzle, and think, *What was all that about?* Then you have to go back and be there for your blokes. You put on a front. Like, 'I know Johnson's lost the top of his head and it's really bad, but we've still got a long way to go on this tour.' I'd play down how I felt.

By the time I got home, a new baby waiting for me... and I didn't like loud bangs, I didn't like my daughter's crying, there were just loads of things I couldn't tolerate. I couldn't stand Lynsey twittering on about crap. 'Look what I've seen in the Littlewoods catalogue, aren't those curtains nice?'

I was like, 'Curtains?'

Or she'd say she'd had it hard, with the new baby. I'd say, 'You had six months in England with a kid, that is f*** all really, compared with what we've been through.'

I knew I was being selfish - she's the one who should have been given a medal, for putting up with me and my negative attitude - but I couldn't help myself. I'd have to get out of the house, and I'd disappear for a week. The only person I felt safe with was myself. You try and phone up your mates who were there with you, and they're going through their own thought processes. Some of them were OK, and wanted to spend time with their wives and families, others wanted to talk.

I was never an emotional guy, but I dwelled on having killed people and I felt bad about it. Really bad. And you feel like you can't talk about it. My wife is always saying, 'You don't talk to me.' Well, I can't explain it to you because you probably won't understand and there are probably things I am going to mention that I don't want you dwelling on, or lying in bed thinking, *I'm married to a jellyhead, here.* Do you want to sit and listen to how I piled nine bodies in the back of a Warrior?

Likewise, I can't go to the pub and say, 'Phwooar, she's fit... and, by the way, I killed a load of people in Iraq.'

You stand there with your civvie mates, or your dad, or your brother. And they're like, 'How was Iraq?'

You go, 'It was alright. I was involved in contact, and took a fair bit of incoming, got someone in my sights and had to put them down.'

They go, 'That's good. Did you hear about David Beckham? And what about Rooney?'

You think, *Hang on, I'm struggling here. You've asked me and I want to get it off my chest.*

'How's that mate of yours, Lewy?'

'Well, not great.'

'He'll get better. Anyway, what about West Ham?'

And I'd think, *You've just asked me how my mate is, he was on bloody fire. At least let me have the chance to finish what I was saying. I want you to understand about pain, about someone being on fire.* They don't understand, and they don't want to know.

But then, at that time, even some of the British Army in Iraq didn't understand. When I was a casualty in Basra, where the environment was pretty friendly, there were people in shorts and t-shirts having parties. They had a bar party with a Hawaiian theme. That was hard for me to see. I was like, 'I've just come from Al Amarah. Have you any idea? We're fighting for our lives down there. Food and water is an issue. Ask Justin Featherstone, we have to deliver it to him.'

You have to live with the consequences of what you did for the rest of your life. You have to ask yourself, *With hindsight, could I have done anything differently?* The answer is actually, No, because we were ambushed and you have to fight your way out. But when you see the damage that our weapons systems can do to people, when you have to put the body parts into ponchos to bring them back, it does play on your mind.

The good thing is the Army now understands the possible effects, and I did see the doctors to talk things through, which was very helpful. And you look at blokes who fought in the Second World War, you look at what they did, where they took a lot of casualties, as well as inflicted them... and you think, *How did they deal with it?*

And how does it affect the Iraqis? I did feel sorry for them. Some of them are poorly educated. You put $50 in front of them and they grab a rifle and try and take you on without realising the fire power you have. The guys in the Danny Boy incident, they were just bewildered when we got to them. The four we arrested, they all went to court and I think they got five years each. Two of them were farmers. I think the youngest was only 17.

I got back and was posted to Winchester as a trainer. It was a case of the Army being good to me and thinking I needed a bit of time and space, and to be nearer my family while the rest of the battalion went to Germany... an easy posting, really. But it made things worse because I wasn't with my own guys. No-one there believed what had gone on during TELIC 4. Nowadays, everyone knows it's like that all the time. If someone came into the mess now and started to talk about what he'd done in Afghanistan, you'd believe him but, back then, people thought I was exaggerating. They were like, 'Yeah... I've been to Iraq, mate.' And they had, but they'd been to Basra before it all kicked off and although the papers back home were doing a good job telling people what was going on, it still hadn't become common knowledge, even in the Army. I felt like I was in the minority, trying to convince the majority. I was like, 'I'll make you believe me, get your kit on, let's get down to Al Majar Al Kabir and let's see how hard you are. See it for yourself.' I wished they could have seen what I'd seen. I got into a few fights about it, to be honest. I remember being dumped on my arse in a pub by some students one night.

The only time that anyone ever believed me, and stood up and took notice, was when I went to visit the Queen at Buckingham Palace. Then they started phoning me up and saying, 'Alright mate? Want to go out for a beer? Want to go out for a chat?'

'Well, no, I don't.'

I carried that attitude through to training. Lads would arrive late on parade, or with an empty water bottle. They'd say, 'It's only water.' So I'd go off on one and start shouting, 'Only water? What about if your mate's on fire next to you? What if *you're* on fire?' I was too aggressive with them, but wanted to make sure they understood the importance of the drills. I didn't want them coming home in body bags. I wanted them to understand that a rifle is only used for one thing, and it makes a mess. I didn't care whether they wanted to be a dog handler or a medic, they would be a soldier first. In the end, I was court-martialled for hitting a recruit over the head with my pace stick. I shouldn't have done it, it was totally wrong and I bitterly regret it.

The court martial found Broome guilty and fined him £1,000, but did not reduce him in rank. Colonel Matt Maer, OC 1PWRR, told the hearing: 'This is a man who repeatedly, in the face of mortal danger, put his life before that of his soldiers. If I was to command Colour Sgt Broome again, I would consider it an honour.'

That was a big wake up call for me. I'd been having flashbacks and things and I needed help, basically. And I did get it and I'm fully fit, now. I went back out to Iraq on TELIC 8, as the CO's gunner. I remember the first time we drove past Danny Boy... it was quite emotional. But then, I'm a human being, and this sort of thing does change your life.

All the citation and the medal and everything is very nice, and I am grateful, but I'm no hero, I'm just an NCO who did the best he could in difficult circumstances, the same as anyone else would have. I did no more and no less than anyone else, it's just that you have got a report there which is all about me, me, me. It is not about me, it's about the blokes. There are too many of them to mention, but my hat goes off to all my team. They worked hard and gave 100% effort... there are guys who've since slipped back in to civvie street, and all they have is their memories of what they did and nothing to show for what they went through or stood for. They are the real heroes, to me.

Getting on with it, under fire, with no questions. If they're reading this, I'd like to say, Lads, be proud, you're my heroes.

I'm proud of what the battalion achieved. We went through something and came out of the other end and we had a hard time. We'll watch the TV one day, and there will be peace and there will be pictures of people shaking hands and drinking tea, as though nothing has ever happened. Shame we can't do that now. So the medal... I said to Lynsey, when I leave the Army eventually I'll probably sell it and give the money to some needy organisation, maybe burns victims or something like that.

Lance Corporal Darren Dickson, MC
The Royal Logistic Corps, Territorial Army

ALTHOUGH the situation was certainly worse further north in Maysan Province, British soldiers in Basra were coming under fire increasingly often.

Darren Dickson was a young bus driver from Edinburgh with plans to enter the priesthood; he was also a lance corporal in the Territorial Army. On May 8 - as Chris Broome and his colleagues in 1PWRR were mounting Operation WATERLOO up in Al Amarah - Dickson was in the top cover sentry role in an open Land Rover which was part of a 1 Cheshire Battle Group detail escorting a convoy of Low Mobility Water Tankers through the southern city.

At just after 6.30am, they were ambushed with a combined IED, RPG and small arms attack, and 22-year-old Dickson - who had only arrived in Iraq a week earlier - suddenly found himself fighting for his life.

I come from Edinburgh, and I'm now 24. My late father was in the Royal Artillery in the 1960s and the regular Army was always an option I'd considered, but I joined the TA instead. I'd been in for a couple of years when Iraq came along and I was compulsorily mobilised. I was half expecting the letter, because I'd been saying I wanted to get out there, but my mum was very apprehensive, and not that keen. The situation, to the general public, was getting a bit more hairy. Personally, I was really looking forward to it. I'd been working as a driver for Lothian Buses, but that was really only a bit of a stopgap; my plan, in the longer term, was actually to go into the priesthood. So I thought I'd save up some money on the buses and then go into the Postulancy in Edinburgh when I got back from Iraq.

I was called up with a composite squadron of about 100 guys from my regiment, the Scottish Transport Regiment, part of the Royal Logistic Corps. We had training and Optag and then went to Catterick to join the unit we were attached to, 8 Logistics Support Regt.

We did a month-and-a-half with the regulars, had a couple of weeks' leave and then deployed, arriving on May 1.

We landed at around 3am. First impression... this is hot. And muggy. We had a few hours sat around waiting for our transport to arrive. And then some guys from the Black Watch turned up. They looked dirty and knackered, and their uniforms were pretty beaten up. I thought, *I wonder what those guys have been through?* Not realising we were very soon to get a taste of it ourselves.

We had three or four days of acclimatisation, doing combat fitness tests and simply walking or jogging round the perimeter of Shaibah Logistics Base where we were located. A good four miles, starting anywhere from 3.30am to 6am. At this stage, the base didn't really come under attack - the first mortar attack I experienced was a couple of days later, up in Basra. I was sent up there with another corporal from my regiment, Cpl John Todd. I was top cover on an open short wheelbase Land Rover, nervous but excited. John had been there before, so he knew what to expect, he knew the sights... it was comforting. He'd drive down the road pointing out such and such a power station or mosque... I felt at least I was with someone who knew where we were. We got to the base and later on the lads were all in a mess tent watching the football on the telly... I think it was Newcastle against someone in a UEFA Cup game. And suddenly these explosions went off, quite close by. I was pretty concerned, but mostly the lads just carried on watching telly. I think a few of them got up to have a look, but they weren't going to let a few insurgents put them off the football.

My main role was as a driver or radio operator, working mainly in Land Rovers. Our troop was water resupply, so we would escort water tankers round our various bases in Basra, and out to places like Al Amarah as well. From time to time, we'd also drive drops vehicles, doing mail runs and so on between Shaibah Log Base and the other camps.

We'd been in Iraq for a week when we were tasked to escort six water trucks out to the main Basra base at Basra Palace. It later became known as the 'Chicken Run' because of the likelihood of being ambushed along the way, which only increased as the weeks and months dragged on. At the front of the convoy was a snatch Land Rover from 1 Cheshire Battle Group. Behind that was my open-topped Rover. Then the trucks. Then a second 1 Cheshire Battle Group snatch at the rear. By today's standards, ridiculously lightly-armoured, but fine for that time as long as it didn't all kick off too badly.

I was on top cover, and I was really looking forward to going out and doing what I felt was some proper soldiering. We left Shaibah as dawn was breaking, and I must have looked pretty excited because I remember the driver, Cpl Chris Garden, a good friend of mine from my squadron in Edinburgh, grinning at me and saying, 'You're enjoying this, aren't you?'

I thought, *Yeah, it's good, this is why I joined the TA.*

And off we set. Shaibah was south of Basra, out in the desert near Az Zubayr, and at that time the IED threat was not so great as it is now, so the drive up was relatively safe. We were still very wary, of course, but essentially, it was all fine. I was quite enjoying myself. Not knowing that half an hour later, things were going to get quite ugly. As we reached the outskirts of Basra, we crossed over a prominent bridge, with a police checkpoint on the other side and the first signs of people going about their business, market stalls setting up, traffic starting to build a bit, the usual car horns sounding and dogs running around the street. The tell tale sign that things are going to go bad is always no-one's about, but it wasn't like that.

We passed a big sign reading, 'New Iraq, New Basra, New Life'. *Very Tony Blair*. I thought, *That's nice.*

And that's when it all kicked off.

First thing, an IED went off... luckily, it was on the opposite side of the road. I just heard this almighty bang, and flinched down, thinking, *Oh, my good God, what's happening?*

The bomb had gone off somewhere behind us, probably around the middle of the convoy. I turned round, and I could see the dust and smoke and debris falling, but everyone seemed to be carrying on going.

Then the gunfire started. For the first few moments, I tried to convince myself that it was just some celebratory fire. People in Iraq were always pointing their guns in the air and letting off rounds. But then I thought... *Nah... it's 6.40am on a Saturday, there's not that many weddings going on right now.*

The infantry escorts engaged the enemy from their armoured vehicles and were "joined without hesitation by Dickson", his citation says.

Locals were scattering, the guys behind me were returning fire and I raised my own weapon and started scanning for targets. There was a 4ft wall on the other side of the road, and people were popping up and down firing AKs at us from behind it. It's not as simple as just looking through your sight and shooting someone... a man stands up, and you've got half a second to locate him, aim and fire before he goes back down. The attacker always has the upper hand - it goes quite well in training, but the real thing is always different.

They were being suppressed by some accurate marksmanship from the Cheshires, though the guys alongside the drivers in the trucks weren't able to return fire because the attackers were on their side. At first, the fire seemed to be aimed elsewhere. But it dawned on me that it was getting a bit closer, both the sound and the rounds... and finally I realised it was directed at us, at my Land Rover.

I identified a couple of targets I'd seen popping up and fired rounds at them. It was all aimed shots... we'd been told very clearly only to fire aimed shots because the last thing we wanted was innocent civilian casualties. I don't know whether I hit the guys I was aiming at, and I'd rather not know to be honest. It's not that I have a problem killing people in situations like that - it was self-defence, and the defence of my colleagues, and I had a job to do. But I certainly didn't want to kill any of them, I just wanted to get them to go away. But they weren't going away.

The convoy had slowed right down by now. The front Rover had dropped off and started to lay down heavy fire to allow the convoy to go through, so we were in the lead. And as we proceeded up the road, the fire slackened off and I thought, *Wow, we've just been through an attempted ambush.* It felt like that was the end of it.

We got to what was either a T junction or a crossroads, where we needed to turn left. And cars started pulling across in front of us, blocking us in, probably deliberately. The last thing we wanted was to be stopped, because then the gunmen could have another go at stationary targets, from cover, where they had much the upper hand. So we quite aggressively managed to push through, with a bit of shouting, beeping the horn, guns on show, and the trucks followed us through and we carried on. We'd gone maybe 100 metres, and my heart started slowing down a bit and I was catching my breath. I thought, *Well, I hope that's it for the tour.*

And then we had a very similar ambush. I heard a loud bang, from another IED; we were on a narrower road now, and the shrapnel was showering down over the trucks. Gunfire, RPGs... one of them took the wind deflector off the roof of one of the trucks and spiralled away, others were hitting but not exploding. Very chaotic. You wonder what's happening.

My vehicle commander, Sgt Tony Belli, was now returning fire, as was the fourth bloke, our radio operator, a regular from 8 Regt called Marcus, a Jamaican guy, I think. He'd radioed in that we'd been hit and then stood up next to me in the back. Bear in mind, we're not in a Snatch. There's nothing protecting us at all. Our vehicle is totally open, just a roll bar.

This second ambush was a lot more intense. The road we were on was narrow and there were high-sided buildings, three and four storey, either side - coming from Edinburgh, they were almost like tenement buildings to me. And you felt hemmed in, and very vulnerable. By now, the three of us are returning fire, trying to locate targets, and so is everyone in the trucks, the passengers anyway. The enemy were everywhere, in windows above us, on roofs, on the ground in doorways... hard to say how many, but I'd say at least 20. The air was just full of the sound of gunfire and rounds zipping past my head or hitting our vehicle. By the end of it all, there were a number of bullet holes in our Land Rover, a lot of them at the front. One went through the frame of the commander's door, another right through the centre of the windscreen.

I was absolutely terrified. I remember thinking, *What on earth's happening. Am I going to die here? I was driving buses round Edinburgh a month or two back.*

I was praying hard, too. There aren't too many churchgoers in the Army, but the old saying is that there's no such thing as an atheist on the battlefield. If you're getting shot at, you won't find many people who don't, for a minute, think *God help me!*

Chris Garden and Sgt Belli were just awesome. They were both ex-regulars, and both tremendously calm, just giving me directions... 'Man at 9 o'clock! Sniper in that window!' And I was trying to follow their lead or find my own targets, concentrating on my drills. They sounded so in control and unfazed by what was happening, and that gave me masses of reassurance. Sgt Belli said, 'Only take aimed shots.' He wanted us to be slick and effective, and not get into trouble by hitting civilians. The trouble was, you couldn't always see where the buggers were hiding, and you wanted to put down suppressive fire but you just couldn't.

I remember small things. Like, it was quite overcast, quite grey, not unlike the sort of sky you might see over Edinburgh. I remember the smell... lots of cordite, and almost... when bad things happen to me, I seem to smell something like chlorine. I know it sounds weird, but I had a bad bike crash, and I could smell it then, too. Well, that chlorine smell was all around. And I had an odd, metallic taste in my mouth. I remember looking at the guy in the truck behind me, Cpl Jock Haldane, also from my regiment, and he was shaking his head. Probably like me, thinking, *What the hell's happening?*

It was very intense and time seemed to have no importance. I've spoken to people who say we were in contact for a good 45 minutes but to me it felt like five. And that was four-and-a-half too many. I don't know where it went, but the time was irrelevant, anyway. All that mattered was staying alive and getting away. I didn't know whether we were winning or losing. I think I thought we'd get out of it, but at the back of your mind, say the truck behind us, the driver had been hit, that would have stopped us all and been problematic.

It was all very well-planned. We were being channelled through a long killing ground, because they had blocked off certain side roads with building blocks, cars, rubbish, anything. And the driver was having to take us round stuff in the road, we were constantly up and down kerbs and it was a very bumpy ride, which made it all the harder to return fire effectively.

I had the sense that the rounds were getting closer and closer, and then I got shot.

The moments before it happened are a blank. Maybe I saw someone aiming, I don't know. It's gone now. I do remember standing there, thinking, *This is a really bad situation we're in now. Please just let it end. How great would it be if the cavalry suddenly arrived? Or we stopped, and the sun came out and everyone was happy?* But it's not going to happen, you have to make it happen.

I just felt this dull thud. People ask what it's like, and I say, 'It's a bit like getting hit with a sledge hammer.' But that hasn't happened to too many people either so it's hard to convey.

I was standing up, leaning against the roll bar with my rifle up, and the impact knocked me over. The round came in from above, went in through my rear deltoid and, we later found out, followed a track down my rib cage and lodged in my back. I was very lucky. It was not far from my jugular vein, carotid artery, heart, head.

I was out of the game for a few seconds. I remember shouting to the guys in the front, 'I think I've been shot.' A bit hysterical, a bit of a squeaky voice.

To which the reply was, 'Well, have you or haven't you?'

I looked down. I couldn't feel or see an exit wound but there was a lot of blood and I just knew that's what it was. I said, 'Yep... I've been shot.'

Sgt Belli said, 'It's probably shrapnel... anyway, get back up and carry on firing... stop being a lazy little sod!'

LCpl Dickson's citation says: "Despite heavy bleeding, he resumed his position as top cover and with no concern for his own safety continued to return fire against the insurgents.

Although a heavy weight of rocket-propelled grenade and small arms fire continued against the convoy, the aggressive fire from Dickson was sufficient to ensure that the enemy's own fire was hasty and inaccurate, with rockets passing between the vehicles."

So I got up. My left arm was completely useless - it was like it'd got the worst case of pins and needles ever, so I couldn't aim properly. But I carried on, doing the best I could. Which probably wasn't all that good. There was no pain at all at this point. Just an ache. The pain only came hours later, after the ops.

A few thoughts went through my head. Mainly, *'Will I ever see my mum again?'* She'd not been keen on me going in the first place, how dreadful would it be if I didn't make it back? I didn't feel guilty exactly, but I'd have been pretty annoyed if I'd died.

By now, we'd got completely lost because of the way they were channelling us, so we were now looking for the nearest camp. The original mission was abandoned.

I'd used my whole magazine up - 30 rounds back then, as opposed to the 28 we carry now - but I couldn't reload because I couldn't move my arm. Luckily, around then it finally started to fizzle out.

I thought, *It's going to be over soon and if I'm not dead yet, I'm not going to die.*

We came to a roundabout and dismounted so we could all regroup and reorient ourselves. There were locals standing around watching us, curiously. A few smiling faces among them, who seemed to enjoy the fact that I'd been hit. Thinking, *Who are this rabble?* We probably looked like something out of the boy scouts rather than the British Army. We didn't really know where we were. The streets all looked the same. You imagine coming to a British city... one street of terraces looks much like another to an outsider, particularly a foreigner. No street signs, unlike back home. Eventually, the commander worked out where we were and we were off again and eventually the old Ba'ath Party HQ sort of hove into view. I could see the sangars and there was just this feeling of, thank God for that. A great sense of relief, we were a matter of footsteps away.

There was a bit of a hold-up getting into the gates - everything was kicking off that morning, everyone was getting it, so Chris told me to jump off and run up to the gate. Marcus must have radioed ahead because there was someone there waiting for me, and he took my CBA off and started undoing my shirt. And then Chris ran over, pushed him out of the way, said, 'This is how you do it,' and just ripped it off. A bit more heavy-handed, he wanted if off ASAP so I could be looked at. My t-shirt and shirt were fairly well soaked with blood and I had a look at the injury. I'm not that squeamish so I was quite interested. It was very red and still oozing blood, but the flow had obviously slowed.

The chap said, 'Right, we need to get you to the medic... can you run?'

I said, 'Er... no, I can't. I've been shot.'

So we walked to find a medic. My main concern now was to get some breakfast, but the medic wouldn't let me eat because I was obviously going to need an operation later that day.

I said, 'But I could be dead by then... can I not just have a bacon roll?'

Clearly, the injury was not life-threatening, so they put a first field dressing on, stuck a drip in my arm and sat me in front of the telly while a doctor came across town to see me. He arrived an hour or so later, he'd had to fight through his own ambushes to get there and the guy was pouring with sweat. He had a look, confirmed I was going to need operating on and said, 'Right, we'll get you down to Shaibah to the hospital there... let's sort out an ambulance.'

Invasion frontline: a soldier of the 1st Battalion The Royal Regiment of Fusiliers about to engage enemy troops with his GPMG on the run-in to Basra. Nearby, Lieutenant Chris Head MC (below) and Lieutenant Ollie Campbell MC, with their men of 1RRF, were taking and holding two vital bridges against near-suicidal Iraqi resistance.

Sergeant Mark Heley MC (r) and Sapper Ginge McLaren disembark their WMIK Land Rover from a helicopter. Below, Heley in the WMIK, with the .50 cal and GPMG mounted. Shortly after these photographs were taken, he and his colleagues were battling through a series of well-planned ambushes.

Lieutenant Simon Farebrother MC (l) poses in a captured Iraqi vehicle with the ubiquitous AK47. Also with him is Jon Whelan, another C Sqn Troop Leader.

Corporal of Horse Glynn Bell MC on ceremonial duties in London
- a far cry from Al Majar Al Kabir.

Lance Corporal Justin Thomas CGC takes a break with others of 40 Commando during the early days of the invasion.

Corporal Shaun Jardine CGC with his medal; he charged straight at a group of enemy gunmen in Iraq, ignoring their machine gun rounds and getting to within a few metres of them before finishing them off.

Major Justin Featherstone MC with 'Tigris, Dog of War',
an Iraqi stray rescued from Al Amarah by the men of 1PWRR
and now living back in the UK with Featherstone.

Warrant Officer Mark Evans MC with his medal: Evans led his young
troops to safety through a rabbit warren of streets in Basra, with a large
force of insurgents snapping at their heels and engaging them with
machine guns and rocket-propelled grenades.

Sergeant Chris Broome CGC (second from left) with (l-r) Private 'Spud' Tatwaka, Sergeant Major Dave Falconer MC, Private 'Rushie' Rushforth and Private 'JC' Fowler: their staggering bravery at the battle of Danny Boy, and throughout their tour, saw the soldiers of the Princess of Wales's Royal Regiment earn a number of decorations.

Lance Corporal Darren Dickson MC (bottom right) just after arriving in Iraq, and just a few days before he was shot when his convoy was ambushed. With him are (back row, l-r) Lance Corporal Tony Gribben, Corporal John Todd and Private Grant Patterson and (front row, l-r) Private Andy Gray and Private Stephen Cogan.

Sergeant Terry Bryan CGC in Basra, two months before he would find himself leading a multiple through the streets of the city, pursued by a howling mob and fighting for his life.

Colour Sergeant Matt Tomlinson CGC, left, with a US Marine Corps colleague; Tomlinson would soon be charging up the riverbank behind him directly at dug-in insurgent machine gun nests.

That was about the scariest thing that happened all day, him saying that. I did not want to travel back by ambulance. Not that long before, an ambulance had been shot up with soldiers in it. And I wouldn't be able to protect myself.

'Don't worry,' he said. 'It's got a big red cross on it.'

Well, that doesn't help... it's like a target!

I eventually went in a Warrior to another camp, before being helicoptered to hospital at lunchtime. You lose your dignity a bit when you've been shot. It was bumpy, I was holding a drip and there was nothing much to stabilise myself with. I ended up almost snuggled into another soldier in the back. I remember him saying, 'You're a fast mover... we've only just met.'

A RN doctor came on the helicopter and put marker pen round where she thought the bullet was. We were in the air for about 12 minutes, which was pretty scary. Again, it's the fact that you can't do anything to protect yourself. There was a door gunner, but he was the same size as my mum, 4ft sod all.

Got to hospital, rang my mum, but the Army had beaten me to it. And visited her the same day. She thought it was my brother on the phone - I have five, but I'm her youngest by 10 years - and went off on a bit of a rant about what had happened.

I said, 'Mum it's not Terry, it's Darren... ' and that was it, she started crying. I met a priest who anointed me and gave me the last rites, as a precaution. Then we had a chat about how Celtic were doing before I got taken away and x-rayed. That was really painful, having to move my arm into position. Then they took me to a ward and gave me some morphine, which I'd not had as yet, and pretty much as soon as they did that I just went to sleep. I was woken up later for my operation, which took about four hours, and finally given some tea and toast. And the bullet.

I travelled back to the UK a week later. Again, there was that sense of vulnerability as we were bussed between Shaibah and Basra air base, but it was fine. I flew straight to Birmingham and into hospital at Selly Oak, where I spent a month or so and had 15 operations to clean the wound, as it became infected. Selly Oak was an eye-opener - guys with legs missing and stuff, a lot worse off than me. I'd just lost my rear deltoid, which I didn't even know I had in the first place.

And then home to Edinburgh for a bit of leave.

The CO, Colonel Kelly, had come to visit me in the field hospital and I'd said to him that I wanted to get back out to finish the tour as soon as I was able. He'd sort of said, 'Yes, of course,' probably thinking I was in shock or something. As it happened, when he came back to the UK on R&R, I had recovered and was sent to Rear Party where I was given the job of driving him. So I took every opportunity to remind him I really did want to go back. It took a few visits to the welfare officer and so on, but I did get back out for the final two months. Of course I was apprehensive but I just wanted to finish off the tour with the other guys - I'd have felt unfulfilled if I'd not done so. It was a personal thing. I did a lot of top cover, we were mortared and things, but it wasn't too bad. Unfortunately, on our last run two private security guards were killed a stone's throw down the road from my vehicle by an IED. A British guy and a South African, they'd literally just arrived in Iraq from Kuwait. Awful. But I'd love to go back to Iraq, or maybe Afghanistan. My mum would probably disown me, but if the chance arises, I'll grab it.

Dickson's citation continues: "It has been estimated that the series of ambushes involved up to fifty insurgent gunmen, and that several were killed or wounded by the heavy weight of return fire. Dickson displayed remarkable fortitude and courage, particularly given his limited military experience and training. His dedication to protect his charges by returning fire despite being shot inspired the rest of the section to maintain

momentum and also return fire. His selfless disregard for his own safety and prompt action undoubtedly saved lives."

The medal came as a shock. The RSM called me at my mum's and said, 'I need to come to your house tomorrow...' and he made up some rubbish about discussing something work-related. And then he turned up with the CO of the regiment, both in best dress, with some champagne. That was pretty emotional, especially for my mum.

I wasn't sure quite why I got the medal; lots of people did very similar things to me that day. Some people from the Cheshires who were out that morning got Mentions in Dispatches, but I thought they did an outstanding job. One thing I would like to think is that it at least reflected well on the TA. We are professional, and the guys put a lot in, a full-time job and their soldiering as well.

The award ceremony was at Holyrood Palace. A very proud day, and very humbling. The Queen's Archers were on ceremonial duty, they're the Queen's ceremonial bodyguard in Scotland, and one of them, an old boy, had a Military Cross on. As I walked past him, he elbowed me and grinned. He looked a lot tougher than I am and I thought, *He must have worked hard for his MC.*

He came up to me afterwards and asked to shake my hand. He had a row of medals right across his chest, and I said, 'It should be me asking to shake your hand.' A really nice moment.

My plans now... I'm still getting rehabilitation at RMTC Chilwell, though I'm OK now, 99% back to how I was. As I say, I'd like to get out to Afghanistan, maybe, and long-term, the priesthood is still there. Maybe not as strong as it was. There's more life experience I would like to get first. But it's very possible at some point in the future.

Sergeant Terry Bryan, CGC
Royal Horse Artillery

AS spring turned to summer and the blistering heat of August set in, the mood on the streets of Basra became darker still, just as it was doing further north.

At around 3pm on August 9, a small group of soldiers found themselves stuck in a satellite base a short distance away from the main UK camp in the city. They were surrounded by an increasingly volatile crowd, and fears grew for their safety,

Eventually, it was decided to send other troops out to cover their extraction.

Terry Bryan led a two multiple patrol to help bring the men in.

However, before they reached their destination, they drove into a clever and carefully-planned ambush.

So began a nightmare ordeal that saw their vehicles destroyed by an enormous weight of rocket-propelled grenades and machine gun fire; Sgt Bryan and his RHA multiples were forced onto unfamiliar streets and into a running battle with hordes of insurgents.

Desperate, they broke into a building; surrounded, and shooting attackers at point blank range to keep them at bay, their ammunition started running dangerously low.

A quick reaction force was sent out to rescue them but, with communications patchy, and the enemy now trying to set the building alight, Bryan and his men, some of them teenagers, began to fear the worst.

I was born in Derby and lived there and in Nottingham as a boy. I never intended to join the Royal Artillery - I actually wanted to become a chef, so my plan was to join the Catering Corps. But the guy in the recruiting office was a gunner and he convinced me that the RA was the place to be.

I joined as a 16-year-old, so the Army is pretty much all I've known.

I was 33 years old when I found myself out in Basra with the Regiment on Operation TELIC 4.

We were based in a fairly small camp, I think it was a former Iraqi naval officers' academy, in the middle of the city centre. This was one of several camps the British Army had established in Basra; it gave us a bit of a toe-hold, a focal point. Most of the regiment was there - around 500 people.

When we first arrived, in April 2004, Basra was relatively friendly. I mean, it was the most hostile situation most of us had ever been to, so you were wary, but on the whole it was not bad.

Initially, our task was to set up and oversee the training of the border police down at the docks. They were impressive, the Iraqi recruits. These were brave guys, who faced a lot of intimidation, and many of them had travelled a fair distance to get there. They were reshaping their own country and I had a lot of respect for them.

We also did low-level patrolling, close to camp, no more than a few Ks outside our gates. The idea was to suppress insurgent activity and stamp our authority on the area while letting the friendlier locals know we were there and approachable if there was a problem. We wore helmets in vehicles - when you're in a military vehicle, even on exercise, you always wear a helmet, because you can get bashed and jolted - but on foot patrol, we'd be in berets or floppy hats. Helmets step up the ante, like you're bringing it on. We'd stop and talk to the locals, through the interpreter, and play with the kids. We got contacted now and then - vehicles I was in took a couple of rounds, an RPG once - but mainly it was a case of being mortared in camp in the evenings. We were very lucky, given the amount of mortars we had, that no-one got badly injured. We sent patrols out at night time to deter them, targeting suspect areas where we knew they were firing from, but it was next to impossible to catch them at it. They have a range of around 800 metres and they're very portable. You can put one on the back of a truck and cover it with a tarpaulin, or hide it in someone's yard. And once they were fired they were gone. They were virtually guaranteed to get away.

You quickly adjusted to the level of threat to the point where you would sleep through the mortar explosions, no problem. The amount of work we were doing during the day, we were shattered.

I'd get up 6.30ish each morning. Work started soon after but you couldn't have lain in bed if you'd wanted, it was just too hot, especially as the summer approached. We were getting temperatures in excess of 50 degrees centigrade. As we got into June and July, things did start to step up a bit. We were constantly being briefed about the situation up north, and there were patterns - if certain things happened elsewhere, you knew copycat incidents would filter down to us later.

On the day in question, Bryan was sent to escort a police General to a meeting a kilometre away, in a multiple of two armoured Land Rover 'snatch' vehicles. On the way back to camp, it was clear something was awry.

Things weren't normal. Usually, there were people milling around - workers, people looking for a job, street vendors, food stalls, taxis, buses, donkey carts. Today, none of that, a real noticeable lack of people on the streets, which immediately got alarm bells ringing. It's as important to notice the absence of the normal as it is the presence of the abnormal. Anyway, we altered our patrol route on the way back, just to be on the safe side.

They got back safely and, after a quick meal, Bryan went to his bunk. He was awoken an hour later, and told to make his way to the Ops Room for a brief on a patrol.

It was a dark little room, the communications and intelligence gathering centre, where what's going off on the ground was monitored. There were six or seven people in there - the Ops officer, Capt Amber Tyson, the Battery Commander, Maj Paul Bates, and a watch keeper and a couple of gunners.

Capt Tyson did the briefing. Apparently, there was a patrol of around eight guys holed up in a small camp a bit further into Basra. A hostile crowd had built up outside and the guys were going to extract. They were in soft-skin Land Rovers and our task was to assist in their extraction, protecting them if anything flared up. Specifically, we would cover two junctions a minute or so from their position; junctions are obviously dangerous points because you have to slow down and turn and you are vulnerable to ambush as you do so.

The plan was that we'd radio in when we got to the junctions and they would then extract. It all seemed reasonably straightforward.

I'd rounded the boys up before I went to the Ops Room - *Get some water down your necks, lads, get your kit together, throw some water on your face, look lively* - and by the time I got back they were all in the vehicles, ready to go. There were four vehicles, split into two pairs for the task. There were four guys in my vehicle and five in the other which would travel with me. This was commanded by my good mate Olly - Sgt Matt Oliver, whom I've known for years and years. Olly wasn't actually scheduled to come out with us, but he'd been lying around getting bored and had decided to come along for something to do. I had enough time to brief the lads, and then the word came through to go.

The other two Rovers left first and radioed when they were in position. Bryan's pair of vehicles then left, heading along the wide dual carriageway, which had an 18 inch concrete barrier dividing the lanes. The soldiers kept an eye out for occasional breaks in the barrier so they could whip round and escape if they were ambushed.

We knew where each break was. Our intention was to get to the junction, turn through the break there and point back towards camp before deploying out of the vehicle and patrolling on foot until the extraction happened. However, as we got to that break and slowed for the turn, we realised there was no longer any break there: it had been closed off by big oil barrels.

Simultaneously, the firing started: it was as though someone had turned a switch on.

I'd experienced nothing to prepare me for it. I know it's a cliché, but it was literally like a hail of bullets hitting the vehicle. *F***! What's happening?*

The guys on top cover came down straight away and closed the hatch and I tried to assess the situation. I could see men firing at us from the tops of buildings, from windows and shop doorways, from behind walls, all over. There were dozens of them, as close as 30 or so metres away. They would run out of a doorway, hose us down with half a magazine or loose off an RPG, and then run back inside. There was no way we could return fire: we'd have been killed very quickly if we'd opened the doors, given the intensity of fire. I could hear hundreds of AK rounds, ticking on the windscreen, the sides and the back of the Land Rover, interspersed with the distinct thud of heavier calibre rounds, probably from a Dushka anti-aircraft weapon. RPGs were hitting us and exploding. But the armour was holding out and, strange as it sounds, I felt quite safe in the vehicle.

We're still moving at this point and I've got my head in a map, trying to plan our extraction route. I can't turn back, because we'll be sitting targets while we turn. I can't reverse, because there's very little rear visibility and, again, we'd be sitting ducks for 300 or 400 metres back along the road and sooner or later one of those RPGs is going to cause some real damage. I can't go right because of the concrete and the oil drums and I can't drive off left, because we've been contacted on the waste ground there once before and I know the Land Rover will get bogged down with the weight of the armour. The only thing we can do, my instant reaction, is to gun it and drive forward out of the killing area.

We were trying to radio for help, but the radio had been damaged and we couldn't contact HQ. We had a patrol mobile phone, but you can't get a decent signal in an armoured vehicle. I could still speak on the short distance radio to Olly in the other vehicle so I told him to follow. *(The other multiple had also been contacted, but they had managed to return fire and extract themselves.)* The road ahead was straight, with a few roundabouts and side streets further on. There were other breaks in the central reservation ahead, too; I thought if we drove on out of the contact area we could find a safe point, get out of the vehicle and phone a sitrep in.

But as we headed on, the junctions and gaps in the road had all been blocked off. We just kept driving, and they kept shooting. I'd gone around two kilometres by this point, with heavy contact the whole way. Clearly, the whole thing had been very well-planned - the angry crowd to lure us out, the break in the barrier closed off, and hundreds of armed men ready to take advantage. Finally, we came to a roundabout. All the exits were blocked and we were forced to drive round it. As we did so, the vehicle was hit on the left side by an IED which blew away the left front wheel. So now we're travelling on three wheels, tyres shot away, still under heavy contact, rounds rattling and pinging off us non-stop, as they have been since it started. I saw that Olly's Land Rover had been hit with an RPG and was on fire at the front.

It was at that point that I started to worry a bit. Still, there's always squaddie humour. I was talking to him on the radio and I remember grinning to myself and thinking, *I bet you're wishing you hadn't volunteered for this.*

I was also still frantically studying my map and listening to my driver, a mature, very bright, very professional young South African gunner called Frank Haman, giving me a constant update on the activity and the state of the road. He was amazingly calm; suddenly, he said: 'There's a break off to the left. I know where I am now... the former Ba'ath Party HQ.'

The Ba'ath Party HQ seemed like a sanctuary to the soldiers. A former British base, it was now full of Iraqi Defence Force troops. With both vehicles badly damaged and options limited, it offered reinforcements and solid walls for cover.

There was this amazing sense of relief. I thought, *Maybe we're going to get out of this, after all.* Then the contact started up from the building itself. Guys in uniforms were shooting at us now - we'd stopped the vehicles, almost, but we were still being hit from all sides. We pressed on but it was getting pretty desperate; 10 or 15 metres later, both vehicles effectively conked out and came to a halt. They were both on fire, and obviously going nowhere.

The thing about being in a vehicle is that you're relatively safe, though less so, obviously, when you can't move and there's 200 people outside trying to get in and kill you. But now we had to get out. It was a hard decision, though in a strange kind of way I preferred being out in the open. A Land Rover is a target, it draws fire; on foot, or lying down, you're harder to hit. For a moment, I worried about the vehicles falling into militia hands. Then I thought, *F*** it, at the end of the day I've not got a lot of choice here*. We needed to get somewhere safer and I couldn't do that in the Land Rovers.

I told the lads we had to debus. They were all very young and inexperienced - most had only been in the Army a year to 18 months - but as soon as I said that the doors were open and they were out into the firefight, all in good defensive positions around the two vehicles, well-dispersed and laying down suppressive fire. Really impressive, given their inexperience. Almost immediately one of the lads killed one of the attackers. This guy was dressed in a police uniform, stood there, reloading an RPG launcher. Although he was quite a distance away, the young gunner dropped him, a nice shot.

At that moment I remember thinking that we were going to have to take lives, a lot of them, to stand any chance at all of surviving this.

Everything was happening at once, at about 100mph. The hardest thing was trying to work out where we were so I could send my sitrep on the patrol mobile. I was very disorientated and I found it hard to gather my thoughts. While I was crouching there, trying to clear my head, an RPG round came in and hit the wall a few feet above my head, showering me in crap. I looked down, and I could see rounds sparking all around us, sending up little dust clouds in the dirt. We were massively, massively outnumbered. But there was a glimmer of hope: they didn't like us returning fire. They were fine shooting at us in the Land Rover from a doorway in the distance, but once we'd got out of the vehicles and started carrying the fight to them, they weren't so happy. A few of them were running off and the fire from the others was getting more inaccurate and wild. The lads saw this, and it boosted their morale.

I'd managed to get through to the Ops Room by now. Normally, I'm very friendly and chatty on the phone - *'Hello! I'm here... be back in 10 minutes... cheerio!'* - that sort of thing. So when the captain answered the phone and saw it was us from the caller display, she was very relaxed. 'Hello, Terry! How are you?'

I just shouted, 'F***ing contact!'

It probably sounded really garbled; I was having trouble speaking because my mouth had gone horribly dry and sticky, like when you wake up after a massive drinking session. I couldn't get my words out properly, I was gagging for something to drink, just to wet my throat. Everyone else was the same, it must have been the adrenaline.

In the background, even above the noise of the firefight, I could hear her shouting, 'Contact! Everyone be quiet!' and everything went quiet in the ops room. 'Where are you, where are you?'

I still didn't know. All I knew was that we had been hit down the road from the point where we'd been sent and we were now some distance away, still under a huge amount of fire. 'Not sure, but I'll tell you shortly. I've been hit by everything, it's a well-conducted ambush, there are hundreds of them out here. I've lost the vehicles, I can't stay here, I intend to move on.'

By now, the enemy, realising they hugely outnumbered us, had become more confident again. They started getting closer, still firing RPGs and pouring hundreds of AK rounds our way. You could hear them cracking overhead, smacking into the vehicles and walls nearby. It felt like it was only a matter of time before one or more of us was hit.

Bryan led his troops on a fighting withdrawal along a dirt track, temporarily losing the enemy. But they were soon contacted again.

We were standing in the open and I could see easily 100 of them coming at us from two or three angles between 9 o'clock and 6 o'clock. With the lads laying down short, two-round bursts of suppressive fire, I headed off for a scout around with the medic. As we ran off, we saw a couple of blokes running towards us, firing. Instinctively, we shot them and laid them down. I didn't feel anything at the time; to be honest, I wasn't thinking much about what I was doing - it was just happening. We saw a building, a semi-detached house with a driveway down one side and the garden enclosed in a wall topped with a metalled fence, and called the rest of the patrol up. We entered the garden, hoping to hide, but we'd been seen and guys started coming over the wall at us. We were shooting them at a distance, literally, of five and six feet. Now we were very vulnerable - one grenade could have taken a lot of us out. So we kicked the door of the house in. Inside, there was a father and mother and three kids, daughters of around six and nine and a baby. The parents were shouting at us, screaming and crying, yelling out of the windows. They must have been terrified. We rounded them up and got them into their cellar, for their own safety. I sat Frank Haman there, where he could cover the back door and also make sure the family didn't get out. We quickly cleared the house. On the outside of the building was an external staircase leading up to a balcony and then into the bedrooms, and there was obviously a danger that the attackers could get into the house that way. In fact, one of my guys was clearing the upstairs and, as he walked in to one of the rooms, a guy stood on the balcony and threw a grenade into the room. The soldier saw it happen, pulled the door shut and shouted 'Grenade!' When it exploded, he opened the door again and shot the guy, who was busily spraying the room with automatic fire. Once we were sure both floors of the house were cleared, the blokes took up the right defensive positions, covering doors and windows where they could look out.

The house was small and very controllable, easy to defend, which was good. Downstairs was fairly open-plan - a small kitchen, which we'd come into when we first entered the building, a big main sitting room and a small spare room. Upstairs there were a couple of bedrooms and a bathroom. There was the balcony to consider and two entry doors downstairs but the house was made with thick, breeze block-built walls which would stop rounds and we were a lot safer inside than outside.

I was still trying to work out where we were. Looking back, we must have headed in a circle after leaving the vehicles, because the house was basically next door to the Ba'ath Party HQ, though unfortunately it wasn't until later on we realised that that was what it was. At first, it was just a big building visible through a large, floor-to-ceiling window.

We could see men leaning over the walls of this building, shooting in at us, just spraying the upper rooms. At that point, strangely, I was shooting back but not wanting to hit them. I know I'd laid men down but I really didn't want to kill anyone else. I just wanted to frighten them off. So I was aiming near to them, hoping they would get the message and p*** off. But they didn't. They'd pop up, spray five or ten rounds from the hip, and pop back down again. Eventually, that realisation - that we were going to *have* to kill people - returned. One guy was just a few feet away, firing at me from behind a chest-high wall. The rounds were peppering all around me but, almost miraculously, missing. I thought, *I'm going to have to take this boy out.* I looked through my sight, aimed and fired. But I missed him, I don't know how - like I say, he was no more than 10 feet away. I saw the bullet hole appear in the wall and thought, *Surely he's not going to be so stupid as to come back up in the same spot, is he?* I kept my rifle trained on the spot, lifting the barrel slightly, and, sure enough, up he popped. He brought his weapon up but I got there first. I shot him in the head and he fell away.

In a brief lull, Bryan took a moment to assess the situation inside the house. The majority of his soldiers were upstairs, with better lines of sight and arcs of fire. He checked on everyone; amazingly, with thousands of rounds fired at them, no-one was injured. By now, they had been in the house for 10 minutes, and it was 45 minutes since the first contact. The fire was increasing, with RPGs and grenades being used in an attempt to break through the walls of the house.

I spent time with the guys upstairs, just telling them little things like to move away from the window, and stand two or three feet inside to make yourself less visible and a smaller target. The guys didn't really want to kill anyone, either. We were having to, but we really just wanted them to leave us alone, just go home to their wives and kids so we could go back to our mates.

Then I went downstairs. I had to crawl down on my belly because of the floor to ceiling window. Down there it was getting really hairy. People were trying to get in through the back door, coming in waves, two or three of them at a time, and Frank was just calmly knocking them back. The door would open and Frank would shoot a guy and kick the door shut. A second later, the dead man's mucka would be there, dragging the body away and picking up his rifle to have a go himself. Frank would have to shoot him as well and shut the door again.

Another lad, Dan Cavidi, was assisting him in keeping them at bay, but inevitably this meant they were neglecting the front door. So I took up a position covering that, just in case. That was lucky, because then they did start trying to get in that way. They had popped the bonnet of a car up and were hiding behind it, getting up and spraying rounds into the room, blindly and indiscriminately because it was dark inside, and quickly getting back down. I knocked two of them away, but I could hear it was getting more intense upstairs again. I tapped Dan on the shoulder and said, 'Look, you're going to have to cover this front door here, I need to get back up there.' He was straight over there; I was really impressed with him and all of them, they were doing brilliantly.

I crawled back up the stairs. I'd given the patrol phone to Olly and when I got to the top I found him reclining on a settee at the top of the stairs, on the phone, looking like he was chatting to his mate on a day off back home. I had to laugh. It was like, 'Make yourself comfortable Olly. Have you noticed we've got a few problems here?'

Obviously, he was onto the Ops Room. That phone was our lifeline: our only link with any potential rescuers. They were getting together a QRF in Warriors and Olly was trying to help them figure out where we were and how they could get to us. Under fire and in a built-up area it wasn't going to be easy for them to get to us. What made it worse was ammunition was now becoming a concern. We'd each started out with 120 rounds of 5.56mm. We had two Minimi gunners with 200 rounds each, we had a few grenades and, in my day sack, I had a further 200 or so rounds. As I distributed these, I could hear the conversation Olly was having. It didn't sound good. He was looking at me, shrugging his shoulders... it didn't look good, either. We'd given them a grid and reference, which pinpointed us down to the house, in theory, but there wasn't a lot of confidence. We got the feeling they wouldn't be able to find us, which was about as low as I've ever felt. Once we ran out of ammunition, or if they attacked in even greater numbers... well, that didn't bear thinking about.

We didn't need to say much; you'd had those six RMPs wasted in the police station up in Al Majar al Kabir and I could see us getting overrun and then either shot, or worse... maybe dragged through the streets by our feet behind vehicles, paraded, tortured, beheaded on the TV, that sort of thing. The same thing was going through Olly's mind and the feeling that unfortunately we weren't going to get out of here was starting to build. Neither of us wanted to fall into the hands of this mob. We decided that, if we were going to be overrun, we would take our own lives rather than fall into their hands. We'd shoot the young lads and then do each other. We were absolutely certain about that.

In between all the fear and panic, there were some bizarre moments.

One of the young lads was shouting, 'I need a p***, I need a p***.'

We shouted back, 'Well, just p*** on the floor.'

He looked around. 'I can't,' he said. 'It's someone's bedroom, this.'

We were like, *Full marks for your consideration, but have you seen what's happening outside?*

Next to where Olly was lounging on his sofa was a shower room. He'd not long ago been in there himself for a wee. 'Use the shower,' he said.

'I can't,' said the young lad. 'That's a shower.'

We looked at each other and cracked up. *Just p*** in your trousers, for God's sake.*

But he wouldn't do that, either. In the end, he went in the shower.

It was hysterically funny at the time; in fact, we seemed to spend half the time laughing, strangely. The rest of the time I was terrified.

Sgt Bryan's citation makes great mention of his devotion to the young men under him, saying: "In debrief, his soldiers stated that his leadership and support was fundamental in maintaining their self-belief and will to win. As the battle wore on, junior members of the patrol became concerned that relief was not coming as time was slipping by; unbeknown to them, the patrol tasked to recover had itself come under heavy attack. Bryan was everywhere, absolutely determined that his position

would not fall. Having been heavily involved in close-quarter fighting himself in the early stages, he now took time to be with each of his men at their fire positions, lending a hand in the fierce firefight and encouraging the young soldiers, pushing them to another level and reinforcing their belief."

I did another round of all the lads to check they were OK. They were just cracking on but there were still all these people outside. I suddenly remembered our grenades. I crawled out onto the balcony. For the first time, I got a really good view of outside and a clearer picture of exactly how much s*** we were actually in. A lot, was the answer. It wasn't a pleasant sight. Crouched down behind the balcony wall, I could see there were absolutely loads of them, firing at us from all directions: they were a mob, really, and they looked to be psyching themselves up to storm the house. I lobbed a grenade into the middle of them. Then I popped up and sprayed them down before getting back inside, crawling along the balcony on bits of rubble and glass and shrapnel and getting myself downstairs. I was really thirsty, so I took a drink out of the kitchen tap. I remember thinking, *This is going to go through me like a Lamborghini later on*, and it did, but I needed something to drink. *F*** it, I could be dead in five minutes anyway.*

I checked the boys downstairs and went back upstairs; Olly's still on the phone, trying to confirm that the Warriors are definitely on their way, whether they'll get to us in time, and I'm back out on the balcony.

I peered down, with my head as close to the wall as I could get - my helmet, which protrudes an inch or two out over your skull, stopped me getting flush up against it. As I did this, I noticed a guy aiming a rifle at me, he must have seen me coming. In that moment, he fired. One of the bullets came between my face and the wall, just above my ear and underneath the overhang on my helmet. Very lucky

- three inches to the right, and it would have gone straight through my helmet and then my skull and that would have been game over. As it was, I felt it go past and heard a massive crack as it hit the wall and showered my face with loads of concrete and dust, filling my left eye with grit and crap. I couldn't see properly - I was disorientated, so I stood up, which sounds crazy, I know. I was staggering around on the balcony trying to get this stuff out of my eye, in full view of all these people below me. Out of my good eye, I saw a guy throw a grenade up at me. I barged back through the door and, as I got halfway in, it went off. The shrapnel hit me on the arm and in the inside of the thigh, right by my bollocks - it felt like a really stinging kick. The floor shook with the blast and the shockwave smacked me down; I looked up to see our medic, Cpl Ryan James, lying motionless in front of me. My first thought was that the poor bastard had taken the full force. 'I don't believe it... the f***ing medic's been hit,' Olly was saying. 'Who's going to sort us out when we get blown away?'

But as we watched, he sat up, grinned and gave us a thumbs-up; he'd just been winded. So naturally we start ripping into him. 'Get up and start fighting, you lazy bastard... any excuse to lie on your belly and get your head down, you medics!'

Once he recovered himself, he showed me his other hand. In it was a grenade. He'd been in the process of following me out onto the balcony, having seen I was in a bit of bother, and was planning to grenade the crowd.

I said, 'Pass it us.'

He said, 'I can't.'

'Ryan,' I said, 'Pass us the f***ing grenade.'

He said, 'I can't... I've pulled the pin.'

We all started p***ing ourselves laughing - thank God he'd not let go of the bloody thing in the impact, we'd all have been screaming in agony or dead.

He crawled over to me, laughing, and passed it to me, being careful to hold it so it didn't go off. I made my way painfully back out onto the balcony and lobbed it into the mob below.

That gave us a moment's respite.

However, there was some seriously bad news. The phone, our lifeline, had gone off for some reason, and Olly couldn't get it to work again. Now we had no way of talking to the QRF. Without that link to the outside world, and the opportunity it gave us to direct the rescue team in, we were almost certainly dead men. Olly nearly hurled it against a wall in frustration but I put my hand up to stop him. We were looking at each other, close to tears. We sat down next to each other, didn't say many words, just counted enough rounds for the lads and ourselves out into our pockets. Olly was cursing the phone. He was going, *'If this was a f***ing Nokia I could work the f***ing thing.'*

Most of the patrol phones were Nokias, but for some reason this was a Siemens.

I said, 'Chuck it here.' I had a Siemens myself. As long as the battery wasn't dead... a minute later, we were back onto the Ops Room. Talk about relief. Even better, they told us the QRF was on its way. I started to think that if we could just hold out, maybe we'd get out alive.

Back downstairs, they had a new problem.

Some of them had set alight the car that was in the drive and had rammed it in the front doorway, trying to burn or smoke us out. But while it filled the house with smoke and it was getting red hot down there, it also meant they had closed off one potential way in for themselves, a way in we no longer had to worry about or cover. And it also provided a new column of black smoke to attract the attention of the QRF, so we passed that on ASAP.

Time passed and I found myself back up on the top floor, looking for targets, knocking them down, trying to make every shot count and cursing myself for shooting to miss earlier. We were down to our last grenade, I think, and were very low on ammunition - 20 or fewer rounds per man. I was worried about the Minimi gunners - they'd only had two or three hundred rounds to start off with and you could fire all of them in a few seconds if you weren't careful. One squeeze of the trigger was 30 or so rounds. But they had proved themselves a vital tool for suppressing the attackers and I didn't want to lose them. I remember at one point kneeling next to one of the Minimi lads, Gnr Jason Bambridge, when a guy appeared and started coming towards us. Bam Bam pressed the trigger and the rounds just literally cut this guy in half.

Then Olly shouted that the QRF had arrived in the area and were looking for us. I went out on the balcony again to see if I could hear them - the Warrior has a very distinctive sound. Somewhere over the sound of the shouting and screaming and firing, I could faintly hear the sound of a Warrior. I nipped back inside and shouted to the lads, 'I can f***ing hear them, they're coming!'

As morale lifted, Sgt Oliver tried to guide the QRF in. But although they were close, they couldn't pinpoint the building that held the Artillery soldiers.

Ultimately, I felt that the only way we would be able to attract their attention was to go to them. So I went down the balcony, past the burning car, through the garden and out into the street, in amongst the Iraqis. I think they were quite surprised to see me, but they soon started firing. It was bizarre - none of them hit me. It was like slow motion. It was very dusty out there, and I could see rounds impacting and kicking up little dust spouts all round my feet... I'm thinking, *How are they not hitting me?*

There were bodies everywhere but a lot of them had legged it when the Warrior arrived - they were firing their co-axial machine gun and the guys in the turrets were firing too - and within moments the enemy were only a dozen or so strong, the rest had run off or been killed.

Sgt Bryan ran back into the house to round up his soldiers as the reinforcements debussed to engage the enemy. With blue-on-blue incidents in his mind, he decided to leave via the back door, approaching the Warrior through the side alleyway. Initially, he had trouble persuading the troops to leave the house.

The boys didn't want to go. They felt safe in the house, they were comfortable with the cover they had and the level of contact they were facing. They'd only seen what was in their little arcs of fire - they had no idea what was outside.

'Come on, we're going.'

'Yeah, right, OK.'

No one moves.

'F***ing come on, we're leaving!'

Eventually I got everyone downstairs and lined up. I opened up the cellar door and asked the family inside in my broken Arabic if they were OK. 'Shlownak?'

'Naam zayn,' he said. Yes, good.

Then Frank said he'd seen some of the Iraqis messing around outside the back door earlier. Maybe it was booby-trapped?

I said to Ryan the medic, 'I'm going through there, stand at the back, if it's booby-trapped and it goes off just f***ing drag me out to the Warrior.'

Then there was a knock at the gate outside, a voice said, 'British Army, we're here.'

I shouted, 'Move back from the door!' and then kicked it down. Nothing happened, except that it opened.

I ran out and through the gate and got eyes-on with the call sign that had come to get us. The Iraqis had rammed cars in like a queue down the very narrow alleyway so we had to climb over the roofs to get out of there. I told Olly to go first, and count everyone into the Warrior, and I counted them out. We all got safely in the back, all lying on top of each other - they're not built to take that many people, and the guys who'd got out of it extracted on foot. I signalled to the commander that we were all in and we moved out. The rebels had regrouped and were starting to attack the vehicle. But we made it out OK.

Within 15 minutes, the Warrior was back at camp. Amazingly, no-one from the RHA had been hurt apart from Bryan, who suffered minor shrapnel wounds and a sore eye (though, tragically, Pte Lee O'Callaghan, a top cover on one of the QRF Warriors, had been killed).

The doc cleaned out my eye and then I went to be debriefed myself. Everyone was really, really high - like you'd been out on the town and had five pints, you're not totally minging out of your head but you're just high. Everyone was getting stripped off and banging these bottles of pop down themselves like it was going out of fashion, some in tears, me included, hugging each other. It was obvious we'd all just shared something massive.

They tried to debrief us but we were all speaking at 100mph so eventually they sent us to the cookhouse, where we got some food, we were starving and we wolfed it down. And we sat around, talking about nif-naf and trivia, while our mates stood around watching us, like we were freaks in a circus or something: *F***ing hell, I can't believe you're still here!*

We went for showers, checked and cleaned our weapons and kit, re-bombed-up, and tried to wind down.

About 10 or 11pm that night, I couldn't sleep, I lay there, sat up, Olly was opposite me.

'I can't sleep.

'Neither can I, mate.'

'Let's go and get a brew.'

So we took our webbing and weapons and went to the TV room where we had the slightly surreal experience of watching Al Jazeera news footage of our Land Rovers on fire. There were Iraqis dancing all over them, firing at the fuel tank, and, in the background, you could hear our firefight going off. About 3am or 4am, Maj Bates, the Battery commander, came in. He sat quietly with us for a while, and then asked us to round the other troop commanders and multiple commanders up and meet him in the Ops Room in 15 minutes. It turned out we'd all been given a new mission - to set up VCPs on the main artery routes out of town to stop movement of weapons or terrorists.

I was in disbelief, a bit. At first, I thought he was joking, to be honest. I thought maybe we'd be given a bit of time off to recover, if only to get some rest. But the worst thing of all was when the Doc told me I couldn't go, that I had to give my eye and the wounds time to recover. My lads were being told they had to go out and risk their lives again, and I wasn't with them. I felt really bad about it, really bad. They were out for a few days and I hated it, felt really guilty. I just wanted to be with the lads.

I also felt really scared and vulnerable - our little area of the camp was empty, so I'd walk the corridors and there was no-one about, just the Doc and his medics and a few other people. I didn't feel we were able to defend ourselves. We got mortared one day around lunchtime and that really affected me. I was fearful of leaving the block to go for a shower or to the toilet, because it meant exposing myself to danger outdoors. I felt sick with fear. I actually stripped off in the corridor and poured bottles of water over myself instead of going to the showers.

Here I was, some people were calling me a hero - something I hate being called, by the way - and inside I felt like a scared little kid. It was bizarre.

I think I was dwelling on what had happened, lost inside my own thoughts and memories of the incident. I needed someone to talk to or something to do, but there was no-one there and nothing to do. It was a difficult time, till the lads came back.

Three or four days, later the Doc told me I was going to the logistics base on the edge of town to hospital. They took me in a Snatch vehicle accompanied by Warriors to The Hotel, and from there I was airlifted to the hospital. I remember sitting in the back of the chopper looking out the back door thinking again how vulnerable we were. We got to Shaibah Log Base and they came out to meet us with wheelchairs, going 'Sit down, sit down!'

I'm like, *No, I can f***ing walk.* I didn't want sympathy and I felt guilty being there too, because there were guys there who were seriously injured, had lost parts of their bodies and were being medevac-d back to the UK. All I had was some grit in my eye and some metal in my arse. Mind you, it could have been worse. One lad there had hurt himself coming down a water slide on operational stand-down in Kuwait. No matter how bad I felt, I felt ten times better than him.

I spent two days there before they said they were not going to operate - the shrapnel in my arm would come out in time and the bit in my leg wasn't dangerous. I couldn't get back to camp, though, because there was a lockdown on unnecessary vehicle movements. But as luck would have it, the Battery was nearby on the edge of town and some of my mates turned up to see me. So I was able to leave with them and join the operation for a couple of days, until it collapsed and we all moved back into camp.

Life returned then to something approaching normality - we were back down the port, with the border police, though less often, more just checking to see that they were carrying on with their training, which they were. I was quite moved, actually, because the Iraqis who knew what had happened to us were really concerned about me, which I hadn't expected. They were very nice.

And we were soon back out on foot patrols around the camp. I remember going on my first patrol and shaking like a leaf - we hard-targeted out of the base and went to ground and I just lay there, trembling. I was terrified but I thought I couldn't show it because I had all these young lads looking to me. My breathing was so shallow, I was panting. But after a little while, 20 minutes or so, I sank back into it and felt comfortable again. The first night patrol was similar, on edge, because obviously you can see less, but then I just relaxed and was OK. But I found I had become very aware, very conscious of everything - very careful just crossing a road, turning a corner, coming to a junction.

Sgt Bryan's citation is very clear as to why he was awarded such a prestigious medal. "They were ambushed by overwhelming numbers and firepower. They were in contact for the best part of two hours and engaged in a hard-fought, dirty, close-quarter battle that all but expended their ammunition and sapped their physical and emotional strength; memories of the massacre of an RMP patrol in Maysan Province came flooding back. The quite exceptional leadership, professionalism and individual bravery of Bryan stood out that day. He is a quiet man, a communications specialist by trade but, in a particularly dangerous and dynamic situation, he demonstrated outstanding skill and personal qualities. He held his men together as they fought for their lives. In doing so, significant damage was inflicted upon a determined enemy and his patrol maintained their defences until assistance arrived. He is also a modest man, but eight others owe him their lives and his gallantry and leadership speak for themselves." That modesty is clear.

When the tour was finally over, we went on holiday. But I couldn't relax. I really felt on edge all the time. Little things. It was around November 5 and the noise of fireworks going off, kids throwing them in the streets, was terrifying. I found myself diving to the ground, you'd be lying there, literally on your belly, shaking. My perspective on life changed. I'd go shopping with my wife, and see people arguing over parking spaces, or mums getting cross with their kids, and just think, *You are ridiculous.* I just flipped, I said to my wife, 'What the f*** are this lot bothered about? Do they understand how little some people value human life?' I would sometimes look at civilians - this is back then, less so now - and think, *When I was shooting people and grenading them, and nearly dying myself, you were probably down the pub, or watching telly, or deciding between a Mars bar and a Twix... you just have no idea what it's all about.* I had a real attitude. Even, to an extent, with other service personnel. There were places in the main camp at Basra where you were out of range of mortars and RPGs so you were completely safe. They didn't have a Scooby what it was like out past the gate.

I had a tough time, but it pulled me closer to my mates and I think I finally came to terms with it when my CO called me in and told me about this award. That made me think, *Yeah, this really was something big that happened, big enough for me to get some kind of recognition. So it's not surprising it plays on my mind.*

And it was a year after it all happened that I finally put it to bed, really.

Still, I felt guilty about the medal. No-one else in my patrol got the recognition I thought they should have. Why me, and not them? They risked their lives the same as I did. I know that's the nature of medals, but you still feel bad. Last night, I went to a Sergeants' Mess dinner, and one of the guys waiting on was Frank Haman, my driver and the guy who kept the attackers at bay at the back door of the house. I'm shaking my head in disbelief, that this guy fought next to me in combat, killed people, came close to death himself, and now he's serving food and drink to people who haven't even seen action. In a way it seems wrong, but that's the reality of Army life. And Frank wouldn't have had a problem with it at all, he's such a loyal person.

It's your mates and your family... I'd like to thank my wife Lorraine, and the kids Bradleigh and Jasmin, and our baby girl, Tilli-Mai. I've put them through a hell of a lot since we've been together. I'd like to thank the lads of 1 PWRR who came out for us, too. They did an outstanding job that day, and lost one of their own in saving our lives. I didn't thank them at the time because of all the adrenaline and stuff, but if you're reading this now, lads, from the bottom of my heart and on behalf of the other RHA boys, thank you.

Most of all... the nine of us who were there that day - myself, Sgt Matt Oliver, Cpl Ryan James, LBdr Shaun Lebeter, Gnr Jason Bambridge, LBdr Dan Cavidi, Gnr Jealous Muteedzi, Gnr Franklin Haman and Gnr Baker, there's a bond between us you'll never break. There will always be in the back of my mind the fact that I've seen and experienced things which other people won't. I think about the incident every single day. I see the faces of the guys I shot. I feel bad about killing people, and it's not a nice feeling, though I feel better as time goes by.

In the end, you have to move on. I did what I did and I had to do it, it was them or me.

I'm a soldier, this is my job, that's the way it goes.

Corporal Terry Thomson, CGC
The Princess of Wales's Royal Regiment

WITH Terry Bryan's ill-fated patrol scrapping for their lives, the Quick Reaction Force of Warriors from 1 PWRR was leaving to rescue them.

Terry Thomson was commanding one of the Warriors in the QRF. He and his colleagues knew that they would be hit hard almost from the moment they left their base - and they were not disappointed: hundreds of Mahdi Army militiamen were lying in wait for them.

What followed was among the most heroic actions in the history of British involvement in Iraq, as the QRF fought its way to the area where the stranded soldiers were thought to be.

Dozens of rocket-propelled grenades and thousands of rounds were fired at them and Cpl Thomson's Warrior suffered severe damage which rendered his radio system inoperable. As a result, he had to fight his vehicle from the turret, surrounded by gunmen firing at him from alleyways, roofs and windows.

Finally, he arrived at the RHA co-ordinates - only to find the soldiers were not there.

I joined the Army in 1995. I was 18, I hadn't done too well at school, I'd fallen in with the wrong crowd and I was constantly in trouble with the police. Undoubtedly I would have ended up in jail, like a lot of my friends did, if I'd have carried on down the road I was on. I was shopping in Brighton with my girlfriend and we walked past the careers office, and I literally thought, 'The Army's my way out.'

I'm not from a military background and I didn't have a clue about the forces so it was a bit of a gamble, but it's worked out brilliantly for me. If you come from a small town or village, like Rustington where

I'm from, you sometimes think you're something special, when really you're not. Then you come to the Army and you meet a lot of people who are bigger and tougher than you and suddenly, you're a small fish in a big pond. It's a great leveller, and that was what I needed.

I haven't looked back since. I had a good time in training, and came away from training with 'Best in PT' in both phases. Relatively quickly after joining the battalion I was a lance jack, and very soon after that I was a full screw, one of the youngest in the battalion. I managed to get my wings up (parachute training) with 5 Airborne, did a tour of Ireland, a tour of Kosovo and went to a depot as a section commander teaching new recruits, which was good for me. It's all been good.

Thomson was deployed to Iraq in April 2004 on TELIC 4.

My first thought was that it was like no other tour: very hot, everything in tents, you didn't have the luxury of accommodation sorted out. But we settled in quickly enough.

B Company, we were down in Basra, whereas the rest of the battle group went up to Al Amarah. For the first month, it was just like a normal operational tour. Quite quiet, the odd shooting, the odd RPG attack, the odd mortaring, but nothing too bad. Meanwhile, we were getting all the reports about the Battle Group up north getting quite a lot of serious injuries and big contacts and obviously, us as a company stuck down south, we wanted to get up there to support our mates. It was bad for morale, actually, and I'd say it did affect us. It certainly affected me - I felt bad about being down south where there was nothing going on, while guys in Al Amarah, like my best mate, Cpl Chris Mulrine, were being hit every day.

Of course, eventually it all came down to us anyway. The first serious attack was when Cpl Si Gower, now a sergeant, got ambushed in his Warrior and suffered shrapnel to the face and underneath his arm. That was the start of the Shia uprising in our area, and then it all started to kick in. After that, more or less every time we went out we got ambushed with small arms and RPGs.

I later served on TELIC 8, so I've got a bit of perspective about the way things have changed. By TELIC 8, they were much more organised and tactically aware; they had a rank structure and a chain of command. On TELIC 4, the enemy were more sporadic and disorganised. A group of guys would grab a few RPGs and a load of ammo, sit at the side of the road and whack you when you came by - not worrying that their mate was on the other side of the road and would end up being killed in the crossfire. That did happen, if they weren't killed by us. That's not to say they were ineffective - they were often committed and dangerous opponents. We'd go out on escort runs or patrols and we'd just get malleted, especially on the Red Route or on the Yellow Route past the top end of the Shia Flats.

I remember one occasion, the Red Route was out of bounds because we'd been hit on it so often, so there was a convoy down past the Shia Flats. The lead two vehicles got ambushed, stopped to return fire and then the first, a Warrior commanded by Cpl Dax Pett, got a mechanical fault and was stuck. So we had to go down to extract them. Meanwhile, the militia had sussed what was going on and took the opportunity to whack us again when we arrived. We took a massive barrage of RPGs from all over, and a lot of small arms. Myself and Dax jumped out and hitched the broken down vehicle to my Warrior, all the while with this stuff going on, and dragged it out backwards while the other Warrior, commanded by Cpl Dan Davies, gave us covering fire. That was just one of the incidents, and there were lots of similar ones.

On August 9th, Sgt Bryan's Royal Horse Artillery patrol were ambushed and, after their running firefight through the streets, had managed to hole up in a house next door to the city's former Ba'ath Party HQ. Surrounded by several hundred enemy, many of whom were being shot as they tried to break in through doors and windows, they were in great danger of being overrun and were fighting for their lives. But they had managed to call for help.

We were on 15 minutes' notice to move. There wasn't a great deal of information about where we were going or why - it was a case of getting the vehicles up and running and get them out of the gate. The 1st Bn Cheshires were already out and had put a cordon in place but were standing off - they had been pinned down by small arms when making the initial attempt to extract them, and because they were in Snatch wagons and Saxons the risk of them going in was too great. There were enemy and militia all over the place and anything that went down to where the Artillery guys were was getting hit. If their vehicles were hit with RPGs... well, it would have been carnage.

My multiple of two Warriors was told to RV with the Cheshires just down from Yellow 7, one of the main junctions on the Red Route before you turned south, so they could brief us. My boss, Capt Ian Pennells, got a face-to-face with one of the Cheshire multiple commanders and told me we were going to push further down the Red Route towards the former Ba'ath Party HQ, which was somewhere near where the lads were supposed to be. We'd get more updates on the way down. Obviously, we knew we were going to be hit as soon as we started moving, so that does get the adrenaline going. The Warrior is a great vehicle, but it won't stop everything, and we all knew we could be in a lot of trouble.

So we started down the road, myself on the right and my boss on the left and slightly in front of me. Straight away, he got opened up on by RPGs from a building covered in what looked like wooden scaffolding. I was out of my Warrior, head and shoulders exposed. I saw the initiation of the RPGs, saw two or three of them strike his Warrior and immediately we lost comms. His vehicle just disappeared in a cloud of smoke. I just thought, *'F***, what's happened to him?'*

His call sign was 20 and I was 21. I started radioing him, 'Hello, 20 this is 21, send sitrep, over.'

Nothing. No casualty reports, no damage report, just silence. While I'm trying to get him on the net, we get hit ourselves on the right hand side, by a bloke firing from 60 metres down an alleyway. When an RPG hits, you feel the bang against the armour and the noise is unbelievable - it almost stuns you for a second. But you soon react and we started traversing the turret to engage the guy, so he just dropped his RPG and legged it. Having said that, both our vehicle and Mr Pennells' were still taking a lot of incoming - small arms and more RPGs. So there were a lot of targets and we started taking them out with the chain gun.

Eventually, the dust cloud died down and I could see the other vehicle was OK, which was a major surprise and a real bonus.

Just then, another Warrior from the company came through at high speed. It came between us and Mr Pennells and just barrelled straight down the centre of the road. As it got to perhaps 20 or 30 metres ahead of us, I saw this massive barrage of RPGs, five, six, seven of them, all hit the vehicle, all at once. It just disappeared in the explosions and I remember thinking, *Those boys are dead.* Speaking to Mr Pennells afterwards, he thought the same.

The smoke cleared and, as we were all still engaging enemy to the left, right and front, I saw someone trying to climb out of the turret. Bearing in mind all the rounds and shrapnel flying around, that wasn't a good idea at all. We later found out it was the B Company OC, Maj Bradley. It was his vehicle that had been hit and he had taken a lot of the blast. He'd been out of the turret, holding his personal weapon, his SA80, and at least one of the RPGs had struck the turret ring just below him. The shrapnel from the blast had taken off a couple of his fingers and smashed his rifle to pieces, which probably saved his life. But he'd taken a lot more stuff in the face and chest, and had been half-blinded, and had been so disorientated by the explosion that he'd tried to get out of the vehicle. Luckily, Pte Yee Lim, his gunner, had pulled him back in. The same RPG had sent a load more fragments down into the back, too, and the medic and the B Company sergeant major had both been hit. The sarnt major took shrapnel straight in the face, through his arm and straight in the top of his leg, and was in a very bad way.

That was them and their Warrior out of the game, obviously. The vehicle was still drivable - how, I don't know - and Sgt Mick Pike and Pte Lim took command and boxed their way back round to Camp Cherokee to get their casualties sorted.

Meanwhile, the Artillery guys were still under fire from militia, still pinned down, and we were still a good couple of kilometres away.

Two more Warriors, with Sgt Kev Marsh and Lt Scaife in them, then shot through, to try and draw some of the fire away from us so we could start moving again, and we followed. It was a bit disorganised, just common sense stuff... they would push through, we would support them, and see where we got to.

We continued getting absolutely malleted all the way down to Red 17, which was where the old Ba'ath Party HQ was and close to where the Artillery boys were supposed to be. We were taking incoming from absolutely everywhere, including across the river, which cuts through Basra at that point.

Thomson's citation describes one massive rocket-propelled grenade strike which caused "complete communications failure." It adds: "This did not deter Thomson from engaging the enemy and providing flank protection for other vehicles attempting to rescue the isolated soldiers. Thomson resorted to hand-signals, which meant exposing himself constantly to direct fire whilst engaging the enemy and fighting his vehicle."

The RPG came in to the right side and knocked all my comms out - all I got every time I tried to get on the net was an electric shock, like a tingly feeling, in my ears and lips, where the mouthpiece goes to the A&R headset. No-one was coming back to me, so the only way I could communicate was by standing up and using hand signals.

In fact, what I didn't know was that the whole comms situation had gone tits up with all the fire we'd taken - no-one had comms with Zero, Brigade Ops. We were a little bit blind and didn't know where to go next. I could actually see one of our Snatch vehicles on fire by the Ba'ath Party building, so I knew we were close, but exactly where they were I didn't know. And realistically, they had maybe only 10 minutes left, so we really needed to find them urgently.

We were on a dual carriageway; Kev Marsh was facing the entrance to the Ba'ath Party, Mr Scaife had pushed down the road a bit further and my boss was a few feet away from me on the other carriageway, across the central reservation. We were taking fire from across the river, so I decided to move round and engage them. Again, I had to stand up and make hand signals - there's no way Mr Pennells could have heard me shout, even though we were so close - and as we moved, I don't know what happened, but I managed to get comms back... though only to Zero. So I can't speak to people 15 or 20ft away, but I can talk to Brigade Ops a few Ks away. Weird. But that was fantastic, because they were able to update me and send current grids for where the Royal Artillery were. If that hadn't happened, it would have been curtains for the RHA boys, I'm sure.

I received the grid and started plotting it on my map to pinpoint where it was, and I realised that I was sitting almost on top of it. It was the burning Land Rover.

Well, it was clear to me that that was not where they were. Whether this was the grid that the Artillery had sent of where they had ditched the vehicles, I don't know.

I sent back, 'That isn't where they are, confirm that grid, I am sat at that grid. At this grid is 1x Snatch vehicle, no military personnel there. All it is is a shell of a Snatch vehicle.'

They came back and confirmed it again. 'That is definitely the grid.'

I went back on the net and said again that it was not right. 'There are no pax there. That is definitely not where they are. There is nowhere that they could go to ground. There is nothing anywhere to say that they are there. I need the grid of where they are.'

By now, the intensity of fire we're taking from across the river is such that all four vehicles are facing that way to give it back. Using the 30mm Rarden, which is a very impressive weapon. My top cover started yelling at me that we were taking incoming from behind us as well and, as he did that, Lt Scaife's Warrior started up and went past us at about Mach 10. Straight out on to the roundabout and just f***ed off up the road. We didn't know what he was doing or where he was going because I had no comms. It turned out that they had taken a casualty, Pte Lee O'Callaghan; he had been on top cover and had been shot in the chest. The round had skimmed his body armour and gone in at an angle; he was just very unlucky. The guys who were in the back of his Warrior said that he died instantly and there was nothing they could do. He was a good guy, Lee. I can't say I knew him very well, because he was relatively new to the company and he wasn't in my platoon, but the lads who knew him well spoke very highly of him. A great tragedy.

Zero then came back to me with a new grid, which centred on a sangar in the back corner of the Ba'ath Party compound. I got back to Zero and asked them to get the RA lads to put smoke up from where they were, just to make sure. Sure enough, some smoke came up from the corner. The entrance to the compound was blocked with big, steel gates, 10ft or 12ft high. I said to my driver, Pte Dan Cooper, 'Coops, do you reckon this Warrior will get through those gates?'

He said, 'I dunno.'

I said. 'Just put your foot down and hit them as hard as you can.'

He put his foot down and we smashed straight through, smashing them open, though with the force they banged shut behind us. Immediately, we were hit with small arms and an RPG from the compound guardroom and it was like, 'Bloody hell, can't they leave us alone?'

They were so close - 20 metres maybe - that the RPG didn't have time to arm and had just bounced off. We started traversing the turret and it got stuck. User error on my part. When we'd been firing earlier, I'd been chucking empty clips on the floor of the turret in all the excitement, instead of chucking them out onto the road, and some of them had jammed the turret. So we started trying to free it up, and the fire to our right side got heavier and heavier. We came under more RPG fire from derelict buildings running along the left hand side of the compound. In the end, I got the driver to move the Warrior right round so the turret was facing the guard room, the way we wanted it to be. But I realised that Kev Marsh was on the other side of the wall, so we couldn't engage with chain gun or 30 mil, which meant me and the top cover had to try to take them out with our SA80s.

There were big HESCO barriers in front of the guardroom and there were guys in there just popping their heads round and firing bursts of AK at us. The rounds were bouncing off the wagon, ricocheting all around the turret. One round smashed one of the periscopes which was sat right next to my kidneys.

I was s****ing a brick. My arms and legs were shaking and I was trying to aim with my right foot on the turret ring. Anyone with experience of commanding a Warrior will tell you that, normally, with the A&R headset and mike, and your helmet on, trying to get your weapon into the aim position is almost impossible - everything gets in the way. I don't know whether it was the stress or pressure, but I lifted the weapon and the optical sight was right where it should be. As soon as my rifle was up, one of them came out of the guardhouse and stood right in front of me. He was no further than 10 metres away - the distance from the turret to the front of the Warrior and then a little bit more. I could see his face, and I remember it very clearly: he had a lot of heavy stubble, a moustache, a bad complexion, with a big, bouffant hairstyle. Mid 30s, trousers and shirt, holding an AK. He came out, we looked straight into each others' eyes, and he started shooting. I just shot him, bang, bang, bang, and he went down. It was so quick; by the time he hit the ground, another bloke had popped his head round the HESCO and I was having to fire at him.

He popped back in and kept firing rounds at us from the guardroom. The doorway was hidden by this chicane of HESCO barriers, and you could just see inside through this little tiny sliver of an opening. I pulled out a grenade, pulled the pin and threw it straight through the gap. It was about 15 metres away, only a few inches wide and there were rounds pinging off all around me, so I was amazed I'd got it through. I remember thinking, *F*** me, I couldn't do that again... that was cool!*

But then nothing happened. I started thinking, *Blimey... did I take the transit clip off?* Because our grenades have this little metal strip, as well as the pin. *Did I even take the pin out?* I was really flapping, so I grabbed another grenade, made absolutely sure I removed the transit clip and pulled the pin and lobbed that one. Again, it went straight through the door. I thought, *F***ing hell, I should have taken up darts!* And the second one in, it wouldn't even have had time to hit the floor before the first one went off, and there was a double explosion which destroyed whoever was in the guardroom. It's weird - they detonated within six seconds, and that six seconds had felt like forever.

We moved the wagon on towards the sangar, still taking incoming. The top cover, through the crew briefing, told me two more guys had come up round the back of the guardroom and had got into another sangar on top of it.

In a way, that was a good position for them, right on the back wall. It enabled them to fire down at us and throw grenades at us and over the wall down on to Kev Marsh's vehicle. My driver was, at that stage, s****ing himself. He was battened down, but the grenades were hitting his hatch and rolling down onto the dirt in front of him.

In another way, it wasn't a good position for them, because there was nowhere for them to go. We neutralled our Warrior round, brought the gun up - because it could still elevate and depress - and got it on to them, and I put a stream of 30mil straight into their position. It was a risk, because Kev was just the other side of the wall and he'd have caught the debris coming off the sangar, but when you weighed it up it was the only thing to do. You do wonder about these people. Once they got up there and started throwing grenades, they had seconds to live, basically. But life was cheap out there and none of them seemed that bothered about dying. They would stand there and fight, when the sensible thing to do would have been to withdraw.

With them out of the way, we cracked on to the back of the Ba'ath Party to pick these Artillery guys up.

By now, the soldiers in the back had managed to dig the clips out from underneath the turret, so we were able to power traverse again. I can say with certainty that I will never throw clips down into a turret

215

again. We're still getting hit left, right and Chelsea and often couldn't pinpoint where it was coming from because there were so many guys in there... at least 50 of them, though it could have been 300 for all I know. There wasn't a second when we weren't being engaged. I dealt with as many as I could, and I took a fair few of their positions out, as did my top cover, but they were moving around so much that you just did your best. You'd take rounds from the left, turn to deal with that, and you'd get hit from the right. You deal with that, someone opens up from in front. It was 360 degrees. I kept pushing on and we got to the sangar. But no-one came out. I got one of the dismounts to open our rear door and give them a good shout. Nothing. I beeped the horn. Nothing. I got on the net and said, 'Look, if they're in this sangar they need to come out now. I am at the grid and they need to make themselves known because I am taking incoming and we need to get out of here.'

Still nothing came, so I made the decision - they are not in there and we were getting out.

As it turned out, the house the Royal Artillery soldiers were in was a matter of feet away, right next to the compound on the other side of the high wall; the grid reference they had given was correct, but the wall kept them hidden from Cpl Thomson and his crew.

I don't know why we didn't have a clearer picture of where they were. To be fair to the Artillery, I don't think they got out on the ground that much because they weren't Warrior, so our knowledge of the ground was a lot better than theirs. They might have become disorientated. I don't know.

I started to make my way back out of the Ba'ath Party, still in major contact. Again, a lot of the RPGs were either not detonating or were striking the ground in front of us and ricocheting over the top, or just missing. The only way out was the way we'd come in, but like I say the gates had closed behind us. I supposed we might have been able to batter through the wall, but I wouldn't like to say. If there'd been no other way, I guess we would have had to. I was looking forward to seeing those two friendly call signs. They'd seen nothing of us since we'd gone in, and the boss said later he was going to give it another 30 seconds and he'd have come in after us. So it's a good job we didn't meet head on. As we smashed back out, I told Zero the missing soldiers weren't with us.

They still insisted they were there and I said, 'Listen, if they're at this grid and are definitely in the compound I'll go back in, but bear in mind, if I go back in there, there's a chance I might not come back out this time.'

It was WO2 Alexander I was talking to, he said, 'Wait out. I'll confirm with the Artillery's ops room that that's definitely the case before you go back in.'

In fact, another Warrior, commanded by Cpl Andre Pepper, had just located the men in the nearby house, and was in the process of extracting them under heavy fire.

I went left and around Kev, and a small pick up truck came from nowhere onto the waste ground to our left. The back was full of guys carrying small arms, and they were jumping off it and engaging us. Before I had chance to say anything to my driver, he just put his foot down and drove straight over the pick up, and the top cover and the gunner dealt with the people on the ground. Another load of them opened up on us from a sangar so I engaged them with my weapon to get their heads down, and then my gunner traversed and elevated the gun so that it was pointed straight at their position and just malleted it with HE. We were probably five metres away - close enough for them to have jumped down onto the Warrior. Looking back, we were incredibly lucky that none of us were hit throughout this whole thing.

WO2 Alexander then got back on the net and said, 'Cancel. One of the other call signs has picked up the eight pax.'

Which was a relief. The boss and Kev and I managed to communicate with hand signals and we moved around to support the extraction - the section in the back of the other Warrior, who were led by Cpl Shaun Robson, were having to make a fighting withdrawal because the Artillery guys were in the back of their vehicle, so we held the ground to enable them to move out.

And although we took a lot more fire, we all safely got out of there and got back to camp. It wasn't until then that we realised that the OC, the sarnt major, the medic and others had been injured. But we didn't have time to dwell on that because Sgt Ben Kelly, a very professional and effective operator, was already taking over the sarnt major's role and bombing all our Warriors back up so we could go out and cover the Cheshires as they extracted from their cordon position. We got a hot debrief, a couple of minutes or so, and we were all back out.

It was later that we learned about Lee's death, which, as I say, was a real tragedy. He was only 20. It was a tough day for everyone. It probably really only hit me how big it had been a couple of years later, when we were back out on TELIC 8 and the Lynx got shot down in Basra City *(in May 2006, when five personnel died)*. We'd been there a few days, I'd moved to A Company after being promoted to sergeant and I was the only guy in the company who had been in Basra. So I got tasked to lead the whole company out to the crash site, and it all started to kick back in. I was a bit apprehensive and nervous, and I started thinking about what happened that August. It was a mental barrier to overcome, for sure.

Of course, you think about what you did - no-one likes killing people, at least, no-one in the British Army does in my opinion. But it's you or them. The guy I shot who I saw close up, as callous as this sounds, it didn't bother me in the slightest, because he was firing at me. I'm not trying to big myself up and say I'm not bothered because that's not the case. At the time, my training stood me in good stead. Later on, you think about it. I doubt I'll ever forget his face, and while I'd do exactly the same again, it does affect you. I could sit here and say it doesn't, but that would be a lie, and there'd be no point me appearing in this book. People want to understand the way that we feel.

Cpl Thomson's citation describes his "exemplary personal bravery, razor sharp initiative, and aggressive action whilst under continuous small arms and rocket-propelled grenade fire for two hours" and says they "were above that expected for a Junior NCO of his experience and service." It goes on: "His actions were all the more exemplary as he was largely unsupported for a great deal of the engagement. His actions were an inspiration to his men and the remainder of the company over what was an especially difficult period following the serious wounding of the OC and CSM. Thomson's bravery and leadership saved the lives of a multiple from another unit, and dealt a significant blow to the enemy allowing casualties to be extracted under fire." Despite those words, he was shocked to be written up.

The medal was a big surprise. I know lots of people who've done what I would say were braver things. The CO had called us all together and read out Chris Broome's name, and some details of what he'd done to get his CGC, and then he read my name out. I was totally shocked. I stood up, went red and couldn't think of anything to say. I didn't even know what a CGC was - my mate Shane who lives nearby looked it up on the internet and filled me in, which was when I realised it was quite serious.

I took my wife Emma, my mum and my nan to the palace for the investiture, which was a massive buzz. I hadn't told my wife or mum about what had gone on, so I had to give them an outline, but until today I've never spoken about it in detail to anyone. And it's been good to get it off my chest.

It bugs me a bit that people don't really understand what we do. I've spent 14 months of my life out in Iraq. But even my own wife and kid here, and my family, don't really have an understanding of what is going on out there. I remember coming back from TELIC 4 and I was at a family do at my uncle's house over Christmas. As stupid as it sounds, there was an argument between my uncle and his sister, my auntie. It was pathetic - my uncle had just had a baby, and he hadn't rung my auntie to come and visit them or something.

And I thought, *Are you really arguing over that? Something just completely irrelevant?*

I said, 'You need to get a grip of yourselves. There's a family sitting round this Christmas and their son, a guy who I worked with, has been killed and they won't ever see him again, and you're arguing over who hasn't rung who?' I had a bit of a pop at them and there was an uncomfortable silence, and I went out for a drive in my car to clear my head.

People arguing about who put an empty pop bottle back in the fridge while there are guys getting shot at and killed every day, that's when it affects you. But you wouldn't be human if you didn't have those sorts of feelings.

Colour Sergeant Matt Tomlinson, CGC
Royal Marines

AS their British allies fought the insurgency in the south of Iraq, American forces were engaged in fighting of their own further north. Some of the fiercest battles were in the so-called 'Sunni Triangle' - a huge area stretching from Baghdad in the east to Tikrit in the north and Ramadi in the west. At the bottom of this triangle is the city of Fallujah.

American soldiers had shot dead a number of demonstrators in the city in April 2003, and the following year a terrible revenge had been exacted on four US contractors who had been dragged from their car in the city. A mob had battered the men to death, set their bodies on fire and strung the remains up from a bridge.

After that, the area had become something of a no-go zone for Coalition forces until, in November 2004, the US Marines mounted a huge operation to retake the city from insurgents. It turned out to be the largest land battle since the Tet offensive during the Vietnam War.

Matt Tomlinson, a British Royal Marine NCO attached to the USMC, was delighted to be allowed to go into action with his comrades.

Once in Iraq, he found himself passing on invaluable 'small boat' skills to the Americans as they patrolled the Euphrates river, seeking to intercept enemy forces and weapons coming in and out of the city.

On November 15, his team were ambushed by insurgents in well-prepared positions on the river bank. As heavy machine gun fire, AK47 rounds and RPGs rained down on their boats,

many people would have fled in terror. Matt Tomlinson pointed his craft straight at the attackers, jumped ashore and ran towards the fire.

I'm 40, and I was born in Bridport, Dorset, but have spent most of my life in Street, in Somerset. I'm married to Sharon and have three children - Ellis is 10, Harvey's four and Daniel-Brian is two-years-old. I've been in the Royal Marines for 18 years, and I specialise in small boats and landing craft. Until Iraq, I'd never come under direct fire. I did a couple of tours in Northern Ireland, Sierra Leone, the Congo, and Afghanistan, but that was working as media security so it wasn't front line. Obviously, we'd still find ourselves in dangerous situations - I spent two-and-a-half years in Hong Kong working with the Anti-Smuggling Taskforce, where we'd chase and intercept speed boats, and that was obviously extremely hazardous, jumping from one craft to another at night at 60mph.

There are a lot of exchange programmes between British forces and NATO allies, and in 2001 I was sent to North Carolina to work with the US Marines. Essentially, I was advising them on small boat ops and amphibious landings, which are a speciality of ours and not something they really do much of - their Navy takes on a lot of those roles. It was really enjoyable. I was able to take my family with me, we all loved the States and the Americans were so welcoming. Where the US Marine Corps is concerned, they know the history of the Royal Marines, they have come across us on exercises and in operations, and they hold you in the highest respect. It's a bit overwhelming, to be honest - they hang on your every word, they're very willing to listen to your ideas and put them into practice. And we can learn a lot from them, too.

Then Iraq happened, and the company I was training were deploying over there for a six month tour. Normally, the exchange agreement involves keeping you out of harm's way, but I had built up a real rapport with these lads and I was very keen to go with them. There was negotiation with the US Marine Corps and the British Embassy in Washington and right back to the UK - and also between me and my wife. Eventually, I was lucky enough to get permission to deploy with them, which was very unusual; I actually went out a couple of weeks later than everyone else, after the diplomatic clearance had been sorted.

As a colour sergeant, I was on the same level as their gunnery sergeants; there was a bit of banter between me and the junior soldiers about them taking orders from a Brit, but it was all good-natured. Like I say, they were a great bunch of lads.

Initially, CSgt Tomlinson's Company was based at Lake Habbaniyah, near Fallujah. But in November 2004, they were tasked to support Operation Phantom Fury, the US offensive against insurgents using the city as a stronghold.

Fallujah was a rough area - in March 2004, for instance, four American security contractors has been dragged from their car there, butchered, set alight and hung up from a bridge. It was full of insurgents and, through guerrilla tactics, ambushes and sheer aggression, they had pushed the US Army out of the city. I mean, effectively, they re-took Fallujah, which was quite astonishing. One problem was that no matter what the Army did, the enemy never seemed to have any problem getting resupplied, getting fighters in and out and so on. It turned out that they were using the Euphrates, which goes right around the back of Fallujah and through the hardcore Jolan district. It wasn't being patrolled, so they could reinfiltrate ammunition, weapons, more insurgents... basically, the back door was open for anyone who wanted to float through it. It was a classic oversight, probably a combination of overstretch, stealth on the part of the insurgents and the fact that the US Army aren't really set up to do river patrols.

When I turned up in theatre, my role was as riverine tactical adviser for the company commander, Capt Dan Wittnam. That first day, they took me on river patrol past Iskandariyah. We screamed up the river, turned around and screamed all the way back and, on completion, Capt Wittnam said, 'How do you think that went?'

I said, 'Fantastic. However, we've passed farms, pumphouses, vehicles, people who we could forge friendships with and gain intelligence from... we need a ground combat element (GCE), integral to the boat group, so that one minute a guy can drive the boat, the next he can carry a weapon on the ground. We can patrol the river from point A to point B all day, but there is so much more we can add. We can dismount on the bank and go 200 to 300 metres inland, so we can appear out of nowhere, when we're not expected, and search houses, stop people, set up snap VCPs.'

The thing is, people expect you to be using the roads if you're setting up a VCP, so when you travel along in your Land Rovers they'll be on the phone and warning their mates. But if you come out of the long grass, they don't know where you came from, who you were or where you've gone, or whether you'll be back. We can collapse it in 15 minutes and be off, and they haven't had time to organise mortars or snipers or whatever. Then you might reappear 100 metres down the road the next day, or ten miles further on, or show up on a different river somewhere else. It's a very flexible, unpredictable tool. We could also pull up and talk to local farmers, do the hearts and minds thing, make friends and gain intelligence.

Capt Wittnam is a top bloke who didn't mind listening to suggestions and was open to ideas. He could see the sense in what I was saying, he understood this was a Royal Marine strength. Straight away, he said, 'How many do you want?'

He gave me ten Marines for the GCE, two five-man fire teams, and off we went and started training, every minute we got, working on VCPs and amphibious landings and covering 'actions on' which would be used for different scenarios as and when they might happen. The young lads were really impressive, very professional, up for anything, and they trained very well. By the end of the tour, they were exceptionally good and we scored some major successes, particularly with the VCPs. We had equipment to find traces of certain pyrotechnics on suspects' hands, and we located some weapons caches - sometimes by accident, we'd just stumble across huge stashes of guns and ammo on the river banks, because they weren't expecting us along there. So it worked well.

In the November, the decision was made to do an all-out invasion of Fallujah, to sweep back through the city and re-take it. It was probably the biggest planned urban warfare operation since the Tet offensive in Vietnam, a real big thing. About 16,000 US Marines were involved, it was a two-week operation and we were employed as the small craft boat company to set up blocking positions on the Euphrates to prevent re-infiltration and escape... we were cutting off that back door.

We had a number of riverine patrol craft, which are 39ft long, each with a pair of silenced 440hp engines; they'll do 38 knots - about 50mph - when heavily loaded. They have some ballistic defence. Three gun positions, front and back with 360 degree arcs. The crew, typically, was a cox'n, a sergeant, sometimes a medic, an engineer and the dismount team. The plan was for us to intercept and interdict, and generally patrol the river.

The operation against Fallujah lasted 15 days, and we were under fire every day - the very first day of the offensive, we were ambushed. It was the first time I'd ever been directly shot at.

It was just getting dark, I was in the lead craft and we took fire on the corner of the river from the Jolan district, Fallujah's hotbed at the time. Probably AK and RPK. They carried on for 15 or 20 minutes and while I don't think they had night vision capability there were rounds coming close enough, passing down the side of the boat and right through the wheelhouse. Given the amount of fire they put down, we were surprised nobody got hit. After the initial burst, we suppressed them effectively to the point where there were just sporadic shots by the end. The weapons systems we had on board dealt such a massive blow to any enemy that it stopped them in their tracks.

I was literally hanging over the side of the craft to get clear fields of fire and managed to get two or three magazines off with my 203 M16. As soon as the fire stopped, we turned around and moved back up river, only 100 metres or so, to an island. It was a couple of hundred metres long and the same wide, and covered in 10ft high elephant grass, so we went ashore, camouflaged the boats, did a head count and had a quick debrief on what had happened. Then we dug in for the night. With all the fighting going on in Fallujah, stray rounds were winging here, there and everywhere, but we stayed low and were fine.

The next day, they'd worked out where we were so we started taking air burst mortar fire, which explodes approximately 20 metres up and throws shrapnel over a larger area. Not a nice situation at all. We couldn't get in the boats and patrol with all that going on, so we dug in and waited. It's not great, you're very vulnerable, it can get you in a trench, and I noticed that some of the younger lads were starting to get quite worried. I think they looked upon the older guys amongst us for reassurance; I was fairly nervous myself, but in these sustained situations of attack you have to try laughing and joking about it a little bit. During a lull, you move around, check on the lads, try to give them a bit more confidence. If we heard a mortar coming, I'd get down low but I wouldn't dive into the nearest trench like they do in the films. If the young lads see you running around like a headless chicken, that panic is infectious. I was trying to look relaxed and chilled out, even though I didn't feel that way, and looking back it probably helped me just as much it did the lads. At the end of the day it's all part of leadership and elements of what we all learn way back in training and throughout our careers.

Additionally, we needed them thinking about a possible attack by insurgents coming across the river, rather than worrying about stuff they couldn't control. The island would have been extremely difficult to defend because it was covered in so much foliage, but then it made it harder for them to see us, too. We sent out clearance patrols, just to make sure no-one was headed our way, and eventually it died down and we were able to leave.

Every day was pretty much a variant on that. We took rounds to the boats and we had casualties, but all of them were fairly light, mainly because we aggressively and quickly suppressed any enemy with superior fire.

The ambushes got heavier as the insurgents were pushed out of Fallujah and started heading south. On November 15, the company was patrolling the Euphrates.

It's difficult not to set patterns on the river, and if the enemy sees your patterns he can lie in wait. On land, you can use different routes, go off-road. On a river, where there are no interconnecting tributaries, you can only go up and down, though you try to minimise the danger by stopping and turning at different points. A couple of days beforehand, we'd done a routine patrol up towards a big, landmark railway bridge approximately four kilometres up river. We'd taken some heavy machine gun fire from a flat-bed Toyota truck which had positioned itself up high on the bridge. During the ensuing firefight, we managed to call in a Cobra attack helicopter. That hit the Toyota with a Hellfire missile, blowing it clean off the bridge and ending that contact.

We avoided that area the next day but on November 15 intelligence reported that there was a weapons location at a small industrial compound up near the bridge, and about 200 metres inland. We were tasked to raid that compound and locate the cache. Capt Wittnam decided to put in a deception patrol, heading past the target, going further up the river to the railway bridge. We'd turn around there and go ashore 200 metres north of the compound and then patrol in on foot. So we set off, around 1300hrs, on a beautiful sunny day: we were line astern, because the river was only 40 metres wide in parts, and keeping our eye out for sandbars near the banks - you don't want to go aground, because then you'd be extremely susceptible to attack. We patrolled past the target, and it was all quiet until we reached the railway bridge where we had taken fire two days previously. We started to put in our 180 degree turn to come back. I was talking to Capt Wittnam on the back of our craft and, for some reason, I looked down. There was green tracer coming right between the two of us at about chest height. We were only a few feet apart at the time. Although the engines are silenced they're still noisy and with the sound of the water and wind rush with your helmet on - with radio headsets - we often just didn't hear the rounds when we were under fire. Usually, the only way we'd know we were taking fire was when the rounds were actually pinging off the ballistic protection plates on the guns, hitting the craft, or we'd see water spouts alongside.

So we're being ambushed. They were engaging us with AK, RPKs and RPGs and had hit us at our most vulnerable, as we were turning and doing about 5 knots (8 or 9 miles an hour, if that). While that made sense for them, it was also their undoing. We'd agreed that if we got attacked while turning we would get straight in. I started straight for the front of the boat, pointing towards the bank, but the cox'n was already on the case, and had immediately turned the boat towards the fire. My fire team realised what I was doing and with literally seconds before the assault ashore they prepared themselves as best as possible. I think we'd taken the attackers by surprise because the fire was going over our heads and to the sides; they presumably expected us to floor it and try to get away downstream, but that would have left our backs exposed to them for a good couple of hundred metres. I perched on the front of the boat, the cox'n rammed in into the river bank at about 10 to 15 knots and did a power stop. I paused for a split second and checked that I wasn't going to jump in the water, because we were breaking through the elephant grass and sometimes you could be in 6ft of water; I could see mud, so I jumped off and started running forwards. Briefly, I turned back and saw Dan Wittnam behind me; he was always keen to get involved, and I knew the rest of my guys would be behind him so I didn't even stop to look for them. I had total faith in them so I carried on.

I could see and hear a massive amount of rounds coming through the foliage around me, lots of tracer and other stuff just chopping the vegetation to bits. Some of it was wild fire from them, and some was heavy suppressive fire from the .50 cals on the boats immediately behind - there was a hell of a lot of noise and smoke.

Sprinting up the river bank, CSgt Tomlinson came across a carefully prepared network of trenches, occupied by a numerically far superior enemy.

It was a very well-prepared ambush. They had dug a network of two-man trenches, four or five feet wide, and they had cooler boxes for their water flasks, blankets and food. They'd clearly slept there for a couple of days after we initiated the air attack on the Toyota, knowing we'd be back eventually. They had cut gaps in the elephant grass to give themselves clear fields of fire and had a lot of ammunition, weapons and grenades in place.

I'd been on the ground about 10 seconds when I reached the first of the insurgents. He was dug in to a trench, just where the elephant grass was petering out, and I ran out and there he was, no more than six feet away, with his RPK. He had been firing it but at that moment he was sort of frozen - I think he was just surprised at the fact that we'd counter-attacked. If he'd had time to get over the shock, I think he would have either legged it or fired at me. How he didn't, why he didn't, I don't know. Anyway, I shot him several times before he had time to do the same to me. At the time, I'm just thinking about pushing forwards, wanting to break through the trench systems, taking out as many as possible on the way. After I took him out I ran past a pump house - the river banks were littered with these for irrigation - and put some rounds through there, through the windows, in case they were in there too, and just carried on. I wanted to keep the momentum going, rather than the Marines behind me catch up and suddenly we're all blocked up in a group. There were more enemy in trench lines in and around the grass to the left and right of me. The other insurgents in trenches nearby were directing most of their fire towards the boats. Not expecting what had happened, they hadn't cut fields of view to the sides and that had left them tunnel-visioned. By now, the other fire team from my GCE had got off the other boat and were coming in behind and engaging them, very successfully.

Despite the fire chopping through the vegetation around him, CSgt Tomlinson charged onwards; suddenly, he came across another trench, with two more armed men in it. Both were firing at him.

I came across two more blokes in front of me, probably 20ft to 30ft away, and I managed to shoot both of them, too. We kept pushing inland. By now, we're about 200 metres from the river, about

45 seconds into the contact. We noticed that there were a lot of enemy to our left, getting out of their trenches and firing at us as they ran back towards a huge railway embankment which was in the middle of a crop field, with a village beyond it. We were outnumbered at least 3-1, I'd say, but it was so very quick that we hadn't had time to call in air cover. We had a bit of situational awareness, and I hadn't had time to do a combat appreciation - where you go to ground, work out where you are, what, where and how strong your enemy is, whether you can take them on, if you can, how you are going to do it - and issue a Quick Battle Order (QBO). And so on. Combat appreciation mustn't be rushed. It can be the difference between mission success and failure.

We'd now pushed inland about 300 metres and managed to set up a base line where we faced the retreating enemy; we're about five metres apart, with a couple of guys keeping up rear protection. The other five man team had landed 50 metres further up stream and had had their own enemy positions to deal with, as well as taking fire from the railway bridge, but they finally managed to hook up with us and in the end we had 10 Marines out on the ground. I now got chance to issue my QBO: *This is what we're going to do, we're going to fire and manoeuvre forward in pairs across the fields and irrigation channels... Numbers 1 and 2, you two guys put down fire support, No4, I'm going to move off, you follow me... No5, you're watching us to the rear at all times... No6, you take up his arcs... Nos 7 and 8, move as a pair and mark our trace and enemy positions with smoke* (this was done on several occasions when the craft could not see our position and when we had no comms, to avoid a blue-on-blue situation when they were providing fire support). *Nos9 and 10, you will cover our right flank towards the village.*

We were still taking and returning fire and now they started firing RPGs at us, including airburst grenades which were exploding about seven metres behind us. I called for the boats to adjust the direction of the fire support they were giving. They opened up with GAU 17, bringing a devastating barrage onto the position of the RPG. The GAU is a minigun which puts out around three thousand rounds of 7.62mm every minute - it's such a powerful weapon that it's only used on extreme occasions. If there are civilians around, for instance, you just can't use it because there could be many innocent fatalities. For that thing to be in fire support, in dead ground where we couldn't see the boats, and the boats couldn't see us, was extremely unnerving and dangerous. My corporal passed on our positions by GPS every time we moved, and we marked the enemy positions and our own with smoke grenades, but even so there was confusion and sometimes it was too close. On one occasion, even though we needed the fire support, I stopped it because I was concerned that we were going to meet up with a hail of GAU 17 rounds.

The enemy were knocked back and confused. In taking the fight to them, we'd really caught them off hook. Sometimes the best thing to do is to do the total opposite of what the enemy expects, and with the firepower we had backing us up it's a good tactic.

But although a large number of enemy had been killed or wounded, they started to regroup, and, with reinforcements arriving, the Marines' position was becoming untenable.

We started taking a lot of fire from our right-hand side. For the five Marines on that side, their fire was obviously drawn that way, but we still had a lot of enemy to the front, so we were dividing our fire power. It became clear that we weren't assaulting a designated position, we were assaulting, or manoeuvring towards, several enemy positions, which wasn't an ideal situation to be in. We'd been about an hour on the ground at this point. Ammunition was a problem. We carried eight magazines of 30 rounds each, and they were quite quickly used up. We also carried bandoliers holding a further 150 rounds each, with 10-round speed-loaders, and had a guy as designated loader filling magazines, but it's quite time-consuming even with the speed-loaders and takes him out of the fight, so we're now down a man pretty much constantly. Meanwhile, the enemy were only going to get reinforced and gather their wits. We could hear a lot of hollering and shouting going on over the other side of the railway embankment. There were tunnels cut through the embankment, and we started to see insurgents streaming through; it was clear they were regrouping to counter-attack and come down on us in numbers. I started thinking about a withdrawal. We took some RPG airburst fire from a palm grove which we managed to mark with smoke and the boats immediately put down a weight of fire in an attempt to neutralise the position. But we had become static: we were making best use of cover provided by the network of irrigation channels, directing fires onto the insurgent positions, but large groups of insurgents were massing in the village just behind the embankment and we weren't making positive progress. The insurgents' weight of fire was increasing, so we began fire-and-manoeuvring across the fields back towards the boats. At times, we'd go firm to engage those insurgents closing in on us, at others we'd be cover-manoeuvring, where you move without firing to save ammunition, because we were down to a few rounds each by then and we needed to save ammo in case we came up against a group of them.

It took ten or fifteen minutes to get back to the boats, and as they got bolder they got closer and louder, shouting and calling to each other. Just from the shouts, you could tell there were a lot of them, and every time I looked back I could see more coming out. We were taking fire from behind and to our side but we got back to the river bank and made another base line, returning fire from prone positions.

I'd called for two M240Gs - the belt-fed, US Marine version of our GPMG - to be brought off our boat that was on the way in to pick us up, and no sooner had the cox'n rammed his craft into the bank than those weapons were brought forward. We set up both guns at the small pump house I had earlier passed during the initial assault and both gunners engaged the insurgents as they appeared over the embankment. We continued to engage those already crossing the field towards our position. The GPMGs put down a stream of covering fire as my 10 man team cover-and-manoeuvred back onto the two craft that had come in to extract us.

At some point, you have to turn and run for the boats; at the end, there was just me kneeling down with the last man in our team. I sent him on while I put down my last magazine and then I legged it after him. Then came the worst bit - the head count. A couple of the guys got on the wrong boat, no fault of theirs, they just climbed aboard. We needed to get out of there. We were down on ammo and we were vastly outnumbered, by tenfold now. All you can hear is the rattle of the enemy guns and the crack of their rounds overhead. I was trying to count to 10 to make sure I had all my guys - you cannot imagine leaving one of them behind - and it's bloody hard to count 10 bodies in a boat as they're scrambling for cover, magazines and a good fire position, especially as we had attached EOD with us that day and they were also in the boats.

You feel as though you're counting in a drunken state, so to speak, and I must have counted them seven or eight times, with the captain and the cox'n hollering at me, 'How many have you got? Have you got all of them?' I totally ignored them because I didn't want to say that I had and then realise that I didn't. During that time, guys are still scrabbling around on the boat for magazines, returning fire into the elephant grass, rounds are screaming everywhere and pinging off the boats.

Eventually, I convinced myself that everyone was accounted for, and we could leave. And we were off, at high speed, performing a hot extraction, where we put a horrendous amount of fire down on the pursuers. They were a really determined enemy and that was a determined counter-attack; they had the numbers and they really wanted us. Just as we were leaving, our forward air controller called in two Harriers, and they dropped some ordnance, including two 500lb bombs. Upon our return to the forward operating base, we received word from the pilots that in excess of 100 insurgents were right on top of our extraction spot just as they initiated the air attack.

We checked ourselves for injuries once we were clear. It sounds strange, but in these situations you could be shot or maybe take shrapnel and not know it, especially with all the adrenaline flowing. We had one injured. A young gunner, Pte Williams, who had taken a gunshot wound to the arm, probably in the initial ambush from the nearest guy, the one with the RPK in the trench that I initially assaulted. He got sent back to the States, and he was OK, a bit of an infection, but he was fine after a few weeks.

Following that ambush, Fallujah was pretty much coming under control of the USMC; we continued to patrol and engage the insurgents as they periodically left or fled the city. Indirect fire attacks continued on our craft, but we remained lucky and were soon re-assigned to Iskandariyah, which again saw us fighting the insurgency on a daily basis.

Three weeks later, CSgt Tomlinson was withdrawn from the US Marine attachment having completed a three month tour. This timeline had been agreed between the British embassy and USMC Command before he was granted permission to deploy. He remained at Camp Lejeune for a further year, training Marines preparing for tours of Iraq and implementing lessons learnt from his own tour.

The memorandum of understanding between the two countries is such that ranks on exchanges aren't supposed to be involved in dangerous tasks, not even in training, and I think the feeling was that I had to go back to the States. Which was a real shame. I didn't like leaving the guys. We'd bonded into a very tight team, especially at the GCE level; I was glad to be going home to my family, especially as my wife was expecting our second son, but to leave the lads was hard to accept. I felt as though I was leaving a job half-done.

But I returned my weapon, packed and flew back through Germany to the States. And the day after I'd left I was shopping in Wal-Mart with my wife. No weapon, no helmet, no body armour. It was horrendous. I was just walking around looking for all this essential kit that had saved my life on a daily basis. And thinking about the guys I'd left behind, probably under fire while I was looking at cookies and ice cream. Don't get me wrong, I was glad, probably overwhelmed, to be at home and see my wife Sharon and our kids.

I'd written a daily diary while I was away, and that had made me think about home, about my wife and the children a lot more, because I was writing to them in case something happened to me and I didn't come home. I had three locks of hair - one from my daughter, one from my first son (my youngest hadn't been born at that point) and one from my wife - in a small bag inside my helmet. I just felt closer to them, and knew that if anything happened to me then they would be with me. Some people might think that soldiers or Marines in combat aren't of that character, but it's the opposite. You're a responsible, mature adult, looking after younger Marines who look up to you, trying to look after yourself, and it's nice to feel that your family are with you, especially a fantastic family like mine. At the end of the day we're just human beings.

When it comes to the taking of life, especially when it's so close you could touch your opponent, you think about your own life, how easily it could have been you, how it would have felt, and how totally shocking and horrendous it must have felt for the insurgents on the receiving end. In a way, you regret taking life, you wish it could have been sorted some other way. Why didn't they surrender? I don't think you can ever decide an end result, or draw the line, those 'What ifs' will stay with you until the day you die. To me, any human should feel bad about killing another. If you get enjoyment out of that, then in my eyes you shouldn't be anything to do with the military, and you certainly aren't human. We don't enjoy killing, we are first-class soldiers, trained very well, and taught how to defeat an enemy. We're also taught how to preserve life and protect people.

I've heard a lot about post-traumatic stress disorder, and I've seen people on the TV who say they have it and I can understand why some of them suffer such symptoms. I don't have nightmares or flashbacks or anything like that, and I'm not saying I have it. We get training now to help us deal with the effects of combat. But, yes, I've certainly changed, as will everyone who has served in a combat situation. I've gone to sleep thinking about stuff, about killing those men, and I still think about it every day, I must admit. I've had times when I get really emotional about them, which is a bit odd. I mean, I had to kill them, or else they would have killed me. But I still feel guilt, which I'm not ashamed of. There is not a day that goes by that I don't think about it, and it makes you feel like a bit of a different person. You have changed the way you are for the rest of your life. My wife says I'm different. I get frustrated very easily. Small things, like I don't go shopping anymore. Shops are a big thing for me. I get very stressed out, especially if it's very crowded. Queuing stresses me out, and I have to go and wait outside. I get very annoyed and cross now with people who moan and whinge about the simplest of things. Unfortunately, people sometimes need a reality check on just how bad things are in other countries.

Doing the sort of thing we do is probably the toughest job in the world, and we all deal with this in certain ways. You try to find avenues to take out your guilt and frustration. I find running a good escape, it gives me time to re-think, sort things out, until next time the images or thoughts are triggered. Sharon tells me when I need a run, her support is a big thing. Sometimes it gets very difficult for her when she has a problem. It'll be something which, to her, needs dealing with, but to me will seem irrelevant. This is obviously unfair on her; she hasn't a clue what actually goes on deep down in conflict. Why should she?

The other thing that really upset me was when we lost one of the Company... LCpl Brian Parello... he was a 19-year-old from New Jersey, a fantastic Marine and a really nice guy who used to drive me everywhere, in the Humvee or the seven-tonne vehicles we used when convoying our boats to different rivers. Sometimes these journeys would be five or six hours long, at night - all convoys were conducted under cover of darkness due to the threat of IED attacks. And Brian was a brilliant driver. I'd sit up front with him and talk to him, keeping him awake as he'd navigate these knackered, bombed-out old roads and keep his eyes peeled for ambushes and IEDs etc. He was always keen to be part of the GCE but never came ashore with us. After I left, he did get out with the GCE. They'd carried out a number of successful raids, and got ambushed on New Year's Day 2005. They turned towards the insurgents and went ashore, as we had a month or so before, but Brian was hit by an IED the enemy had placed at the river bank. It was a terrible loss.

My family and I had decided to travel back to England for Christmas. I went out on New Year's Eve with Sharon, and something didn't feel right. I could see all these young people out there getting drunk and making fools of themselves, like we all do, and I said to her, 'I can't do this at the moment.' Just knowing what was going on, as we sat there, just knowing what I had seen and done, and what people were going through on a daily basis. I didn't really blame the people I was watching - how can most ordinary Brits know or think about Iraq? It doesn't affect their daily lives. But it's fair to say they don't realise how lucky they are to be able to sit at a bar getting drunk. Anyway, we decided to go home early and Brian was killed in Iraq roughly at that time, which was strange.

I didn't find out until we got back to America on January 6. They'd already had his funeral. Brian had driven me on those convoys, and had always got us to the other end safely, and I'd very much like to have been there to pay my respects. I wrote to his parents, telling them what a fine young Marine he'd been. I felt a lot of guilt. He was one of the team. Had I been there, maybe I might have done things differently, or would at least have been there to best deal with the situation. But it's unfair to try and predict what would have happened.

His family travelled down from New Jersey to the small craft company to meet us and the lads when they returned from Iraq, and when we left the States and came back to England on the completion of my tour Sharon knew that I wanted to go to Brian's grave and say my farewells. So we drove from North Carolina to New Jersey, which is a six or seven hundred mile trip. It took a couple of days. I met his parents. His mum gave me a dog tag engraved with his photo, which I keep in my car. We visited his resting place. He was buried next to a lance corporal from the Vietnam war which in some ways was heartening. I said a few words, and then we drove back down to Washington for our flight back to the UK.

Despite the occasional bad feelings, and they are inevitable after you go through a tour, I'd love to go back out to Iraq or Afghanistan. To experience that immense camaraderie with your mates and colleagues throughout a tour in a war or troubled situation is unique and addictive. The feeling of responsibility, and knowing that lives depend on each and every one of you in the section, or troop or whatever, fills you with pride and honour. Whatever the cause, whether you are fighting for freedom, or fighting terrorism, or fighting to improve peoples' lives, looking after each other always comes first.

Currently, I'm back in the UK testing new equipment for the Amphibious branch of the Royal Marines. It feels like a bit of a sleepy hollow. I'm always on the phone trying to see if there is anything doing. It's not because I want to get in a firefight or anything like that at all, that's the last thing I want. I just want to do something to help out, to get involved and feel a sense of being and importance.

The medal's a bit of a strange one. The Americans initially wrote me up and wanted to give me a Bronze Star. But the British Embassy wanted me to get an award that I could wear on my uniform. Whoever it comes from, it's a massive honour, which obviously makes me proud. But I hardly ever talk to people about it. I certainly don't brag about it, because it's nothing to brag about. To be honest, the Marines and the Paras... in fact, all of the British forces are very professional, we're all trained and expected to perform to a high standard... you look at the troops currently fighting on the ground in both Iraq and Afghanistan, performing unbelievable acts of bravery and heroism 24-7... they don't get written up that often. I know 19 and 20-year-old Marines who've done some real brave stuff and haven't had any recognition because it is expected of you. It's happening on a daily basis, we just never get to hear about it. Most of the Marines don't even know I got it, just my mates, and they never talk about it, either. This is probably the first time I've really sat down and gone through it. I've been asked about it a couple of times, and I find it embarrassing. I really don't know what to say. I just say, 'Oh, I did

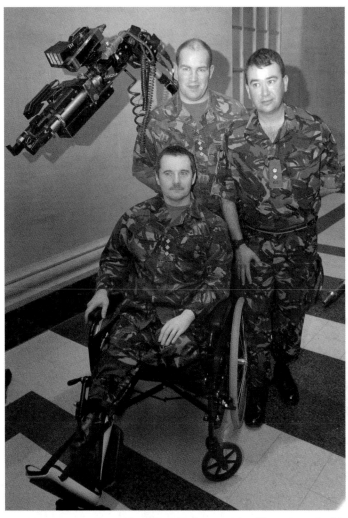

Captain Simon Bratcher MC (back, left): he won his Military Cross for his bravery in dismantling a huge IED north of Basra. With him are Capt Peter Norton GC (front) and Lt Col Robert Seddon, CO to both men in the Royal Logistic Corps. Capt Norton won his George Cross for outstanding actions in Baghdad. While at the scene of a bomb blast which had killed four US soldiers, he was terribly injured by a secondary device; despite losing a leg and part of an arm, he ordered medics to keep clear until he was sure the area was safe.

Sergeant George Long is ablaze as he bails out of his Warrior;
Sgt Long was part of a cordon surrounding a Basra police station
where two kidnapped British soldiers were being held hostage.
As petrol bombs, RPGs and AK47 rounds rained down on them,
Major James Woodham MC (inset) and others were being held inside
at gunpoint by Iraqi insurgents and rogue police officers.

Colour Sergeant Jim Harkess CGC at Camp Abu Naji,
prior to taking his Warrior out on patrol.

Private Michelle Norris MC in Basra, where she saved Colour Sergeant Ian Page's life. Page had been shot in the face, and Norris climbed up onto the top of his Warrior, under fire from snipers and RPG teams in the middle of one of the biggest battles fought in Iraq by British forces, to give him emergency medical aid.

Wing Commander Sammy Sampson DSO in front of his Harrier.
On one mission he killed a large number of Taliban who were
about to overrun a convoy; in all, he flew over 100 sorties.

Flight Lieutenant Matt Carter MC, who was decorated after leaping from a
flying helicopter, at night, straight into a firefight with the Taliban.

Lieutenant Hugo Farmer CGC (far left) with others of 1 Pl 3 Para;
four places to his left in the front row is the bearded Corporal
Bryan Budd VC, who would die in action days later.

Lieutenant Tim Illingworth CGC (standing, second from left, wearing cap)
with other members of the OMLT in Afghanistan. He would later charge
Taliban positions alone, getting to within 20 metres of them,
after Afghan soldiers with him were killed or fled.

Lance Corporal of Horse Andrew Radford CGC, with local children near the town of Naw Zad; his close friend Lance Corporal Ross Nicholls (left), 2nd Lieutenant Ralph Johnson (centre) and Capt Alex Eida (right) tragically died when their Spartan armoured vehicle was destroyed by a Taliban IED. Radford braved a hail of bullets and RPGs to save Trooper Martyn Compton's life.

Major Mark Hammond DFC flew his casualty evacuation Chinook into two huge firefights on the same day, bringing out badly injured soldiers and returning on a third mission in a new helicopter after his first was damaged by Taliban machine guns.

Lance Corporal Chris Balmforth MC relaxes in an accommodation tent in Basra; days earlier he had been involved in a huge firefight with insurgent ambushers.

Corporal Terry Thomson at Buckingham Palace with his CGC:
he showed 'exemplary personal bravery, razor sharp initiative,
and aggressive action whilst under continuous small arms
and rocket-propelled grenade fire for two hours.'

something that was a little bit stupid, but I only did it because of the guys who were with me.' It doesn't matter what you get, a CGC or a VC, or a campaign medal, you don't achieve these awards independently, it's practically impossible. There's always going to be somebody with you, who helps and assists you and is there to provide confidence for you to achieve what you do. It's nothing spectacular that I did. Anyone would have done it, I only did it because the other Marines and Dan Wittnam were behind me. I knew that if anything happened to me I would be looked after. I knew that no matter how many trenches we had to fight through all the lads would be behind me to the very end.

I don't see myself as a hero at all, but if you are going to use the word about people... one thing I wish is that the British forces were recognised a little better, and that the word 'hero' was saved for serving and retired members of the UK forces, and people like the police, and firefighters, and ambulance crews who put their own lives on the line on a daily basis for the freedom of our people. The day I got my award, the papers were full of Bruce Forsyth getting something like an MBE for service to showbusiness. I didn't want any recognition for me, so I'm not complaining on a personal level at all. But for the services as a whole, that seems wrong, somehow. Currently, the word 'hero' is used far too freely - you read the tabloids, and some footballer is a hero because he scores a goal. He's earning in a week what it would take a Marine three years to earn, which makes you think.

Captain Simon Bratcher, MC
The Royal Logistic Corps

THE Iraqi insurgents and militia gunmen have always come off second best in firefights with British forces, whose superior training, tactics and discipline enabled them to win against apparently overwhelming odds on many occasions. However, there is one weapon in the terrorist arsenal that tips the balance the other way - the Improvised Explosive Device, or roadside bomb.

These have proved devastating against British armoured vehicles, with tragic consequences.

Frequently - through skill, intelligence or luck - IEDs are found before they can be detonated. When this happens, men like Simon Bratcher are called to the scene to defuse them. This is an incredibly dangerous job which requires huge bravery, great skill and very steady hands.

Talking on a sunny, spring morning in Oxfordshire, Bratcher - a quietly-spoken and extremely modest man - seemed a million miles away from the heat and dust of the Iraqi roadside where he found himself on Monday June 6, 2005.

A patrol had reported a suspicious object - 'some wires and an antenna' - and he had deployed to the area, intending a rapid 'remote render-safe' of the device. But the IED waiting for him was out of the ordinary - a massive, highly-sophisticated, victim-operated bomb. He could have destroyed it. But he decided to risk his own life to recover it intact, to allow forensic scientists to look for clues to the maker.

I'm 30 years old and I was born in Dorset. I grew up in Hampshire, but Dorset is and always will be home. I don't have a military background, other than the usual grandfathers who fought in WWII. I was thinking of joining the RAF, where I had an uncle, but he told me not to be so stupid and to go for the Army instead. I signed on at 15. They sent me through 6th form and then university and I joined in August 2000. I'd wanted to be a Royal Engineer, but according to them I was dull and uninspiring so I ended up joining the Royal Logistic Corps instead. I don't regret this at all - I would not have had the opportunities that I have had anywhere else.

The RLC's primary role is to supply everything that the Army requires - food, water, fuel, ammunition, the post - here in the UK and out in theatre.

However, that's not all we do. I started off in stores and then trained as an Ammunition Technical Officer. It's a 16-month course where you learn about ammunition, from cradle to grave... its history, design, how it works within weapons systems, its construction, storage and transport, how to keep it in usable condition and how to dispose of it if it goes past usable condition. We then learn about conventional munitions disposal - such as where someone has found an old German bomb dropped during the war, or a stockpile of our own stuff which has been forgotten about many years ago has been uncovered.

Following on from that, we go to improvised explosive device disposal. IEDs are home-made weapons which try to mimic an actual piece of ammunition, like an anti-tank mine. Because they are improvised, they are more unpredictable than off-the-shelf weapons.

This basic course qualifies you to work in the UK only. After working at home for a year, I went on a six-week course which qualified me for 'High Threat' environments overseas. Typically, this means the perpetrator is prepared to kill his target and, if he can, the person who will try and render the device safe. Or is using much more sophisticated devices than a simple blast bomb. In the old days, that meant Northern Ireland; now it means Iraq and Afghanistan.

I passed the course in February and went to Iraq on a four-month tour in the May.

I found the prospect exciting. All soldiers want to go and do their jobs properly; I knew I would get some good jobs and I was looking forward to pitting myself against the bomb-makers. We generally all enjoy what we do. We get a buzz from putting our training into practice.

IEDs were being used against British troops more regularly as the insurgents found they were the only way to get to soldiers in Warrior armoured vehicles. Capt Bratcher was briefed on the likely threats before leaving.

They were generally using radio control or command wire to initiate the devices. They liked the RC type better because that gives them a non-physical link to their bomb - they can detonate it from a transmitter in their pocket, for instance. They would adapt a child's radio-controlled car, using the servos in its motor to trigger the device, or use walkie-talkies or mobile phones. In turn, we would use electronic counter measures to jam their frequencies. Eventually, they can fall always back on command wire - a physical link to the detonator which allows them to set the device off by simply connecting it to a battery. It's old-fashioned, but it's very simple and it works and is something that they will always go back to as we develop counter measures for everything else. Of course, it puts the operator at more risk; the wire can be hundreds of metres long, and we've come across them a kilometre or longer, but in an urban environment they need line of sight so they're usually nearby. Plus there's the risk of a patrol seeing you lay the wire, or discovering it buried in the sand or whatever.

The bombs themselves were typically dug in at the sides of roads. They were using military ordnance - sometimes C4 plastic explosive, but often artillery shells, where they would remove the fuse and put a detonator straight in. Where you use a shell, the advantage is you have less 'building' to do - the thing is already designed to maim and kill, and can take out a tank... it has the explosive and the metal casing to produce the shrapnel you want. They were using multiple artillery shells, which we called 'daisy chain' bombs, linked down the road, which meant the blast could cover a much bigger area.

Up to that point, with the drills and skills we had learned, particularly in Northern Ireland, and the vehicles that we had, casualties hadn't been that bad. They were just ramping things up, though, and unfortunately they did start to have some success.

I was based in Basra initially, where it was all pretty quiet at the time. I had a couple of falses, where people thought they had found a device. Better safe than sorry, I got called and they turned out to be nothing. We would always try to use Wheelbarrow - a tracked, remote inspection vehicle - first. It has three or four cameras on the vehicle itself and you can zoom in, spin round and have a look at different aspects. If it turns out to actually be a device, you can try to disrupt it by firing a water shot into it. Or we have manipulators with cutting blades, and we can snip wires, that sort of thing.

Shortly afterwards, Capt Bratcher was moved up to Camp Abu Naji near Al Amarah as part of the Maysan Battle Group, 1 Staffords.

Almost straight away, we had to clear a device from a road - we put in place the first joint cordon run by the Iraqi Army and British

Army working together, so it was something different. It then went quiet for about a week, little bits and pieces, but nothing happening, which is good because it means people's lives are not being put at risk.

That all got ruined on May 29, when LCpl Alan Brackenbury, a 21-year-old from the King's Royal Hussars, was murdered. He was on top cover duty in a Land Rover which was part of a convoy, basically just driving down the road, when an IED functioned and killed him. It was a hell of a shock. An awful day for everybody concerned, and it was the start of things to come. Having not been there long, I'd not met Cpl Brackenbury, but he was a popular soldier and his loss hit everyone very hard.

When a device has functioned, someone like me has to go to the seat of the explosion to clear it, to say it is safe, and to look for evidence. If anything, I found the experience increased my resolve a great deal. You think, *You bastards, you are not going to bloody do this. We will be better than you and we will defeat you in what you are doing. You are not going to win.* Along with the shock, there was a massive determination to find out who had done this.

This particular bomb was the first to be set off with radio-controlled, passive infra-red - the sort of sensor that automatically switches on your outside security light at home - in our AOR. It was a victim-operated device; it would have sat there at the side of the road, switched off so other people can drive past it, while the enemy watched. When they saw our convoy approaching, they switched on the sensor from a distance and it would have been triggered by the corporal's Land Rover. We hadn't seen the charges before, either. They were EFPs, Explosively-Formed Projectiles, which means using high explosive to transform a steel or copper disc into a slug of metal that travels at exceptionally high speed and can penetrate an armoured vehicle. We believe the bomb was disguised with either plaster of Paris or expanding foam and made to look like a rock - there were rocks and rubbish at the side of every road - so it blended in. Later, we found others which had been painted beige and then had local sand poured over them while still damp to disguise them further.

A week later, on June 6, another patrol was using the same road, heading south to meet elders in a nearby village.

They decided they were going to put in snap VCPs along this road with the Iraqi police, just to give some security and dominate the ground. A young second lieutenant called Richard Shearer was in charge, and he randomly picked a point on this dead straight, five kilometre road. Totally arbitrary. As the guys in the back of one of these two Warriors dismounted, the youngest of them - the newest guy in the Battle Group, who had only been out of training for three weeks, this was his first patrol in theatre - stopped and said, 'I don't like the look of that... something's wrong.'

He'd spotted a wire leading to a bit of a box. They instantly mounted up and left, pushing one vehicle forward 200 metres and another the same distance to the rear so they could put in a four Cs operation (confirm, clear, cordon and control). The idea is that you are far enough from the device for safety and also stopping anyone else from approaching. Particularly, we don't want to leave it so the bomb-makers can just come back and remove it. That's where we come in. I got on to the ground at about 4pm. It was starting to cool down a bit from the hottest part of the day, but we were still probably talking about 40 or 50 degrees. It was hot. I sent Wheelbarrow forward, got some eyes on the thing and started to uncover a bit of it. Unfortunately, the terrain meant it could only do so much. But we managed to uncover what we thought was most of the firing pack - I could see three main charges, and they were EFPs, very similar to the device that had killed Cpl Brackenbury. But that was all we had to compare it to.

It was then time for me to earn my money. I needed to work as fast as it was safely possible because the longer we were on the ground the more attention we were attracting. There were always people watching us, studying our movements through binoculars, talking on their mobile phones - we called it being 'dicked'.

Capt Bratcher would have been quite within his rights to perform a controlled explosion to render the device safe, but he was determined to recover it intact so that it could be examined for evidentiary and intelligence purposes. This meant dismantling it by hand. He had no way of knowing whether the onlookers 'dicking' him were simply curious locals or were members of the bomb-making team, watching and waiting for the right moment to detonate the device; the 'right moment' was likely to be as Capt Bratcher worked over it. This was a terrible prospect which would mean certain and instant death. Additionally, he was also well aware that insurgents often booby-trapped IEDs with secondary charges designed specifically to kill bomb disposal operators. Finally, as his citation emphasises, he exposed himself to the risk of RPG or small arms attack as he worked. He showed "exceptional calmness and selfless bravery" in an "exceptionally dangerous" situation.

It wasn't ideal. We were in a static position, so mortaring us would have been easy enough. Looking back, I suppose it was quite exposed and dangerous, but I put that to the back of my mind. As it happened, nothing came our way. I've had interesting times since. Pot shots here and there, mortars incoming while I'm trying to work. It certainly focuses the mind. The people watching, yes, they might be insurgents discussing setting off the bomb, but who knows? Nothing we can do about it, anyway. We can't shoot people for talking on their mobiles. I went down - we call it 'The Longest Walk' - and one of my guys, Cpl Ian Holt, came forward with me, close-ish but not as close as me obviously, to provide the electronic counter-measure cover. The idea is he will hopefully be able to jam it if they try to set the thing off by RC means while I'm working over it. He also offers me a bit of personal protection. We'd had cars try to come through cordons before, and the danger there is obvious: I had my pistol but I couldn't carry a rifle because of the suit I wear. This is kit designed for Northern Ireland, a big, dark green thing which weighs 29kg and has a large plate protecting your torso, and a helmet with visor. It offers you some protection as you walk to and from the device.

As I walked down there, I was going through a mental checklist. *I must do this, and then this, if this happens I'll do that...* a lot of it is obviously thinking on your feet. No one knows at that point how big the device is - it looked like three linked bombs was all I knew. Also, you're trying to avoid getting too knackered. You're sweating - you're nervous, obviously, so you sweat whatever the conditions... I've been in the suit in six inches of snow and still been sweating buckets. Really it's nervous excitement - *I'm going to go and do my job. I'm going to do something that is good.* But the more tired and dehydrated you are, the more frustrated you become and you can make mistakes. Plus it might be a lengthy task and as soon as you've completed it you might be called to another device somewhere else in town. Also in my mind was that we needed to get the infantry off the ground. It wasn't like they had just come out with us. They'd been out in the sun for a few hours by now, so they were tired and dehydrated, and they may well have had to go back out again later.

I managed to completely separate the component parts by hand. The most crucial thing was to make sure that the firing pack was no longer connected to the detonators, which would start the explosive train. These are very sensitive, and you want to make sure they are nowhere near any batteries or power sources. So I cut the detonators off - they were taped on, so I had to be careful not to ruin any forensics like fingerprints or DNA - and removed the detonating cord from the three main charges that I could see. They were tubes, maybe 6in in diameter, with 30 copper discs in the front, to form the projectile, and 4lb of C4 as the explosive. Quite heavy and very nasty. My plan then was to ease them away from the sand, but they were stuck fast.

OK, I thought. *Maybe it's caught on something underneath it?*

I gently started to scrape away the sand with my trusty B&Q garden trowel, and I found they were linked to another main charge. That made four. But that wouldn't come out, either. So working from the side, going down through, I found another one. Five. With the amount of explosive there, the suit, the plate and the helmet wouldn't have done anything for me so, for comfort and ease of working, I took them off. I had probably been down for the best part of an hour by now but it wasn't too bad - we still had a reasonable amount of light to work with. I carried on digging away and eventually I realised there were ten of these things in total. *Bloody hell.*

At that point, the batteries in my equipment were alarming so I needed them replacing. I also needed a break and to let other people know what I'd found. I couldn't communicate back to the guys on the cordon; we don't have radios, because detonators don't like radio frequencies. In any event, with a very significant incident like this, you can't just start talking about it on the open net.

I headed back to the incident control point so I could talk to the team - my Number Two, an ammunition technical corporal called Jamie Mills, Ian Holt, Cpl 'Johnno' Johnson, our driver, and a weapons intelligence specialist, Cpl 'Fin' Finlay. A great bunch of lads. It was nervous giggles time for me. I said, 'Guys, you know we thought there were three? Well, there are *ten*.'

There was a bit of disbelief. I got a lot of water down my neck and cooled down a bit while we came up with a further plan of what we were going to do. You always talk it through with your team, bounce ideas off each other... and that's what the team's for. I also had a quick debrief with Richard Shearer, the infantry commander. I said, 'It's a device all right, Rich. I think I've got most of it safe. However, I'm going to need more time to deal with it.'

Rich was fine with that.

It was always possible that they had arranged it to detonate if it was disturbed so I worked quite slowly, photographing everything as I went. At the back of the thing, I found 15.5 metres of coiled detonating cord, which was a good moment; they had used exactly the same thing in the bomb which killed Cpl Brackenbury, so we knew we were onto our man. Det cord is highly dangerous stuff. It's crush-sensitive - it can function if you drop something on it, or cut it with pliers.

The IED, it transpired, was a "professionally manufactured and highly sophisticated explosively-formed projectile device controlled by complex sensor and telemetry modules."

We finally finished taking everything apart and bagging it up for further analysis by 8.30pm. It was a great example of teamwork - from the youngest squaddie in the Warrior spotting the thing, to me, and then to the highest level of forensic science. Getting it out in one piece helped enormously with the development of counter-measures, so it was obviously very satisfying. Anything we can do in our trade that can help protect the soldiers on the ground... that is the greatest feeling. We are protecting the guys who, in turn, protected us when we were on the ground.

Tragically, shortly afterwards, 2nd Lt Richard Shearer was himself to die in a roadside bomb attack along with Ptes Leon Spicer and Phillip Hewett. He and Pte Spicer were 26 years old, Pte Hewett just 21.

That was an enormous blow, the worst day of our tour. I had got to know Richard; he was becoming a friend and was a very popular guy. He had a habit of locating IEDs - some of them were falses, and we would tease him for it: 'I can't believe you got me out of bed for this, Rich.' But most often he was spot on the money. A very good soldier - as were the two privates - and an excellent young officer. The team got to know him and got to know his call sign. It was horrible, awful, when we had to go out to the device which killed him.

Going out to Iraq and doing this job... things like Richard Shearer and the other blokes dying... it makes you think. I don't like hearing people have a go at soldiers for doing their job. That is very frustrating. Some people don't like what we do, maybe don't like us being in Iraq. Well, I'd rather they kept it to themselves. I think we're doing a good job out there, and the people who criticise often have very little idea what the guys are going through. And they never will.

I don't have flashbacks or bad dreams or anything. It helps being around people who've seen what you've seen. My other half is an ex traffic copper, so I can talk to her, too. She's seen some pretty bad things. I had one bad moment when I was out in theatre. I happened to see somebody else's job pictures and I suddenly smelt the blood, the explosives... it's an indescribable smell... metallic, cloying. Horrible. That was from seeing the aftermath on a monitor.

My outlook on things is pretty fatalistic now, I'd say that was one change in me. It's either your time, or it isn't. You can do everything you possibly can to protect yourself, but what we are all doing is inherently dangerous and whether it is luck, your time, whatever you want to call it, you can do everything right and still be killed, or you can have a lucky miss.

None of it makes me regret joining the Army, even for a second. It's the greatest job in the world - the camaraderie, the life. Saving other people's lives, making a difference. It's a brilliant feeling.

Capt Bratcher's citation makes clear his Military Cross was awarded for his "exceptional calmness and selfless bravery"; his courageous actions "led to the arrest of suspected terrorist perpetrators and moved the counter measure process on significantly."

I feel extremely humbled to have been awarded the Military Cross. I don't think a single other person in the trade would have done anything different. It just happened to be me and my team. I was there and it was my job to deal with it, and that's all there is to it. In my mind, the medal is for everyone who helped me do my job, and also for the trade itself. There are guys all over the world doing this on a daily basis, and many of them do far braver things and pay a dreadful price, like SSgt Chris Muir, who died during TELIC 1. Look at Capt Peter Norton, who was awarded the George Cross: he lost an arm and a leg to a bomb but told the medics to keep away from him because there was another nearby. There are lots of other guys who've done amazing things; if my award, and this story, lets people know what we do, then I'm happy. It is grudgingly that we talk about our work, but it's important that people realise the commitment the guys give.

Major James Woodham, MC
Royal Anglian Regiment

ON September 19, 2005, two British soldiers were arrested by Iraqi police after shots were fired near the infamous Al Jameat police station in Basra. The two men, who had been working on counter-terrorist surveillance, were bundled away to the police station for interrogation.

British troops were quickly on the scene. With elements in the Iraqi police linked to the militias, it was feared that the pair might be passed on to terrorists and either used as bargaining chips for the release of insurgent prisoners or even executed.

But the police refused to release the soldiers, claiming they were Israeli spies, and a mob of angry Iraqis began forming outside.

Petrol bombs were thrown - one setting a sergeant on fire in pictures that were beamed around the world - and then shots, RPGs and anti-tank missiles were fired.

James Woodham, a married man from Norwich and now a lieutenant colonel, was a major at the time; he had good links to the Iraqi Police, so he was called to the Al Jameat to try to negotiate the release.

He and his team found themselves trapped inside the building, with the atmosphere rapidly deteriorating and turning very ugly.

I was a Company Commander during Op TELIC 6, working for 12 Mechanized Brigade from April to November 2005, based primarily in Basra. The Brigade's job was focused on supporting the Iraqi Provincial Government and developing the Iraqi Security Forces to a level where they could be responsible for the security of the area. Until that was done, we also had to undertake security operations in order to maintain a relatively safe environment to enable the reconstruction and development to continue.

Basra was relatively calm, but it would be fair to say that the average Iraqi was growing a little tired with the lack of progress that the Iraqi Government was making in turning the country around. Some of that frustration was aimed at the British Army as we were seen locally as the organisation which was most likely to deliver the changes which would make Iraqi lives better. The war itself had actually caused very little damage to the infrastructure in Basra, which is something I think many people don't realise. Most of the damage had been done over the previous years by a lack of investment during the time of Saddam's regime. And indeed, where possible, we were trying to assist with the reconstruction work. But the security situation began deteriorating significantly during our tour. There had been occasional IEDs early on, mostly aimed at the Iraqi Security Forces. But during the summer the threat changed considerably and we started seeing a significantly more potent and lethal IED being used which damaged a number of vehicles and led to a series of fatalities. In turn, this meant that towards the end of our tour more of the Brigade's focus and resources were aimed at security rather than reconstruction and the training of the Iraqi Security Forces.

We undertook a spectrum of operations, everything from framework patrolling to reassure the locals and gather information and intelligence, all the way through to carrying out highly-focused arrest operations aimed at removing particularly bad people from the city. The performance of the British soldier in Iraq, certainly during Op TELIC 6, was outstanding. There has been much comment that today's soldiers are not like those of yesteryear, not hard or physical enough, but my experience is that, when given the challenge of operations, they rise to that challenge and perform admirably. We had occasions of intense military activity during Op TELIC 6 when our soldiers responded very well and showed that they still had all of the spirit and fortitude of our forefathers.

On September 19, two soldiers were involved in a shooting incident while on a surveillance operation; they were arrested and taken to the Al Jameat police station in Basra.

I was having a relatively quiet day in Brigade Headquarters when we received reports that two British soldiers had been involved in a chance encounter with a unit from the Iraqi Police, some of whom were in civilian clothes. Each thought the other was suspicious, shots were fired and the two soldiers were eventually arrested. It is in the public domain that there were members of the Iraqi Police who had allegiances to other organisations, in particular to the Shia militia of Moqtada al-Sadr. These were the Mahdi Army, or the Jaish al Mahdi, often known to the soldiers as the JAM. During 2004, the JAM had been involved in a serious uprising which had led to problems, particularly in Al Amarah and Basra. Some of that was full-on war fighting *(which is covered elsewhere in this book)*. The JAM was a dedicated and ruthless organisation, and some police officers' allegiances were being split between their day job and their night time illegal activities. So when these soldiers were arrested and were being held by the police there was a great deal of concern about their fate.

British Army patrols had sought to reach the Jameat to make contact with the captured men, but had been refused entry and a stand-off was developing. The Iraqi police were very jumpy. They had deployed machine guns on to the roof, which was very unusual, and they were not allowing access.

I'd been dealing as the Army's liaison officer with the police units at the Jameat, so I had reasonable relations with a number of them and they knew me quite well. So it was decided that I should use my contacts to gain access and ascertain that they were indeed holding the British soldiers and that they were still alive and well.

I called my contacts in the police station and asked if I could come down to visit them. They wouldn't talk about the situation but they were happy to receive me, so I grabbed a small team of my soldiers, including an interpreter, and deployed by helicopter. It took about five minutes and we landed 300 metres from the police compound.

The Jameat was in an urban residential area of the city, a large, walled compound with security posts around the outside and guarded gates, front and back. The police station itself was a three-storey building which contained a prison cell which one can only describe as being on a par with the Black Hole of Calcutta; this was where the Iraqi police held what they considered to be their most dangerous terrorist suspects. Behind the main building were a number of large prefabricated Portakabins, which a number of different Iraqi police and intelligence units used as their offices.

The Basra City Battlegroup, centred on 1st Battalion The Coldstream Guards, had formed a defensive cordon aimed at stopping anyone leaving with our soldiers. At that point, I think there was approximately a Company present - around 100 men. But as things developed throughout the day, that grew to the best part of a Battlegroup, with about 600 men on the ground.

I was met from the helicopter by a patrol, quickly orientated and I made my way on foot to the police station. Things were strangely tense. A crowd had built up at the front gate and it was clear that the police were on edge. But I was allowed access, and I quickly found my contacts inside. I then started the usual Arab way of doing business, formal introductions followed by small talk before slowly moving to the business in hand. It was very frustrating; I just wanted to find out whether the two soldiers were there and to get to see them, but if I had gone in and tried a more direct manner I would have got nowhere.

The Iraqi Police confirmed that they were holding two Western men and said they had concerns that they were Israeli intelligence operatives on a bombing mission in Basra. I said, 'Well, I think, actually, that they might be British soldiers. Can I see them?'

Eventually after much consideration we were taken to see them. They clearly were two of our soldiers. They were being held in an interview room in an upper floor of the main police station building, and had been roughly treated - each was sporting decent cuts and bruises - but were otherwise OK. They were being model prisoners and saying very little, but were pleased to see us; it meant that the British Army knew where they were and that people were trying to secure their release.

However, it was clear that there were going to be real problems trying to get these guys out. An investigating judge had arrived to deal with the case, and I began to negotiate with him. They were taking the legal route and my knowledge of the Iraqi legal system was pretty basic so it was apparent I needed a lawyer alongside me pretty quick. I called the Brigade Headquarters on my mobile. They said they'd send our Brigade lawyer, Maj Rabia Siddique, so I went back outside to await her arrival. I'd been on the ground about an hour at this point.

Outside the police station, it became apparent that the crowd was building and there was significant tension within it. They were being orchestrated and whipped up by a few individuals and were getting quite aggressive towards the soldiers on our cordon. It's very hard to control a crowd in that environment, and it gets harder the more excitable they become. Every soldier is forced to make fine judgments over how he acts - starting off being polite but firm but being able to ramp up the levels of aggression to ensure control is retained, all the time being careful not to exacerbate and further inflame the situation.

Imagine you're a young private soldier, perhaps on his first operational tour, and you have a seething mass of people in front of you, moving towards you, chanting in a language you can't understand, waving their fists, looking very angry... at any moment, someone with an AK47 might appear from within the crowd and fire at you, or a device could be thrown. The noise is such that you perhaps can't hear instructions on the radio too well; you might not even be able to hear the man next to you. It's very hot and your adrenaline is up. You're nervous, probably frightened. It's in this sort of situation that the control shown by the British Army and the soldiers on the ground is at its greatest; they were doing a sterling job of holding their ground in very trying circumstances.

Before too long, the lawyer, Maj Siddique, arrived. Also at this stage it became clear that my military interpreter was suffering with a heat injury and was unable to come back into the police station with me. So I grabbed a locally employed Iraqi interpreter from the troops on the cordon and he accompanied Maj Siddique and me back into the police station. We made our way to the interview room containing the two soldiers, and Maj Siddique continued the negotiations. She managed to get the investigating judge and the police to agree that they would release the soldiers when they received a signed letter from the Iraqi government ordering them to do so. I requested the letter and behind the scenes intensive work ensued in Baghdad and in Basra to get the letter signed and back to the Jameat. Eventually the letter was produced and handed to the Commanding Officer of the Coldstream Guards. Lt Col Nick Henderson, who was commanding the cordon. He then had the interesting task of trying to march the letter into the police station, through what was now a violent and volatile situation.

The soldiers outside the police station now had an extremely dangerous situation on their hands. Rocks and petrol bombs had been thrown from within the seething crowd, and now shots were being fired; before long RPGs and even anti-tank missiles would be used against the British. Soon, the aggression spilled into the building. "Negotiations became fraught," says the citation, "and the atmosphere was highly charged and extremely volatile." Woodham and his team found themselves trapped.

The situation was brilliantly captured by those famous press photographs of Sgt George Long bailing out of his Warrior with his clothes on fire. RPGs and small arms were also being used. In the course of defending themselves, the cordon troops had shot a number of people. The relatives and friends of some of these people were now getting into the police station. They were protesting about their relatives and friends being shot and injured or killed, and they wanted to vent their anger on the man they perceived to be commanding the operation, which was me and the team inside the building.

I think it was around this time that my second interpreter decided he was best off out of there, and he also left the police station. Which wasn't tremendously helpful.

The police found it very difficult to control the situation at this stage. They had lots of angry armed civilians coming into the police station and, at that point, the investigating judge also decided he was going to leave. He appeared concerned for his own safety. As he left, there was a subtle change in who was in charge. One minute we were negotiating with the judge, and the second he left the void was filled not with the police commanders but with locals - religious and militia leaders. The police had effectively lost control. That ratcheted things up for us quite a lot. We were physically ushered away from where the two soldiers were being held. Outside, I could hear shots being fired and see explosions from petrol bombs and so on; one began to wonder, for the first time, about one's own safety. In 2003, six Military Policemen had been killed in a police station in Maysan Province *(at Al Majar Al Kabir)*. While that incident didn't go through my mind at the time, having subsequently spoken to others involved in the operation, it was at the back of other people's minds.

Woodham found himself staring down the barrel of an AK47; the man holding it was screaming at him, his finger twitching on the trigger. There were up to 30 angry, armed men in the room by now; his citation says he "was left with no alternative but to recommend to Brigade Headquarters that the cordon should be pulled back, and he did so fully aware of the increasingly isolated position in which this would leave his team."

It became very chaotic. There were now lots of armed people milling around, not many of them in uniform, carrying a mixture of pistols and AKs. It was very hard to work out who was who. Who was an angry relation, who was a policeman, who could you trust, who couldn't you trust? Three of the soldiers who were with me got split up from us. Myself and Rabia were escorted down the stairs and outside, round the back and into a Portakabin where we found ourselves very much on our own with a bunch of very angry people. At one point, a very angry man armed with an AK47 burst into the doorway and started screaming whilst aiming it at me. I was looking at him looking at me over the sights of the weapon.

I remember thinking, whilst searching for something resembling hard cover, *Is he going to pull the trigger?*

I'm a married man, and at the time I had a two-and-a-half-year-old son, and you do think the unthinkable, if only for a fraction of a second. It was a worrying moment, but I had nowhere to go and there wasn't anything I could do if he chose to shoot. For some reason, he chose not to.

That was just a vignette in a very tense period.

Eventually, the three soldiers who had been split from us managed to force their way in to where we were. In the process, an attempt was made to take their weapons and equipment; I think they lost a radio but they got to us. So now we were all together, but in the corner of this Portakabin with lots of armed people shouting and arguing amongst themselves about what to do. Shots were being fired outside the Portakabin, and I was extremely aware, as I think we all were at that point, that we were one decision away from something that would have been very untidy.

All we could do was to remain extremely calm; I was doing lots of talking, whilst those behind me watched the armed crowd surrounding us and were doing so in a way not to cause an undue reaction.

I think at that point, just getting ourselves out of this pickle was the priority - gaining the release of the two soldiers had become a secondary priority. There comes a time when you have to become pretty brutal about the whole thing; I genuinely felt that my small team was in mortal danger and I decided that we had to look after ourselves for now.

There was then a slightly bizarre moment, when a local Iraqi journalist climbed in through the Portakabin window - he squeezed in through what was no more than an eight-inch gap and started taking photographs. It was rather surreal and put a slight smile on our faces. I'm not sure the Iraqis found it very funny; he was quickly and forcibly ejected, and there were reports that night that a journalist had been killed by men dressed in police uniforms. We put two and two together and thought it was probably the same chap, though we had no proof.

Even though it was clear, in retrospect, that the police allegiances were split, and they were being heavily influenced by the presence of those who were closely linked to local militia, there were glimmers of positive behaviour by members of the police.

When the chap was aiming the AK47 at us, he'd eventually been calmed down by members of the police and moved out of the way. It was another of those glimmers of hope that I was able to capitalise on. Present in the Portakabin room with us was a policeman with whom I had developed a relationship over the preceding three months or so. I grabbed him and said, 'Look, I trust you and you trust me. You have got to get us out of here before this goes badly wrong.'

And luckily, he organised a team of people he trusted to form a human shield between us and the more angry members of the crowd, and they moved us out and into another Portakabin. That was the key moment, where I felt the high threat had been somewhat defused. It was calmer, and quieter, and we were able to continue more reasonable negotiations with the leaders - members of the police, the local community, the provincial government - without the attendant shouting and assault rifle-waving.

Funnily enough, the policeman who helped us out of the room on that day was actually a bad apple; it was more than slightly ironic that he was the one who was instrumental in our move to relative safety. My only explanation of his behaviour is that because we were his guests in his police station he felt a responsibility to assist us. This is an aspect of Arabic culture and on this day we were very grateful for it.

There was still no agreement to hand over the two captive soldiers. With the men outside still struggling with the angry crowd, plans were drawn up for armoured vehicles to smash their way into the building and force their release.

Negotiations continued and I remained in constant contact with Brigade Headquarters. Eventually, late in the evening, I informed the senior policemen that if they didn't hand over our two soldiers then all available means would be used to ensure their safe return to us. We were laying it on pretty thick, in the knowledge that the military strike force was close and poised to take action. Unfortunately, the threats didn't work. They agreed that we could leave but said they could not hand over the other two.

This was enormously frustrating; we were very concerned for the two soldiers at this point. We'd not seen them for the best part of four or five hours and it was now dark and perhaps as late as 9pm. So we moved to the rear of the compound and left by the rear gate, reporting to the commander of the strike force that we didn't have the two soldiers. At that point we jumped into the back of the armoured vehicles and shortly afterwards the same vehicles entered the compound through the walls in what was, effectively, a raid on the police station: they quickly established that the two soldiers were no longer there.

What was interesting was that as we had moved out of the back gate streams of policemen were also leaving in their cars and, looking back, something had changed. The tension had evaporated and they were just leaving like it was the end of the day. As it turned out, the soldiers had been bound and moved out of the police station in the boot of a car to a residential house about a mile and a half away. At some point, the police had handed them over to the local militia. Two days previously, we had arrested the leader of the JAM in Basra and our assessment is that the pair were either going to be killed in retribution or used as bargaining chips to secure their leader's freedom. Whichever it was, intelligence was forthcoming as to their location and, having checked the police station, the strike force moved to the house and found the two soldiers tied up in the bathroom of the house. So it all ended reasonably well, though 19 British soldiers were hurt on the cordon, which they had held for the best part of ten hours under extreme provocation, and during which a number of Iraqis were also injured or killed.

"In an exceptionally dangerous and unstable situation," says the citation, "with himself and his team held at gunpoint and threatened, Woodham provided a cool head and calm leadership, despite the imminent danger to life; one mistake could have triggered a blood bath, but this was prevented by his courageous leadership and exceptional presence of mind in the face of extreme danger." Woodham is typically modest about the part he played in the successful outcome to the day.

I had no idea that I'd been written up for a medal. The following year I took a strange phone call and was asked to go up to London with my wife. When I got there I was informed that I had been awarded the Military Cross.

I experienced a mixture of feelings. There was a sense of shock and pride, but primarily I was embarrassed. I was only one of a large number of people involved in operations conducted by 12 Mechanized Brigade on that day. I just happened to be in the middle of it all. I wasn't alone: it was absolutely a team effort, from the people with me, those manning the desks and controlling the operations back at the HQ, and to our soldiers on the cordon. It was rather humbling to be selected from that group of people for recognition.

Colour Sergeant James Harkess, CGC
The Princess of Wales's Royal Regiment

IN 2004, The Princes of Wales's Royal Regiment had clashed with the militiamen of the Mahdi Army in some of the fiercest and most brutal fighting the British Army had seen in modern times.

Jim Harkess, a Platoon Warrior Sergeant in C Company, 1 PWRR, had been on that tour, and had also been in Iraq, attached to the Royal Regiment of Wales, the year before.

In 2006, Harkess found himself back out there for the third time, deployed with the Queen's Royal Hussars Battle Group in Al Amarah on Operation TELIC 8.

Like Chris Broome before him, CSgt Harkess, a Nottinghamshire miner who had joined the Army after the pit closures of the 1980s, was later awarded the Conspicuous Gallantry Cross for "bravery in the face of the enemy" on three separate occasions. His citation says he "demonstrated immense courage, repeatedly exposed himself to enemy fire and led his platoon with real bravery, gallantry and leadership."

I've been in the army for 15 years. I'm originally from just outside Mansfield in Nottinghamshire, and I went down the pit straight from school. I'd been a miner for seven years but they started closing the mines and I found myself at 22 wondering what to do. I couldn't see myself working in a factory so I applied for the Worcestershire and Sherwood Foresters and got accepted. My first posting was to Cyprus and I loved it - it was a brilliant place to be for a young lad. I was there for two years, I've done tours of Northern Ireland, Bosnia, Kosovo and two and a half tours of Iraq.

I'd been on TELIC 3 with 1RRW and part of TELIC 4, when we'd had a lot of trouble around Al Amarah, but the reports ahead of TELIC 8 were that the situation wasn't too bad, which for me and my lads was a nice thought. We were looking forward to having a peaceful, relaxed tour and then getting back home. We took over from the Scots Dragoon Guards and they said it had been fairly quiet. They'd had a few guys killed by IEDs, and one guy shot, but then they used to do a lot of foot patrols, which we found surprising.

I'd say about 25 or 30 of our lads had been under fire in Iraq before, which helps because they knew what to expect. But it also meant we had to train really hard because we knew what could happen if it really did kick off. We wanted our guys to be a little bit harder than if they'd gone through a normal Ops package, or done some light training prior to deploying.

The tour started in the April, based at Camp Abu Naji near Al Amarah, which brought back a few memories. It had been supposed to close on TELIC 7, but had been extended on to 8; the plan was for us to be there for six weeks and then extract out.

We got small contacts from day one. Patrols were kept to a minimum, so as not to incite the locals, but we had to cover supply convoys and we'd go out to the local police stations and make sure they were all up and running so that when we pulled out they could take over properly. We'd take a lot of incoming mortars and rockets, mainly at night, but we had no casualties early on.

Out of Al Amarah town, it was OK, but once you got to the outskirts you could feel the tension, and the atmosphere got nastier every day. There was more graffiti on the walls than there'd been before, and a lot of it was in English, saying things like 'British Forces Get Out'. And while we'd been quite friendly with the police before, you could see them start to take a step back from you. A bit more distanced. They wouldn't do any joint patrols, which they had done on

TELIC 7. Interpreters didn't want to come out on the ground with us, which was also telling us something. But we still went out ourselves; it was about freedom of movement, which we were saying we had.

We would be stoned as we drove, but you don't mind that too much because, generally, if you're being stoned you're not being shot at. That said, they'd do things like mix a few grenades in with the rocks, and if one of those gets down past you and into the vehicle, you've lost the vehicle. So the turret commanders like myself would constantly be scanning the crowds; your adrenaline is up and you're extremely alert.

You trust your gut a lot. We'd be at a police station and if I felt it was alright we'd stay a fair while; if not, we'd be in and out in 10 or 15 minutes. If trouble's brewing, you can sense it. Say there are normally kids around, and suddenly there are no kids. Or there's no traffic coming up or down a given street. The police aren't hanging around outside a particular police station. Then you start seeing cars blocking off the road, and you start to think about routes out of there to avoid contact. There may be no other way, it may be that you have to smash the cars out of the way, which is what we did in one major contact. You'd try to avoid this, because you're going to have to go back the next day or the next week and you don't want to needlessly wind people up. You try to have a bit of courtesy towards them. But if they refuse to move, we move them.

On May 23, 2006, CSgt Harkess deployed in a strike operation against a Mahdi Army stronghold.

The day hadn't started well, there was something in the air. My platoon of three Warriors had been out on a patrol to a police station in the morning, with another platoon just outside the town covering us as a QRF in case it went off. And straight away it was wrong. We actually changed our route about three times as we came into town, though we arrived at the objective without any real bother. But there was no-one out on the street, and the police had all vanished as soon as they saw us coming. My boss and the platoon sergeant went inside - very dangerous, no-one knows what's waiting for them in there - leaving us covering the frontage. I put dismounts up on the roofs to cover them, and look for snipers or other potential danger. Cars started blocking the ends of the street, at which point the interpreter jumped straight back in the vehicle. I got in after him and asked him what was going on. He'd overheard a conversation between a taxi driver and the police, saying there were two snipers on their way.

I passed this on to my boss, and he was back out within a few minutes. We remounted up and started to move out and we were confronted by about 150 people and a full-scale riot, with lots of bricks and stones being thrown. The baton gun came out and I popped a few rounds at targets, trying to disperse them. We managed to break out and we stayed out of town for a good couple of hours after that. But clearly the mood locally was a bit feisty.

That afternoon, we were tasked to support 7 Platoon who were going to go into a particular shanty town-type housing estate on the northern side of Al Amarah, which was known to be full of JA Mahdi. They went up one side of the town and we mirrored them on the other; the net was full of reports of heavy stoning but our side was quiet. They had to cross one of two bridges across the Tigris - we called them Green 2 and Green 3 - to get to their location, and we were to stay on our side of the river and be available in case of trouble. It was well known for ambushes and even before we went static I started hearing contact over the net.

A heavily-armed, 50-strong group of Militia had attacked in an attempt to isolate the lead elements of the Company; CSgt

Harkess ignored a torrent of heavy fire from small arms and RPGs to take and hold a position to allow his comrades to extract.

Sgt Geordie Davison, callsign M1-2, was reporting. I've known Geordie for 15 years, he's probably my closest mate, so my ears pricked up and the hairs on the back of my neck started standing up. Straight away, I stopped the platoon, all gun turrets turned, and asked him what he wanted. He was about a kilometre away, on the other side of the river and inland by about 600-800 metres. He needed us to cover the bridges for his extraction so we pushed down there. And we got contact straight away. They threw the lot at us - RPG, small arms, heavy machine guns and even mortars. I sent my two front vehicles down to support one bridge and reversed by myself to cover the second; not knowing which way he was going to extract, we had to cover both. They were about 800 metres apart, you could just about see one from the other and we could support each other, too.

I could hear rounds hitting the back door, AK and heavier stuff, so I traversed the turret across the river which was where the fire was coming from. But we couldn't ID anyone - there was a crowd of 40 or so people milling around, and no obvious gunmen, so we had to sit there and take it. It was one of their favourite SOPs - the crowd parts, the gunman fires and the crowd closes again. It's a high stakes game for them to play, but they know our rules of engagement. Of course, it's very frustrating; we could have hosed them all down and the problem would have been solved. People ask why we don't do that, just open fire and *claim* we have located the shooter. But if we were like that then we wouldn't class ourselves as British soldiers, and the British Army would not be what it is today. Could I live with that on my conscience? No, I don't think I could.

One unfortunate side effect of this is that the Iraqis, wrongly, perceive it as a sign of weakness, and that encourages them. If you can respond to aggression with more aggression, they respect you for it.

I noticed that the crowd were massing around the end of an alleyway, so you knew the shooters were around there somewhere. Then an RPG was fired. You see the flash and you know it's incoming, but you've no chance of getting out of the way - you just have to hope. The grenade dipped onto the back deck of the Warrior, very close to me, and skipped away, so I was very lucky. I got the driver to start jockeying left and right, trying to lure the RPG boy out to have another go so that we could get him. As we're doing that, another RPG hits us from behind and explodes. The vehicle is designed in such a way that the shrapnel should fly upwards, so it wasn't particularly dangerous to me, but it's obviously a bit unsettling. So you don't think about it. You go into your own world. You know everything that is happening around you, but you're just thinking about what you have to do at that moment in time.

By this stage, we started to locate the shooters across the river. I put my chain gun on to three or four targets and the gunner, 'Chappers' Chapman, got on with them. He'd been a dismount on TELIC 4, Chappers, so he knew the score; he found a lot of targets and kept a lot of our boys alive throughout this tour. On this occasion, he'd quickly dropped three or four, which knocked the stuffing out of them a bit. Once they see what a 7.62mm chain gun can do - I mean, it will just cut you in half, or take your arms and legs off - they're a bit less keen to have a go. While all this is going on, I'm still conducting everything on the net with 7 Platoon and passing reports back to my OC and sitreps down to my platoon commander so that everyone was kept informed.

7 Platoon were in heavy contact; their dismounts were on the ground, also in heavy contact, and time was marching on. The longer these things take, the worse it is, because the enemy pins you down

and starts encircling you and then it's only a matter of time. We ourselves were now caught in a 360 firefight, and we couldn't break contact because of 7 Platoon on the other side of the river. My gunner was identifying targets and taking them, as I was with my rifle. There was a stoppage on the chain gun, and I saw seven guys and two RPG teams move into a building, slightly to my rear right. I shouted down to my platoon sergeant, Sean Wardle, that he needed to take them down, because it was too close to use the 30mm. At that range, the shells would just keep on going and explode somewhere else, and we're not here for that. He opened the back door, stepped out and managed to put two or three of them down. But then another RPG came in - luckily, it landed short and exploded on the bank - and he had to get back in. It was pointless him being out there that exposed. Mind you, it's bloody bad enough being in the back of a Warrior in these situations, with rounds pinging off the back door. You feel very exposed and helpless.

The gunner got his chain gun cleared and started concentrating on taking targets down. 7 Platoon had started to extract slowly and we could see enemy reinforcements trying to cut them off. The fire intensified: some of them were just charging us, running towards the Warrior with their AKs blazing. You wonder what possesses them, but they've been brainwashed and a lot of them are given drugs and told it's some sort of invincibility potion. Unfortunately for them, it doesn't work.

Despite hundreds of incoming rounds and grenades, Harkess held the vital ground under prolonged pressure from the enemy. Eventually the Company safely extracted. "His action prevented the isolation of British soldiers, and denied the enemy the opportunity to close," says the citation. "He regained the initiative and almost certainly saved lives."

Eventually, Geordie and his lads broke clean, so we set about extracting ourselves. I started to move forward, picked up my other two vehicles and headed down the Yellow routes. As we came back round on to the main street, lorries had been parked to block us off. We just rammed through them - a Warrior weighs 25 tonnes, and it just dented the bar armour a bit.

We hit a small ambush but just diverted off down a little track we'd found, which ran alongside the river. That took us to Black 11 where we got ambushed again. It doesn't take long for them to set one of these up, they've all got weapons at home and they just get on their mobiles and say 'They're coming down your way.'

So we fought through that and then had to stop to change batteries in our ECM gear. We realised that we'd lost certain parts of the ECM in the various contacts, which meant Geordie had to come and take us back, so we were within his ECM bubble. It was only a couple of kilometres back to camp and before long we were back.

You check to make sure that all the blokes are alright, clean weapons, check ammo and see how much has been fired. Interviews then have to take place. Who fired at what, how many rounds were fired, how many enemy killed? It's a big demand, and it has to be done straight away, while it's fresh, to cover us in case of complaints.

I spent a bit of time chatting to my boys, making sure they were OK. A couple of my young guys were very nervy. They'd never been in a major contact before, they were only 18 or 19, and it's a lot to ask of them. I'd tell them, 'No matter what happens, no matter how bad it is, I'll always come and get you. I *will* come and find you.' And that was some comfort, I think.

We later got a message back from the JAM via some intel source, saying, 'We tried you, we tested you, you are strong, you didn't leave. You are better this time.' May 23 was their test. They wanted to see how we would respond. We knew from that point that the attacks would get heavier and heavier, and they did. And my lads of 9 Platoon always did me proud.

On June 11, 2006, C Company conducted a ~~major~~ search operation in Al Amarah.

We had been taking some heavy mortars and rockets - big barrages of thirty or forty plus, daily - so we launched a search operation to find them and take them out. Around the same time, a Lynx chopper had been shot down in Basra and men had been moved down there, so we were short of blokes. My platoon had been stripped - we were left with two dismounts per vehicle, so I'd been refilled in the back with the search team and the snipers.

We had target areas north and south: 7 Platoon was tasked north and 8 Platoon was tasked south. My tasking, 9 Platoon, was to drop off the snipers for target area north and the search teams for the south. My second tasking then was to satellite and deter. Meaning cover the searches to interdict and deter any insurgent attacks.

We started out in the early hours of the morning. 7 Platoon went off first and, as they started hitting Black Nine, prior to turning left to go down the Reds to their target area, they were contacted. Fast and furious, but they were coping OK. I had to go down that way, to drop the snipers and search team off for that location.

We broke down Black Nine, heading towards target area north. We were getting reports of enemy snipers and RPG teams up on the rooftops and, sure enough, once we got into the built up areas and got near to 7 Platoon, all the rooftops and alleyways just opened up on us, like it was bonfire night. I pushed my two lead vehicles forwards and started fighting the alleyways. I also got two of the lads up on top cover in the mortar hatches and they started engaging people to the rear and watching the alleyways after we'd gone by, making sure someone didn't step out of the shadows and hit us with RPGs from the back. Myself and the gunner dealt with the front. It was dark, still about 3am, but there was street lighting; we didn't take it out, because we were still moving, and we were wearing night vision, which gave us an edge.

We got out of the contact area and I reached Geordie, who was pulled over at a sort of crossroads, with alleyways either side. We had a quick face-to-face and he told me his turret system and comms were down. His platoon had pushed on and he was covering these alleyways for the rest of us coming through. So we continued, encountering one or two more contacts, till we reached the target area. Then we chucked the snipers out and set off down to target area south to drop off the search teams.

We made it OK, though there were reports coming through all the time, contact, contact, contact. We dropped off the search teams, about-turned and set off to carry out our second tasking. We got sidetracked by reports of a flat-bed truck which had been used to fire mortars somewhere around the prison, but we couldn't find it, so we carried on. And for a while, things were reasonably quiet - just the odd bit of small arms fire here and there.

Then a Warrior bogged, leaving it stuck and highly vulnerable. CSgt Harkess quickly secured a key junction, a pivotal position he held in the face of a series of determined attacks.

7 Platoon reported they had a vehicle immobilised in a ditch. There were massive open sewerage ditches running down the centre of the streets and the bank of one had crumbled as a Warrior had been turning, and it had slipped in. It was literally in the s*** - obviously a nice, big, static target - and we needed to get it out.

The position was very vulnerable. We could be attacked from either direction along the road in question, there were alleyways and junctions leading down to where we were and lots of overlooking buildings, including a large mosque. We knew the enemy wouldn't take long to find out what had happened and they had lots of cover from which to attack. We got the Warriors set up covering the position as best we could, with mine covering two approach roads that intersected with the one we were on.

The 7 Platoon dismounts had fanned out around the mosque, and they started taking fire. We could see figures flitting around in the shadows, and you'd see muzzle flashes; we located, identified and dealt with a dozen or so guys, I'd say. And then it really started.

The ensuing battle lasted six hours, and was the largest and most intense in Iraq since 2004. Over 200 Mahdi Army soldiers assaulted the British troops, using the narrow alleyways and roof tops as cover as they engaged with rocket-propelled grenades, heavy small arms fire, snipers, blast bombs and grenades.

It was absolutely knackering. Like a fool, one of the alleyways I'd chosen to cover was the main one they were feeding themselves down. Within about five minutes, I was in another 360 battle. It was constant. There was no let up, and I was firing all the way through.

I'd say my vehicle and crew took down 50 enemy in total, easily. There was me with my personal weapon, the gunner and two guys in the back with Minimi and UGL. We all went out with 240 rounds of 5.56, and the Minimis had 800, plus 10% spare in the back, and by the end of it all we were pretty much out. I had 54 rounds of 7.62 left out of 1600 for the chain gun, and I'd used up all my 9mm pistol ammunition as well. They were coming at us in waves - at one stage, you could see bodies stacked up where we'd been killing them. Guys would jump up on rooftops above you, only five to ten metres away, and start firing down at you, so you'd put them down... then some more would be there a minute later.

RPGs were a constant threat. We later worked out that between 50 and 60 were fired at our vehicle alone. I remember there were four RPG teams in particular, a team is a firer and a spotter with an AK. They were in a hardened area, a building off one of the alleyways about 600 metres away. We'd put SA80 in there, Minimi, waxed them a few times with the chain gun and UGLd it a couple of times, and we just couldn't get through to them. So I said bollocks to it and we let them have the 30mm cannon. We put half a dozen shells down and that was that. One of my guys in the back had a bit of a problem with that for a long time afterwards - he'd been looking down his sights and he saw the enemy basically exploding, which can't have been very pleasant.

As it wore on, local people started coming out and we had crowds of non-combatants getting in the way and preventing us returning fire. But we had a Lynx chopper from 847 Naval Air Squadron overhead, flown by a US Marines Major on exchange, William Chesarek. He kept flying past, low and slow, drawing fire and luring the gunmen out, as well as acting as a Forward Air Controller for the fast air and letting us know what he could see. He did me a lot of favours... 'You have men appearing now on the rooftop in front,' and so on and so forth. Bearing in mind this was only a few weeks after a Lynx from the same squadron had been lost in Basra, it was pretty brave. Well, very brave. He was up there for five hours in total, and was nearly RPGd on at least one occasion. He won the Distinguished Flying Cross for that, the first American to do so since WW2, and it was well deserved.

Harkess's citation says: "Communications were poor, and Harkess exposed himself to enemy fire in order to dismount, speak to, direct and reassure his men. He led repeated counter-attacks, (and) opened up so that he could maintain situational awareness and simultaneously engage roof-top gunmen with his rifle. Strike marks peppered his vehicle, yet he refused to take cover. His example inspired others and demonstrated immense courage in the face of the enemy."

It was noisy, obviously, and at various times I had to get out of the turret and stand on the vehicle to shout to the lads on the ground, to either reassure them or direct them. In my citation for the medal, it talks about this being evidence of 'immense courage' but to be honest anyone would have done exactly the same, and they probably have at various times. It wasn't as though we even had time to be nervous or scared. It was so intense... man left, bang, RPG right, bang, AK to the front, bang... you just don't have time to think about anything else. And I've always said to the boys, and I believe this, when your number's up, it's up. It's going to get you one day, here, or somewhere else in 50 years' time. So don't worry about being shot, don't worry about being blown up, worrying might make you hesitate and that *will* get you killed. Plus you could get through all this, go home and then get run over by a bus. Are you never going to cross the road again?

The ammo situation got concerning, particularly as there were people getting to within a few metres of us. But if we'd been completely out we'd have just run them over - they were never going to get to us. And it started to calm down at the sort of six-hour point. I think we'd taken so many of them out that they were being neutralised. We'd been identifying them too quick and eventually it must have sapped their will. We recovered the bogged Warrior and got ourselves extracted back to base.

It was only then, when the adrenaline started to leave you, that you sat back and thought, *Crikey.* There were strike marks and blast marks all the way around the Warrior, loads of them within inches of where I'd been standing: you felt that someone, somewhere, had been looking out for us. The men I fought with that day are some of the bravest I've had the pleasure to know. The two guys who'd been in the back were completely in shock, so I gave them 24 to 48 hours off. They were quiet and completely withdrawn. Doing that much fighting, for that length of time, seeing first hand what a 30mm shell can do to a human body, taking grenades, RPG, heavy machinegun, taking small arms coming in all the time, while you stand there exposed... they were only young lads, and it had taken it out of them.

We were worried about Ian Page, too. *(CSgt Page had been shot in the face during the fighting, and his life had been saved by the female medic Pte Michelle Norris MC, who had climbed out onto his Warrior, under fire, to administer emergency first aid.)* At that stage, nobody knew whether he was dead or alive, and he's a good mate. But, luckily, thanks to the work of the young girl medic, he was OK. He was casevac-d back to Shaiba log base and then back to the UK. It'll take a long time for him to fully recover from that day, but he's a fighter and he's on the mend. Good luck, Ian.

On July 30, 2006, CSgt Harkess was deployed as part of a night-time Company operation protecting a re-supply convoy; as the convoy approached the town of Al Maymunah the enemy sprang a complex ambush on him and his men.

It was a major convoy, 200 vehicles or more, bringing in food and water to Abu Naji and also beginning the process of extracting our kit out as we prepared to hand the base over to the Iraqis. They'd ambushed the last convoy which had come in, this one was an even bigger target and we needed to go out to escort it in. The rest of the company would be on that, and my task was to leave the camp late, re-clear where the lads had already moved through to make sure that nothing had been placed in behind them, and then hide up in the desert outside Al Maymunah, about 10 kilometres south of Al Amarah. Once the convoy was past, I would shoot down into the town and picket the area to look for any enemy.

Al Maymunah had been a little sleepy town, nothing ever happened in it. But as they went through, the guys got bottled, bricked and blast bombed and the OC was injured. So we knew the convoy was going to get hit. I got a call on the net to get back into town and get the dismounts out to start covering the alleyways, and so forth. 8 Platoon were coming in from the southern side to do the same.

We were about 300 metres from them when we heard them get contacted. They were out of sight, round the road and among some housing, but you could hear a weight of fire suddenly start up and then the reports began coming over the net.

I had a new platoon sergeant, a gleaming lad called Ferguson. I said, 'Get the boys out, dominate the alleyways while we hold the main road with the three Warriors.'

We pushed one vehicle back, sent one forward and I stayed in the centre. The dismounts got out and as soon as they'd closed the back doors we started taking sniper fire. There were three of them set up, and unfortunately we had stopped in their main killing area - wide and flat, with waste ground either side of the road, well-lit up with street lights, because it was pitch black at the time.

"It was a complex ambush," says the citation, "and with fire coming from all directions the situation was confused. Despite enemy fire, CSgt Harkess accepted that he could not withdraw his Platoon without exposing the convoy to greater danger, and he repeatedly exposed himself in order to find the enemy in the face of machine gun and sniper fire. He was steadfast under extreme pressure and he led his Platoon with real bravery; his gallantry and leadership were critical in ensuring that the convoy got through."

We couldn't move, because the convoy was coming through. 8 Platoon were still in their own contact down the bottom of town. We had no comms with camp, which was 15 to 20 kilometres away, so we had no air support. The other platoon couldn't come to help us, because they were covering and protecting the convoy, which was now three or four kilometres away. I'm wondering what to do, and the fire starts intensifying - now there's a bit of AK and light machine gun fire too. All the dismounts were pinned down fully. Fergie couldn't move - every time he tried to he would get rounds landing very near to him. The thing is, ordinary small arms aren't that much of a drama. I know that sounds ridiculous, and obviously if an AK round hits you it can take your arm off, but I've seen literally thousands of rounds fired at us over the course of my time in Iraq and it tends to be point and spray stuff, hardly anyone actually does get hit. Snipers are a different matter. You could hear the shots, single, aimed, probably using a Dragunov, a pretty accurate rifle loosely based on the AK. When they weren't trying to pick off the lads on the ground, they were having a go at us - a round would ping off the turret next to you and you'd hear the *crack!*

Once again, we're in a bloody 360 degree battle. Which I was getting tired of by now. At least the guys were used to it and they knew what to do, which was locate and kill. They were fighting their own little battles, up and down the alleyways, so I decided to concentrate on the snipers. I stood up in my turret, trying to draw a bit of fire, hoping to see the muzzle flash. Rifle up, managed to locate one, put the 30mm straight on to him and neutralised him. We located another three or four people on the rooftops who were firing down on to the boys, we waxed them a couple of times and no fire seemed to come from that location again. The gunner was clearing all the rooftops and balconies, using the 30mm or the chain gun, depending what was needed. The two guys on top cover in the back were fighting another battle to my rear left and rear right. My main concern was the other two snipers. I was taking quite a bit of heat from them, had a few come past my nose, so I wanted to find the bastards. But I couldn't see them. It's quite hard to find people, in contact and at night, but I just caught sight of one of them moving, like a bent-over run, on the parapet of a roof to my right. He was trying to get a better position on me, or on the guys on the ground. I turned the turret around and let him have the 30mm. The rooftops all have thick walls round them, they can be hard to get through with a rifle or even the 7.62, but the Rarden just goes straight through. I saw him blown over and crawl around on the roof, a bit disorientated, maybe looking for his weapon. Then I saw him come back up again. The gunner had already flicked the turret back and was engaging elsewhere, so I took the guy with my rifle.

I couldn't locate the third bloke for a while. He was somewhere over to my left but I wanted to get him, because I'd called Fergie on the net and told him to get his lads back inside, they were too exposed. And I didn't want them picked off as they got in. Most of the dismounts managed to get back to their vehicles, but my boys were completely pinned down in an alleyway to my side and in doorways. Every time they stepped out, they were getting fire coming down on them. Most of it was coming from rooftops opposite, so I said to Fergie, 'I'll put a load of 7.62 tracer up there to keep their heads down... as soon as you see that, move.'

But when he did, he had to dive for cover again - they were firing AK at him from a point almost directly above him. I told Fergie, 'I'm going to send three rounds of 30mm straight above your head... stick your fingers in your tabs, it's coming hard and fast.'

The 30mm did its job and they were able to extract out, with a small running battle till they reached the Warrior.

My main concern then was the last sniper. I started to move my vehicle back and forward, to draw him out, tease him with a target he couldn't resist. So we moved forward, moved back, moved forward, moved back... and, sure enough, he started firing. The gunner dealt with him and as he was doing that Fergie, down inside the back of the vehicle, started tapping me and telling me we were taking fire from the right. So I turned and dropped another one there with my rifle. I was out, so I popped down to change mag, and a guy with an AK just stood up right near us, out of nowhere. I was like, '*F***!* Where did he come from?' I dropped my rifle, pulled out my 9mm and basically emptied it into him.

Then we heard fast air arriving. They came over low, dropping loads of anti-missile flares which lit the area up. As that drifted down, the guys were able to identify groups of men moving on the rooftops and take them out. It was a free-for-all, and that really finished their plans off for the night, I think. Shortly after that, day broke - there's no dawn to speak of out there, one minute it's pitch black, then you get a quick, yellowy-pink sunrise, and then it's daylight and it starts to really warm up. And the fighting pretty much stopped, apart from one or two optimists with AKs rattling off half a mag here and there.

The convoy came through, having been held outside the town until it was safe, and we tagged on the end and were back in base half an hour later.

Once again, no-one killed, which felt like a miracle in some ways.

And again, check ammo, check the vehicles, clean the weapons and check on the lads, who were all feeling the after effects of a long and very dangerous contact, under sniper fire, at night, with rounds skipping off walls next to them. But they were a fantastic set of lads, some of the best men I've ever worked with, and they'd all coped brilliantly.

The citation says the three separate actions, were "each worthy in their own right of the highest recommendation for bravery in the face of the enemy." Jim Harkess himself is less sure.

It wasn't till much later I found out about the medal, and I'd have preferred a crate of Guinness, to be honest. I was upset that more of my blokes didn't get anything. I wrote quite a few of them up and I think they all earned my medal, not just me. Actually, if I could just say to them, to the men of C Company, you are the finest men that I've ever had the privilege to work with and fight with. There's no 'I' in 'team', be proud of what we've done and what you'll do again. To my lads, of shiny 9 Platoon, boys, you are the best. To my crew - Chappers, Reevie, Steve, Chris, Fergie, Stan, Richie, Butler - thank you for everything. To the boss, Lt Lyons, we always made a good team, good luck in the future. To M3-3 and M1-3, thank you for everything.

People ask me what it was like going to Buckingham Palace. Honestly? Crap. You go there, you get rushed in, you get split away from your family, they get stuck in a hall where they have to sit for two and a half hours, you eventually get called through, have your two or three minutes with the Queen, your medal's pinned on, then you're straight out, you get your medal taken off you and put in a box, you're pushed back round into the hall and then they rush you back outside. It's a bit like a fast food operation. Don't get me wrong, it was a proud moment, but more for my family, my mum and dad, than me. For me, I'd not joined the Army to win medals. I'd joined to do this sort of thing, to get out to places like Iraq and Afghanistan, and I was just doing my job.

Another thing people ask is how has it all changed me? Well, I basically don't give a f*** anymore. What can people throw at you? Your attitude does change. You can't experience what we have and not be changed. There's something wrong with you if it has no effect. Little things that might have wound you up before, now it's like, *So what?*

I enjoyed my tours, and I'm looking forward to going out to Afghanistan soon. I love being in the Army, basically. I love the camaraderie with the lads - during some of the major contacts, me and Geordie and others would be laughing and joking with each other... 'Your turn to get the coffees on,' or 'Am I coming to save your fat arse again?' Lots of banter, amid all the contact reports. Which I think helps keep the blokes calm.

To me, it's like being down the pit all over again. I just changed from an orange suit to a green one - the danger was there, with gas and collapses, and the *craic* with the lads, having a laugh and going out for beers, is the same. Although PWRR being a southern outfit, they're mainly shandy drinkers. Apart from that, it's one of the finest regiments there is. The guys are second to none.

Private Michelle Norris, MC
Royal Army Medical Corps

WHEN British forces first went into Iraq, Michelle Norris was a schoolgirl. Just three short years later, she was sitting in the back of a Warrior armoured vehicle at the centre of one of the biggest battles British troops fought in Iraq.

It was June 11, 2006, and she and her colleagues were engaged in a night-time search operation aimed at arresting key Mahdi Army figures and seizing their weapons and ammunition. It had erupted into full-on war fighting, with hundreds of enemy fighters surrounding the British troops.

A few hundred metres away, Jim Harkess was engaged in one of the actions which would see him awarded the CGC, and many other soldiers were fighting hard.

Pte Norris was just 19 years of age, and only recently out of basic training. During the heaviest of the fighting, CSgt Ian Page, the commander of her Warrior, was shot in the face and seriously injured.

Without hesitation, Norris dismounted and climbed onto the top of the vehicle to administer life-saving first aid, while under sniper fire and with heavy small arms fire and rocket-propelled grenade attacks continuing around her.

I joined the Army in November 2004, and went out to Iraq on TELIC 8 eighteen months later. I was 18 at the time, and I'd wanted to join the Army since I was really little. I'd always been a bit of a tomboy - I like playing rugby, and I follow the Worcester Warriors - but I'm not from a Forces background. One of my uncles did his national service and then stayed on for a few years with the Royal

Logistic Corps, that's it - but I remember watching all the war films and documentaries with my dad and I guess it sprang from there. I joined the cadets when I was 13, and I really enjoyed that so I joined up after college.

When I was in the cadets, I developed an interest in the medical side of things. Both my parents worked at the local hospital, and my brother was in the Red Cross and the St John Ambulance, and I found I really enjoyed learning first aid. I progressed to teaching it as I got older, and found it was something that I was quite good at.

When you put the two together, I suppose it was inevitable that I'd joined the Royal Army Medical Corps, though my initial plan had been to go into the Royal Artillery.

My job is combat medical technician, which means dealing with casualties anywhere from immediately after they get hit - on the front line, if you want to call it that - to bringing them back to hospital or dealing with them once they are actually in the hospital. On any given operation I could be out with the troops or back at the hospital; on TELIC 8, I was a company medic out on the ground all of the time, whereas on my next tour I'll be working in a hospital.

There were two medics, myself and a lance corporal, in our Warrior company - four Warriors in each platoon, three platoons to the Coy. We'd each travel out in different vehicles and the idea is that if someone gets shot we are on the scene to give whatever immediate treatment we can; the initial period, what we call the Golden Hour, is very important in surviving major trauma like gunshot wounds. As a medic, you might have to go to someone who has been injured and expose yourself where everyone else is taking cover. That is a scary thought, but we are trained to make sure the situation is as safe as possible before we move.

I went out to Iraq on April 12. I was with 1 Close Support, and in the January they had asked for volunteers to go out and I put my hand up. I thought, *This is why I joined the Army, it's an opportunity to see and do things I wouldn't have otherwise.* I had no idea what to expect. You see stuff on the telly, and you get your briefings and chat to guys who've already been out there, but I went out with a clear mind, determined to experience it for myself.

My first thoughts were how hot and dusty it was - a lot different from back home. And there was the cultural shock of seeing how other people live... the sounds of the praying from the mosques, the sights and smells. Very different.

On June 11, C Company 1 PWRR, to which Norris was attached, went out on a night-time search operation in Al Amarah. It turned into the largest and most intense battle in Iraq since 2004, a war-fighting engagement where the soldiers found themselves under very heavy, accurate and sustained attack from a well-organised Mahdi Army force of over 200.

We were going out to look for weapons caches after a series of recent attacks. I was obviously nervous before we went out; pretty much every time we went out we were shot at, and the anticipation of that isn't nice. But it wasn't as scary as it had been the first time; you just got more used to it, eventually. We were out all night and there were lots of contacts. Warriors were being shot at all over town, I could hear the reports coming in over the net and part of you is thinking, *When are we going to get hit?* You're reasonably safe sat in the back of the vehicle with the dismount troops, protected by all the armour, certainly against small arms fire, that's no problem at all; multiple RPG strikes or IEDs, that was what we were really concerned about.

We got through most of the operation without too many problems. But then, just as it was getting light-ish, it came over the net that we had to go to this particular place where there was a crowd gathering around another Warrior which had become bogged down in a ditch. So we set off, and as we got closer I started hearing things bouncing off the Warrior, little pings and dings. I thought it was just kids throwing stones, because that's what it sounded like, but then I heard the turret getting hit, and that was clearly rounds. The turret is where the gun is, and the gunner and the commander.

Ian Page had taken a round to the face.

I shouted up, 'Is everyone OK?'

There was no answer, but I could see movement - they had the hatches up, and there was some daylight coming in - so I thought nothing of it. I reached for a bottle of water, and the driver, Pte Nani Ratawake, shouted down to me that the vehicle commander, CSgt Ian Page, had been shot.

I got on really well with Pagey. He had his birthday while we were out there and I said, as a joke, 'Blimey... you're old enough to be my dad!'

He said, 'You cheeky so-and-so!' and ever since then we'd walk past each other and he'd say, 'How are you then, daughter?' and I'd say, 'I'm alright dad, how are you?' He was a nice man, very good to the younger soldiers and if I wanted to talk about anything I could always go and talk to Ian. You don't go to Iraq to make friends, you go to do a job, but sometimes it happens. You can't help it - I just got on really well with him. So when I heard he'd been hit I was really concerned.

In the back of a Warrior there's a cage around the turret mounting - the turret can traverse through 360 degrees and obviously you don't want the soldiers in the back falling into the mechanism, or the guys in the turret getting their legs caught in it... hence the cage. You should be able to open it to get into and out of the turret, but it was jammed. I tried for a moment or two, but it wouldn't open, so I shouted to Nani to stop. The only way I could get to Ian was to get out of the vehicle and up onto the top of it.

This was obviously an extremely dangerous action, and one which put her own life in immediate and serious risk. The area was full of people, many of them armed, and the sniper who had shot CSgt Page saw her emerge from the vehicle. As she clambered on top of it, he began trying to shoot her as well. Despite this, she continued to administer first aid through the commander's hatch, until the gunner pulled her into the turret for her own safety. In addition to the sniper fire, heavy small arms fire and rocket-propelled grenade attacks had continued around her, yet she deliberately ignored the danger to her own life in order to save CSgt Page.

I told the lads in the back to move out of the way to let me out. They opened the door for me, and I think one of them shouted to me, 'Be careful.' I jumped out. From that moment on, it's a bit of a blur. I ran round to the side of the Warrior and climbed up on to the top, using the bar armour as a ladder. I stood over the turret and looked down. Pagey looked up at me, and I could see this massive hole in his face. There was blood everywhere, he was in a lot of pain and you could see the fright in his eyes. He wasn't speaking, I don't think, but over the noise of the engine and the gunfire and the people I don't know if I'd have heard him anyway. I shouted down through the turret to get one of the lads to chuck my med bag up while I was having a closer look at him. He'd been standing up, with his head out of the turret and his rifle up, scanning his arcs for targets. A round had come in, hit the rifle, come through the other side and gone into his cheek. As it turned out, there was also an exit wound but I couldn't see that for all the blood and tissue. I had to assume it might still be lodged inside his head, so that was another complication. If it had lodged in the back of his throat, say, it might obstruct his airway; if it had deflected upwards, it could have led to a brain injury. I just didn't know.

I realised I wasn't going to be able to do anything up there on top of the vehicle, so I told the lad with my med bag to get back down inside. Up to that point, it was strange, like time had accelerated. I have no idea how long I was out there, but the OC said it was something like three or four minutes. If that's right, it's amazing - it didn't feel anything like that. But then things started slowing down again, and I started hearing rounds cracking off right by my head. I thought, *Maybe I'm getting shot at here?* One of them hit the radio mounting a few inches away from me, and pretty much at that moment one of the lads pulled me down into the turret.

I slid down in with Ian. There was a lot of blood and I needed to get him into the back with the rest of the lads so I could treat him properly. I was thinking out loud, and I said to myself, 'What do I do now?'

Pagey said, 'Traverse the turret.'

Those were his only words - the rest was just mumbling, really. He was in a lot of pain.

I got the gunner to traverse it, the dismounts inside pulled the cage open and dragged both of us down through the turret into the back.

I applied a first field dressing to try to staunch the blood, and then had a think. I couldn't give him morphine for the pain, it's not allowed with a head wound as it has effects on your breathing and blood pressure which can make things worse. So I checked his vital signs, his pulse, his respiration, his pupil dilation, the colour of his skin. It wasn't easy. There's not a lot of light in the back of a Warrior - it can be pitch black at times, but there was some light coming in from one of the mortar hatches, which are used for top cover, and there's a small red light inside which might have been on, too. He looked OK, considering, but he was my first real casualty so I had nothing to compare it with. I'd never seen a gunshot wound like that before. I was crouched over him, talking to him all the time, trying to make sure he didn't lose consciousness. As long as someone is awake, you can get feedback to your questions. *Where does it hurt?* They can point. *Is this helping?* They can nod. They can squeeze your finger once for yes, twice for no, even if they can't speak. He never lost consciousness, which was good. I felt that he needed fluids put into him, given the blood loss, so I told him that and he pulled away, which was a good, strong response. He'd understood me and knew he didn't fancy a line being put into him.

While all this was going on, the driver was heading as quick as possible to the nearest HLS so we could evacuate Ian and get him to hospital. I have no idea how long it took us to get there, but the helicopter would have been airborne almost immediately and it was actually coming in to land as we drove into the camp. We stopped and a medic from the Light Infantry ran over. I did a quick handover, told him what I'd done, and we got Ian onto a stretcher and onto the chopper and away.

Despite the fear and shock she must have felt, her citation says she "immediately and without hesitation then remounted the Warrior and returned to the battle" for the remainder of the action. "On return to camp, she and the gunner helped to clean the large amounts of blood and human tissue from the turret. Even on being told that someone else would do this psychologically difficult task, she insisted on continuing."

I went back to the Warrior. I sat in the back thinking, *What if I haven't done something I should have done? What if I could have done more? What if he dies?* I got myself quite worked up and worried, with all sorts of stuff going through my head. *What about his poor wife and parents?* I didn't have too long for that, because we needed to get straight back out onto the streets, continuing patrolling until the operation was officially over.

When you get back to camp, you have to strip down the wagons and get everything out. In our case, the vehicle was obviously full of blood. The sergeant major came over, pointed to a load of lads and said, 'You, you and you… go and clean that Warrior.'

I said, 'I'll come and give you a hand.'

The lads tried to stop me but I wanted to do it. I couldn't just sit around because at that stage I didn't know whether Pagey would survive and I knew I'd just break down if I had nothing to do. So we cleaned it out.

The doctor phoned me later on in the evening from the hospital and said Ian had come out of theatre, he was fine and was making good progress. He said, 'If it wasn't for you getting to him in the time that you did and doing what you did he would have died.' I just broke down and cried.

It was a bit embarrassing later on. In the cookhouse and places like that, people kept coming up to me and shaking my hand and saying, 'Well done.' Everyone loved Pagey, and they all kept saying what a good mate he was to them, and how long they'd known him. I was only doing my job.

I remember someone saying that because the operation had involved such a lot of fighting that it might be on the news, so I phoned my mum and said, 'Something happened today, mum. It might be on the telly, but I just wanted to tell you that I'm OK.'

I went on R&R for two weeks not long after. It was really weird being at home, when just a day before you've been in Iraq surrounded by a lot of people who would kill you if they got the chance. I just chilled out as much as I could, still thinking about the lads who I was working with, the people still out there, but trying to enjoy myself as much as I could. After Ian got shot, I realised for the first time how special and fragile life is, and how you can be there one day and gone the next, so I just spent as much time as possible with my family.

When I went back out, the story of what had happened came out in the papers. There was a lot of stuff written that wasn't true - like saying I got shot through my rucksack, which I didn't. I'd seen it on the internet and I phoned home and said, 'I think I'm in *The Sun*, mum.'

She said, 'Do you know how much hassle you've caused me?'

I said, 'Me? Why?'

She said, 'I've got news reporters knocking on my door and phoning me up and trying to talk to us.'

After the incident, I was a lot more nervous when I went out. Basically, I was scared of having another casualty to deal with and not saving a life or doing the right thing. Before this happened, I was basically an infantry soldier for seven months and I was always thinking, *I want to do my job*. And then that happened and I thought, *Actually, I don't want to do my job*! I mean, I love it, but if it's quiet it means that the lads out on the ground aren't getting injured or killed. He was actually the first and last casualty that I dealt with on the tour: most of my time was spent dealing with blokes who'd got insect bites and stuff like that. Thank goodness - if I never see another soldier with a gunshot wound I'll be very happy.

We got back to Germany and we had to queue up at the barracks to hand our body armour back in. I was standing in the line and I head someone say, 'Cheers, Pagey!'

He was the Company Quartermaster Sergeant who deals with all the stores and stuff, but I didn't know he was back and in the office. I walked in and he dropped his book and said, 'Private Norris!' and he walked over and gave me a big hug and a kiss and said, 'Thank you.'

I had tears in my eyes. It was all I could do to say, 'Thank God you're OK.'

As I say, I hadn't really thought about dying or death before that. There were times... I still think about it now. Do you remember the young girl who died not that long ago, Eleanor Dlugosz? She was in a Warrior, doing exactly the same job as me, and it was blown up. She was one of four who died, including another girl. Eleanor was a few weeks behind me in training, and I knew her. My friend phoned me up and told me that she had been killed, and everything just came rushing back again. It is hard. You do try and forget about it but there are certain moments when you can't just forget about it. You have to sit down and have a think, or have a cry, or talk to someone about it. The Army's like a family, especially in a small regiment, and something like that affects so many people.

But there has never been a moment when I've regretted joining up. It's a really good thing to get into. You can be skint at the end of the month, but you'll still have a roof over your head, three square meals a day and all your friends there to watch your back. And you're learning a trade. I think you grow up a lot quicker than you do in Civvie Street. You have to look out for yourself, get yourself up for work, wash and iron your kit, look after your money... stuff like that. You can't rely on mum and dad. I see some of my civilian friends back home, and they're still asking their parents for things... 'Can I have this, can I do that?' I feel so much more independent. Yes, there's danger. I'm going back out in December and while I won't be going back out on the ground again, there's still mortars and rockets, you can't do anything about them. But if it's going to hit you it will, and if it doesn't, it doesn't. It's just one of those things. That is what I signed on the dotted line for: to get sent anywhere in the world, any day. I'm looking forward to being back in Iraq.

I couldn't believe it when I was told I was getting a medal. After the contact had finished, my sergeant major said, 'You'll probably get a Mention in Dispatches for that.' I didn't even know what one of those was. I read up about MiDs and thought, *Well, that would be nice*, but it wasn't something I wanted or set out to get. Afterwards, when it came out that I was getting a Military Cross, I thought, *Bloody hell.* I was gobsmacked, and when the 2IC came up to me and said, 'Do you realise you are the first female ever to win that award?' I didn't know whether to laugh, cry... I didn't know what to do.

Of course, I'm very proud, but, honestly, anyone would have done what I did, and people did lots of far braver things and didn't get medals. Look at Pagey - he had exposed himself by standing up in his turret and letting them shoot at him. How brave is that?

She may not see it herself, but her citation is clear. "Her actions were extremely courageous," it says, "and certainly saved CSgt Page's life. Her total disregard for her own personal safety to save the life of a comrade showed incredible bravery, particularly for a soldier so young and inexperienced."

I was only allowed three guests at Buckingham Palace, so I took my mum, my dad and my older sister. It was hard to pick between my granddad, my brother or my sister. Because it was up steps, and my granddad has bad legs, it was between Peter and Tina. They put their names in a hat, and Tina's name came out, so she came down.

It was mad. We were waiting upstairs, and there was a screen where you could watch people being invested. I could see my family in the audience and the next minute I was walking through and was in the queue myself. And I was like, *Oh my God! That's the Queen!*

When my name was called, I walked forwards and curtsied and shook her hand and she was really nice.

She said, 'I am really proud to be giving you this. You must be proud of yourself.'

I said, 'Yes, ma'am.'

It wasn't as though she was just talking to anyone, she really seemed to care. She wanted to know where I was based and whether I was going back out to the Middle East, and when I said I was she wished me luck. And that was it. She shook my hand again and said goodbye.

It was great for my mum and dad. They say they're proud of me but I can't imagine how proud they are. There's only so much words can say.

Wing Commander 'Sammy' Sampson, DSO
Number 1 (Fighter) Squadron, RAF

ALONGSIDE Iraq, Britain's troops have been heavily involved in Afghanistan.

Sammy Sampson served on two tours of operational duty there between December 2004 and May 2006, flying 103 missions during "high tempo operations, in demanding climatic and environmental conditions," and in the face of "a significant and hostile level of enemy activity."

He was awarded the Distinguished Service Order for a combination of the way in which he motivated his pilots and ground crew and his own actions in combat.

"Through his inspirational and composed leadership, justifiable pride, impressive self discipline and unreserved application," says the citation, "Sampson instilled an outstanding level of drive, morale, mission focus and singular determination in each member of his unit."

I'm 40 years old, married with three children, from Plymouth, and I'm known as 'Sammy' to everyone, apart from my mother who insists on using my real name, Martin.

I'd wanted to be a pilot for almost as long as I can remember. My favourite cousin emigrated to Australia when I was three and we went to the airport to see them off, and it was the first time I had seen aeroplanes - from that point onwards, I was hooked. When I was in my teens, there was a series on TV about fighter pilots and that turned my mind towards the military side. I joined the Air Training Corps and, finally, the RAF. And it has been a dream job. So many of my friends from school are doing their jobs because they have to, whereas, for me, every day is as good as the first and I would not change a thing. To fly in the RAF is a massive privilege, and to be flying single seat aeroplanes, and the Harrier, which is such a unique aeroplane, is fantastic. If you'd told me when I was 16, when I walked through the door to the careers office, that I'd fly Jaguars over Iraq post Gulf War I, that I'd fly with the US Marine Corps, fly Harriers and be the boss of Number 1 squadron, I'd have said you were mad. I have been very lucky.

The terrain in Afghanistan is vast and, in places, extraordinarily difficult for the troops on the ground to travel across. Ten miles is not 30 minutes - it may be three days, particularly if it's through the mountains or during the winter months. You can't just get onto the limited roads and tracks and drive from A to B because the enemy will place IEDs on frequented routes, so a lot of the time our troops are travelling off road. The terrain is no impediment to an aeroplane, so fast jets were requested to provide close air support and recce in support of ground forces, and the UK decided to put Harriers into Afghanistan in 2004. Number 3 squadron went in first and handed over to Number 1 on 29th December 2004, which incidentally was my birthday. We held that commitment for a shade under five months, and we returned the following year for exactly the same period... post-Christmas to the end of May. In between times, the other two squadrons at Cottesmore, 3 and 4 Squadrons as it was then, rotated through at regular intervals.

We were based at Kandahar airfield, then home to 6,000 to 8,000 troops, most of them American. Back then, it was a rough old place. The roads around the base were just dirt and there was a lot of ex-Soviet equipment, trucks, missiles, guns, aeroplanes, helicopters, just lying around, trashed. Primarily, it was a garrison for the troops and a staging point used to fly supplies in and out, although there were some helicopters based there, too. Fast jets were a new thing to KAF and understandably when we arrived there wasn't very much of an appreciation of fast jet operations and their needs and requirements. It was a shocking winter, the country's worst for 50 or 60 years, very cold and very wet. We stepped off the transport aeroplane, after a 28 hour journey, and the whole of our engineering site was under 2ft of water. Without hesitation, the engineers immediately started dismantling and putting it back together. It took three or four months to get it right - they put up defensive walls and raised the ground by a couple of feet with hardcore and rocks, with the pilots who were on alert helping out and digging trenches and drainage ditches. We began by living in tents, there was no drainage, electricity or running water and regularly went for many weeks without hot water. So we had *some* appreciation of what the lads out on the ground were going through. Because of the harsh winter and snow, quite often the fuel trucks couldn't get in so at times we didn't fly regularly. We just held alert status, normally waiting a couple of hundred metres away from the jets, ready to scramble... ring the bell, run like hell, a throwback to the Battle of Britain procedures. Or if we sensed that something was likely to happen, we'd sit in the aeroplanes, with the engineers ready to go. On the signal to launch, you'd start the engine and taxi out in about five minutes.

For almost the first two years of operations in Kandahar, the Harrier was the only fast jet that could routinely take off and land there. The runway was of old Soviet construction, nothing had been done to it for years and it was taking a fair beating from heavy aeroplanes moving all the troops and supplies. As a result, it was breaking up. I remember one occasion where we'd just got some guys airborne, and just the force of the aircraft taking off had left a 40ft by 30ft hole in the runway, down to a depth of about six inches. It looked like a knocked-over jigsaw puzzle. We had every single person who was available, pilots, admin people, flying clothing people, the engineers, about 150 of them, all out on the runway, brushing it and picking up pieces of tarmac and concrete, trying to get it clear before the aircraft had to come back. One little lump of something, if missed, could completely trash an aeroplane, and that means one less to support the ground forces, which could mean somebody loses their life. The upshot was that, most of the time, there were only small portions of the runway which were available to us. But the Harrier only needs a small strip - it can operate from 1,500ft, where other jets may need 7,000ft or 8,000ft. The big transport planes were not affected - they have big, fat wheels and stand much higher off the ground so they're not as susceptible to potholes or bits of runway jumping up at them, whereas fast jets can be damaged, or potentially even lost, by debris. So we were absolutely paranoid about maintaining the capability of the aeroplanes.

Wng Cdr Sampson flew more than 100 missions over the two tours.

The Afghanistan environment is not like a traditional air campaign. We never went out to bomb bridges, roads or buildings; we didn't even have pre-planned targets 99.9% of the time. Our role was to go out and support the ground forces.

The missions were hugely varied and unpredictable. There might be a convoy going from Kandahar to a base a couple of hundred Ks away, so we would provide top cover for them throughout their journey... we'd fly just ahead of them, talking to the guys on the ground, spotting for them, because the terrain can be very undulating and, at ground level, you may only have 200 metres visibility. So we'd be on the net... 'There's some activity just ahead of you... there's a road block here... there's a group of people off to the side of the road there.' The hope is you give them that little bit of thinking time. Plus, of course, we would help out if they were ambushed. We'd fly in pairs, though one might run out of gas first and have to head back, because he was flying lower than the other, or had a different weapons fit - so we'd handle it singly for a while until we were relieved.

We might support troops who were sweeping through villages - we'd provide overwatch. They might be planning to travel through a particular unknown area - maybe somewhere up in the hills, 100 kilometres off and 10,000ft above sea level. We would fly over and use our recce pod to photograph it to give the guys on the ground a heads-up, to see what the environment is like and what's going on there.

Generally, we'd fly out of range of RPGs or hand-held surface to air missiles, at a reasonable height. But it varied. You might be at 35,000ft, you could then re-fuel at 25,000ft, and you might be down at 5,000ft shortly afterwards. We tailor our flying to what the guy on the ground needs. They might be feeling threatened... sometimes, the mere presence of a fast jet is enough to calm the situation. They might say, 'Can you make some noise over that village five kilometres ahead of us so they know we're coming in?' So you'd dive down, put full power on and zoom back up again. Or if they've had someone take pot shots at them, they might have us fly over as low as 100ft at 480knots, or 500mph. If we've not advertised our presence, by staying high, and then all of a sudden we come straight over the top of you, it's a real shock... quite often, the enemy would think twice about engaging the guys on the ground once they knew that our troops had this firepower to draw upon.

Our whole purpose was to support the troops and the Afghan government, with imagery, presence or weapons. And also to help people like the Afghan National Army and the Afghan National Police. The sheer scale of Afghanistan means that the soldiers can't be everywhere all the time. There may be a district governor who is very pro the Coalition, pro the government, and not sympathetic towards the Taliban or the other anti-Coalition factions, who is being pressurised by strangers coming in. For him to be able to call in fast jets, and have a presence day and night, sends a very powerful signal to the locals. For instance, one night we took a call four or five hours after our flight period had finished - we would fly for a 12-hour period, with obviously work before and after that to get the jets ready. HQ called to say a governor in a particular village was in difficulty and that the district police headquarters had been overrun. There were no Coalition troops anywhere around and he really needed some support. I was asked, 'Can you do anything?'

I was airborne within 30 minutes and overhead the village 15 minutes later, using night vision goggles to have a look. I flew over the top of them and just the presence of a jet calmed the situation down. The local leader can say, 'I made a call, at night, and the jet arrived...' It makes him look very powerful, and it certainly would make most people think twice about challenging the authorities.

The second tour was busier in terms of ordnance actually used.

About 5% to 8% of the time, we were expending weapons. I'd have been happier if it was 1%, or never, because we only ever used our weapons when all other avenues were exhausted and the guys on the ground were in trouble. You would rather measure your performance as, How many times did you arrive and your presence stopped shots being fired? It was always better to come back with your bombs and your rockets on, than come back without them. When you came back without them, it meant that your guys had been in a combat situation and there may have been casualties.

You have to remember that the Coalition forces are there at the request of the Afghan government, and the situation, particularly in the north, is fantastic compared to how it was. The schools, getting girls into education, the hospitals, the road building, the regeneration and rule of law and the ability of people to vote provincially and nationally - all of that is hugely impressive progress. And there is a lot of good work going on in the south, too. All the military can do, and for us we're only talking about six Harriers, all you can do is support the Afghan people and their government to create the right conditions so that they can move on. Dropping weapons is the absolute last resort and if you didn't have to do that then it would be great.

"Wng Cdr Sampson's Squadron doubled its sortie output, without compromise to standards, through his comprehensive leadership," says his citation. "Driving his people hard, but with a compassionate eye when required, he reduced the combat turn round time of his aircraft from sixty minutes to twenty and drove the unit to outperform by two hundred per cent the output expected of it; the additional missions generated stand the Squadron out as the most dynamic operational Close Air Support contributor of all the Coalition units within Afghanistan."

I was very lucky in the team of people I had on the squadron. They were an intelligent bunch, massively motivated, they knew what the job was and to be their boss was an absolute pleasure.

The difference for airmen in Afghanistan, compared to any other place, is that we were living in the war zone. We were being mortared and shelled - a Harrier was hit on one occasion - and we were eating with and talking to the guys who were going out and being engaged, and with the medics who were treating the casualties. We'd sit in the coffee shop, and chat to the various nations and forces that were going out on the ground... Americans, French, Australians, the whole lot. It made us feel really part of it, as opposed to flying over them miles up and landing back home at a base miles away in the rear. There were only about 200 Brits there, out of 8,000, so if the Harriers had been out and protected a convoy or dropped some weapons and saved some lives, people knew that was us. We regularly had people coming up if they heard a British voice, it could have been the young SAC, it could be the squadron commander, they would come over and say, 'That was awesome, thanks. We were in real trouble and it was a real comfort to have you guys there. It was a bit tense and we saw the jets and it was fantastic.'

Or they would make a point of coming into the Squadron ops room and saying, 'Can you tell me who X call sign was on X date at X time, because they helped us out in the Sangin Valley. If they hadn't pitched up, I wouldn't be here now.'

It's tremendously rewarding; the effect that has on a young aircraft mechanic, say, is huge because it really drives home that when he goes out to fix that aeroplane, he personally is helping to save lives, because he's meeting the people whose lives he's helping to save.

To re-emphasise that, we would get all the ground guys together and show them our weapons drops on video, talk them through exactly what happened, in intimate detail, so that they felt part of that, too. The more they know, the better they understand and can adapt and become better at what they do. They might think a little differently after you have described something to them, and they might say, 'We can change our procedure here, and that would make it a little easier or better.'

Time is life, and a minute can be crucial... that's what we could bring. Yes, we had massive firepower, but the most important thing is that we have speed of response. But there's no point in tearing off at 500mph if, when you come back, it takes an hour to dot the i's and cross the t's. So the engineers changed the rostering to brigade more people for the high tempo periods, they pre-positioned the bombs, we changed the procedures as to where we could store weapons so that they were right beside the aeroplane, so it was like a pit stop crew for a racing team. Yes, you have to adhere to safety issues, but there is a lot of pre-preparation you can do.

I recall one of the guys pointing out that the thing that took the most time was fuel, because the bowser drivers were civilians contracted by the Americans. And their procedure was that you could only phone up and order fuel when the aeroplane had landed and was ready to be refuelled. They would then send the first available guy and it might be 30 minutes before he arrived. Their procedures were based on transport aircraft, when it matters less - whereas for us, as I say, time was critical. The engineers tried to change them, and sometimes there is a bit of resistance to change, and the 'rules is rules' mentality. So they were smart, and invited some of the drivers down for a barbecue and a game of five-a-side and got friendly with them. And then they pointed out why we needed the fuel quicker... it wasn't that we were queue-jumping, or wanted to be first for first's sake, it's because, out there on the ground, soldiers are under fire and we can get back to them quicker if you refuel us quicker. So how about if the aircraft calls us when it's ten minutes away from landing, and you send someone then? And they saw our point and were happy to change.

The engineers changed our maintenance procedures, doing certain things at the same time or coming up with new procedures, rather than doing things the way we do them in peacetime, where it's - quite sensibly - slow, methodical, one thing at a time. We kept safety paramount, but if we could find a suitable way to do different tasks at the same time, why not? Even to the extent of them coming up with a scheme for where we parked the jets which reduced the time involved in launching them.

The number of times the guys didn't eat... it took 15 minutes to get to the mess hall and then the time to sit and eat, and they didn't want to leave their posts for that long, so they went and chatted up the guy who ran the mess hall and had them provide hot takeaways for us.

The *only* problem I had was making sure they weren't breaking themselves by being too keen. They worked so hard, 12 or 14 hours a day or more for up to 27 days straight, doing demanding, difficult work in often very bad conditions. The aeroplanes needed to be ready about three hours before flying, and when they got back there was more work to be done on them. Then there is scheduled maintenance, things that have to be checked every 50 hours flying, or 100 hours flying... those little jobs might take four or five hours, and that would need to be done in the dead of night since we flew during the day, mostly. And they had to work in low light... big floodlights would attract attention, so they would work with helmet torches, which made it harder and more wearing. Freezing cold, maybe mortars landing not far away, knowing that if they drop that little component inside the aircraft it's grounded. A lot of responsibility rested on the shoulders of the engineers.

The squadron engineers and the admineers did all of our guarding, so that was another task that was rotated through.

So the main concern I had was that it was a marathon, not a sprint. It was great to raise the bar to such a high level, but we needed to be able to find a way to keep ourselves going over such a long period of time. I had to keep them as fresh as possible. So I'd get people together quite regularly and say, 'Let's take a good, hard look at each other and make sure we are not asking too much of ourselves.'

There were lots of bugs, dysentery and stuff, around because it wasn't a clean environment... we had a couple of pilots and a lot of engineers who got stomach bugs and they were out for five days, maybe a week. So the other pilots and engineers picked up that tasking. I said, 'We're all going to have to dig a bit deeper, so all we can afford to do for the next seven days is fly, sleep and eat... don't go faffing about on the computer, don't go down playing video games in the R&R set-up, don't go down the gym. We're going to have to park all that and stick to the basics.'

I said to everybody, 'You have the power to look anyone in the eye, including me, and say, *'You can't fly'* if you don't think they are fit to fly.' It was the same for the engineers and, whilst it never came to that, the fact that everyone had that power was important to me.

I like people, I like being part of the service, the banter, knowing everybody's first name and using it... I like to know when Geordie has been wound up by Sharpers or Tanky over whatever. I don't need to be in their face all the time, because people need their space, but I liked to go and chat to the lads, and buy them a coffee, and I hope that they knew they could come to me at any time. To me, the job of youngest and most junior guy in the Squadron was as important as mine. And it wasn't just me, obviously. The senior NCOs and junior NCOs, the flight lieutenants and other officers, they were all fantastic. Everybody had their finger on the pulse. People who had issues at home which couldn't be dealt with from afar, we created reasons to swap them over with other people. We spent ten months out of 15 in Afghanistan; the troops would do six months, very hard ones, of course, and know they weren't likely to return for some time. When our guys went home, they knew they were coming back out soon - it was only seven months between our two five-month deployments. Guys would say, 'I don't want to go back early, I want to do the whole five months.' But we had to insist - partly, they needed the rest, partly we needed to expose others to the environment we were in. Their commitment was inspiring.

As well as being a leader who could get the best out of his personnel, Sampson is "also a fearless and courageous airborne warrior; a report from one of the 103 missions that he has flown illustrates this point. When scrambled to support troops under extremely heavy fire on 30th April 2006, Sampson engaged targets while under intense fire and at low level. His complete and inspirational command of Number 1 (Fighter) Squadron on operational duty in the face of a persistent and hostile enemy reflects his exceptional personal courage, outstanding flying skills, comprehensive understanding of the tactical environment, and his supreme leadership of men in the field."

It was getting towards the end of the day, an hour and a half before dusk. Two of our jets were airborne and were diverted to a troops-in-contact situation around nine minutes' flying time away.

The two jets had each dropped a bomb and it was clear this might develop further, beyond the point when they'd have to return to refuel. So I ran down to tell the engineers to get two more jets ready. Of course, they'd anticipated my call, and had already got two aeroplanes bombed up, gassed, and ready with the power plugged into them to warm up all the systems. I got one of our corporals to go and find me another pilot and Fin Monahan, the 2IC, my executive officer, met me down there. *(Sqn Ldr Monahan was awarded the DFC for his actions on a different sortie.)*

We jumped into the aeroplanes and started listening in on the radio. There was a real sense of urgency about the radio traffic, and fuel was running out, our guys were going to have to leave station. I wanted to get out to them before they left, so that they could tell us what had been going on and point positions out to us from an aerial perspective. I gave the signal to Fin to start the engines. You're not allowed to launch unless you're told to by HQ so we got on the net to them, told them we felt the need to go and they gave us the all clear.

As soon as we were airborne, we started talking to the guys who were on station. We arrived and circled above them as they pointed out where their bombs had landed, used the craters as reference points for the friendly positions and described the ground units, their vehicles and their composition.

They were Coalition forces with some Afghan Army; they'd been out on patrol, they'd become separated and were dispersed in three groups over a fair distance, say six or seven kilometres. One vehicle, with a JTAC forward air controller (Joint Terminal Air Controller, the same as a British TACP), was stuck on the eastern side of a wide river, with no obvious crossing back. The main convoy, perhaps a dozen vehicles strung out in a line, was on the western side. There was a second JTAC there. At another position, a little further off, was another vehicle or two.

It was very difficult for them to get back together and get the sufficient mass to move on. And they had come under heavy fire from numerous directions. They were low on ammunition, close to being surrounded, and it wasn't looking good.

The enemy were firing RPGs, heavy machine guns, mortars... it was difficult to tell how many of them there were from where we were.

There was a building on the western side of the river which was obviously being used as an ammunition store - they could see the enemy forces going in empty handed and coming out carrying stuff. The troops in the main convoy asked me to take that building out, so I put a 500lb bomb onto it which seemed to calm the situation.

As the other two aircraft left, low on fuel, the JTAC on the eastern side of the river came on the frequency. He sounded agitated, saying, 'I'm getting signals that people are preparing to attack us over here... I'm feeling pretty vulnerable.'

So I spoke to the guy on the western side and said, 'We're going to move six or seven kilometres over there to help out, are you happy with that?'

'Yep, we're happy.'

So we pressed over. Below us, I could see their vehicle, exposed and pinned down and now well under attack. I could see incoming RPG fire from three separate positions, I could see the explosions, and every time the JTAC tried to talk I could hear the blasts through his mic. It's a strange feeling, you're out of harm's way yourself but you can see blokes in, basically, a fight for their lives. He was returning fire with his .50 cal while trying to point out the enemy positions and talk me on to them. There were three teams of enemy forming quite a wide arc around him, so while he was engaging one, he was being engaged by the others. It was all very co-ordinated. He couldn't move, because to move he'd have had to stop returning fire, and he had no support from his guys on the other side of the river. They had no mortars or artillery - he was on his own and in a difficult position.

As luck would have it, Fin's radio had packed up, so he couldn't hear any of this, though he could still hear me. The guys wanted an airburst 1,000lb bomb dropping on one of the RPG positions, so I relayed the info to Fin who said he was happy to tip in. I called him in hot, the guy said, 'Yes, cleared hot and make it quick.'

There was real desperation in his voice, the fire was getting closer to him and he was in danger of being overrun.

Just as Fin began his dive, I had a feeling that I needed to follow him so that I could drop a bomb quickly if he missed or something else happened. And as he tipped in, he had a system failure on his aircraft and couldn't drop the bomb, so he pulled off and said, 'I'm off dry.'

The JTAC, seeing no ordnance, just started screaming, 'I need some weapons, I need some weapons now!'

So I just rolled in without formal clearance, just using the previous clearance, and hit the position myself with a 500lb bomb.

I came off. The guy called, 'Good hit!' and then he started taking fire from the other positions.

I asked if he was happy for me to talk Fin on to them, given that I could see where they were coming from. Without his radio, Fin was lacking situational awareness... he could see things going on down there, but there was a lot of it, and who was doing what to whom?

'Are you happy for me to clear in hot?'

He said, 'Yes, all targets, any weapons.'

Fin dropped a 1,000lb onto one of the positions and silenced it and, with the guy on the ground telling me he was running out of ammo and needed the last target dealt with, too, I talked him onto the final one, cleared him and he put a laser-guided bomb on to it. That ended all the attacks on the eastern side of the river, and cheered up the guys over there quite a bit.

As the laser-guided bomb went in, I looked west and all I could see were rockets, tracer, machine gun fire, explosions... just the biggest firefight I have ever seen in my life. So I just legged it over to the other position at full power.

They weren't even calling for us at that point - they couldn't talk because they were too engaged.

The friendlies hadn't moved far, they were just trying to regroup. So when I looked down on the ground, I could still see every vehicle that I'd seen before. It was dusk, and I could see all the outgoing fire and tracer from those vehicles, and the incoming, which was helpful.

I switched to that JTAC's frequency and tried to call him, but all I could hear was machine gun fire and mortars going off, and lots of shouting. He just about managed to say, 'Wait out!'

I circled around and flipped back to the other JTAC and said, 'Are you OK over there now?'

He said, 'Yes, great job.'

I said, 'OK, I am now supporting the other guys, who are in the middle of a massive firefight.'

He said he would lend support wherever he could, and I flipped back to Fin's frequency and told him to come in above me and find me. Then I switched back to the western side's JTAC frequency. I was orbiting; I could see maybe 50 enemy scattered in an area a few hundred metres from the friendlies. There was a string of bushes and trees following the line of the river, some isolated buildings and a track running up to some compounds. They were mostly in there; I could see a mass of criss-crossing fire coming from the tree line and the buildings - mainly muzzle flashes and RPG burns. The RPG initiates with a large flame which then dies off, but I could see where they were being fired from, and I could also see the hits, which were getting closer and closer to our troops and the Afghan soldiers. There was also a mortar being fired about 400 metres from where I thought the main body of enemy was.

OK, so I have a rough idea where many of the enemy are. I went round again and spoke to the JTAC. I said, 'I can see where they're firing from, but I'm going to need a talk onto them.'

I needed to make sure there were no unknown friendlies located closer to the Taliban positions.

He said, 'Stand by... I can't... there's too much fire coming in.'

I went back and said, 'I'll put one rocket down, and you tell me where to go from there.'

He acknowledged me, so I came around and rolled in. I had a pod of single rockets, and a pod of ripple - which fires 19 all in one go - and as I came down I put my PIPA sight on the centre mass of where I thought things were and called in 'Hot!'

The JTAC said, 'Cleared all weapons.'

As I was about to fire the rocket, I saw four or five RPGs all fired from the same spot around 150 metres away from where I was aiming. I deselected single shot, selected the ripple pod, moved my PIPA on to that and put a pod of 19 rockets into it. I was pretty much at minimum range, and flying at very low level at that point - maybe 2,500ft to 3,000ft - and they travel very quickly, about Mach 5, so I saw them hit. They're a very effective weapon - designed for anti-ship warfare, actually. There's a steel rod inside each one, and that, the incendiary and the casing... the blast and the shrapnel have a devastating effect. I pulled off, reselected the single, and as I banked I could see the spread of the weapons - they don't all hit the same spot, they give you a pattern, and I'd covered a good area.

The JTAC said, 'Great hits, great hits!' All the fire stopped coming from that area immediately.

A mortar then went off from about 400 metres away. Again, I saw the initiation, a wide flash at the base, and then I saw the impact. Not far away from the friendlies. The firers were nestled in the left-hand corner of a compound. I kept my eyes on their position and extended off a little bit to give myself a better run-in. As I did so, I called the JTAC. 'I can see that mortar, I've got six rockets left, that's all I have, I'm ready to engage it if you want me to.' I explained where the mortar was and he said, 'Standby.'

I went into the overhead, and they hit the position with their .50 cals.

And then it calmed down a bit and the bloke could talk to me.

I said, 'I've got another 20 minutes I can be in the area.' I'd sent Fin home because he was out of weapons and told him to get gassed and bombed-up and be ready to come back again. On the way, he would be able to talk, calmly and clearly, to the guys in the alert jets sitting on the runway waiting to replace us if need be... tell them, as we'd been told, what the composition and disposition was of both the friendly and enemy forces.

The guys on the ground managed to regroup. The JTAC said, 'Look, we need some air cover for our transit back to our base because we're very low on ammunition, now.'

It was around 50 minutes back for them, in trucks and Humvees. I said, 'My guys are nine minutes' flying away, I will leave at X time, based on my fuel level, and I'll get them to launch at that time minus ten minutes. We'll have one minute in the air together, so they can familiarise themselves, and then I am going to hand you over. You can have air cover for the whole of the journey back.'

Then I called back and said, 'Launch them.' They came up airborne, I handed over and the convoy made it back with no casualties.

My citation says I engaged the targets while under intense fire, but to be honest I wasn't aware of anything coming close to me and I certainly didn't get hit. I think from the ground it probably looked more dangerous than it was. I did have RPGs fired at me a few times over the two tours, but they never hit - they're very slow and short range. That's not to say there is no threat - Afghanistan is one great big ammo dump, lots of the old Soviet equipment is still there, so you'd have to anticipate that they could have access to hand held SAMs, you couldn't discount it. And you could, I suppose, be brought down by small arms fire if you were flying low, by a lucky shot. So you can't recklessly launch yourself and fly around at low level everywhere. It is not so much about your own safety as, if you lose an aeroplane, that's one less aeroplane for supporting the ground troops and, ultimately, that's what we're there to do. Because, relatively speaking, we are much safer than the guys on the ground. Mainly because we can dynamically traverse altitude and distance in very short periods of the time. You can go from 3,000ft to 15,000ft in a matter of seconds.

I occasionally get asked how I feel bombing people. My overriding feeling is that it isn't about taking life, it's about saving life. When you're overhead, and seeing the urgency of a particular situation, and the difficulty that our troops are in, you are potentially saving their lives when you release your weapons. We are not there as the aggressors, we're there at the invitation of the government; if people decide to take on the Afghan and Coalition troops, then our job is to help deter or stop them. Unfortunately, sometimes the enemy just want to stand and fight.

It's obviously a great honour to receive an award. But it's not a medal for me, it's a medal for every single one of the guys who was out there with me. You can't fly jets without someone putting gas in them and everyone, *everyone*, played a massive part in two successful tours.

There are people in the RAF, Navy and Army who are doing things which are extraordinary, pretty much every day. That's the stuff that the taxpayer and the public should be really proud of - just the fact that there are 19 and 20-year-olds who are willing to go out to places like that with no days off, and work, if necessary, 20 hours a day to get the job done. Doing their job professionally and keeping their mates going alongside them. Looking after their mates as well as looking after the reputation of their unit, their Service, the armed forces and, ultimately, their country. There is so much done out there on operations that is really good, and if anyone can get a glimpse of that then I think it will be quite a humbling experience for the general public. It makes you incredibly proud, when you see the things our people do, day to day, in conditions that most people really couldn't appreciate... if the general public can just see a little bit of that then I think that it would be a really positive thing.

Flight Lieutenant Matthew Carter, MC Royal Air Force Regiment

AS Sammy Sampson's story shows, air power can be the difference between life and death for troops on the ground in Afghanistan.

It is, of course, vital that the bombs, shells or missiles delivered by the aircraft hit their intended targets; flying several thousand feet up, at high speed and with British troops and Taliban attackers often separated by a matter of metres, the potential for tragic errors is clear. To minimise the risk, specialists are used on the ground to speak to the pilots and 'talk them on' to enemy positions.

Matt Carter was one of those specialists - the Tactical Air Control Party (TACP) officer with 3 Para Battle Group HQ.

This is a dangerous trade; necessarily, the TACP will be near the front of the fighting at all times.

Carter was involved in a number of major contacts, directing "close and accurate fires immediately, without prompting and with devastating results." His citation adds that, "without regard for his personal safety, he was determined to join the forward line of troops, and gallantly and repeatedly exposed himself, during all contacts with the enemy, to a very high risk of being killed."

Among the many actions he was involved in, the citation picks out two.

In the first, Carter found himself metres from the Taliban, with himself and his colleagues in grave danger.

I'm 33, and originally from Worthing, West Sussex, but I now live in Bury St Edmonds in Suffolk with my wife, Ali, and our twin boys, Jack and Harry.

I have no military background or family, other than my brother-in-law who was a captain in the Royal Marines. As a young lad, I'd chat to him about forces life and it sounded appealing. I was a sporty type, so I decided I'd join the RAF, with the intention of becoming a PT instructor. While I was thumbing through the leaflets in the recruiting office I came across one about the RAF Regiment, liked the sound of what they did and decided to go for that instead. That was nine years ago, and I've never looked back.

When I left for Afghanistan, Ali had not long had the twins. They were three months old and Jack, the elder of the two by one minute, had just been diagnosed with two holes in his heart; he was going into heart failure, and needed an operation, so it was a massive wrench to leave them all, absolutely horrible. The hope was that the op would be carried out during my R&R period, and I was obviously worried that the two might not coincide and that he would end up needing the surgery sooner. As it was, he didn't have it until I got back, thankfully, and he's now fine and catching up with his bigger brother. It gives you some idea of what the families of servicemen and women put themselves through; it was really difficult for Ali, and I always say she's the one who deserves a medal, not me.

I was nervous about going to Afghanistan, as I guess most people are. I'd never been in contact before, and the most dangerous thing I'd done with the forces to that point was skydiving or parachuting - nothing on operations. The only Middle Eastern place I'd been to before was Kuwait, where I just got a nice tan.

A TACP's job is fairly complex. If you imagine a 3D battlefield, there are friendly and enemy positions on the ground and then numerous air assets in and around the area, at various heights and over various points. The TACP ensures that the air assets don't come into conflict with each other, or with friendly mortar or artillery fire, and that they don't fire on friendly forces or civilians. I might be getting fast jets to drop bombs on enemy positions, or to fly low for effect. Other times, I might be talking an AC130 Spectre or some Apache attack helicopters on to targets. There could be six or seven different friendly positions, and you are talking to these guys, responding to their requests for assistance, plus talking to the air assets, or to Chinooks coming in to drop off men or ammunition, or to evacuate casualties... you are under fire, in the middle of the battle, so it's quite challenging. In a place like Afghanistan, where the terrain provides a lot of cover, a lot of the houses and compounds look very similar and there is a civilian population living in the area, you have to be extremely careful.

We deployed to Camp Bastion, which was only just being built, so we were the first conventional British troops into the Helmand region. Bastion was an outpost miles out in a flat, barren desert. There was nothing there except sand. Pretty inhospitable. No people nearby. But no enemy, either, unless they came looking for us. At that time, it was pretty small - it took about 20 minutes to run around the perimeter - but it grew hugely in the six months that we were there, with many more units coming in. We had some time acclimatising and training before our first patrolling actions a month or so into theatre, when we started seeing the real Afghanistan, of the sandy-coloured compounds, green valleys and poppy fields.

My first patrol was an overnighter with A Company of 3 Para down near Gereshk. We tabbed out into the sticks about four kilometres, and we started having teething troubles with our radios. They weren't working, so we all had to go to ground in a poppy field and hide there while we tried to sort the problem out. It couldn't be sorted, so at around 8am the decision was taken to tab back in to base.

It was early May: the heat hadn't been too bad during the night, but it was murder even that early in the morning... 30 to 35°C, and I'm carrying 90lb-worth of kit. That was an eye-opener to the sort of conditions we were going to be facing. That day, we mounted a big security operation to cover the CO, as he was going to meet the Gereshk Chief of Police for the first time. So I got myself up on top of the police station, controlling a couple of top cover Harriers while the CO was talking to the chief. All very quiet, sitting there in the sun, with the jets circling overhead, the lads patrolling down below and no enemy at all. And I thought most of my job would be like that... providing top cover, rather than dropping lots of bombs. That was generally the story from Iraq and, although I'd never been there, that's where our latest operational experience was from.

As we left Gereshk, we got ambushed. Nothing massive, probably two or three blokes with AKs just spraying a magazine each in our direction, but it was my first contact, the first time I'd been shot at, and I'll never forget it. I was terrified. There were a lot of rounds fired, and the closest to me hit a wagon that was 20 metres away, so I was in no immediate danger, but my heart was racing... you don't know what's coming... is there going to be a big ambush? Are they in those buildings? Behind that wall? Have they got IEDs planted?

I just dived for my radio, because I knew I needed to talk to the Harriers to try and get support in straight away. We had no idea where the shooters were, so we couldn't react to it and go forward and neither could we use the Harriers to bomb them. So we had to withdraw out of the town and we did it under the cover of a Harrier coming in at 100ft.

It was a real shame, because as we patrolled through Gereshk town there were young children coming up and kissing my hand, and most of the local people genuinely seemed happy that we were there. I thought, *Wow, they really want our help and we can do a lot of good here*. And, no doubt about it, that was our full intention, and we really tried to do as much good as we could. We did things like going to the hospital and plumbing-in washing machines... stuff that made an immediate difference to people's lives. The trouble was that the Taliban did have supporters, usually very small factions, but they had power over the local community. So sons and fathers, who actually just wanted a quiet life, would go and fight for the Taliban, because if they didn't they would be shot. And we couldn't plumb in washing machines while under fire, so the first thing we had to do was deal with the Taliban. And once the Taliban saw what we were trying to do, they realised that if we helped the local community then it would massively favour us, so they started coming in and making it harder for us to do things like that. It was very difficult.

On June 4, 2006, Flt Lt Carter was attached to Patrols Platoon and deployed on Operation Mutay. Intelligence reports had identified a Taliban compound outside the town of Naw Zad and the plan was for Carter and his colleagues to cordon it off, break in and search for weapons or Taliban fighters. They came under heavy contact three times, during which Carter was targeted with small arms and RPGs at very close range. "Without regard for his personal safety," says the citation, "he exposed himself to significant risk, forcing his way forward into the front of the heavy firefight to direct precisely attack helicopter cannon fire against a determined enemy, a mere 30 metres in front of friendly forces."

It was a Taliban area and there was intelligence from the Afghan National Police, via the Gurkhas who speak a very similar language, that a large weapons cache was being stored in a compound on the outskirts. The plan was for Patrols Platoon, Paras in WMIK Land

Rovers, to set up a cordon to the south, the Gurkhas would cordon the north and a Chinook would bring A Company in to conduct the searches. We drove up the day before, about 70 kilometres from Bastion, stayed in Naw Zad District Centre and then headed out in the morning to form this cordon. My signaller and I were in the back of an open Pinzgauer; the signaller's job is to protect us with his rifle, because I can't fire and concentrate on my job, plus listen in on the Battle Group Net and help me know how the wider battle is going while I talk to the aircraft.

Our cordon was supposed to be set up on the fringes of Naw Zad, in a semi-rural location. As we arrived, we came around a corner and took immediate and heavy incoming RPGs and small arms from four or five guys in a building some 50 metres away. It was totally unexpected. 3 Para tried to put rounds back down, but unfortunately some of the ammunition wasn't to the best standards - it's in the public domain that we had these problems, and they have now been rectified - and their guns jammed, so we then had to withdraw as quick as possible. I have no idea, to this day, how no one was hit - it can only have been because we never really stopped moving. I could see the rounds hitting the walls behind us, and an RPG came in and hit a tree above my vehicle, showered us with branches and twigs, and detonated in an airburst on the other side of a wall, so that was a close call. I scrambled to get on the net and get hold of the Apaches and at that moment the Gurkhas were also ambushed. They were about a kilometre to the north of us, and they had a Forward Air Controller with them who was also trying to get on to the Apaches. It became very confusing... lots of different people dropping call signs at the same time... I suppose we didn't expect that everyone would be in contact simultaneously, and it was a good lesson. The next operation we did we changed our procedures and it worked perfectly well from then on in.

I managed to get on to an Apache. The Taliban who'd first opened up on us moved off, planning to come round and outflank us after we pulled up maybe 300 metres further down the road, where there was a wall to give us a bit of cover. I talked the helicopter on to where they were, he saw them and he destroyed them with a burst of 30mm cannon. Really loud, really devastating, and we knew that had solved the problem.

That was the first time that a British Apache had been used on operations, and knowing that they were up there, and that I was having an effect on the battle, was a brilliant feeling. Otherwise, you're just some bloke cowering in the back of a Pinzgauer while other people are fighting around you. Their deaths never troubled me at all - they were trying to kill us. My job was to save *our* lives. If they didn't want that to happen, they should have stayed at home and not fired on us in the first place.

After dealing with them, we started out again. There was a brief lull and then we drove into another, longer ambush. We were on a narrow track, and for around 300 metres or so, at every compound we passed, people would start firing at us. AK, more rocket-propelled grenades... luckily, this bunch were not that good with their weapons. The RPG is not all that accurate at the best of times, but they were missing at ranges of as little as 50 metres; you'd hear the *whoosh*, and the next thing you know something has gone straight over the top of you like a very big, very quick firework. And thank God they were missing... if one hit and detonated, it would destroy a Pinzgauer, no problem. Just a blind impact would do an awful lot of damage. But I thought the small arms fire was more frightening, because it was more accurate and because of the sheer amount of it flying around.

You never get used to being shot at, but you get more comfortable. You accept that not every bullet is going to hit you, but it's still terrifying. I remember the last Op I did, we went into Sangin, getting the Marines in to replace us, and there were high crops around us, well over head height. We were patrolling through these, and we could have been ambushed at absolutely any minute. And you're thinking, *This is spookily like a Vietnam war film, and I know what happens next!*

It was almost as though the whole village, in this particular area, was infested with Taliban. There were little groups of men off to our left, scurrying to and from cover, firing rounds at us and then moving, and clearly trying to out-manoeuvre us. You could hear small arms fire coming in from all sorts of angles and we had a couple of grenades thrown on to the road in front of us - I saw them come over walls and bounce in front of us, and you just hope that the driver stops in time so they don't go off underneath the wagon. My signaller is returning fire at targets and I'm trying to keep a clear picture in my mind of what's going on and where everyone is.

Mark Swann, the captain in charge of the Patrols Platoon, was trying to organise his troops, but it was a hell of a difficult job for him. Vehicles would stop for a few seconds so that the Paras could jump out and engage a given group of enemy in a particular walled compound... they'd deal with them, we'd move on again and the same would happen a few metres down the road. They did extremely well, took a lot of people out, and eventually we got out of that second ambush area and halted at a slightly sheltered location with a bit of cover. From there we had a period of respite while Capt Swann formulated a plan, and we still were trying to put in our cordon when A Company arrived and came straight into contact of their own. So now the plan needed revising, because we had to put the cordon in and also, if we could, get to A Coy and aid them. And then we came under another heavy contact, this time from a number of men in and around a tree line and a farmhouse.

We had a reasonable defensive position, with vehicles in cover in order to provide a bit of depth, but we were not able to make much progress. If the enemy are using cover well, popping up and down from behind thick walls and moving around in trees, it's extremely hard to deal with them. We got to within a few metres of the house, but then we were effectively stuck in two groups behind two walls separated by a gap of 50 metres or so. Every minute this continues gives them chance to call for reinforcements, to get round behind us... we had no idea how many we were fighting but it felt like this whole suburb of Naw Zad and we didn't want to get surrounded. It became clear that we needed some air support to deal with the Taliban in the trees and this house, but I needed to get closer because the distance from the Paras to the Taliban was danger close and I had to be absolutely spot on with my instructions to the Apache pilots. So I had to run across the open space and through fire coming from the tree line to establish exactly where the Paras were so that I didn't talk any of the Apache fire on to them.

Running across the gap was terrifying. The Paras had been doing it, pushing blokes forward, and I'd watched them go with the rounds kicking up the dust around their feet. I knew I'd have to go, too. There was a Para sergeant who tried to stop me, but I had to say to him, 'If I don't go you'll get no air support.' So he waved me on. I don't know how quickly I'd normally cover 50 metres in, but I reckon Linford Christie would have been hard-pushed to keep up. The adrenaline is pumping, you're so focused on what you have to do... the only way we were going to get out of this was if I called fire down, and that was a much greater factor than the fear.

Immediately I set out, the Taliban started shooting at me, but I made it across safely and slumped down behind the wall. Absolutely gasping for breath. As soon as I could, I had a look over at the house just across the way; a lot of the guys next to me were firing into it and there were a lot of rounds coming back from the people in the building. I could obviously see it easily, but the Apache pilots... they're a lot further away, the building looks pretty much the same as all the others in the area, they can see people running around, but it's absolutely vital, literally life and death, that they identify the enemy position and not ours. And when the gap is only a matter of metres it's obviously danger close - too close for missiles, with the danger of fratricide, and close even for the 30mm cannon... when you think that the shells are coming in from several thousand feet up, you can see why. Plus the helicopter has to be in exactly the right position to fire, we don't want him firing above our heads into the building, so I needed both to mark the building for him and also describe our position, so that he fires from a point parallel to us. Part of the skill of Forward Air Controlling skill lies in telling the pilot where he can come in from, and they are obviously very good at that as well.

I told Mark Swann I needed to mark the building, so the guy next to me, a Para called Bash, picked up a Light Anti-tank Weapon.

I got on the net and told the Apache that we were going to mark the building with a LAW.

The pilot came back and said, 'Confirm... with a LAW?'

I confirmed it, Bash fired the missile and a second or two later, the pilot came back, 'Yep, I've got the building.'

I said, 'From that building, look X metres south, you'll see a wall and a load of Paras stuck behind it.'

'Roger.'

And then this hail of fire rained down into the enemy building and killed or injured all of the Taliban fighters inside and silenced their guns. It felt as though the whole world around us was erupting... I remember thinking, *I wouldn't want to be on the receiving end of that.* It's a fantastic bit of kit.

That allowed us to withdraw, though we still took quite a lot of fire from the trees as we did so; unfortunately, we couldn't call fire in on those Taliban as we weren't sure where A Coy were and couldn't risk engaging them. Another part of my job is to manage the airspace for the company Battlegroup op, not just call in fires. So as we withdraw, I'm also talking to the other FACs who are in contact and teeing assets up for them. For example, Sean Fry, a Corporal of Horse attached to 3 Para as a FAC, called an A10 in to strafe an enemy location and he could do that because I had told him where our friendly troops were and because I'd talked the aircraft on to where he was.

I could then turn my thoughts towards helping A Coy. I controlled a B1B over the top of their location at about 5,000ft so the enemy there now know, *Right, they've got a bomber capable of doing a lot of damage over the top of us.* It's a demonstration... cut contact now, or we'll drop a load of bombs on you. That sort of thing worked early in the tour - one time in Gereshk, in our first contact, we brought a Harrier in very low - but they got used to it and it had less effect as the weeks wore on.

Carter had placed his own life in serious jeopardy to aid his comrades. The citation says: "Attack Helicopters had not been fired by UK forces to this proximity before; he was therefore also in great danger from the friendly helicopter fires themselves. But this risk was essential given the ferocious weight of the fire incoming from the Taliban. His direction of these fires proved critical and, once this enemy location was destroyed, he remained with the most forward troops and took part in the immediate compound clearance with the lead dismounted elements of Patrols Platoon. Carter repeatedly exposed himself to a significant chance of being killed and made a decisive contribution to allowing the Patrols Platoon to regain the initiative."

Once it was all over, we sent a small patrol back into the building we had hit, to clear it, and I went as part of that to advise air cover. We found lots of blood and some flip-flops and other bits and pieces, and a number of blood trails where the dead or injured had been removed. The Taliban are amazingly quick at taking away their bodies.

A Coy went in and were able to carry out the search, with the Paras and Patrols Platoon drawing a lot of the enemy away, and it was a success, they did pick up a major cache of weapons. The whole thing, three big contacts, was spread over six hours. To this day, I don't know how anyone wasn't hurt on our side. Bash, the Para with the LAW, did get shot in the chest with a tracer round... it went off and started glowing in his CBA, but he was basically OK. We confirmed 21 Taliban killed in our battle, and we were only one of three elements.

On 14 July Carter participated in Operation Augustus, a deliberate Battle Group operation to capture or kill a high value Taliban leader near Sangin.

There was a key Taliban figure in a compound to the north of Sangin.

The plan was for us to go in at night, land as close as we could, 100 metres away, use the element of surprise and stop the guy escaping.

There were three CH47 helicopters involved and, unfortunately, they heard us coming, so we landed in a hot HLS.

It would never have been a straightforward landing... at night, 40 blokes on each chopper, with gear and ammo. Heavy loads. And lots of ditches and bumps in the ground, not a nice, flat field. Under fire, obviously, it was massively harder and it was very intense for the pilots. They did, and are still doing, a consistently brilliant job out in Afghanistan - returning time and time again to hot areas, flying into firefights, taking an awful lot of punishment... very brave people doing an outstanding job.

On this occasion, the first thing we knew about the enemy fire was when the door and tail gunners started going for it as we came in to land. Obviously returning fire. Very scary. You're in an airborne petrol tank, there is a lot of very effective tracer fire from a heavy machine gun flying around, plus RPGs whizzing by, and there's nothing you can do. You're at the mercy of the guys with the machine guns and RPGs, and the pilots. Fortunately, no-one in my aircraft was shot, but there were people in the other helicopters who were. I believe two of the Paras were hit, one got a nasty shoulder wound and had to be forced to stay on the helicopter because he *still* wanted to get off and join the fight. They're mad, those lads... absolutely bonkers.

Our landing was very heavy. The idea is, as you land on you immediately run off the ramp. We had Afghan National Army with us, they weren't used to the environment, were probably a bit panicky and weren't holding on properly, so when we landed they all fell over in the back. So it took a long time for us to get off. My signaller and I were the last two to get off, with the Battery Commander's ACK, the NCO equivalent of a Forward Observation Officer, and a Mortar Platoon colour sergeant ahead of us. I think there must have been a bit of a misunderstanding between the pilot and the loadmaster, because as the ACK and the sergeant stepped out the pilot took off. So the two guys just fell off the ramp in mid-step; one broke his leg and the other broke his hand.

As the helicopter rose ever higher, and with tracer and small arms fire all around, Carter and his signaller leapt off the aircraft into the darkness below, ignoring the obvious risks to their lives.

You couldn't see the ground. We looked at each other and thought the same thing. *We've got a big part to play in this battle... and can you imagine the ribbing we'll get if we stay on the Chinook?* We've got to go. So we just jumped out. We were probably about 15ft off the ground at that point, so we just had to hope we didn't hit anything hard when we landed. As we went, the chopper sort of took our feet from under us, so we ended up doing mid-air somersaults and landing sort of on our backs. Luckily, the earth below had recently been ploughed, which meant it was broken up and softer than it would have been otherwise. I was carrying a 90lb Bergen, almost half my own weight again, and I'd hate to have landed on a load of rocks. But it's a good job we went when we did. The helicopter was moving quickly and if we'd hesitated for another second or two we would have been another 10 or 20ft up and well away from the rest of the guys, which would have been very dangerous for a number of obvious reasons.

Once we were on the ground, it took a moment or so to reorientate ourselves. And there was just total confusion. Rounds and RPGs were coming in from several directions and we were all spread out and in cover in a number of ditches. Their fire was pretty ineffective, but we couldn't return effective fire of our own because we couldn't be sure our own guys weren't in the way, with lads all sprawled out and keeping their heads down, and being hard to identify. There was lots of shouting, people trying to link up with whoever they were supposed to be with, tracer fire screaming overhead, a lot of noise from weapons.

We hadn't been exactly sure which compound our man was in, it was one of three or four. But I could see a big line of green tracer following the departing Chinooks and that identified the enemy for me. We had an AC130 Spectre above us. This is a fabulous bit of kit, a Hercules fitted with a 105mm artillery gun and 40mm and 25mm cannons. I talked to the AC130... he had great night vision, he could see our positions, he could see the enemy positions, and I was able to talk him on to the heavy machine gun and other locations.

Carter calmly and effectively controlled the Spectre Gunship's heavy fires, which were landing very close to his own position, and destroyed the Taliban position that was only metres away. Once this position had been defeated, the initiative was regained. This "significant and gallant contribution" proved to be decisive by allowing the remaining aircraft to land the rest of the Battle Group to successfully complete the mission.

I think I fired sixteen 105 rounds and a load of 40mm grenades at different targets all around us, and that won us the firefight, allowing a second lot of Chinooks to land on. We then went on to carry out the operation to search the compounds; the guy unfortunately had managed to make his escape, but he was tracked from there by other means and later killed.

Back home, I think... during Op Augustus there was a guy there filming for a documentary, and some of his soundtrack was apparently broadcast on the radio in the UK. So the first Ali, my wife, knew about what was going on was when she heard my voice calling in the AC130, with the sound of all this gunfire in the background. So she was desperately worried, and didn't really have a clue. But then, generally speaking, I don't think people back home have the first idea of the intensity of the fight over there. And I think that was the hardest thing when I came back, to understand that people were just living their everyday lives. And to fit back into normal life, without the intensity of life over there, and people not informed, unaffected, quite naturally and totally understandably... it took me a while to adjust. Lots of our friends had been killed or injured but the papers... well, you'd read about the deaths, yes, but not the serious injuries, the horrendous burns. We don't even see much of it ourselves; guys are casevac-d back to hospital and then whisked back to Birmingham, where they get very good treatment. But it's not in the papers and I think people would argue that's a shame... Simon Weston-type scenarios are reasonably common, you see things you wish you'd never seen, and yet people don't seem all that bothered.

Carter's citation says that "his ruthlessly efficient prosecution of air-delivered fires, in the closest of proximity to a determined enemy, single out this brave and courageous officer for very high public recognition."

A while after we returned my Wing Commander said, 'You've got to go to London with your wife for a drink with the Chief of the Defence Staff.'

Bit weird, I thought, but then he said a few people who'd been out in Afghanistan had been chosen to meet him. We went down to a hotel, and I met Mark Hammond and Hugo Farmer, both of whom I knew from Afghanistan, and I started thinking, *Something strange is going on, here.* Then they sat us all down and read out all the citations - it was the first I knew that I was getting an award - and Ali heard the full story. She was a bit shocked. She kept saying, 'You did what?' She was gobsmacked, actually.

Personally, I was a bit embarrassed. I do consider that I was just doing my job. I mean, what choice did I have? I know lots of people who have done brave things, and medals are a bit of a lottery... they're only awarded to people who are lucky enough to be written up. Your 3 Para Tom, whose mate has just been shot, but he still goes out the next day and patrols round the streets of Sangin, knowing that the chances are very high that he will be in contact again... that's horrendous. So brave. An 18-year-old lad who's seen his mate shot the day before. Yet he might receive no award, and for that reason, I felt a bit embarrassed. Of course, it was also a huge, huge honour. I believe it was the first Military Cross for 50 years awarded to someone serving with the RAF Regiment, so I obviously felt proud. It's lovely to have things you've done recognised, and great for the Regiment too.

It's a cliché, but I couldn't have done any of what I did without my signallers. SAC 'Sausage' Lucas was my sig on the Chinook incident... he's just left the forces to become a tree surgeon. And SAC 'Rusty' Whitehouse was my sig for the majority of the time. Rusty was firing back at the Taliban constantly, enabling me to call in the fire, so any praise I get is for them, too.

Most of all, the person who deserves a medal, to me, is Ali. Like all the wives and families, she had to get on with life on her own for months, not knowing where I was or what I was doing, and in her case she had baby twins, one of whom was actually quite poorly. It's a shame that sort of contribution can't be officially recognised because without the support from back home we could do nothing.

Lieutenant Hugo Farmer, CGC
The Parachute Regiment

IN an attempt to push the Taliban back, British troops set up bases in District Centres - government office compounds - in a number of towns in Helmand. One of these was Sangin, a settlement in the north east of the region, below the strategically vital Kajaki Dam. Situated in the middle of the country's opium fields, and home to around 15,000, it is a typically Afghan collection of dusty, pale yellow, stone-and-mud buildings and narrow, winding alleys.

Hugo Farmer, a young Lt with 3 Para, led his men in to the Sangin DC for what was intended to be a whistle-stop visit to extract a wounded local leader. 3 Para ended up spending weeks there, and lost a number of men in the process, including one of their best, Cpl Bryan Budd VC.

They were rocketed and mortared in the DC and ambushed every time they left to go on patrol; Sangin became a byword for savage fighting, danger and death.

Lt Farmer commanded 1 Platoon A Company in some of the most intensive engagements of the tour; he "consistently demonstrated outstanding leadership and gallantry," says his citation, and regularly "led assaults on enemy positions."

He won his CGC for several actions, including that on the day Cpl Budd won his posthumous Victoria Cross.

I'm 27, and I joined the Army in January 2004. I have no Army background, other than that my grandfathers fought in WW1 and WW2, as most people's did, and I had no desire to join up. I went to university in Bristol and, to be honest, my main focus then was just to earn as much money as possible. I was very mercenary. In my penultimate year I did an internship with a bank, got an offer to start training as an investment banker, and took it. I had the usual six month honeymoon period, where you go through that learning gradient and begin to understand what the job will entail for the next few years. And I realised that I didn't find it very enjoyable. It was dull, sitting in an office for twelve hours a day, at the least, often doing 'busy work', work for work's sake that achieved nothing. I hated it. After 18 months, I changed team, thinking I might have another honeymoon period and find my niche. But I didn't, and in fact it just got worse.

I remember thinking to myself one day, *I need to do something else.*

I had a look on the internet and found myself thinking about the Army, and decided to apply to the Parachute Regiment. I actually quit my job before I made the application. Fortunately they sponsored me, and I went to Sandhurst in January 2004. I managed to get into the regiment in December 2004, did my Special-to-Arms training, the Platoon Commander's battle course, then P Company and then my jumps course.

And then I went straight out to Iraq, on August 1, 2005. I was very lucky. Some of my friends in different regiments in the Army have yet to go away or command a troop or platoon. Within 12 months, I was a full lieutenant *(Farmer is now a captain).* Iraq was a nice introduction to how to command a platoon on operations, patrolling the Iranian border, out in the middle of nowhere on long range patrols for a week or so at a time.

I came back in November 2005, had two weeks off, and then went straight into pre-deployment training for Afghanistan. We flew out on April 17, 2006.

A Company was in Sangin three times. Some of our guys spent nine weeks there, give or take, which is not an inconsiderable achievement because it was a pretty grim place at times.

We were based in the district centre, the local government HQ, which was a group of buildings in a compound about 120 metres by 120 metres square.

Defensively, it was poor. The main building was a large, one-storey house with thick, robust walls and stairs going up to the flat roof. About 20 metres away was a two-storey building which was home to the FSG (Fire Support Group), because it offered better arcs and views over the town. There was a canal, brought off the Helmand river, going across the top of the camp, and there was a third building on the other side of that. Finally, there was a little wooded area, a pomegranate orchard; the Afghans are very into their gardens and agriculture - when we were out patrolling we'd see row upon row of tomatoes and limes and oranges.

The canal acted as a natural barrier on one side, and there was a two or three metre wall on the other but that wasn't particularly secure - there were gaps you could squeeze through, until we filled them in. To the west was open ground down to the Helmand River and the wide river valley, with hills in the distance. To the north were woods pushing out towards higher ground two or three kilometres away. To the south and east was Sangin town, and the main road, Route 611, from Gereshk in the south all the way up the Sangin Valley to the Kajaki Dam at the other end. The road was about 700 metres from the centre point of the camp, and between it and us were lots and lots of buildings, with narrow, winding alleyways and trees which allowed the Taliban to get very close with good cover.

The first time we went there was in mid June. It was supposed to be a quick, in-and-out sort of thing to go and pick up a relative of the local governor who'd been injured in a firefight with the Taliban. Although we'd never been there before, we knew Sangin was a hotbed of trouble and a real danger area - people talked about the place almost in awe throughout our training. Still, we were hoping we could get in, pick up this guy and get straight back to Camp Bastion.

It didn't work out that way.

We got in without a shot being fired, which surprised us massively, and secured the area. The man was driven down to us. He was in quite a state - I think he'd been shot through the stomach. It was around then that I realised we wouldn't be leaving quite as quickly: I was on the net to my Major doing sitreps, and it became clear that it wasn't just us who were shocked that we got in there so easily. HQ were pleasantly surprised, and suggested we stayed in Sangin, now we were there, using it as a base from which to operate.

We'd packed and gone out expecting three or four hours on the ground, and we ended up staying there for just over three weeks that time. Initially, re-supply wasn't a problem because, for all the talk earlier, it wasn't a terribly hostile environment. We'd secure the HLS, they'd bring the rations in and it was fine. We had good freedom of movement around the camp and we were doing the good old hearts and minds stuff in the streets outside. The local people were interested in what we were doing. It was quite funny, some of them thought we were Russians... 'The Russians are still here!', that sort of thing. It was all good, though we weren't complacent. We worked to build up the defences in the compound, patrolled into the town, set up meetings with the elders about how we could improve their lot. Trying to show them we were the people to side with, rather than the Taliban. Basically starting, in all the right ways, the counter-insurgency battle that we had been trained for. And they were receptive.

Then, a week or so in, it all changed. There was an operation going on a couple of kilometres away to the south one morning, and it developed into a big firefight. You could see and hear it for some time; I remember there were two A10 Tank Busters in support, and they were like a pair of angry hornets over the enemy positions for a good two hours. Eventually, it stopped and we went out on patrol, but, instantly, the mood of the locals had changed. They were annoyed, irritated: the operation seemed to have knocked out part of the power grid and I think there'd been disruption to water. They were coming up to us and saying, effectively, 'You talk a good game, but what are you doing? You're blowing up our facilities.'

All we could say to them was, 'It's not us. Rest assured, we're here to help.'

But they started to get hostile and a day or two later the camp first came under attack; from then on, we were under constant threat. It started with people attacking the base with small arms and RPGs. Then it escalated to 107mm Chinese Rockets. These are big artillery shells - fortunately, they didn't have the gun to fire them, but they would rest them in the earth, aim them roughly and use fuses to ignite them. Only three hit, and two were blinds, they didn't go off. The other did, and it was devastating. It went through the top of the FSG building, where we had our machine guns, anti-tank systems and surveillance systems, and killed three people - an interpreter and two soldiers from the Royal Signals, Cpl Peter Thorpe and LCpl Jabron Hashmi, who were attached to us - LCpl Hashmi was the first Muslim British soldier to die in the conflict. At the time, we were under the impression that they had some kind of super weapon, maybe a recoilless rifle... first time it's used, direct hit, three dead. But we later dug a shell up in a garden when we were digging defences and managed to work out that it wasn't as much of a threat as we'd thought.

Most of the locals started moving out of Sangin and it really became just us and the Taliban. There was a buffer zone, a 500 metre radius around the camp, where no-one lived any more. Later on, when we went out patrolling, it became a no man's land... we would always be engaged in that 500 metres. There were only two entrances and exits so they didn't have much to cover. The initial 200 to 300 metres was safe, because we were covered by the FSG, but as soon as we'd get out of sight it would all kick off.

Initially, I wasn't impressed with the Taliban. It was all spray and pray stuff at the camp, and it wasn't until much later on that we were regularly being taken on on the ground, but by the end of it they were impressive. They were digging trench systems, their marksmanship was very good, with initial bursts of machine gun fire from 80 metres consistently going into blokes' chest plates. Body armour saved a number of people's lives; it wasn't until I got back from Afghanistan, and put all my kit together, that I noticed all the bits of shrapnel and stuff in the plate of my own body armour. By the end, the only thing that really separated us was our discipline. They were fighting a very effective, light-scale insurgency. Our blokes were far more disciplined and professional, but we noticed a vast improvement in them towards the end.

In early July my platoon was ambushed on patrol, resulting in the death of Pte Damien Jackson, a young and very popular rifleman from the North East. Usually, our patrol skills were so good that we could consistently outwit the enemy and upset whatever plans they may have had, but on that day our luck ran out. As we were securing an HLS for a re-supply, the enemy initiated a well-planned ambush and Damien was hit in the stomach. He was 19 years old and his 20th birthday was only four days away. His death brought into focus the harsh reality of what we were doing.

Around that time, A Company was replaced in Sangin by B Company for two or three weeks, while we went back to Camp Bastion for some respite.

July 27 was the day we went back in. B Company's methods had been slightly different to ours. They'd done less patrolling, and consequently had hardly been in contact, though obviously they had their reasons and were doing a very good job in their own way.

A Company went back in with a new company commander, Maj Jamie Loden. He wanted to do a familiarisation patrol, so we pushed down into the town, set up some VCPs and started engaging the locals in conversation, getting ourselves seen on the ground. People were a bit shifty and grumpy, but it wasn't as hostile as before; I got the impression that the locals just didn't want to be seen to be having much to do with us in case the Taliban were watching, which they probably were. We did that for half an hour, and headed back to camp. When we got back to the buffer zone, it went totally quiet. No car engines or horns, no kids playing, there was no one even walking... a major combat indicator.

We were on the corner of the open air market. No-one around at all, just us. Then one of my lead scouts, a guy called Pte Pete McKinley, shouted that he had seen a number of men scurrying across the roof of the pharmacy with long-barrelled weapons. Probably 100 metres away. We'd obviously come across an ambush that was in the process of being set. We got into cover, and I briefed Cpl Bryan Budd, the commander of the lead section, about how we were going to take the enemy on. We always wanted to take the battle to the enemy, and make sure they came off second best.

I sent the first section forward and went with them with my radio operator, while Maj Loden stayed back, at the very front of the second section, so he could see what was going on. As we were approaching, McKinley saw the guys a second time and engaged them. And all hell broke loose. Within the first five or ten seconds, Pte 'Eddie' Edwards was hit in the thigh. I didn't know how badly, initially. He was lying on the ground, unable to move, with the Taliban trying to finish him off. Rounds landing very nearby. Bryan Budd led an assault on the enemy positions, which included a breeze block-built public toilet in the middle of the road, and succeeded in driving them off, while a Fijian soldier called Pte Balivanalu dragged Edwards into cover and started doing immediate first aid on him.

I brought up another section from behind me to use with 1 Section and we fire-manoeuvred and engaged the enemy as they retreated. It wasn't clear at the time how many we were hitting or killing, though later on we got reports that there were two dead and five injured.

I got back to have a look at Edwards. Hs injury was pretty much the worst that I saw out there. He had been hit in the femur with a 7.62 and either the bullet had shrapnelled on the bone, or, more likely, the bone itself had shrapnelled as a result of the bullet going through. The whole of the inside of his leg had been split and was just folded open, like big slabs of meat. Balivanalu had put a tourniquet on him and we tried to suggest to Edwards that he didn't look at the wound, but he already had.

Our casevac plan worked well, and we got him packed off back to base in a Household Cavalry Scimitar; he was there within about 12 minutes of being hit, being seen by the RMO. Initially, I thought he'd lose his leg, and I later found out that the doc, Phil Docherty, thought he would die of bleeding, but in the end he lived and he also kept his leg. There's muscle wastage and scarring, but he's undergoing physio now and there's no reason why he shouldn't make a full recovery. He is still in 3 Para.

It was only when he'd gone, and I was checking that everyone else was OK, that Pete McKinley said that he'd been hit, too.

I said, 'What do you mean?'

He said, 'I think I've been hit in the back.'

We had a look, and there was a slit in the top of his back where he'd taken some RPG shrapnel. A load of it had gone through his webbing and cut the straps; he was very lucky not to have been more seriously injured.

He was quite happy with that, he was walking wounded and still able to function, and when we got back to base he was put on a chopper with Edwards and taken back to Bastion. A few days later he returned, all smiles and patched up. He was bored and wanted to come back.

Over the next few days, I don't remember a specific incident but we were attacked a lot. We didn't take any casualties, we didn't score any decisive victories. We patrolled and came under lots of fire.

On July 30, Farmer's platoon was attacked by Taliban with multiple RPGs and small arms fire. He ordered the Platoon to respond with suppressive fire and then personally led an assault onto the enemy position. Not expecting such a tenacious and rapid response, the Taliban abandoned their position and fled. Farmer's prompt action regained the initiative.

Every now and again, you would come face-to-face with the opposition but the conditions were not right to engage. For example, one of my sections was moving through an alleyway, with buildings on either side, and they saw six or seven Taliban walking across them, right to left, completely unaware. They were armed with RPGs and rifles, legitimate targets... but the section commander, Cpl Huw Hanson, didn't feel that he could engage them properly because, with the section unable to manoeuvre themselves into a good position, he couldn't bring every weapon to bear. You might have the front two guys shooting, but there are six or seven of them and if they get into cover quickly and start returning fire then you're in a lot of trouble. And comms were poor, with all the buildings, we didn't have eyes on Huw's section to be able to support... so he let them go. A very sensible decision by a young section commander showing wisdom beyond his years. Having commanders of that quality, thinking guys, was another reason why we were able to perform to the standard that we did.

In fact, with 1 Platoon I had an absolute wish list of corporals. For 1 Section, I had a guy called Prig, Cpl Quintin Poll, I'm not sure he likes people knowing his first name. He left to go to Catterick as an instructor and was replaced by Cpl Bryan Budd. Those two are probably the best section commanders I've ever seen, and certainly the best I've ever worked with. In 2 Section, I had Charlie Curnow - very solid, very sound, someone you could really rely on. Not very old but a good head on his shoulders. In 3 Section, I had Huw Hanson later on in the tour. Cpl Waddington was another man of the highest quality, as were all my corporals, and as a platoon commander, when you have those guys and a sergeant as good as Sgt Dan Jarvie, life is very easy.

The frequency of attacks on the base was high, to the point where the counter-insurgency campaign needed rethinking. It was all we could do to defend ourselves and prevent the Taliban from having total freedom of movement in Sangin. The danger that brings is that, as they get closer, they develop better firing positions, better ambush positions and it's only a matter of time before they start to bear fruit. By that point, every time we went out it was an advance to contact. It was not a question of *if* we would meet them, it was a question of where and when, and ensuring that when it happened we used the ground and our superior training to defeat them.

I don't think anyone relished the idea of going out on to the ground. Originally, yes, because it's exciting and new, but when you see people getting injured and killed, you start questioning. But the blokes had an ability to suppress their fear and concentrate on the job. Admitting to fear is not a sign of weakness; conversely, being able to admit to it and carry on regardless is a sign of strength.

On August 17, we were going to move down south, just over a kilometre from the camp. We were platoon strength, with a mortar fire controller and some interpreters. We went out under cover of darkness and laid up until first light, when we moved into an area called the Gardens. I suppose if you weren't dressed up as an infantryman advancing to contact, the Gardens would be quite pretty. There were fields of maize up to 8ft high, making observation very difficult, and others of various kinds of vegetables, with trees everywhere and irrigation channels feeding the crops. I'm a great fan of the English countryside, and this was verdant and lush and very interesting. There was lots of cover from view, and some cover from fire in the ditches and mud-walled buildings which were dotted around. These walls were very robust, solid, compacted mud, akin to concrete, and over a metre thick at the base in many cases; they would easily stop bullets from a rifle and it would take you a while to cut through one with a GPMG. In fact, it would take a little while to go through one with a .50 cal gun. We found we had to use a significant amount of plastic explosive on our mousehole charges to get through them, and only really had guaranteed success with bar mines, which are used to blow up tanks. Which gives you some idea.

Because of our rules of engagement, the Taliban could escape at any time by putting down their weapons and walking out of a given situation unarmed. But they had to store them. The plan was to look for weapons caches: we believed they were using the Gardens to cache weapons to pick up later. There were three patrol lanes, and each section was going to move through one of them, checking the culverts, ditches and hedgerows for weaponry.

We'd received intelligence that the Taliban were recceing our patrols on motorbike and, sure enough, a couple of blokes suddenly appeared on a bike moving slowly down a farm track. Bear in mind it was just after dawn, there was no-one else around. No farmers, for instance. They were very interested in what we were doing, so we stopped and detained them. As the blokes were restraining them, I happened to look away and, through a gap in the corn, 60 metres away, I saw the heads of two guys. Just walking along, laughing to each other. I assumed they were farmers and that perhaps it *was* clocking-on time, after all. Then I looked again and saw the heads of four or five more behind them... I thought, *No, the direction they're going leads to waste ground, I know that area, there's nothing over there, they're not going to work.*

Then the gap widened and I could now see from their knees upwards. And they had webbing on, they were carrying RPGs and AK47s.

I had a split second decision to make; I could either engage them and see what happened, or I could warn the blokes. I decided to warn the blokes first. They hadn't seen them and were busy with the arrests. I turned and made the sign for enemy, a thumbs-down, and pointed in the direction of the six or seven Afghans. We all looked over, and as we did they looked over at us, and then there was a big, simultaneous contact, a good, old-fashioned firefight. Lots of rounds going down.

They had obviously been coming in to take us on but had no idea we would be so far from base. We had gone into their heartland and we had the element of surprise. I often think to myself, *Would I have been better off just having a crack myself?* That does play on my mind. But then I think, *Don't be silly... I warned my blokes, and not a single one of them was injured that day.* And there was no chance that I could have killed all of them.

We then launched a very satisfying co-ordinated platoon attack. The mortar controller started bringing in fire on them and we advanced along a ditch till we got within grenade-throwing distance, about 35 metres for me. I used to be a javelin thrower, and I played a lot of tennis at school - it's the same action as the serve, so I'm famous in my platoon for having the longest throw. Sometimes, the blokes would call me forward if the enemy were just out of reach and I would throw the grenades. We were getting good 'mini H hours' - rapid fire from the FSG on to the target, allowing the other sections to manoeuvre.

Cpl Budd went forward for the assault. He was always champing at the bit to get forward, and we pushed them back and they fled. We found no bodies, and no blood trail, and that pissed me off. I'd have liked to think that we'd hit some of them and at least injured them. But the platoon had worked well.

Then I thought, *We've used quite a bit of ammo, and now everyone knows we're out here. We're a kilometre away from base.* Clearly, we needed to abandon the initial mission and extract, because it was very soon going to be a very dangerous place to be.

We shook out and started to move off, and within 60 seconds we were engaged from the other side of the river. It sounded like two gunmen, but we couldn't get to them and, with the high maize, we couldn't see them, either. It was very difficult to see where the fire was coming from. Very hard for us even to return effective fire. From their point of view, it's a different proposition: they know there's a body of men spread over, say, 100 metres. If they spray that with 250 rounds of RPK, they might hit something. That they didn't was down to a combination of luck and the fact that the blokes were well up on using cover, and not at all shy about crawling round in the mud. We got into the irrigation ditches, in places they were 6ft deep, and started wading back through them. We had some Household Cavalry Scimitars standing off us at a wadi for fire support, and I had a quick look at the map, revised the extraction plan and decided to head for that. If we got under the cover of their 30mm Rardens, a nice piece of kit, that would be handy.

The Taliban were pursuing us in numbers from the direction in which we'd chased the original lot off; they were firing a lot of rounds.

We'd called for air and, as we were moving out, it came in, and it was fast jets. It's a lottery what you get. We'd like to get A10s every day of the week, second choice would be Apache, and then everything else after that is much of a muchness. It's difficult terrain for a fast jet to work, hard to get situational awareness and work out who is exactly where at 600mph, and they didn't have a great day. The air power, generally speaking, was very good but on this day they made a number of mistakes, and some of them were very dangerous. That is just a fact. We all have bad days, and generally speaking they were excellent.

I didn't have a great day myself, air-wise, either. I let off smoke to show the planes where we were, which is doing it by the book, but in hindsight we had actually broken clean at that point. The Taliban were wondering where we were, and then they saw the smoke and instantly thought, right, and headed for us.

They were putting in a very determined effort to get to us and, again with hindsight, it was clearly because they thought we still had the two detainees. As it happens, both of the men had been kneeling down in the field right in the firing line during the initial exchanges, and had both been killed by their own side.

They got so close to my rear section that the lads could hear their footfall and breathing and calls to each other, and we had to mount a number of snap ambushes to keep them off. We inflicted significant casualties on them in these ambushes, shooting them at ranges of a few feet at times, and that was good; it gives the blokes confidence, knowing that they're doing a good job, and obviously keeps the enemy at bay and gives him something to think about. Even so, rounds were pinging overhead and around our feet all the time.

Eventually, we reached the Scimitars and peeled off behind them and got back into camp, with 2 Platoon up on the Hesco Bastion covering our withdrawal in. It got to a point where we knew we were safe-ish and the adrenaline started to ebb away.

All in all we were in contact for about an hour and 45 minutes, and not just a little contact here and a little contact there, it was sustained. We used a lot of ammunition that day, even me, and generally I don't fire my weapon, because if you're busy shooting then you're not thinking about the platoon. I got rid of about two and a half magazines, which indicates how intense it was.

We were all totally knackered. A kilometre doesn't sound a long way, but believe me, it is. It was already hot, even though it was early in the morning, we were carrying a lot of kit, which was all water-logged, and we'd been under a lot of stress. People had been shouting, they had been concentrating, the terrain was difficult - up and down ditches, stumbling through the baked mud... all the while thinking, *I hope no-one gets hit.* Because if one guy gets shot, the whole platoon gets bogged down, with the best part of a section taken out with the carrying and the protection of that carrying.

We were all shattered, but we got in and it was one of those days when all ended well and we all had some good stories to tell.

On 20 August, 1 Platoon's lead Section became engaged in a heavy firefight with the Taliban.

We didn't go out again until August 20.

We had a mobility problem when leaving the base, because they knew where we were likely to go. You try and throw in as much deception as possible, and try and prove them wrong, but there were only so many routes we could take through the place so, inevitably, if you patrol for long enough you will run out of luck.

My OC said, 'The problem is mobility... what is the solution?'

I thought for a while and then I said, 'Why don't we create more routes?'

He said, 'What do you mean?'

I said, 'Well, just go and blow some walls and buildings down, and that way we'll increase the number of routes in which we can move around the town.'

I'm talking in areas where all the locals had left - it's not as though we were suggesting damaging occupied property and the idea was, once we'd finally got the Taliban dealt with and pushed them out, it could all be rebuilt.

He thought that was a good idea and, as importantly, the blokes thought it was a *really* good idea. They were feeling vulnerable and this was a plan. They were all over it.

We decided we'd start on the 20th by increasing the mobility corridor due north. I'd identified a number of walls that we needed to go through, and every one of them was covered by the FSG building. That meant we could use them to go into town, but if the Taliban decided to use them to come the other way then they were covered with fire.

We were using mines because of the thickness of the walls I spoke about earlier. I pushed 1 and 3 Sections north while 2 Section placed the explosives. We set the first mine and as soon as it blew I heard contact from the front right, which was 1 Section, Cpl Budd. I took 2 Section round and we got up to the back of 3 Section, who had been front left, so I could get a sitrep. As soon as I arrived, I saw casualties coming back from 1 Section. Pte Balivanalu was carrying Cpl Roberts, the Mortar Fire Controller, who had been shot through the shoulder. A guy called Pte Steve Halton, who has since gone to 1 Para, he was coming back half-carrying Pte Lanaghan. Lanaghan had only come out in May, because he was only 18... a real young bloke, but an exceptional soldier with a very bright future ahead of him. He had also been shot in the shoulder and I don't know how, whether it had ricocheted off his body armour, but the round had travelled up and hit him in the nose. So they were both bleeding quite profusely and Lanaghan, particularly, looked in a bad way. As it happened, neither of them were hit through the bone or anything, and both later made full recoveries. And Lanaghan has a fantastic scar, which I'm sure he's very pleased with.

It turned out that both the other sections had come under fire at a similar time.

Cpl Budd, the Section Commander, was reported as missing, having continued to assault the enemy position on his own. Farmer quickly reorganised his Platoon and led two attempts with his remaining Sections in an attempt to locate the missing Section Commander.

I said, 'Where's Corporal Budd?'

And it was Steve Halton who said, 'I don't know, boss. Last time I saw him, he was going forward but I lost sight of him and I don't know where he is now.'

I thought, 'Oh, s***.'

Some of his section had peeled back and joined the other section, so I went forward to them and asked, 'Is Corporal Budd here?'

Same answer: last seen charging towards the enemy and he'd not come back.

I spoke to his 2IC, trying to piece the picture together. Everyone was saying that Bryan had seen Taliban and had launched a section attack. That was something we'd made clear in the orders; given that the sections were going to be separated, if you got enemy pre-seen - i.e. they haven't seen you, but you've seen them - the section commander was to use his experience, which by now was pretty considerable, to do whatever he thought right. Bryan had organised his troops and engaged. Later on, I saw a number of enemy dead, so it had obviously been successful. But in the after action review, we felt that his section had not noticed a flanking position - for good reasons, just an opportunist behind a wall - and he had opened up and strafed them, with devastating results... hence those two injuries. Plus Pte Sharpe had taken rounds to his chest, but the body armour had saved him. He was knocked over and shaken up, as you can understand, but he survived.

So I'd rapidly got to the point where one of my sections was pretty much out of the game, and the rest of us were bogged down and in a firefight with the Taliban. The enemy were in a line of buildings ahead of us, with good firing points. No idea how many of them there were. If I was guessing, I'd say somewhere around 10 at that point, though more were arriving. We were taking whatever cover we could find and returning fire.

At this point I thought, *My hands are tied now.* It was very straightforward. *Cpl Budd is not here, what are we going to do? We are going to get him.* And everyone would have felt the same way. I spoke to Steve and he gave me Bryan's last-known position, down to within 20 metres or so. On the fringes of the buildings, where they met a field of high-standing maize. I thought, *Chances are he is probably still very close to there.*

At this point, I was already fearing the worst. It's been several minutes now, and no-one's heard from him. Worst case scenario, he was dead. Next worst, he had been captured. At best, I felt he might be lying up somewhere, maybe injured, unable to attract our attention because of his proximity to the enemy.

We made several attempts to make headway, struggling to get forward because we were out-positioned. I had guys on their belt buckles, or firing and manoeuvring... even if it's not accurate fire it gives you a good psychological boost. There were lots of rounds flying around and the seconds and minutes were ticking by.

But we had to do something. We had to bring Bryan back; we couldn't let him be kidnapped. We know what the Afghans are like when it comes to dealing with enemy dead or captives, and we had intelligence to suggest that they were looking to kidnap one of us, cut off his fingers, gouge his eyes out and give him back alive. I wasn't going to let that happen to anyone.

I had a look and I thought there was a possible way around to the right. So I got my radio operator and some of the blokes and we tried a right flanking option to get around to where he'd last been seen. It meant leaving the relative safety of what little cover we'd found, and I knew we were taking a risk; it was the only thing I did in the whole tour where I thought, *This could go badly*, but it was worth trying.

We moved up forward to a stream which ran in front of us along the line of the cover that we were receiving fire from, with other guys giving us some flank protection and suppressive fire. We were quickly out of sight of their main position, but we were exposed, and I felt very vulnerable. I didn't want to ask anyone else to do what I wouldn't do myself so I was at the front of the section. We were almost creeping, really slowly, like something out of *Dad's Army*, trying not to be spotted. All the time, looking around, thinking, *There's some cover, if I get fired upon that's where I'm going*.

As I went forward, there were Taliban dead along the bank of the stream. Bryan had very thick, dark hair, and a dark beard, and the first body I saw, all I could see was his head and his arm. I thought, *Is that Bryan?* Hoping it wasn't. I got closer and closer and eventually I could see the webbing and clothing were wrong.

There were other dead littered around. You're supposed to follow a rigid procedure to check they are dead, because you don't want someone you've just walked past popping up with his AK and nailing you from behind. So you go in a pair, disarm them and then jump on their back and turn them over to make sure that they're not booby-trapped. But in the heat of battle, you don't have that time. In most cases, the injuries were such that you just knew... gunshots to the head, major trauma to the chest, that sort of thing.

Around this point, I looked up; there was a building ahead and I could see rifle muzzles poking around corners. Not towards us, just as though there were several guys there thinking about sticking their heads around and having a look. We were in, effectively, a pipe range. The stream to one side, with a building on the opposite bank, and a wall to the other. About 10ft in between. We were totally exposed and I thought, *Jesus, I could be in trouble here.*

As I was thinking that, we were engaged by machine gun fire. The initial burst hit Pte Briggs, my radio operator, in the chest plate and knocked him over. He was just behind me, to the left; a foot higher and he would have been very dead. A foot higher and three feet to the right, and it would have been me.

He was shouting, 'I've been hit, I've been hit!' but he was shouting it so firmly and strongly that I knew he must be OK.

I turned to him and said, 'I know that, I can hear you, but you sound alright to me so let's get the f*** out of here.' It was quite funny, looking back.

I'd got myself down behind the only thing I could find, which was a small tree, and got hit in the arse by a piece of bullet shrapnel which must have split off on his chest plate. I got some in both boots, too, but I think that was from other locations.

Cpl Curnow, 2 Section commander, was behind me and he got a shrapnel wound, quite a lot of shrapnel, to his lower leg so he turned around and started moving back. McKinley and a guy called Pte Randle provided cover for us to extract and we did the same for them, fire-manoeuvring out of there.

So we ended up pretty much back where we started and we obviously weren't going to get to Bryan that way.

By this point, Maj Loden had sent out a Quick Reaction Force under the command of Andy Mallet, a composite of Paras, Engineers, Household Cavalry and even RMP. Some of these guys would never have dreamt of being in this sort of infantry fighting, but there was no choice. Maj Loden had gone round basically saying, 'Right, you, you and you... get your kit together, you're going on the ground.' On foot and straight into a big contact, so that took a lot of balls from them. And every single one of those guys went out and performed well, and it was very good to see.

Andy Mallet tried to push through but the weight of fire from the enemy just got bigger and bigger and bigger. We'd been out on the ground for an hour or more since the wall was blown, and they had obviously been coming from left, right and centre to get a piece of the action. We were stuck.

All my thoughts were about Cpl Budd and getting to him. I can't justify this on a moral basis, but I knew I'd accept casualties - obviously not dead, but injuries - to get him back. The worst thing for us and his family would be for us to leave the battlefield not knowing where he was.

He was a really good soldier, Bryan, exceptionally good, and half the guys were expecting him to pop up in the canal with a reed to breathe through hours later. But I knew.

As Andy Mallet tried and failed to make much headway, I was being warned by Maj Loden that intelligence suggested that we were about to be surrounded. I looked behind me, and there was the River Helmand. I said on the net, 'Good luck to them, if they're that f***ing good. There's a river behind me.'

He said, 'Oh, alright then.'

And about 30 seconds later, they started firing from the bloody reeds! So we were in a genuine 360 degree firefight. We'd had that before, but not with this weight of fire. But a number of our corporals had the presence of mind to bring down very effective 51mm mortar fire onto the position in the reeds, so that threat was actually dealt with very quickly.

Then we entered something of a stalemate. We were in organised packets, in cover. Admittedly, we couldn't move forward, but we weren't getting hit, either. Andy was pinned down, I tried and failed to move forward again and I was getting stuck for ideas. At that moment, Maj Loden came onto the net and said, 'You have two Apache helicopters with you in two minutes... I've given them your frequency, their call sign is X... just use them.'

I'd learned my lesson from the maize field. I did pop smoke to mark our position, but I popped it into a high-walled compound close by so it was largely contained and not visible to ground elements. One of the pilots asked where the enemy was, and I gave him an eight-figure grid-reference, which was a building where the centre mass of the enemy forces were located.

He said, 'What effect do you want us to have?'

I said, 'Just f***ing level it.'

He said, 'I don't have the right ordnance to do that.'

I said, 'What have you got?'

He said, 'Cannon.'

I said, 'OK, strafe the southern and western aspects of that building.'

So they started that and within three or four minutes it was clear that the Taliban were withdrawing. They'd put up a decent fight, had had good positions and had held us, but there wasn't much they could do about the helicopters. We saw them moving back, but I was painfully aware that time was not on our side.

His citation reveals that Lt Farmer personally led troops into an area of high standing corn - where enemy gunmen might be hiding - to search for Cpl Budd.

I organised a section to go out into the maize field to try and find him. That was risky, because there could have been anyone in there, waiting for us, or IEDs or whatever.

Within 20 seconds of moving forward we found Bryan.

There were Taliban dead all around him.

One of the guys picked him up, put him on his shoulder and started running back to a casualty evacuation point we'd set up in cover about 150 metres away. As soon as I saw him on the back of that guy's shoulder, the sense of relief was incredible. He was very pale, and limp, but he threw up as they ran back, and the Combat Medical Technician had a look at him and he said he had a slight pulse. So there was some little hope, but the pulse and the vomiting were really only a physiological response to his body being picked up and moved.

By this point, the Taliban had regrouped and we started getting mortared. We had 800 metres or so to get back to camp, so Bryan was put on the back of a quad bike and driven back by the sergeant major. We collapsed, I let Andy go first with the composite platoon, and then my platoon followed. And we pretty much did a best effort run over the open ground, almost an exact simulation of the two-miler in fighting kit which we do in training. They weren't able to adjust the mortars to keep up with us, but there were mortars hitting the casevac area we'd taken Bryan to. I was running back, thinking, *Thank God we do that run... there is a point to it, after all.*

Tragically, Cpl Budd had succumbed to his injuries. Lt Farmer's citation says: "However, Farmer's considerable courage and personal example under fire inspired the soldiers around him in a dangerous and confusing situation where casualties had been sustained and there was a real danger of being outflanked. Apart from convincingly defeating the

Taliban by taking command of the additional forces sent to him and calling in attack helicopter fire, his firm leadership and dogged determination to press forward in the face of intense effective enemy fire to rescue Cpl Budd ensured that all casualties were extracted from the firefight. There is also little doubt that his actions contributed to the fact that no further casualties were sustained."

We got back to camp and as soon as we got there I was told he was dead.

He was the second guy I'd lost, after Damien.

I went to see Lanaghan and Cpl Roberts to see how they were, how the others were, too. Everyone was very shaken up. Bryan was very popular, even though he'd only been with the platoon since June. Popular not only for his outstanding professionalism, but also for his humility. He was a family man, and an all-round nice bloke. I spent time with the blokes and, to be honest, I wasn't really concentrating on what was going on outside after this. Everyone was back in and Maj Loden organised more air power. We had A10s in, all sorts. They could see Taliban from the air and they thoroughly neutralised them, over the next two or three hours.

The terrible thing is that that day I was going out on R&R, so I was in a position where I was going to have to leave my blokes in Sangin just after this had happened and fly home to the UK. I'd like to have stayed, but the Army is very clear about the need for us to get rest so I was lifted out with the casualties. The Taliban had regrouped and attacked the base, they just kept on coming, and we were extracted under fire - it took a lot of balls for the Chinook pilots to come in.

It was surreal. Three or four hours later, I was in Bastion, pretty much as safe as houses, and a few days after that I was back home in the UK.

I didn't like leaving my blokes, but R&R at least gave me the opportunity to go to Bryan's funeral. That was very difficult. I was going to read the eulogy, and I'd have been honoured to do so, but in the end it was done by an officer who had commanded him in the Pathfinders. A few days before I'd been three thousand miles away, laughing and joking with him, and then going out and fighting in a real high-tempo... well, it was just war, at that point. Then here I am at his funeral.

I still think about Bryan a lot. I'm not just saying this because he died in action, he was a very, very high quality corporal. The thing about Bry was wherever we were stopping he would put pictures of his wife, Lorena, and his daughter, Isabelle, on the wall. I remember more than once, totally unsolicited, we were having a bit of down time, I was between planning or writing orders, he came up to me and said, 'Alright, boss? Hey... have you seen these?' And he showed me their pictures. 'This is my wife. This is my darling little girl.' He was so incredibly proud of his family and was looking forward to the birth of his second child only a month later. He was admirable in every single way. I would have done the same thing on the day for any one of the blokes, but I had a real soft spot for Bry. And I obviously get emotional thinking about his death, sometimes. But it makes it easier the more you talk about it.

Cpl Budd was awarded a posthumous Victoria Cross for his tremendous bravery on both July 27 and August 20. His citation, in part, reads: "Cpl Budd's conspicuous gallantry during these two engagements saved the lives of many of his colleagues. (On the second occasion) he acted in the full knowledge that the rest of his men had either been struck down or had been forced to go to ground. His determination to press home a single-handed assault against a superior enemy force despite his wounds stands out as a premeditated act of inspirational leadership and supreme valour."

The recognition Bryan got was awesome and totally deserved. My own medal, I don't think about at all. It's in a safe in battalion HQ, and it was a nice day out at Buckingham Palace for my parents. It was part of a collective, a group of achievements that everyone made that day. But Bryan, he really earned his all on his own. There's a tradition in the Parachute Regiment where, if someone wins a VC, then they get an oil painting of themselves in whatever action they won it. I know that I'll be able to walk into a mess somewhere when I'm older, maybe 60 or 70, and point to an oil painting of Cpl Budd engaging the Taliban and say, 'Yes, he was my section commander.'

And that thought makes me so proud, much more proud than anything I did.

The breakdown of my platoon, we got a VC, a CGC, two MCs, three MiDs and some Brigade Commander's Commendations. For all sorts of bits and bobs. It's an indication that we had a very interesting, and very tough, tour.

It's funny. Back here in England... I was born in York, and lived there as a child, but we moved to Leicestershire and I live near Loughborough now. I used to love the countryside, I was a real country bumpkin, loved nature and all that sort of stuff. Now I can't look at a hedgerow or hillock without thinking, *That's cover from fire or cover from view, or an approach route.* Particularly early on, I'd be walking through the fields thinking to myself, *Look left, half left, possible enemy position, buildings over there, possible Taliban...* and then you think to yourself, *What am I doing? I'm walking the dogs, for goodness' sake!*

I told my parents some of what happened, but not everything. I'd tell mum everything was quiet, nothing was going on... she was horrified to read my citation. I keep a journal, so I can give it to her one day.

That's the job. It's all-encompassing. It's a vocation. I think differently to how I used to, and I've learned more in the last four years than I ever did before - about myself, definitely, and that's a good place to start, but also about the world. Things aren't black and white, everything is context-dependent. When I was young I was always science-driven, and there always seemed to be a clear explanation for things. As you go further into science, you realise that that's not quite true - everything is an approximation. And life's a lot like that.

It's only when you understand yourself and your capabilities and skills that you really understand other people. It's something that I am very, very glad I have done. It certainly beats sitting in front of a computer for 12 hours a day.

Lance Corporal of Horse
Andrew Radford, CGC
Household Cavalry

WHILE Hugo Farmer and his men were fighting the Taliban daily in Sangin, others were engaged in battles of their own in and around the town of Musa Qala to the north west. The administrative centre of the Musa Qala region - a sparsely-populated area made up of many small villages concentrated in the valley cut by the Musa Qala river - had been held for some time by soldiers of the Pathfinders, the elite forward reconnaissance element drawn mainly from the Parachute Regiment.

In scenes reminiscent of Rorke's Drift, they had fought off wave after wave of Taliban attacks, running desperately low on food and water, before a Danish column had eventually fought their way through to reinforce them.

Now the Pathfinders were being extracted, and a group of Household Cavalry armoured vehicles was sent to assist them.

Andrew Radford, a young father of four from the Potteries, was part of that convoy.

The convoy had reached a village just south of the town on August 1 last year when a huge Taliban bomb exploded, destroying the vehicle in front of LCoH Radford's.

One of the four men inside was his close friend Ross Nicholls; another vehicle further ahead was now being engaged with rockets and machine gun fire.

Radford was about to perform an act so brave it would earn him the British Army's second highest decoration.

I come from Stoke, and joined the army aged 16 - I'm 25 now. It was something I'd always wanted to do, like from the age of four or five. I'm not from an Army family - maybe it was seeing stuff on the telly, maybe the first Gulf War... I don't know, it just really interested and inspired me. I went straight in as soon as I could, and joined the Engineers at first. I spent six years as a combat engineer but was actually planning to leave until my wife persuaded me to stay in. I think she realised I'd be lost outside - I certainly didn't know what I'd do when and if I left.

I scoured all the different websites for the Army - I must have gone through every regiment - and in the end I went for the Household Cavalry, based in Windsor. The regiment's role just really appealed to me. There are two sides to it - armoured and ceremonial - and I knew that if I ever felt like a change from the armoured side I could do the mounted stuff. You can swap between the two.

The armoured side is formation reconnaissance. We go out on recce patrols, the furthest forward you can get for non-Special Forces troops, looking for the enemy and gathering intelligence on him.

We're split into troops, and within each troop you have four vehicles: the troop leader's vehicle, commanded by a troop Corporal of Horse, which is our equivalent of sergeant, and two more with a corporal in each. I was a lance corporal at the time *(he is now a Corporal of Horse)*, so I wasn't commanding a vehicle - I was the troop leader's operator, a gunner.

We were in Scimitars. This is like a small tank, with a crew of three - a driver, a gunner and a commander. It has a 7.62mm machine gun and a 30mm cannon, the same as the Warrior's except that the Warrior's is chain-fed and we have to load ours manually. The operator works them both, though obviously not at the same time. You move from one to the other by flicking a switch.

We arrived in Afghanistan on June 20 - the day after my daughter was born. She's my fourth, I've got three boys as well, and I saw her born the night before we left. I was able to hold my little girl and be with her for a few hours, and got on a plane the next morning. It didn't feel good, leaving, but it was one of those things and I was just glad that I had been able to see her.

Afghanistan was like nothing I had ever seen before in my life. I'd spent a lot of time on the internet and watching the news about the country before I went out there but what that can't do is prepare you for the heat. We were there in the summer and it was absolutely outrageous. By 11am, you couldn't actually touch anything on the vehicle - you would burn yourself if you put your hand on the metal. And they're not air-conditioned, so you sweat like anything inside.

But it's funny how quick you get acclimatised. We spent three weeks in Camp Bastion getting used to the conditions and, to begin with, you were drinking water constantly, litres and litres of the stuff. You couldn't put a bottle of water down. By the end of the tour, it was like being back in England really, your body just got used to it. So it didn't degrade our ability to fight.

I remember the first time we left camp and went out on a limb. It was quite a nerve-wracking time, because although I'd read up on Afghanistan and we'd had intensive briefings before leaving, I still didn't know exactly what to expect. I knew it wasn't going to be a quiet tour, that's for sure, so I'd say I was nervous and excited at the same time. You'd see civilians and wonder, *Could they be Taliban?* You can't tell who's friendly and who's not, because they all dress the same. But after a while you get used to it and go with it.

We were out on patrol a lot of the time, sleeping out, doing whatever we'd been tasked to do, coming back to fix the wagons, maybe have a couple of days in camp if we were lucky, and then go back out again. I think the longest we spent out of camp was three-

and-a-half weeks, up in Naw Zad giving fire support to the Fusiliers. We did a few MOGS (Mobile Outreach Groups) too, integrating with the local population, trying to see what they needed. The local population loved to see us, particularly the children... we'd always give them sweets or food. On one occasion, we were on a hill overlooking Naw Zad and a man drove up on a motorbike with two small children on the back. They had both been badly injured by an old piece of ordnance which they'd been playing with and which had blown up in their faces. Both of them were seriously burned; we arranged to have them flown to Camp Bastion for medical aid. Sadly, one of them died a few days later but I believe the other made it. As a father of young children myself, that sort of thing really got to me, obviously.

We tried to avoid the towns and villages where possible, and stayed off road as much as we could because of the threat of IEDs, though the nature of the terrain meant that, sometimes, you had to use roads. We'd mostly be moving through the countryside. It was a strange mixture of flat plains and big mountains; there was miles and miles of barren, rocky desert and suddenly you'd come upon a few buildings, with irrigation channels, and the area would be green over with opium poppies and other crops.

We'd heard about Naw Zad, and how busy it was, and how the Paras and Gurkha Rifles had had such a bad time up there, and we were initially sent up there to give them a bit of protection with our firepower. We went up there as a squadron complete - that was four troops, three of Scimitar and one of Spartan, a troop carrier with a small crew in the back which can fulfil an infantry role if needed. But when we got there there was nothing going on - not a single shot was fired, and we wondered what all the fuss had been about. And really we saw very little to worry about until we got moved - all except one troop, which stayed in Naw Zad - to the Musa Qala area at the end of July.

There was a camp there in the heart of the town, with members of the Pathfinder Platoon there. Some Danish forces had gone in to reinforce and then replace them and our mission was to cover the re-supply of the Danes and assist in the extraction of the Pathfinders - mainly by providing a diversion. A squadron of Scimitars knocking around makes a lot of noise and you can definitely see them coming. We were just going to do that, make some noise in and around the area, to get eyes on to us and off them. Plus, obviously, recce any possible Taliban activity.

The whole of Musa Qala was infested with Taliban and they were determined to retake the town. Afghans suspected of collaborating with the British had been publicly hanged along entry routes and huge caches of weapons and ammunition were being built up. On the morning of 1 August 2006, the Troop moved through a small village to the south of Musa Qala. As they reached the middle of it, the lead two vehicles were ambushed by Taliban forces with a combination of RPG fire, heavy machine guns and a large IED.

There were three vehicles within the ambush area - two vehicles in front of mine - and probably another three behind, with others further back still. Probably 12 vehicles in total. It was a well-planned ambush. In fact, from their point of view, it was perfect. They knew it was our only route through the area and they also knew we were in the area because we'd had a mine strike the night before and one of our vehicles had been taken out - luckily, no-one was injured.

At the time, because we didn't think the threat level was that high, I had my head out of the turret scanning my arcs. On a normal day-to-day basis, when you don't feel threatened, you stick your head out and have a look around. The commander was to my side, and the driver down below, also open. We'd stopped short of this village a couple of minutes previously and the commanders had had a brief on what we were going to do - I think it was simply who was going to go where as we were going to go through this built up area. It was a series of compounds, houses with walls going around the garden. Maybe five or six of them, but with more than one house to a compound. From memory, they were on our side of a ditch, and there was a bridge across the ditch.

We drove through, and almost immediately the first vehicle got hit. We saw the first RPG hit him, and heard the vehicle commander, CoH Mick Flynn, on the net, saying, 'Contact. RPGs.' He's not so much talking to us, because we can see what's happened - they were probably only 50 metres ahead of us. Basically, it's an instant heads-up for HQ, to let them know we've been attacked.

His mic button stuck so we could hear his whole conversation and everything that was going on in his wagon. He was really out of breath, trying to tell the driver where to go, and talking to the gunner, telling him what to do. They decided to move back through the ambush area because they were isolated where they were and they were still being engaged with machine guns and RPGs to the front.

They took a second RPG as they were trying to fight their way out, though we had reversed out of the line of sight by the time that one hit. There's no point in trying to drive through if you aren't in the ambush yet.

Then the second vehicle, a Spartan, got hit by a huge IED. I saw a massive, literally huge, fireball and then a billowing cloud of smoke and dust.

By this stage, we'd moved forward again, with other vehicles, and we were putting down maximum fire power, trying to get the first vehicle out.

We knew that the second vehicle had gone. There was no way that anyone could have survived that blast. It was on fire, well ablaze, and the whole of the back had been blown off. They're all my close colleagues in there, as they are in the Scimitar, but you can't allow yourself to think about that just at that moment. It's like, *Forget that for now, put it to one side, our job is to try to help the first vehicle to get out.*

There were Taliban with machine guns about 75 metres ahead, and to the right there was a little wooded area where the RPGs had been fired from and where we later discovered the IED had been initiated from, by command wire. There were probably only about three or four enemy in each of the two positions, but we were in such a small area that that was enough. Luckily, we had left two of our own vehicles short of our position before we were driving in, to cover us. They were on high ground and had a good view into the town and beyond. It turned out the Taliban had held a number of motorbikes and Toyota Hilux-type vehicles, all kitted out with men with RPGs and AKs, in reserve. They had tried to come around the right hand side and take us all out but our lads behind had wiped them out.

We'd been hearing all the chat in the front vehicle, as I say, and it suddenly all went quiet. We couldn't see them for the smoke and flames from the Spartan, so I just presumed that they had gone as well. I just kept firing while my commander assessed what was the best thing to do.

I remember thinking about my family, and especially my little daughter who I'd only seen for an hour or two. I didn't want to die here and have her never know her dad. I think it spurred me on. As soon as you think about your kids... well, you'll do anything to stay with them.

Then something sort of caught my eye. I noticed someone moving around over at the base of the wooded area. We assumed it was one of the enemy at first, but when we looked really closely we could just make out that it was one of our boys. As soon as I realised he was one of ours I knew we had to go and get him. There was no way that we would leave him there. No way. The Taliban are evil, and they don't treat prisoners well at all. We couldn't drive the vehicle closer, because the threat was too high in that situation. The vehicle attracts rounds, you don't know whether there are more IEDs in the area, it's just too dangerous.

The citation makes clear just how brave Andrew Radford was, acting in the highest traditions of his regiment and the British Army. "Without hesitation or prompting from the officer commanding his vehicle," it says, "and seeing the imminent danger that the injured soldier was in, Radford dismounted his vehicle and, under sustained enemy fire from the Taliban fighters and with total disregard for his own safety, ran into the ambush killing area towards a gravely injured man."

My boss, Lt Tom Long, turned to me and I think he was just about to say, 'One of us is going to have to go and get him,' but I'd actually already started putting my helmet and webbing on. I jumped off and just legged it down towards him. As I was running, there was a lot of incoming fire, I don't know where from because the noise was so great you couldn't tell the direction. I was putting as many rounds down into the trees as I could with my SA80, away from the lad and off to the side, just suppressing fire. I didn't stop to aim. I couldn't have stood around.

As I ran towards him, I looked into the back of the destroyed vehicle. One of the guys in there was LCpl Ross Nicholls, one of my closest mates. They were obviously all dead. It wasn't a nice sight. I remember seeing two of the crew of the first vehicle running in my direction. I think they thought I was coming to help them, and they were trying to let me know they'd extracted OK. I shouted something like, 'You've got to put rounds down... there's one of our guys up there.'

They started firing into the tree line and I carried on running. I'd got to within about 20 metres of the injured man when Mick Flynn, the commander of the first vehicle, appeared.

As a senior NCO in his 40s, and a Falklands veteran to boot, CoH Flynn was the old man of the troop though his fitness levels and fighting prowess were those of someone twenty years younger. He had left the Army to run a village post office but had rejoined after six years. Alongside Radford, he was about to win a Military Cross to go with the Conspicuous Gallantry Cross he had already won in Iraq during Operation TELIC 1.

Mick's wagon was stuck in the ditch and they'd had to abandon it. He shouted, 'What are you doing?' And he joined me while his driver and gunner gave us covering fire with their personal weapons.

A few seconds later we got to the injured guy and did a quick assessment. He'd stopped moving, and I actually thought he was dead. I could see that it was Tpr Martyn Compton, the driver of the Spartan. He was burnt to a crisp, with all his clothing sticking to him or burned away. He'd also been shot twice in the legs. But as we started moving him, he began making noise... moaning but not really speaking. He managed to say, 'Radders... help me,' just about, but he wasn't really with it. It was distressing, seeing him like that, especially such a good bloke like he is. You can never be trained for this exact experience I don't think, but all my instincts for personal survival and to get Martyn out of there really kicked in.

Mick was checking his gunshot wounds and I got my morphine out. He was clearly in absolute agony. But because he was in such a state I didn't know whether the morphine would just finish him off, so I put it back in my webbing. He looked like he was on his last legs, to be honest. I didn't think he was going to make it. We picked him up and put him over my shoulders and I sprinted as fast as I could back to my wagon.

Taliban machine gun fire and RPGs kicked up the dirt at his feet as he ran.

You find strength that you didn't know you had - I didn't even notice I had him on my back.

By now, the whole thing had probably taken about half an hour, tops.

The weight of fire was massive, with the lads in the vehicles covering me and Mick, and we made it back without being hit ourselves. I laid Martyn down on the front decks of our vehicle as best I could, the other three from the first vehicle jumped on alongside him, and we drove off to where we'd left the HQ element, probably two to three kilometres away. We took our time because it was rough ground and we didn't want to hurt him any more than we had to, because he was in such a bad way.

I was brought up in a religious family and I think I said a prayer of thanks at this point.

We had a brilliant medic attached to us, a lad called LCpl Paul Hamlet, and he did some really good work out there. I think he administered morphine to Compo while they called in the casevac Chinook and he was taken away.

I still didn't think for one minute that he was going to live.

After we had got him back, we had a quick brief. The squadron leader explained what had happened, for anyone who didn't know, and basically hit us with it, that we'd have to head back down there and retrieve what we could. The company that was on QRF in Camp Bastion got crashed out on a couple of Chinooks, there were Apaches in the air and some 105 guns further away were also giving fire. There was fast air. It was a massive operation to go back in. I didn't personally come across the enemy again, though - I think the Apaches saw them in and around the area as we were extracting and they had sorted out anything that was needed.

We did manage to retrieve the bodies of the dead from the second vehicle. You cannot imagine what it's like. You see things on the television, but it's not the same, and you never think you'll ever see the things that you're seeing. Absolutely unbelievable. Ross Nicholls was one of them, as I said. Ross had transferred over from the Royal Signals at the same time as I did, and we'd done a few courses together. We were very alike and we had just bonded straight away and been great mates ever since. He was a really nice bloke, a Scottish lad with a very dry sense of humour. Married, had a young boy and a young girl, the youngest born a couple of months before my little girl. All you could say is that he wouldn't have known anything about it. I was amazed that Martyn Compton had survived. I'd assumed he'd been blown out of the vehicle and landed where we found him but it turned out the explosion from the IED had caved the front decks of the vehicle, basically the bonnet, down onto him. We're talking aluminium armour, really heavy stuff. And he'd managed to push it off himself. It must have been pure will to survive. He was on fire - totally ablaze - and he rolled around on the floor to put himself out and crawled to where we saw him.

We got back to Bastion a day later. I rang my wife as soon as I could. She wasn't happy. She'd seen it on the news, the initial 'three soldiers killed in Afghanistan', but there are so many of us out there that she didn't really worry about it too much. Then she heard that two were from the Household Cavalry *(the other men who died were 2nd Lt Ralph Johnson of the Household Cavalry, 24, and Capt Alex Eida of the Royal Horse Artillery, 29)* and that did worry her because there were 88 of us out there, so she knew there was a 1-in-44 chance I was involved, and she hadn't heard from me.

When I phoned her, and she found out how close to it I had been, she started sobbing.

They'd sorted out the bodies and put them into coffins and I actually managed to put Ross on the plane; I was one of his pall bearers. I followed him up to Kandahar and they had a huge ceremony up there. All the Americans and all the NATO Forces lined the airport. But I wasn't able to come back to the UK, which was a shame.

And then we were all just in camp, fixing the wagons again. We all talked a lot, shared our experiences of what happened, because everyone can give a little bit more information and it does help. We had a remembrance service for the guys who died.

I was nervous when we went back out again. I didn't fancy it, but we were asked if we were ready and if anyone hadn't been they would not have been sent back out. My feeling was, if you put it off you're just going to keep putting it off, so the quicker you do it the better. And that was the general feeling. We got back out, there were initial nerves but after a couple of days you know that that sort of thing is not going to happen every day.

When I got back home at the end of the tour, I was dreaming about it every night. I've only just stopped to be honest. My wife would wake me up some nights because I was distressed, and she'd say I was talking in my sleep.

I still think about it every day. I see Ross's wife Angela quite a bit. I think it helps us both to talk about him, though I don't really talk about that day in particular. I've not actually spoken about it before now to anyone, really.

The Army are quite good about helping you with this sort of thing now. You're offered the chance to talk to people, like the Padre, the doctors and other specially-trained people. It's definitely there for anyone who wants it. But I didn't want it. I'm quite philosophical - it's one of the risks of being in the Army. Death is part of the job. You know when you join the Army that things could happen, and Ross would have known that. Onwards and upwards. I certainly have no plans to leave because of what happened. I get asked about the people who laid the IED, how I feel about them. The thing is, life is cheap out there. They had the Soviet invasion, there's all the inter-tribal stuff, they've been doing this sort of thing since they were little boys. It's all they know, I think. I don't feel anything towards them, not hate, not anything. Obviously, I wish it hadn't happened, and it does sadden me, but it's part of being in the Army.

Martyn Compton is making a good recovery. I think technology now, what they can do compared to what they could do maybe twenty years ago, is amazing. When he got back, they initially sedated him so that he was unconscious and I think he was in an induced coma for at least a couple of months. He'd only been out of that for about a week, I think, when I got back. I went straight to see him and he was still in a terrible way, physically. He was still in a wheelchair because of being shot in the leg but now he's walking around again. Morale-wise, he seems to be totally sound. I think the plans are for him to stay in the Army if he wants to, and he's making damned good progress. He's extremely strong, mentally and physically, and you can only admire and respect him for how he has coped throughout the whole ordeal. I was at a party last Saturday for our awards and Martyn came to that and he was drinking with me and having a good time. We've talked a bit about what happened, but not in any detail. It's awkward for us. I think it's a bloke thing. I'm not sure whether he wants to talk about it, and he's not sure whether I want to talk about it. I'm sure one day we will.

LCoH Radford's citation is very clear as to his awesome bravery: "He showed a complete disregard for his own safety and acted completely on his own initiative. A father of four young children, he deliberately put himself in harm's way to rescue a fellow soldier. He showed an almost superhuman effort to rescue Trooper Compton and extract him uphill the 70 metres back to his own armoured vehicle... all the more remarkable as he was still under fire from a mixture of AK-47s, machine guns and RPGs. At no point did he think of himself, utterly focused on saving his fellow comrade in trouble, who had suffered horrendous injuries. Without doubt, his immediate action saved Trooper Compton's life. It is this act of selflessness, conspicuous gallantry and bravery in the face of a well co-ordinated and sustained enemy ambush that merits public recognition."

I am very proud to have received the CGC, but if I hadn't received anything it wouldn't have bothered me in the slightest. You don't do things for medals, you do them for your mates. I'd like to think that if that had been me lying there that someone would have come and got me. In the Household Cavalry, we are all very close and we look after each other and look out for each other. Mick Flynn got a Military Cross, and he'd already got a CGC from Iraq, too, so there's plenty of braver blokes than me out there. And it was down to the efforts of every man involved that day that the Taliban didn't kill any more men than they did.

My wife is happy and proud of me, but she reckons it was a one-time offer. My luck might run out next time. But she knows that I have a huge love for the Army and always will. She knows it's my life, so if I died that way I would have died doing something that I love.

My mum was the same - not happy, to say the least, but very proud. She knows the job I'm in and she appreciates what we do.

I say I think about the incident every day, but now it's not from a bad point of view. Whenever anyone mentions Afghanistan it's in my mind, but it doesn't trouble me. It did at the time. Just seeing that sort of thing, and coming so close to dying, is not good. Not something that you expect. When you come so close to death you start to think about whether you're in the right job, and what's all this for? I got over that. It was just the nerves of, *This could happen again*. But just last week a lady died in a car accident down the road from our barracks, while walking her child to school. Who expects that? When your time's up, your time's up.

One thing about what happened, it definitely makes you realise that there's more to life than people think. You laugh at people who think they've got worries. There are people out there doing a hard job in very difficult circumstances, and I don't think the British public really appreciate that.

Major Mark Hammond, DFC
Royal Marines

WHEN soldiers such as Martyn Compton or Brian Budd are hurt, it is to the helicopter pilots that their comrades turn. Injured men need urgent medical assistance and the only way to achieve this is through aerial evacuation. This means - as often than not - landing in a hot LZ, with enemy fighters blazing away at you with machine guns and RPGs.

It doesn't take much to imagine how dangerous - and frightening - this would be. Yet at the very moment when the danger is at its greatest, the steadiest of hands and nerves are required.

Mark Hammond is something of a rarity; a Royal Marine Chinook pilot. But his flying - leading the Immediate Response Team (IRT) and Quick Reaction Force for the Operation HERRICK Helmand Task Force, based at Camp Bastion - was in the best traditions of his elite Corps.

Like the other Chinook pilots and crews, and the surgical teams who travelled with them, Maj Hammond regularly put his own life in danger to save the lives of others.

I joined the Royal Marines in 1989, aged 21. As a young officer, you go through Commando training, become a troop commander and then you can go off and specialise. There are three distinct specialisations within the Marines: Mountain Leader, Special Forces (Special Boat Service) and pilot. I chose the latter, joining what was 3 Commando Brigade Air Squadron in 1994, later re-commissioned as 847 Naval Air Squadron in 1996. I trained on the Gazelle, transferred to Lynx and then was lucky enough to have an exchange to the States, where I flew Cobra Attack Helicopters. I now fly Chinooks.

We went out in early 2006 to do prelim ops associated with the build-up of Camp Bastion and the preparation for the main force, 16 Air Assault Brigade with 3 Para, coming out. We spent two months ferrying engineers, troops, stores and equipment out to Bastion and various other places in the triangle. We were flying six to eight hours every day, but there was no trouble, it was a milk run. Our sister flights from 18 and 27 then rouled through, and it was while we were back in the UK that it started hotting up.

We deployed back out to Afghanistan at the end of August, and the whole situation had completely changed. Our guys were holed up in district centres in towns throughout Helmand, like Musa Qala, Naw Zad and Kajaki in the north, Sangin below them and Garmsir down to the south. The guys were on the ground in what had become bandit country, basically.

We were based at Kandahar, from where we'd carry out regular resupply runs or assist in the rotation of troops in the district centres. And we had a forward base at Bastion, with Chinooks forming the IRT and the QRF. You would do a certain amount of roulemont - you'd rotate through on a cyclical basis, spending a number of days doing the tasking lines, and then you'd go forward to Bastion and do a number of days on IRT or QRF.

Of course, pretty much wherever we were going was a fixed site - you're going into the same landing zone every time. You can approach from different routes, and you can come in from different angles, but your ultimate destination is the same. And the Tellytubbies are not stupid. They know where you're going, so they'll set up and wait. They'll have a pop at you on the way in and the way out and if you spend any more than 30-60 seconds on the deck you'll get mortared. A Chinook is a 99ft long helicopter and while it's not that slow - it will top out at 140-150mph - it's a big and relatively easy target. Having said that, we have one of the best defensive aid suites on British helicopters for missiles and we wouldn't go anywhere without Apache top cover. They're very good, the Apache boys. I'd say there's a lot of mutual respect between us - we know they're keeping us alive, and they know we're going into the zone. And, believe me, our respect for the guys on the ground is 10 times greater, because they're sat there being shot at 24 hours a day. At least we get to go back to the relative safety of Bastion or Kandahar.

On the night of September 6, Maj Hammond and his crew were holding the IRT standby when the Sangin base was attacked with mortars and small arms. One soldier suffered a critical, life-threatening injury. The IRT aircraft, accompanied by a pair of Apache attack helicopters, was scrambled to retrieve the casualty. As he lifted off, Hammond knew of intelligence reports that the Taliban intended specifically to target Chinook helicopters using the Sangin landing site, and that anti-aircraft weapons were in place.

September 6 is not a day I'm ever going to forget.

I'd been in theatre for about a week. The guys we'd replaced had been taking some fire - just after we arrived, for instance, they took a round through an engine cowling. So everyone knew the danger. It wasn't an exercise and it was very likely that we were going to be shot at.

We had the Kajaki mine incident in the morning-gusting-afternoon, where we'd sent two IRT helicopters out to Kajaki because unfortunately members of 3 Para had moved into a minefield. The lads went out to try and give assistance but, unfortunately, due to the steepness of the slope, the Chinooks couldn't land. It was reported in the press that the downwash of the helicopters had set off mines, though it didn't, but there were still five casualties and one fatality - Cpl Mark Wright GC, who unfortunately died after being extracted.

Cpl Wright won his George Cross - the equivalent of the Victoria Cross, though awarded for actions of extraordinary bravery carried out when not in the teeth of battle - after he and other soldiers were injured in a minefield; he had continued to reassure and encourage his men, despite having suffered severe injuries which would soon claim his own life.

I came up IRT at about 1600hrs. The helicopter has a full medical and surgical response team in the back - they can operate on guys in the air - and its protection. Say 10 people in all. There would normally be four or five of us... myself, my co-pilot and two or three crewmen who can operate guns on the sides and the ramp. The IRT is there 24 hours a day, on short notice to move during both day and night.

At about 1700hrs we had a call and we legged it across the road to the command post to find out what was going on. Lt Col Stuart Tootal, CO 3 Para, ran that... a very good officer, he was awarded a DSO. We were told that a soldier from the Royal Irish, LCpl Luke McCulloch, had taken shrapnel to the head in a contact in Sangin, and was in a bad way. He was a T1 casualty, which means he will almost certainly die if he isn't reached and given proper medical help within the 'golden hour'.

Obviously, every time you send a helicopter out to an event like this you are risking the aircraft and the lives of the people on board. The other end of the stick is that we want to get our people out and save their lives if at all possible. It ends up being a call for someone of the rank of Lt Col Tootal. If there's an ongoing, full-scale battle it may be that we simply can't go. But things were reasonably quiet, so we were given the go-ahead to launch.

It's not something you can do immediately. The medics need briefing on the injuries, the Apaches need briefing so they can clear you into the zone, you need to co-ordinate with the ground call signs reference your approach direction and when you'll be there. Sangin was between 20 and 45 minutes away, depending on the route we took.

Flt Lt Mark Daffy, a very good operator, was my co-pilot, sitting in the left-hand seat, doing the navigation, the comms, monitoring the engines, telling you where you're going. Our Number Two crewman was Sgt Dan Baxter, who was manning the guns on the right hand side. Sgt Sam Hannant was my Number One down the back, operating the ramp to get everyone on and off and manning the ramp gun.

It was dusk as we arrived at Sangin, and I remember seeing outgoing fire from the position, friendly troops firing tracer at the enemy. According to the guys on the deck, we were fired on as we were trying to get in, though I have to say I don't really remember that because I was concentrating on getting us on to the landing zone. As we landed, one of the Apaches said, 'You might want to hold off for a minute, it's getting a bit warm in there.'

I said, 'Actually, it's a bit late... I'm already in the zone.'

We loaded up the casualties, lifted out and I remember Dan shouting to me that we were taking fire to the rear right so I broke right to come over the top of it. I saw the rounds coming up through the 11 o'clock, big fat tracer within a few metres of the aircraft. The Chinook is armoured but Dan and Sam were stood at the side door and ramp, very exposed. They fired at the position that was firing at us, and that keyed everyone in down on the ground. Within a few seconds, you could see this huge weight of fire bearing down on the Taliban position, and that was that as far as they were concerned.

We climbed up to height to keep it as smooth as possible, hot-hoofing it home as fast as we humanly could, as fast as the cab would take us. Meanwhile, the surgical team was in the back, already operating on LCpl McCulloch, trying to save his life.

A full surgical procedure in a speeding helicopter, starting a few moments after they've landed in a hot LZ under fire. I was mega impressed with the surgical team. It's easier for us flying the thing - they have to sit in the back watching the rounds go past the window and there's nothing they can do.

Unfortunately, they did not save his life.

We landed back on and got the guys off and I remember speaking on the mic, and saying, 'Good job, lads - we've done it. We got him out.'

Then the doc came back on board, put the headset on and said, 'Sorry, guys, he died on the ramp.'

It was a real downer. I remember just shouting some expletives down the microphone. It just wiped the crew out for a bit, because we'd tried so hard to get him out. There's been the elation of getting in and out, and no-one's been hit, and then... But you have to crack on. We lifted to reposition to our parking spot, thinking we would go down and be back on short notice to move. So we landed on and we'd just started refuelling when an old mate of mine who flies Apaches, Lt Cdr Dave Westley, jumped aboard and stuck his head through the hatch. 'There's another one in Musa Qala,' he said. 'You've got to go straight away.'

With Musa Qala, the district centre was even tighter, more enclosed by houses, than Sangin. The lads there had just been mortared and taken fire and there was a T1 casualty who had taken a gunshot wound through the neck. And various other people had been injured as well.

The ground commander wanted us to go in from the north-east so we had a quick brief with the Apaches - this is our route in, this is your call to say the zone isn't hot, and so on. We went out, climbed up, we were wearing night vision goggles by now because it was dark, and we dropped down to low level just on the outskirts of the town.

The only available landing site was directly adjacent to the compound that had just been attacked. As Hammond approached, his aircraft was engaged from numerous firing points.

I was 50ft up, with houses below, trying to get in, and it all kicked off. It's a cliché, but it really did go into slow motion. I remember Dan calling, 'RPG!' and a few moments later Sam called, 'RPG!' Subsequently, I saw the video footage shot from the Apaches above us - it shows one grenade passing 10ft above the aircraft and the other one passing 10ft below. If either had hit us, that would have been curtains. And there was a lot of small arms fire coming our way, too. But I remember there was no shouting, no screaming, it was immensely calm and professional from all the boys.

Sam and Dan suppressed the RPG firing points with their M60s, which was some brilliant shooting - 50ft up, at night, on the goggles, doing 120 knots, while I'm throwing it around all over the place, and they took out the two firers, both of them. They were RAF crewmen, specialists in the job; the RAF gets a bit of stick from time to time, but these boys were extremely impressive.

Then we felt a shudder through the air frame. Mark turned around to me and said, 'I think we've hit a bird.'

At night, with all this firefight going on around us.

I said, 'I think we have, yeah.'

And it did feel like a bird, but then Mark said later that he'd seen something flash up in front of the cockpit.

We were still trying to get in to the zone but at this time both the ground call sign and our Apache escort gave the codeword to abort the landing and go round. It was just too hot. There was stuff flying around everywhere. I was on short finals to come into the approach, just slowing down, just bringing the nose back up so that I could put the rear wheels on. About a quarter of a mile out. I contemplated ignoring them and just going down, but if they're telling me not to there might be something I don't know. We climbed back up to height and I spoke to Dave on the radio and said, 'Listen, we're going to have to go home and rethink this because it is not working, not with RPGs flying around.'

So we went back and got into the CP with Lt Col Tootal. We subsequently learned that we shouldn't have gone in from the north east because that's where most of the Taliban commanders lived. They have sentries that stay up all night on watch to make sure that the important guys don't get snatched by the Americans. They had a Dushka, a 12.7mm anti-aircraft weapon, plus a load of machine guns in fixed positions to make sure that they are protecting their commanders, so it wasn't a good route in.

The casualty had stabilised down to a T2, because they'd managed to sort out his neck, but he still needed picking up. I remember, we came off the cab and the medics were all sat down the back. Their boss was a colonel - he was pretty ashen-faced, and I had a smoke with him. We were sucking down this smoke, and I said, 'You do realise we are going to go back?'

He took just about the longest drag I've ever seen, stubbed it out and said, 'Yeah, I thought we might.'

And he just walked off. Immensely brave - one, for just sitting in the back of the helicopter and getting shot at and, two, for then cracking on with your job, trying to save lives. Amazing guys, absolutely amazing.

We were given a lot more assets, and it became a deliberate operation. We had a gun group out in the desert, so we had an artillery fire plan. We also had an A10 tank buster, which was going to do its business, and they were calling for other assets as well.

It was while we were planning all this that the engineer who'd just been looking over my helicopter came over. 'I'm sorry, sir,' he said, 'but you can't take that one. It's got four bullet holes in it.'

One of which had gone up through the blade root - that was our 'bird strike'. Another had gone through a blade in the rear and another had hit somewhere just above Mark's head. That aircraft was obviously out of commission.

Maj Hammond's citation says: "At this stage, it would have been simple for him to declare that the threat was too high to return, and, indeed, the risks were so extreme that he was put under no pressure to do so. However, without hesitation he decided to attempt another recovery using a new aircraft. His flight commander was able to witness first-hand Hammond's calm decision-making and leadership of the joint force planning for the recovery mission."

I spoke to the crew and asked if they were happy to go back. They all said they were. We added a Number Three gunner, Sgt Spence Donnelly, and launched off.

As soon as we got near, the enemy started firing at us again. There was the DC, then a safe zone, and anything in there was fair game. The civilians had all left, it was just baddies, surrounding our guys 24/7, like a siege. So the A10 let them have it. The A10 has a bad reputation with friendly fire, but if you want to quieten someone down then it will. And it did. It just ripped the place apart. It has a 30mm cannon with a phenomenal rate of fire, and it levelled the opposition. I remember looking to my right as we were flying up and just seeing a glow where a big Tellytubby ammo dump was going up. It was amazing.

We dropped down to low level again.

People ask me, 'Weren't you scared going back into Musa Qala for the second time?' To be honest, the only thing I was worried about was making sure that I didn't pork the landing up. A Chinook has a lot of downwash and you're coming into a dusty zone. If you get the landing wrong you end up in what is called 'brown out' where you can't see the ground. If I ended up having to go round again we would have lost the element of surprise.

We took some incoming, but nothing hit the cab this time. We did the landing, got the casualties on board and we were facing south. We were in the zone for 30 seconds, tops.

There was a big building to my right and Dan, my Number Two, said, 'Which way do you want to go out?'

We were going back out over my right shoulder. I said, 'I want to go left.'

He said, 'Don't you want to go right?'

That was the shortest way out.

I said, 'No, there's a building there. I'm going to go left, over my left shoulder, back round and out.'

He said, 'OK.'

So we lifted off and I went over my left shoulder and round and back out over the desert that way. We climbed back up to height, got the lad home and he survived.

One of the Apache guys said to me afterwards, 'Did you see the RPGs?'

I said, 'No... what RPGs?'

He said, 'It's a good job you didn't go right when you took off.'

If we'd taken the shortest route, the belly of the Chinook would have been exposed and the whole helicopter would have been right in front of two RPG firers. Somebody was obviously looking after us that night.

We landed and the great thing was... it's a military thing, an infantry thing... whenever we landed with a casualty, Colonel Tootal and the RSM were there at the back of the ramp to help get the casualties off, which meant a lot to everybody.

And everyone started winding down. People react differently to stress. I smoked a lot of cigarettes, we'd all BS a lot, sit around and try and get back into a normal state of mind. You will de-brief it, you'll talk through what happened, have a cup of tea, smoke some more cigarettes, watch a movie, listen to some music, maybe write a letter home. There's a lot of banter and p***-taking, though obviously it would have been different if we had lost the casualty - it was awful losing LCpl McCulloch, that really did affect us. But as soon as you get your next task underway it's... not forgotten, exactly, but put to the back of your mind for a while.

And then eventually you realise that, potentially, you'll have to do it all over again tomorrow, so you have got to get some sleep.

You tend not to think about your own mortality. I never thought, *My number's up, I'm going to die here*. Maybe when I do, I will, if that makes sense? Before you deploy, you think about what's going to happen if you croak it, but you could walk across the road and be hit by a bus. I ride motorbikes, and I've felt more danger on a bike with someone pulling out in front of me than I have with flying helicopters in Afghanistan - maybe that's the way my mind works, I don't know.

We did seem to attract a lot of RPGs. By the end of the two-month tour - they're short because of the dangers of pilot fatigue, when you're flying eight to ten hours a day - it became a bit of a running joke between myself, Dan and Mark Daffy. Whenever an RPG was fired, at least one of us was in the targeted helicopter. We couldn't work out who the RPG magnet was. My money was on Mark Daffy!

Maj Hammond's DFC was richly deserved, according to his citation. "His personal example to his crew was outstanding," it says, "and the confidence that they placed in his leadership and ability was clear and humbling. Any one of the three separate engagements on the night of 6th September would have been sufficient to shake most men, but Hammond remained calm and dedicated throughout."

Getting a medal was strange: whatever I did, I know all of the other blokes on my flight would have done. There were a lot of very brave things that went on in the aviation world out there during my time - the Apaches looking after us did some amazing stuff - that were not recognised. Mark Daffy was sat beside me the whole time and got nothing, though Dan Baxter got a Mention in Dispatches and Sam got a CJO (Commander, Joint Operations' Commendation).

When you get an award like this you get a host of congratulations letters coming through. My old CO, a two star General, wrote me a very nice letter saying, effectively, remember that your medal is for the crew. And he was spot on. I was the captain, but we made decisions as a crew. I'm the lucky one that gets to wear it and put the DFC after my name and meet the Queen, but it is for everyone who was on board those helicopters that day.

I think people's understanding and comprehension of what is going on out in Afghanistan is lacking, and hopefully this book is something which will address that a little. People only read or see what the media gives them and sections of the media only tend to report certain things in certain ways. Stories about our blokes doing a great job, and aren't they very brave, don't seem to sell papers. They want to read about people being abused, or supposedly under-funded kit, or kit that doesn't work. Or Chinooks setting off mines - that was rubbish. One of my mates was quoted as saying we were flying ancient helicopters. He never said it. I believe in the mission in Afghanistan. Your standard Afghan wants peace. He just wants to make sure that his kids don't get blown up and that he can eke out a living in his patch of desert which he hand tills. Him and his mates have hand-dug a 14-mile irrigation ditch to get water to this little patch of dirt, and they all just want peace and stability. I firmly believe that we are there to help reconstruct their country and give them a better life. The problem is that you have got the Taliban, who don't want that, so you have got to deal with them first.

I believe people need to understand what the guys are going through out there. You come home and you see David Beckham and Posh Spice all over the papers and the telly and you think, *You have completely lost the plot here, people.*

I find it quite interesting that, having done TELIC in Iraq, and with the ongoing casualties, that now a death in Iraq or Afghanistan is somewhere on page 4 or 5 of the papers, and that's a great shame. I find it difficult to believe that people are more interested in what Posh is wearing rather than a soldier paying the ultimate price, but that's the way it appears sometimes.

Lieutenant Timothy Illingworth, CGC
The Rifles

THE British forces in Afghanistan are only there with the blessing of the country's government. Ultimately, it will fall to the Afghans themselves to defeat the Taliban and ensure their country's future. To that end, while our troops have been involved in heavy fighting themselves, the long-term aim is to equip the Afghan police and army to take on the fight.

Tim Illingworth, a young officer with The Rifles, was a member of the Operational Mentoring and Liaison Team (OMLT), working with the local forces to improve their capability.

He had deployed to Afghanistan in April 2006, and quickly fell in love with this wild, rugged country.

On September 10, Lt Illingworth deployed with a small force of OMLT in support of a joint Afghan Police and Army operation to recapture Garmsir District Centre in the face of heavy and continuing resistance. His bravery and example over seven days was well beyond the call of duty. His role was to mentor rather than fight, but he "consistently placed himself in positions of utmost danger. He showed outstanding courage, leadership and selflessness, and such inspiring and raw courage from a relatively young and inexperienced officer is richly deserving of the highest recognition."

I'm 27 years old, and I'm from an Army family. I was at university but it wasn't going all that well because I'd got myself on the wrong course and was bored to death. So my father said, 'Why don't you think about the Army?' I thought it through, and then I quit Uni and joined the Light

Infantry, now amalgamated as part of the The Rifles. I was commissioned in 2002. Since then, I've served in the Falklands, Cyprus and Iraq, and in 2006 I was put forward to join the OMLT in Afghanistan.

The OMLT was there to train up the Afghan Army - how to drive, how to mount VCPs, how to man a sangar, how to patrol, weapons, tactics, everything - and then to advise them 'on the job'.

I went up to Kabul in April to meet my battalion - they call them 'Kandaks' - and watch them pass out after their 14 weeks of basic training. They were a decent bunch, young men who were used to a hard life, who had been brought up with automatic weapons in their homes and whose ancestors had been fighting since time immemorial... the British, the Russians, tribal battles, the whole lot. They were pretty hardy, some even outright scary, and there were one or two officers who would not have been out of place in the British Army. There were obviously others who were less impressive; I think the main thing was that they were very young, like their whole army. After passing out, they were driven down to Kandahar, where a battalion's-worth of vehicles - 40 or so sandy-coloured Ford Ranger pick-ups donated by the US government - were waiting for them. We had a bit of a problem with locally-born blokes going AWOL, just jumping over the fence and disappearing, so we quickly moved them on down into Helmand. Helmand was a much less friendly area, and no-one was likely to wander off too far down there.

All of them seemed genuinely anti-Taliban. They also tended to be anti-Pakistan. I think they saw Pakistan as sponsoring the Taliban, which may or may not be true. They were certainly convinced that northern Pakistan and the border formed an enemy refuge, due to the fact that they could cross with impunity where we could not. But to be fair to the Pakistanis, controlling that area would be a mammoth task that would mean committing the majority of their armed forces, which, given their own situation, isn't a realistic expectation.

So the starting point for the Afghan army was young, inexperienced but willing. We were there to provide them with additional training. However, the key word in Operational Mentoring and Liaison Team is 'Operational'. These guys were going to be put on operations and our job would be to be there while they were taking incoming, advising, assisting.

The officers, particularly, needed giving confidence, and their blokes needed confidence in them. Afghans have a tradition of guerrilla warfare, where everything is a Chinese parliament and the chap with the biggest gun wins the argument. Here we had guys put into a position of power over others - as happens in the British Army - and they weren't quite sure how this conventional concept of military command worked. Some of them were very good at it, others were not - some company commanders would rule by debate, and often get overruled by their men. We were trying to get across that, while it was very sensible to seek advice from experienced NCOs, and to make decisions based on their knowledge, it wasn't acceptable to have soldiers standing around the battalion ops officer, saying, 'No, your plan is rubbish and we're not moving.'

Shortly after their arrival in Helmand, the first Kandak was deployed out and the bulk of the OMLT with them. Various smaller, four-man OMLT teams deployed with groups of Afghan Army to places like Kajaki, Musa Qala, and Naw Zad. It wasn't ideal, because you had four men in isolated positions effectively at the mercy of the Afghan Army. But the situation at the time was fairly quiet - the first rounds had yet to be fired in anger on that tour. The remainder, around 20 of us, were placed in Forward Operating Base Robinson, in the north of Helmand, and given the job of 'seizing' Sangin, a fairly lawless town of around five to eight thousand people, 100 kilometres or so below the Kajaki Dam. It's a big opium-growing area, strategically important because of its size and its geography. The intelligence was that the town was held by the Taliban and the local police were corrupt, and we expected some very stiff resistance on the way in. So we took a fairly substantial number of Afghan soldiers, with Patrols Platoon from 3 Para and various other add-ons, and went down there. But the Taliban aren't stupid, and they did what they did every single time we went into a new area, which was melt away, sit back, look at us, watch how we operate and plan their attacks to suit them.

We sent out a lot of patrols into the surrounding area, and I was left behind in the District Centre with a guy called Capt Leo Docherty from the Scots Guards, a driver, Pte Finau and signaller, LCpl Bow. There was a platoon of the Royal Irish, led by a guy called Sean Williams, to give us some security, and we had five or six Afghans and a couple of interpreters with us. We got ourselves shacked up with the district chief, with the Royal Irish lads next door. The chief had a 60-man militia, all armed to the teeth and usually drugged up - they lived, don't forget, in a country where opium and marijuana grow in the streets like weeds. We were at his mercy, but as long as he was onside we felt everything was OK. We'd dine with him every night and during the day we'd get into Sangin and try to find out what was going on and what the local people were thinking. The more we found out, the more we realised that we were in the wrong place, living with the district chief. He and the chief of police were very unpopular. They were both corrupt, and in a confrontation over extortion rights of the local opium dealers. People felt they couldn't go to the police, because often the police were behind whatever problems they were having, and they'd end up having their livelihoods taken away, or even getting raped or murdered. They said, 'We go to the Taliban, because if we complain to them then things get done.'

The Taliban, being somewhat idealistic, did at least tend not to be corrupt... the local people at least knew where they were with them.

It was all a bit of an eye-opener to the scale of the problems involved in driving out the Taliban. One realised it was not going to be a simple fight. Another eye-opener came when one of our interpreters said to Capt Steve Jones, 'We really don't want to stay with the district chief any longer.'

He was asked why, and said, 'The chief is on the phone now telling somebody what troops you have, what your reaction times are, how long it will take helicopters to get here.'

We all pulled out and went back to FOB Robinson, and started doing regular patrols in the town from there. Hearts and minds stuff and generally trying to find out what we could do to help. One of the things we could do to help was replace the entire police force, which we did.

We had a few incidents to deal with. One sticks in my mind particularly. I was sitting on a roof in the late afternoon sun, looking at the fairly spectacular scenery and enjoying an iced tea and a rare few moments of down time with a couple of mates, Capt Jim Philippson of 7 RHA and Capt Jimmy Slaughter of the Royal Artillery. I'd not met Jim that long before, but we got on very well and spent a lot of time working together. We'd re-routed a patrol to find an unmanned surveillance plane which had gone down on the far side of the river and word came in that they had been ambushed. So the iced tea was dropped and we quickly put together a QRF to go out to help. I was delayed when my Humvee got razor wire wrapped round its axle leaving camp, and by the time I met up with the QRF, it had dismounted and was being engaged by the Taliban.

During this contact, Jim was killed. As a late arrival, I wasn't 100% sure what was happening so I headed towards the front to find out and actually ended up helping to extract Jim's body, although I didn't realise it was him until we got him out from under the trees and into the moonlight. Covering fire throughout was being given by a small team of OMLT which was nearly out-flanked and surrounded. It was for his actions here that WO2 Tommy Johnstone was awarded a Mention in Dispatches. We loaded Jim into a Humvee and then made the decision to head back to camp to re-group.

There wasn't a lot of time to stop and think about it, we still had to get back out and relieve the original patrol. It was all hands to the pump, even some of the guys from UAV unit jumped in, and we went out again. On the route out we were ambushed from the side as we drove along a canal, a barrage of RPGs were fired, most of which, fortunately, went too high. But there was heavy machine gun and AK47 fire, and we were very lucky not to take many casualties. One guy, Sgt Maj Andy Stockton from the UAV callsign who had jumped in, did get badly hurt. An RPG went through his door and took the lower part of his arm off, luckily without detonating. I take my hat off to him, he was pretty good-humoured about the whole thing. His driver or top cover put a plasti-cuff over his arm to staunch the bleeding, and we got out of there. Eventually, we linked up with the other callsign at about 3am. They'd taken one casualty and by all accounts had been fighting pretty hard throughout the night, though by the time we got there it had all calmed down. We consolidated on the position and just waited for daylight, and in the morning a company of Paras from the Airborne Reaction Force flew down and escorted us back to camp.

Obviously, once you get a moment, you think about Jim. He was only 29 years old, a really great guy in the absolute prime of his life, and his death was a tragedy. I think for me, it was mostly the shock of how quickly everything had happened. One minute, you're on the roof having a laugh and an iced tea with the guy, the next you're helping to carry his body out of a firefight. It brought home the fragility of life.

He was buried while we were still in Afghanistan, and we had a memorial service up in Sangin on the day of his funeral. We all got together, had some whisky and said a prayer, which was our way of saying farewell. The Afghans who'd worked with Jim... they see death very differently to us, but they were clearly very sorry that he had died, and they consoled us, but they also saw it as a matter of pride that he had died for their country. Mixed in with that, I think there was some guilt, the sense that it should have been one of them.

I came home for R&R shortly afterwards, and went to visit his grave, which is in a beautiful spot in the grounds of St Alban's Cathedral. An emotional moment.

Shortly after that incident, the Parachute Regiment inserted a company into Sangin district centre - as Hugo Farmer details earlier - and began a long series of battles with the Taliban. Illingworth returned from leave and began working with a new Kandak which had just finished its training.

My sergeant major, Tommy Johnstone, sat me down and introduced my company commander for the second half of my tour, a Capt Daoud Sherzad. I dealt with Daoud every day for the next month or so, and, to be honest, he didn't need any mentoring. He was about my age, 27, and a real soldier's soldier. He was very switched on. For instance, one day I told him we needed to instil some structure, such as having his weapons serial-numbered and allocated to named individuals. He just opened a file, put the paperwork in front of me and said, 'I've already done that.'

If there were things I thought should be done differently, we'd sit and discuss them, in my poor Dari or his better English, or with the interpreter. He was very open to suggestions, almost like a sponge soaking up the way we did things - not so that they could do it exactly the same, but so that he could take the ideas and adapt them to the Afghan culture and ways of working.

When we weren't working we'd sit and just chat away together. We played a lot of chess, chatted about our families and our lives away from war, and I got very fond of him.

His men knew he was good and were tremendously loyal to him. I'm not sure how much they trusted me, but they trusted me through him. So, if I said, 'Come on, let's go and kill some Taliban,' he'd turn to his men and say, 'Are you coming, or are you going to let me go alone?'

He was one of the few Afghan commanders whose men would follow him unequivocally; he was the sort of man that the Afghan Army needed for the future of their country, a born leader, with tactical nous and a lot of balls.

The town of Garmsir, further south, was a key crossing point on the Helmand river. It had recently fallen into Taliban hands and it was decided to mount an operation, involving the Afghan National Army, Afghan police and OMLT support, to clear them out.

A detachment of the Afghan police - effectively, a paramilitary force with older and more experienced blokes than the army, generally - had been involved down there for some time. They'd been getting thoroughly malleted, had basically had enough and had withdrawn to Lashkar Gar. They are tough operators, hardy individuals, well used to fighting the Taliban. Many of them would happily walk into a wall of bullets, firing back. So if they had pulled out, it sounded nasty. It was two weeks from the end of the tour and we were all about to go home, our flights were booked, and there was a feeling of, *Is fate about to catch up with some of us, here?*

But it had to be done. There was nothing between Lash and the Pakistani border except Taliban territory. Apart from the strategic importance, the governor of Helmand felt embarrassed, and wanted us to get it back; we were there to support him, so his wish was our command. British troops were heavily involved up north so it was decided that it would be an Afghan solution, with British mentors. There were 17 Brits, with me as the Afghan Army liaison, Doug Beattie of the Royal Irish with the Afghan police and Capt Paddy Williams in overall command. We had something like 80 army and 80 police with us, and 10 Estonian explosive ordnance disposal guys, who were brilliant. About 200 of us, all told. Initially, Daoud had not been with us, but he was later tasked to join us and having him and a few of his blokes around gave me a lot more confidence.

The local intelligence suggested there were 300 to 400 Taliban in the town and its immediate environs, though as it happened the Taliban hadn't actually occupied the town itself. They had occupied positions out and around but hadn't had time to consolidate their position since the police withdrawal. We came up with a sensible plan to break in, with the police doing the first wave, the army pushing through and then shaking out and sweeping all the way down through the town. And we went down there on September 10, in a long convoy. It took a hell of a long time and we arrived and laid up in the desert about five or six kilometres outside the town during the night. Not easy trying to be inconspicuous, when you have 200 Afghans to herd around like cats. Actually, they were fine; they'd been well-briefed by their commander, and understood what they were going to do.

The next morning, H hour was 5am. We got ready to launch our first assault, on a bridge over a canal which led into the town. Then the Afghan police commander, General Nabijan, decided unilaterally to change the plan and attack a completely different position, an old fort further north. So we took that, and then had to loop round and go back to assault the original canal crossing point, which was now quite heavily defended. The terrain wasn't ideal. The river was to our right and the canal to our left, and beyond the canal was a large area of urbanised farming land and that was full of Taliban. There was a lot of stuff coming across the canal from there, and it took us probably four or five hours to get across the canal, with some pretty hard fighting. But once we got over, it quietened down. Over the other side was a sporadic series of farm buildings, houses and old forts, all the way down to Garmsir, or Kuchnay Darveshan as it's known locally, five klicks away. The houses to the north of the town were still inhabited; like us, the Taliban were fighting a hearts and minds campaign, and wished to avoid including families and residences in their war. They didn't want us kicking in doors because one of their blokes had fired a couple of rounds at us. But we still had to clear them, which was a bizarre but interesting experience. The Afghan Army would go in to a given house and find a family with kids cowering inside... very sensitive, women are untouchable, a massive no-go area, so there would be lots of apologising. Then I'd find some of them had gone missing and they'd be having a slap-up lunch in another house down the road. Mid-operation. Mostly, the Taliban were nowhere to be seen. We managed to clear pretty much all the way down and into the town with very little opposition.

We got down to the District Centre, shook out the Afghans so that we had a footprint on the ground and a defensive position, and then I met up with the rest of the Brits and talked things through with them. The town centre itself was almost empty. It wasn't really residential, anyway - there were shops, businesses, an agricultural college, government buildings - and anyone who might have been there had fled much earlier, during the battles between the Taliban and the police. There was mortar and rocket damage everywhere, and you could quite see why they'd left. I sat down with Gen Nabijan and Maj Kareem, the army commander, in the police headquarters which had been overrun and abandoned a few days earlier. They got their chai on and we sat there for a while, drinking. Maj Kareem was saying things like, 'Victory is ours... the war is won.' I got the impression he thought the job was finished. But that was only the end of day one. Our next task was to push down another three kilometres south, to force the mortar line back and allow people back into the town behind a new buffer zone.

Next day, the Afghan police cracked on. Gen Nabijan was a powerful and charismatic leader, they were a tougher bunch than the young soldiers and a lot of them were from the Garmsir area; they saw it as defending their own patch. The Afghan Army were slightly more reluctant. Maj Kareem was not a massively inspiring chap and I had to bypass him and use Daoud to get the lads moving.

Doug Beattie carried on pushing down south on day two, down the eastern side of the town, and his Afghan police were doing very well.

I started pushing down on the western side with the Army. Almost immediately, we hit some pretty stiff opposition. Right on the edge of town was a Taliban position in two buildings in a thickly wooded area, and they were dug in with three or four machine gun positions. They opened up as we advanced and the Afghans took one killed and two injured, including one of the company commanders. And when he was shot, his company almost stopped fighting. Working with the Afghans, it's very much down to loyalty. Once they were without the commander they respected, it was a challenge to get them to do anything. I tried to get them to push on but it was like banging my head against a brick wall.

So I grabbed Daoud and his blokes and followed Doug Beattie the way he'd gone, providing some relief for him and pushing on down south-east. It did mean we were unbalanced and potentially liable to outflanking, but there was nothing for it. By the end of day two, the

Afghan police had pushed all the way down to another bridge about two kilometres south of the district centre and we occupied that crossing point and a string of three nearby buildings.

I had done a lot of firing myself, clearing buildings, taking out positions in ditches, in clumps of trees, in fields. And there had been a lot of incoming fire, some of it very close. I'd move my head and a round would ping off a rock just beside me, where I'd been a moment earlier. That must have happened a dozen times during the day. You go through your training at Sandhurst and on exercise in Brecon, and they drum it into you... fire a couple of rounds and move, fire a few more rounds and move again. And you go, 'Yeah, yeah,' and you just lie there and fire, because you're cold and wet and thoroughly fed-up. But when you're under fire, you find yourself doing it without even thinking. Thank God for the training.

I'd been shot at before, in Iraq during TELIC 2, where we'd come across hijackers and had had a bit of AK or the odd grenade come our way. But nothing like this. It was constant, it was all day and it was draining. You can't think about it too much, because if you start the *what if, what if, what if* process, you'll end up doing nothing. So I made the decision, early on, that if I was going to get it, then I was going to get it and there wasn't a lot I could do about it. There were rounds literally everywhere... if you get shot then you get shot. Every single one of the guys out there was exactly the same. One of the JTACs attached to us, Bombardier Sam New, had the wire shot off his radio while the handset was pressed to his head. He looked down and there it was, just dangling. The round would have missed his head by three or four inches. With that amount of lead in the air, it is 90% drills and 10% blind luck.

I could see Taliban fighters, and I could see my rounds hitting them and them going down. Not a particularly nice thing to have to do, but if you're in the Army that is part of the job, I'm afraid, so I didn't let it affect me. Sitting here now, some months later and with the luxury of the time to think about it, I feel more emotional about it; back then, I was just reacting to what was in front of me.

We must have killed an awful lot of Taliban that day, but we didn't see many dead, if any, because by the time we reached whatever position we were assaulting the dead and wounded would have been dragged away. They were assiduous about that - often, you'd find pools of blood, or blood trails leading off into the opium fields, but never the actual bodies. We only managed to take one POW during the whole tour: if you saw Sean Langan's *Dispatches* film about this whole period, he was the guy in that film who was brought in in quite a bad way. He'd been shot through his lungs and he was furious, as furious as you can be when you're in that state, that his mates had allowed him to be taken. He'd been led to believe that we would torture him and kill him, and he was amazed that we looked after him and patched him up. I went back later and visited him in a British hospital in Camp Bastion and my sergeant major, Tommy Johnstone, also spent a while chatting to him. He couldn't believe his guys had left him behind, he said that just never happened; it was one of the quicker attacks we mounted, and I think they just didn't have time. He also gave us some useful intel - they were working in 10-man teams, and he confirmed there were about 400 of them in the Garmsir area which, whether you take his word or not, was a pretty interesting figure. Though to us on the ground it didn't change the price of fish, and we still had a job to do and we still had to get on and do it.

Day two ended - we were generally fighting dawn to dusk, as the Afghans had no night-vision - and it had been quite a successful day on the eastern side, less so on the western where the troops had come to a standstill after taking the three casualties.

The following day, September 13, an Afghan Police/OMLT patrol was ambushed and pinned down by heavy and effective enemy fire, causing one British casualty. In an effort to relieve the pressure, Lt Illingworth led his Afghan company commander and a foot patrol to neutralise the enemy position. The ANA were unwilling to advance on the heavily-defended enemy position; to stall at that stage would almost certainly have resulted in further casualties so Illingworth took a calculated risk, personally leading the attack in an attempt to inspire the frightened and uncommitted Afghan soldiers.

First thing on day three, I took 17 Afghans and re-cleared the buildings pretty much all the way down from where we had started off the day before, to make sure that they were unoccupied. That went pretty smoothly and by 8.30am I'd linked up with Daoud's guys where I'd left them the night before. By that stage, Doug Beattie had taken his Afghan police and started pushing further down, trying to get to the 3K point to create this buffer zone for the town, so Daoud and I started following, trying to catch up with him. The terrain Doug was in wasn't great for vehicles, so his WMIKs were in an open field. Unfortunately, whilst in the open he was heavily engaged by Taliban hiding in a wood line to his front and a sandy-coloured, broken-down building to his right hand side. One of the drivers, a TA sergeant major, had been shot in the arm and they needed assisting, so we tried as best we could to get a move on. I was on foot with the Afghans and Tommy, and we moved forward to a position where I could see Doug Beattie and the enemy. We holed up in an old stone barn which looked down onto the tree line, and used anti-tank weapons and small arms fire to suppress them while the shot TA guy, Joe, I think his name was, was extracted. Doug co-ordinated an air strike by French Mirages, and they raked the woods but they weren't particularly effective. We'd had

A10s over the day before to deal with an intractable group of Taliban in a different palm grove and the cannon fire from that had literally torn the trees down and removed the problem. The Mirages didn't have the same capability. They made a second pass, but again were not decisive and we had a bit of a stalemate. I had a chat with Doug over PRR, and it was clear that we needed to get those Taliban out of there because it was within our three kilometre line.

I turned to Daoud and said, 'Right, we're going to have to go in and clear that wood line.'

I outlined a quick plan, he relayed it to his blokes and we all jumped up. There was a track running away from our building down through a field of 8ft tall maize, with a ditch on its edge. The idea was to get into the maize and move down to the end of the track, where there was a kind of T-junction, a point from where we could attack the flank of the Taliban positions. The maize would provide us a bit of cover from view, but not from fire. We got to the end of the track, within perhaps 50 metres of the enemy position, and shook out onto the edge of the field in front of them. It was a marijuana plantation... loads of three-foot high ganja bushes. Almost immediately, we came under RPG fire from the tree line and the other position in the sandy-coloured building.

Three days' heavy fighting saw the resolve of the Afghan troops fail again. Seeing this, Lt Illingworth moved straight to the front of them and moved alone to within 30 metres of the first enemy position under heavy enemy fire. The ANA company commander, Capt Daoud, joined him.

The grenades were high but as they screamed overhead the Afghans went straight down, most of them into a ditch which ran past this T-junction. That's not the idea. The idea is to return fire, try to suppress the enemy, and *then* go down, in cover, from where you can continue to fire... it was just inexperience and youth. The trouble was, that enabled the Taliban to increase their fire, and it immediately got very heavy... maybe three machine guns, small arms, more RPGs coming in. Probably two or three launchers, at a range of 50 metres. An RPG detonated 10 metres to my right between two of the Afghan lads and fragged them both in the legs. Another came in, heading straight for me. They're big old rounds, slow enough that you can see them but quick enough that you can't move out of the way... this stuff in films, where guys see one, yell, 'RPG! Incoming!' and dive for cover is nonsense. Once it's in the air, if it's that close, forget it. I just had time to think, *Oh no!* I'd seen the other go in and detonate a moment before, the guys are on the ground, screaming, and I actually thought that I was about to die. It landed right beside me, missing my foot by a metre or so, and didn't explode - it just ricocheted over the head of the sergeant major behind me and out over the maize field where it detonated in mid-air. All I heard on my radio was, 'What the *f**** was that?'

I thought, *Well, maybe it's my day today.*

Rounds were zipping and cracking through the air and landing all around, left, right and centre, and we were not returning fire effectively at all... people were just pointing their AKs over the top of the ditch and pulling the trigger. They were almost more dangerous to their own side. The RPGs, and seeing the rounds landing, clarified it in my mind; I thought, *Let's just get on and sort this mess out.*

The enemy were difficult to see. They were moving between their positions, and the trees and the marijuana bushes gave them lots of cover. Plus we were heavily out-gunned - we had light weapons, and that was it.

Daoud managed to get three or four of his blokes out into firing positions, but others were hanging back or even running away - the sergeant major had to stay at the rear and try to stop them from legging it back to the building. He stemmed the tide and then came up over PRR and asked if I wanted him to try and get them to right-flank the Taliban positions. I remember saying 'That'd be nice!', though it probably would've caused more confusion than anything. I was left with Daoud and a few of his guys. He grabbed an RPG off one of them and we pushed further forward together, with a couple of Afghan privates alongside.

We got to within 40 metres and Daoud thought he could see one of their machine gun nests.

He got the launcher up onto his shoulder and as he knelt up he was shot in the heart and went straight down.

Probably a lucky stray round, possibly aimed, we'll never know.

I had about half a second to think,

And then I carried on returning fire.

He didn't die immediately, but he was out of it and obviously very near to death. His soldiers pretty much gave up, then. They seemed to forget that there were people still shooting at them and started wailing, 'He is dead, he is dead.'

I scrambled back to the ditch with the two soldiers. The other Afghans were all sitting there in shock, pretty much out of ammunition because they had just sprayed it willy-nilly over the top of the ditch. It was clear that this attack was going nowhere. The only commander who knew what he was doing was dead. We didn't have the men, we didn't have the ammunition and they certainly didn't have the will to fight.

I grabbed another captain, Ahmedullah, and four other guys, and told them to take Daoud's body back to the house. I tried to explain that the rest of us would carry on fighting until they got his body back, and then we would withdraw. It was hard getting the message through, because Engineer, my interpreter, had stayed with the sergeant major. But they nodded, in a dazed sort of way.

His citation says: "Illingworth took up the commander's rocket launcher, firing three rounds into the main enemy position in full view of the enemy while exposed and under withering fire. The Afghan force abandoned him, but in spite of his isolation he attempted to assault the enemy position, expending seven magazines of ammunition in the process. However, the enemy fire was unrelenting."

I saw a few of the soldiers pick up and carry off Daoud's body, back along the track by the side of the maize field, and then I grabbed the RPG launcher and a handful of rounds and pushed back forwards, waving to the others to follow me. It took me a couple of attempts to get the first RPG off. I'd seen them used but I had never fired one before, and I didn't realise that there's a small nut that sticks out of every round that you have to make fit into a nick in the barrel. I'd just rammed the thing in, knelt up and tried to fire, and nothing happened. I got back down again, played with it, found out what was wrong, got up again and tried to fire it again... but this time the safety catch was on. I flipped the safety catch and fired and it went way high, over into the trees. Not terribly impressive, all told.

I fired two more, one went into the sandy-coloured building and the second went into the wood line, and that did quieten the Taliban down. I got back onto my rifle, moving forward, identifying individuals if they left cover and shooting them if I could. I finished my magazine, went to change it and that's when I noticed no-one else was firing. I changed the mag - it was my seventh and last, which is an indication - and turned round. And there was not a soul in sight. Which concerned me slightly.

Looking back, I think Daoud's men had heard the word 'withdraw' and had got confused and just pulled out. I was now probably 25 metres away from the positions that we were originally supposed to be assaulting. Most of my rounds would have been fairly accurate, and had kept their heads down. But as soon as I stopped to change my magazine, and the firing stopped, it was obviously a matter of moments before the Taliban worked out that I was on my own. Then it was going to be game over, basically. Quite a worrying moment.

The other problem was that the last thing Tommy Johnstone had heard me say on the PRR was 'Daoud's dead!' He'd then tried to contact me but I was back down in the ditch at that point, and my radio reception had gone. He told me afterwards that he assumed I was gone as well, and he was busy thinking about how he was going to recover my body.

None of that was in my mind at the time, of course. I was just thinking I wasn't going any further into this hornets' nest. I turned around and went back the way I had come, back on the track and then back into the maize field. As I retreated, the Taliban opened fire on me again, so there were rounds chopping the maize down all around.

Then I stumbled upon Daoud's body, lying on the earth with a solitary Afghan soldier next to it, crying.

"Understanding the importance to Afghans of not leaving behind their fallen comrade, he made repeated attempts to drag Capt Daoud's body back with him. Finding himself under increasingly heavy enemy fire, exhausted and running out of ammunition, he finally abandoned attempts only when he saw the Taliban about to cut off his escape."

I got down next to him. I couldn't leave Daoud there, so I gestured to this guy to help me drag him back. A dead body is never an easy thing to handle, and Daoud was six feet tall and well-built, so he was heavy. I was knackered and carrying a considerable amount of kit, and the Afghan bloke was hard to persuade. I'd heard that they have a cultural thing about touching dead bodies - though it didn't seem to stop the Taliban - maybe that was it. Anyway, it took me a while to get this guy to take a leg but eventually he did so and we managed to pull him a bit further back towards our own building. But we started getting a lot more rounds coming in, probably because they could see us moving the tops of the maize, and at that stage the guy decided enough was enough and disappeared. So I was now on my own, trying to drag Daoud, inch-by-inch, with one foot in both hands, tug-of-war style. After a minute of this, and about five metres covered, I realised that it wasn't going to work, and that the Taliban were going to be in the maize field any moment and we'd then have two bodies, probably after a lot of torture and unpleasantness for me.

It was something I'd never had to deal with before. You don't leave a man behind. Certainly not if he's wounded, there's no question, especially in somewhere like Afghanistan or Iraq where the enemy are not going to respect the Geneva Conventions. A dead man... you'd still move heaven and earth to get him back, because of your respect for him, but you have to weigh that up. Ultimately, would you trade another life - your own or someone else's - to get a body back? No, and it would be stupid to, and the dead guy wouldn't have wanted it, either.

I was alive, he was dead. Nothing was going to change the fact that he was dead, but something might change the fact that I was alive. But it was still the hardest decision I've ever had to make, bar none. I sat there for a minute, or maybe a minute and a half, it seemed like forever, with rounds zipping over me, thinking, *I'm going to have to leave him*. It was a decision I hope I never have to make again. Here was a guy who had died doing what I was mentoring him to do. I'd got him into this situation, and I really wanted to get him out.

I left him, and made my own way back through the maize,

crawling initially and then, deciding that I wasn't getting very far, running. Weirdly, I heard this dog whining somewhere in the maize and I thought, *I'd better stop and help the poor thing.* And then I thought, *What the hell are you thinking? Just run like buggery.*

I got back to the building and the sergeant major was there. He was slightly pleased to see me. And the first thing Capt Ahmedullah did was come up and say, 'Where is Daoud's body? What have you done with it?'

He was very abrupt, and I rather lost my temper with him. Tommy restrained me, made me sit down and said, 'We're not accomplishing anything here... let's work out what we are going to do.' A very good NCO, Tommy. A top man.

We were under no immediate threat. We could have defended the building we were in with about five blokes and a handful of ammo, but we needed to extract the casualties from the RPG strike and another lad who had been shot. I sat down for a bit and got my thoughts together. I wanted to get some more Afghans and go back and get Daoud out, but Doug Beattie and the sergeant major, quite sensibly, said, 'You're not going anywhere... you've done your best. They left him, it's up to them.'

I briefed Maj Kareem as to where the body was and the best route in without being seen. Lo and behold, I don't think he took my advice. We took the casualties back to the district centre to get them patched up while Kareem took a load of guys off to recover the body. We heard some firing and explosions in the distance, and half an hour later they turned up with a flatbed truck full of very seriously injured guys, missing arms, their legs all in pieces. They were Kareem's guys: I think something like an SPG9 anti-tank rocket must have detonated fairly close to them. They did get Daoud's body back, though it left another five guys very seriously injured. That's the Afghan mentality. They could not leave him there, and that's the price they paid.

They all survived, I think, thanks to Ant Cowley, our medic. I went and visited them back at the British Hospital in Bastion after we got back... they were all there, missing a foot or a bit of a leg, but all smiling and happy to see us.

After Daoud was killed, we spent another three or four days down there but it was a battle to get the Afghan Army to do anything, because morale had gone. They didn't trust me, because I had got one of their commanders killed. But my tour was over anyway - I pulled out, with the Royal Marines coming in with a new set of Afghan Army to take over our role.

It sounds strange, but I love Afghanistan. I spent six months of my life there, and that's long enough to develop an emotional attachment to a place and its people. It's a breathtakingly beautiful country, and one of many contrasts. Kabul is in a staggering spot, almost a crater surrounded by mountains, with this endless blue sky stretching out forever. Sangin is in a lush, picturesque valley, irrigated by the Americans after the Russians left, with more of these purple and beige hills off in the distance. But some of the camps we were living in, like Bastion and Tombstone in Helmand, were surrounded by absolutely flat desert, like the surface of the moon or somewhere. And extraordinarily hot - we hit 60°C one day, according to the thermometer outside our hut. And the route we took down into Garmsir was different again... we had to divert because we kept hitting drifting sands, 30ft-high dunes. Like the sort of thing you might expect to find in the Sahara desert. I would go back like a shot. I'd love to see the country develop, I'd love to think the job that I was doing down there was important, and that it made a difference. That, one day, the Afghans will live better lives. I'm sure the rest of the guys on the OMLT would say the same. We were working with a bunch of unusual and surprising people, sometimes good and sometimes bad, but always interesting.

Of course, I saw and did some things out there which have had an
effect on me. Killing people... I was only 26, 27, I've seen friends die.
It feels... actually, I still haven't worked out how it feels. Losing friends
is massive. Having partaken in an operation, having killed people,
having shot people, having blown people up, called in fire missions on
houses... though I wouldn't think twice about doing it again, because
the situation you're in demands it. Jim dying... I wasn't there when it
happened, which I regret. Daoud, I was right next to him and I saw it
happen. There's a feeling of helplessness. I had a close bond with him,
he was awesome. For a long time, I felt... in fact, I still do feel
responsible for him being where he is and me being where I am. It's a
pretty weighty responsibility. But he died doing what it was he was
supposed to be doing, leading his men from the front and doing it
well, and I do feel some pride in that, for me and for him. It isn't a bad
way for a soldier to go. Of course, it's in my mind that I led him into
that situation. If I hadn't, he wouldn't be dead. But there was no
question that it had to be done and it could easily have been him trying
to drag my body out; if the gun that shot him had been pointing
approximately 2mm to the right it would have shot me, given the
range. Two millimetres - the difference between me dying and me
sitting here now, talking to you and planning to go to the pub later.
That's how it goes.

I bumped into Paddy and Doug in Camp Bastion as I was waiting
for my flight out. We went from fighting out in Garmsir to sitting
back in the UK in about a week. It wasn't an easy adjustment to make.
One of the problems we had, as an OMLT, was that we all came in
from different units. Once it was over, we dispersed very quickly. We
didn't get the chance as a unit, or a bunch of people, to talk things
through over a few beers and get it out of our systems, and do the
whole bonding thing that gets you through these times. If you go
somewhere with your regiment, you come back and you're all

together. This was different. But we had an OMLT reunion in Edinburgh later on and, although not all the guys could make it, it was great to be able to sit down and talk to people who'd been through the same thing as you. It did help settle pretty much all of the questions I had in my mind. It's all very well talking about it with friends, family, your girlfriend, but it's not the same as people who were there.

The guys in that OMLT, and some of the Afghans, it truly was a privilege to work with them, and the lessons I took away from the medics, the signallers, all of those guys, were just as valuable as what the Afghans took away from us. Coming together and forming a mentoring team in that way, and then getting into heavy and protracted contacts, was something none of us had done before, and will probably never have the opportunity to do again. But the way that they conducted themselves, and the support that we gave each other, was just outstanding.

> The citation details why Lt Illingworth was awarded the British Army's second highest gallantry award. "His bravery and example over seven days were well beyond the call of duty. His role was to mentor rather than fight. However, understanding the importance of Garmsir, he placed himself in a position of utmost danger to influence events. His outstanding courage, leadership and selflessness in pressing home his attack undoubtedly distracted the enemy ambush and saved the lives of both ANA and British soldiers. His attempt to recover Capt Daoud's body was an act of cultural significance, which has forged a lasting bond between the ANA and their OMLT mentors. Such inspiring and raw courage from a relatively young and inexperienced officer is richly deserving of the highest recognition."

The medal, to me, is simply a recognition that I did my job as well as I could have done. That's all it is. If I could have given an award to every man who was in the OMLT I would have done and I feel very privileged to have been singled out for the CGC. It's an enormous honour, and it's nice to get recognition. But then Daoud - if he had been in the British Army - would have won a Victoria Cross, because he was leading his men from the front, taking them to enemy positions in the face of very heavy fire. But because he is an Afghan he gets little or no recognition.

I was trying to find out what happened to him. The last time I saw him, I was zipping him up into a body bag and loading him onto a helicopter. But I met a guy when I got back to England, having a drink just before Christmas, and he said he was on the plane that took his body back up to Kabul, which is where he was from. He saw his family, his wife and children, come and collect him, and they were handed a couple of bin bags full of money, compensation for him having laid his life down. That was something that had been bugging me for a long time after I got home: I wanted to know that his family had been looked after. These things can get handled badly in Afghanistan, and I was very pleased to learn that he had got back to his family and they had been taken care of by the Afghan system.

The people I was with, I'd like to mention them by name, because they were outstanding: WO2 Tommy Johnstone AAC, WO2 Chip Davidson TA, CSgt Si Hewer PWRR, Sgt Jason Tomlinson The Rifles, Sgt Ronnie Docherty TA, Sgt Michael Elgie AAC, Cpl Aaron Galtress, R SIGS, Cpl Anthony Cowley RAMC, Cpl Steve Emeny RLC, LCpl Steve Chambers RM, Pte 'Fi' Finau RLC, Pte 'Chilly' Chilcott RLC and Sig 'Robbo' Robertson R SIGS. They were brilliant. The experience they will take back to their units, regular infantry advances to contact with Afghans instead of British troops, is just unreal and they performed all the way though. They were outstanding.

The real lesson I took away from the tour was that the Afghans are not all that we expect them to be. If you start to impose British or American standards and methods of doing things upon them then you are going to come up against a brick wall every time. We are not there to create another British Army; we are there to help them create their own and allow them to defeat their enemies themselves.

GLOSSARY OF TERMS

A10 A slow, ugly and unglamorous American close air support aircraft nicknamed 'The Warthog', the A10 is much beloved of troops on the ground for its extraordinary firepower (its GAU gun can fire 3,900 armour piercing shells a minute and it can also carry bombs and missiles). Highly durable and very popular with its pilots.

AC-130 Spectre This is a heavily-armed ground attack aircraft used mainly by Special Forces. Based on the C-130 Hercules transport plane, it is powered by four turboprops and its armament ranges from 20mm Gatling guns to 105mm howitzers. Because it is slow, it is vulnerable to ground fire so is used at night only.

AK-47 The world's most common assault rifle, with over 100 million manufactured, it fires 7.62mm ammunition and is effective at up to 300 metres. Cheap, simple to operate and easy to acquire, it is also robust and able to withstand rough handling in dusty conditions, and is the weapon of choice for insurgents and guerrilla fighters around the world.

Apache The AH-64 Apache is the United States Army's principal attack helicopter, and is also in service with British forces (built under licence by Westland). It is armed with a 30mm M230 chain gun and carries a mixture of rockets mounted on its stub wings; it is used against ground targets in support of ground troops, and as a top cover for Chinooks.

B1B US replacement for the B52 long-range bomber.

BATUS The British Army's Training Unit Suffield, part of a vast training area in Alberta, Canada, which is used for huge live-firing exercises.

BMP A Soviet-built armoured fighting vehicle, best described as Iraq's version of the British Warrior. Equipped with a 73mm smooth bore gun or, in later variants, a 30mm cannon, the Iraqi Army had 800 of them prior to the war.

British Army Units A Regiment (Regt) typically contains around 650 soldiers; some Infantry Regiments have more than one unit of this size; these are 'Battalions' (for example, '3 Para' is the 3rd Battalion of the Parachute Regiment). Each Regiment or Battalion will be split into several Companies (Coy), each commanded by a Major and typically consisting of around 120 soldiers. Companies are broken down into Platoons, under the command of a Lieutenant, each with around 24 men. Each Platoon will be further composed of three Sections of around eight men, each under the command of a non-commissioned officer. A multiple is a small unit of around 10 men.

CBA Combat body armour, incorporating a protective ceramic chest plate covering the heart and capable of stopping shrapnel and small arms rounds.

CH-46 Sea Knight A 'small Chinook' medium-lift assault helicopter used by the United States Marine Corps to provide all-weather, day-or-night assault transport of combat troops and, occasionally, supplies and equipment. Used to carry British forces during the invasion of Iraq.

CH-47 Chinook The Boeing CH-47 Chinook is a versatile, twin-engine, twin rotor heavy-lift helicopter used for troop movement, artillery emplacement and battlefield resupply.

CQMS The Company Quartermaster Sergeant (CQMS) in the British Army and Royal Marines is the company NCO in charge of supplies.

Challenger 2 The British Army's 62 tonne main battle tank. Equipped with a 120mm gun and two 7.62mm machine guns, it is protected by classified Chobham armour and its 1200 bhp engine produces a top speed of close to 40mph.

Cobra The Bell AH-1 Cobra is an attack helicopter which shares a common engine, transmission and rotor system with the famous 'Huey' of the Vietnam war. It was the backbone of the United States Army's attack helicopter fleet until it was replaced by the AH-64 Apache. Upgraded versions continue to fly with the United States Army National Guard and other users.

Dragunov A Russian-designed sniper rifle, firing 7.62mm ammunition and effective at 1200 yards. Most insurgent snipers in Iraq are believed to use the Dragunov, which was manufactured under licence in the country during Saddam's time in power.

Dushka Colloquial name for the DShK, a Soviet-made heavy machine gun originally designed for anti-aircraft use but employed in Iraq and Afghanistan as an anti-personnel weapon.

ECM Electronic counter measures, a means of interrupting the electronic signals which are sometimes used to detonate IEDs.

FIBUA Fighting in a built-up area.

Full Screw Colloquial term for a corporal.

FV432 Outdated British armoured personnel carrier, dating from the 1960s.

GPMG The L7A1/2 General Purpose Machine Gun used by the British Army and the Royal Marines since the 1950s. Much-loved by its operators, and colloquially called the 'Gimpy' by some, it can be used as a light weapon, mounted on a bipod, or in a sustained fire role, mounted on a tripod and fitted with the C2 optical sight. It fires around 750 belt-fed 7.62mm rounds per minute and is effective to a range of 1800 metres.

Harrier The world's first vertical/short take off and landing-capable fighter aircraft, it is in service with the RAF and is used in a close air support role in Afghanistan, delivering bombs or missiles onto enemy positions, or strafing them with cannon fire.

IED Improvised explosive device - a 'home-made' bomb placed at the side of the road and detonated as British forces pass.

Lance Jack Colloquial term for a lance corporal.

LAW The Light Anti-armour Weapon is a disposable, one-man-portable, High Explosive Anti Tank (HEAT) missile system capable of destroying armoured targets at ranges up to 500 metres.

Lynx A highly-agile, very quick attack helicopter in service with the Army Air Corps and the Fleet Air Arm. A British Lynx from 847 Naval Air Squadron was shot down over Basra on May 6, 2006, killing all five on board, including the Commanding Officer of 847 NAS.

LZ/HLS Landing zone, helicopter landing site - described as 'hot' if fighting is ongoing as the aircraft arrives.

Milan A medium-range, anti-tank missile system, comprising a launch and control unit and a disposable launch tube containing the missile. The operator must keep the cross hairs of his sight on the target, while the computer in the control unit steers the missile in to a target up to 2000 metres away.

Minimi/LMG The FN 'Minimi' is a light machine gun firing 5.56mm rounds at a rate of 725rpm to a range of 1000 metres.

Mirage A family of French supersonic attack aircraft, later versions of which have been operated by Coalition forces in close air support of British troops in Afghanistan.

Mortar Mortars are muzzle-loading indirect fire weapons which fire shells at low velocity over short ranges, with high-arcing ballistic trajectories. Relatively simple and easy to operate - the operator drops the shell into the barrel and the firing pin detonates the propellant as it strikes the base of the tube - both Iraqi insurgents and the Taliban in Afghanistan have used them heavily against British troops, often firing from flat bed trucks. British forces are themselves adept with mortars.

MT-LB Soviet-built armoured personnel carrier; Iraq had 500 of them.

Net The radio network linking troops on the ground with others in command posts.

OPTAG The British Army's Operational Training and Advisory Group, which helps prepare soldiers for operations.

Pinzgauer A highly-capable, all-terrain vehicle used for carrying troops or equipment.

Predator/UAV The Predator is an American-built unmanned aerial vehicle (UAV) in use with US and British forces. It is used in a reconnaissance role and can also engage enemy forces with its Hellfire missiles.

PRR Personal Role Radio is a small transmitter-receiver that allows infantry soldiers to communicate over short distances, increasing their effectiveness.

RPG This acronym is a catch-all term for a number of rocket-propelled grenade systems which, as with most arms used by the Iraqi insurgents and the Taliban of Afghanistan, originated in the Soviet Union. The most common RPG in use in the two conflicts is the RPG-7, which dates from the early 1960s. Simple to use, freely available and highly portable, despite its relative antiquity it can be devastating against unarmoured or even lightly-armoured vehicles and, obviously, personnel. The RPG-7 brought down the two Blackhawk helicopters shot down over Mogadishu in the *Blackhawk Down* incident, and it has since, unfortunately, claimed a number of British lives.

RPK A Kalashnikov-designed light machine gun, based on the AK-47, firing 7.62mm rounds at a rate of 600rpm.

SA80 The standard rifle of the British infantryman or Royal Marine. So-called for 'Small Arms 1980s', the original SA80 suffered from reliability and other problems but the current SA80A2 variant is a popular weapon. It uses 5.56mm ammunition and is effective at 400 metres, or 800 metres in a light support role.

Scimitar A lightly-armoured, fast and agile armoured vehicle used primarily in a reconnaissance role. Armed with a 30mm Rarden cannon and a 7.62mm machine gun, it has a crew of three.

Snatch Wagon A lightly armoured Land Rover, originally developed for Northern Ireland, which can withstand small arms and, sometimes, RPGs.

Spartan A derivative of the Combat Vehicle Reconnaissance tracked vehicle used to carry specialist troops such as mortar fire control teams, anti aircraft teams or as engineer command/reconnaissance vehicles.

T55 The Soviet Union's main battle tank in the 1950s and early 1960s, Iraq fielded a large number of these obsolete vehicles - as well as newer T62 and T72s - against the invading Coalition forces in 2003. Many were destroyed.

Top cover Soldiers travelling in Warriors or Snatch Land Rovers, with rifle or Minimi at the ready, to deter and engage the enemy if attacked.

Tornado Main UK jet fighter and ground attack aircraft, a 1500mph aeroplane in service since the 1970s but now being replaced.

Tracer Illuminated rounds, enabling the firer to see their trajectory and adjust his aim; also used to 'spot' targets - tracer will be fired at the target to identify it for others.

UGL The 'Under-slung Grenade Launcher' is designed to be mounted beneath the barrel of the SA80 and can fire 40mm high explosive rounds, smoke and illuminating rounds out to a range of 350 metres.

VCP Vehicle checkpoint, a roadside stop where soldiers can carry out searches for weapons, ammunition or suspects.

Warrior The British Army's main infantry fighting vehicle, equipped with a 30mm **Rarden** cannon which can destroy light armour at a range of 1500 metres and a 7.62mm co-axial **chain gun** (a chain gun is a motor-powered chain-driven weapon which does not rely on recoil to reload; it is thus more reliable and more flexible in terms of rates of fire). Warrior has a crew of three - a commander, a driver and a gunner - and can carry seven dismounted troops ('**dismounts**'). Rarden, a contraction of Royal Armament, Research Department and Enfield, fires armour piercing and high explosive incendiary rounds to a range of four kilometres. Now fitted with additional **bar armour**, bolt-on armour which offers more protection against RPGs.

Webbing The 'Personal Load Carrying Equipment' worn by all soldiers and Marines.

WMIK The WMIK (Weapons Mounted Installation Kit) is the combat patrol variant of the Land Rover. Used primarily for force protection and recce purposes, it is agile, robust and extremely powerful with GPMG and .50 cal armaments.

.50 Cal What is referred to in this book as the '.50 Cal' is actually the L1A1 12.7mm heavy machine gun, an updated version of the Browning M2 'Fifty-cal'. It fires up to 635 rounds a minute and is effective at a range of two kilometres.

203 M16 Main US infantry rifle, with 203 grenade launcher.

ALSO OUT NOW FROM
MONDAY BOOKS

PICKING UP THE BRASS

Eddy Nugent (Paperback, £7.99)

IT'S 1985, The Smiths are in the charts and Maggie Thatcher is in No10. Eddy Nugent's in Manchester, he's 16 and he's slowly going out of his mind with boredom. Almost by accident, he goes and joins the British Army. Overnight, he leaves the relative sanity of civvie street and falls headlong into the lunatic parallel universe of basic training: a terrifying (and accidentally hilarious) life of press ups, boot polish and drill at the hands of a bunch of right bastards.

Picking Up The Brass is a riotous and affectionate look at life as an ordinary young recruit – the kind of lad who doesn't end up in the SAS or become an underwater knife-fighting instructor.

'Eddy Nugent' is the nom de plume of two former soldiers, Ian Deacon and Charlie Bell. Closely based on their own experiences, it's a must-read for anyone who has served, anyone who is planning to join up or anyone who's ever thought, 'Surely not every soldier in the Army is trained to kill people with a toothpick?'

'Laugh-out loud funny' - **Soldier Magazine**
'Hilarious' - **The Big Issue**
'FHM- approved' - **FHM**

Available from all good bookshops, or direct from the publishers at <u>www.mondaybooks.com</u> or 01455 221752.

WATCHING MEN BURN
A SOLDIER'S STORY

Tony McNally (Paperback, £7.99)

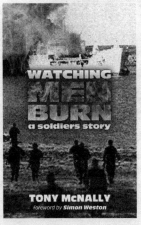

++ The Falklands ++ 1982 ++ TONY MCNALLY is a Rapier missile operator, shooting down Argentinean planes attacking British troops and ships. And it's a tough job - the enemy pilots are fearless and they arrive at supersonic speed and breathtakingly low altitude.

But Tony's war is going well...

Until they bomb the Sir Galahad - a troop ship he is supposed to be protecting. His Rapier fails and he watches, helpless, as bombs rain down on the defenceless soldiers. Fifty men die, and many are left terribly injured.

Tortured by guilt and the horror of the bombing, Tony has relived the events of that day over and over again in his mind.

Watching Men Burn is his true story of the Falklands War - and its awful, lingering aftermath.

Available from all good bookshops, or direct from the publishers at <u>www.mondaybooks.com</u> or 01455 221752.

WASTING POLICE TIME...
THE CRAZY WORLD OF THE WAR ON CRIME
PC David Copperfield (£7.99)

PC DAVID COPPERFIELD is an ordinary bobby quietly waging war on crime...when he's not drowning in a sea of paperwork, government initiatives and bogus targets.

Wasting Police Time is his hilarious but shocking picture of life in a modern British town, where teenage yobs terrorise the elderly, drunken couples brawl in front of their children and drug-addicted burglars and muggers roam free.

He reveals how crime is spiralling while millions of pounds in tax is frittered away, and reveals a force which, crushed under mad bureaucracy, is left desperately fiddling the figures.

His book has attracted rave reviews for its dry wit and insight from The Sunday Times, The Guardian, The Observer, The Daily Mail, The Mail on Sunday and The Daily Telegraph;.

'Being a policeman in modern England is not like appearing in an episode of The Sweeney, Inspector Morse or even The Bill, sadly,' says Copperfield. 'No, it's like standing banging your head against a wall, carrying a couple of hundredweight of paperwork on your shoulders, while the house around you burns to the ground.'

"A huge hit... will make you laugh out loud" – **The Daily Mail**
"Very revealing" – **The Daily Telegraph**
"Damning... gallows humour" – **The Sunday Times**
"Graphic, entertaining and sobering" – **The Observer**
"A sensation" – **The Sun**
By PC David Copperfield – as seen on BBC1's *Panorama*
www.coppersblog.blogspot.com

Available from all good bookshops, or direct from the publishers at www.mondaybooks.com or 01455 221752.

429

SO *THAT'S* WHY THEY CALL IT GREAT BRITAIN

How one tiny country gave so much to the world
Steve Pope (Paperback £7.99)
PUBLISHED APRIL 2009

IT COVERS less than half of one per cent of the earth's land mass, but is responsible for more 40% of the world's great inventions. The first car, first train, and first aeroplane *(sorry, Wright Bros)* came from Great Britain, as did the steam engine, the jet engine and the engine of the internet (the www protocols used online).

Britons created the first computer and the first computer game *(noughts and crosses)*, as well as the telegraph, the telephone and the television *(and the mousetrap, the lightbulb and the loo roll)*.

In almost every sphere – from agriculture and medicine to politics, science and the law – we have led the way for centuries.

Most of the world's major sports originated here – along with William Shakespeare and Jane Austen, The Beatles and The Stones, *Fawlty Towers* and *The Office*.

This book shows – without boasting, and with tons of humour, unknown facts and weird stories – just why our country is called GREAT Britain.

Available from all good bookshops, or direct from the publishers at www.mondaybooks.com or 01455 221752.